JIMMY CARTER'S ECONOMY

William H. Becker, editor

JIMMY CARTER'S ECONOMY

W. Carl Biven

Policy in an Age of Limits

THE
UNIVERSITY
OF NORTH
CAROLINA
PRESS:
CHAPEL HILL
& LONDON

© 2002
The University of North Carolina Press
All rights reserved
Manufactured in the United States
of America

Designed by Julie Spivey
Set in Adobe Caslon and Syntax
by Keystone Typesetting, Inc.

The paper in this book meets the guidelines for permanence and durability of the Committee on Production Guidelines for Book Longevity of the Council on Library Resources.

Library of Congress
Cataloging-in-Publication Data
Biven, W. Carl.
Jimmy Carter's economy : policy in an age of limits / W. Carl Biven.
    p. cm. — (The Luther Hartwell Hodges series on business, society, and the state)
Includes bibliographical references and index.
ISBN 0-8078-2738-x (cloth: alk. paper)
1. United States—Economic policy—1977–1981.
2. United States—Economic conditions—1977–1981. 3. United States—Politics and government—1977–1981. 4. Carter, Jimmy, 1924–   . I. Title. II. Series.
HC106.7.B58 2002
338.973′009′047—dc21
2002003093

06 05 04 03 02   5 4 3 2 1

THIS BOOK WAS DIGITALLY PRINTED.

IN MEMORY OF

Mary Cletus Edgington

John Ewell Duncan

Ronald Allan Borland

AND WITH DEEP AFFECTION FOR

Allan Monroe Biven

Samuel Duncan Biven

THE FIRST IN A NEW GENERATION

CONTENTS

- **ix** Preface
- **xiii** Acknowledgments
- **1** CHAPTER 1
  How It Ended: The 1980 Campaign
- **15** CHAPTER 2
  How It Began: The 1976 Campaign
- **39** CHAPTER 3
  The New Administration: The Process of Economic Advice
- **61** CHAPTER 4
  The Stimulus Package
- **95** CHAPTER 5
  The Mondale Mission and the London Summit
- **123** CHAPTER 6
  Strategy for Inflation
- **145** CHAPTER 7
  The Bonn Summit
- **163** CHAPTER 8
  Bonn and Oil: The Internal Debate
- **185** CHAPTER 9
  The Worsening Inflation
- **209** CHAPTER 10
  Government Actions and Inflation
- **237** CHAPTER 11
  Enter Paul Volcker
- **253** CHAPTER 12
  Jimmy Carter and the Age of Limits
- **265** Notes
- **321** Bibliography
- **339** Index

ILLUSTRATIONS

- **47** *Carter and Charles Schultze*
- **48** *Carter and James McIntyre*
- **50** *Carter and some members of the economic policy group*
- **91** *First meeting of the Quadriad*
- **132** *Carter and his advisers at a meeting with George Meany*
- **153** *Bonn summit*
- **187** *Alfred Kahn with Stuart Eizenstat and John Wright*
- **190** *Carter awaiting the start of his October 24, 1978, inflation speech*
- **192** *Carter at an inflation breakfast*
- **195** *Alfred Kahn addresses the cabinet*
- **205** *Meeting on budget revision, early 1980*
- **238** *William Miller and Carter*
- **243** *Paul Volcker with William Miller and Alfred Kahn*

PREFACE

It is my intention to do two things in this book. The first is to tell a story, the story of how economic policy was developed and carried out during the presidency of Jimmy Carter. It is a story that should have a broader audience than historians or other scholars specializing in this particular time period. There are similarities in economic policy development and execution among all modern presidencies. Each chief executive must make decisions on objectives and decide on steps to achieve them. This is never a neat process. There is the challenge of balancing the claims of competing goals, the uncertainty in predicting the probable effects of actions taken to implement policies, the ambiguities that surround all decision making, and the dynamics of the interactions among those participating in the decisions as well as the effect of these interactions on the final choices.

While the problems that must be addressed have a certain uniqueness for each president, they tend to overlap across administrations. Forces operating on the economy are not segmented into four-year periods that coincide with presidential terms. Starting in the late 1960s the American economy suffered a series of shocks that had impact before, during, and after the period of the Carter presidency. The inflation with which Carter struggled began during the latter part of the Johnson administration, continued through the Nixon and Ford terms, and crested under Carter. The threat of a return of this inflationary pressure affected the conduct of policy during the Reagan, Bush, and Clinton administrations as well as the patterns of behavior in the private sector. The story of the Carter years can be thought of as a case study that provides general insight into the complexities that all chief executives face in managing economic policy.

It has been said that "the task of analytical economics is not to describe reality in its texture and richness, but to provide an ideal type of how transactions might be arranged if Everyman were indeed Economic Man."[1] The first purpose of this book is to add the texture that is missing from abstract economic theory to the portrait of economic forces operating during the Carter years.

The second purpose is to advance a specific theme. The coalescence of a number of events created problems that the administration had limited capacity to solve and which basically shifted the political parameters. To begin with, the double-digit inflation of the 1970s altered the essential macroeconomic problem that had faced the Democratic Party for the previous half century. The 1930s were the decade of the Great Depression. The 1970s were the decade of the Great Inflation. Dealing with serious unemployment requires a series of actions almost the opposite of those applied to dampen inflation. A full employment policy means an activist government, with increases in public outlays and with tax cuts, along with easier money, to stimulate private spending. An anti-inflation policy requires the fiscal discipline necessary to control public spending, to restrain the growth of government, to accept limits on the expansion of the welfare state, and to postpone popular tax cuts, and it requires the commitment to limit the increase in bank credit. When Carter made price stability the top priority in the latter part of his administration, he reversed the traditional position of Democrats along the spectrum of trade-offs between inflation and unemployment.

Perhaps more important than the inflation shock—and one of the most significant economic events of the last several decades—was the decline in the rate of growth of output per worker. Productivity gains are the key to improvements in the standard of living. An increase in the average amount of output available per person has to come from a gain in output per worker. Over the 1970s and 1980s the average hourly wage of American workers, adjusted for inflation, barely increased—an event described by one observer as a "quiet depression."[2]

By the time President Carter took office, the increasing abundance that characterized the golden age of growth of the 1950s and 1960s was over. Why this slowdown occurred, we do not fully understand. There are signs that the productivity growth rates of earlier decades returned in the last half of the Clinton administration. Whether this is a permanent shift, it is too early to say. But perhaps in this information age a "new economy" has evolved with the capacity to return the nation to an era of faster growth. If so, the problems faced by future presidents will be different from those faced by Carter.

There is another effect of a decrease in the rate of productivity growth. In an era when national income increases at a generous rate, new government programs can be financed by growth in revenues without higher taxes on the incomes of the majority. When the growth of the economic pie slows down and personal incomes are affected, voters become resistant to taxes and the cost of new public initiatives. Distributional disputes are minimized in an age of abundance, but the politics of productivity, so successful in the 1950s and 1960s, broke down in the decade of the 1970s.

There were two parts to the Democrats' traditional commitment to their constituency: full employment and the protections of a welfare state. The first commitment was diluted by the inflation of the 1970s; the second commitment was eroded by slower economic growth. A key theme in this book is the argument that Carter understood better than most Democrats the need for rethinking the party's traditional priorities and for moving toward the political center.

At the same time that the administration was faced with the twin domestic problems of inflation and slower growth—a combination that came to be labeled "stagflation"—international economic constraints were becoming more compelling and posing new challenges for American policy. By the time of Carter's election, foreign trade had become a larger proportion of total national economic activity. The competitive challenge from the German and Japanese economies, which had risen from the ashes of World War II, and from the emerging third world countries, particularly those along the rim of the Pacific Basin, was pressing hard on American industry and labor, which had formerly enjoyed overwhelming supremacy. In addition, the dramatic dissolution of the Bretton Woods arrangement, the international monetary system that had governed world financial transactions since the end of World War II, took place only three years before Carter's inauguration. One economist has written that in international terms, "the period from the early 1950s to 1973 must be rated the greatest and most stable boom in world history."[3] In the period 1971 to 1973, the financial system that supported that prosperity collapsed. The Carter administration was presented with a new international monetary regime vulnerable to volatile foreign exchange markets—a volatility intensified by an explosion of international capital movements—and whose workings were not yet fully understood.

In an effort to define Carter's place in history, a number of students of the era have pointed to the economic forces that battered his presidency.[4] In this book I examine those economic forces in detail.

Whenever minimum understanding of economic analysis is needed to follow the decisions of the administration on some issue, I have provided background suitable for a reader with limited exposure to economics. Throughout the book I have carefully annotated my sources for scholars who have a professional interest in the Carter administration or in the policies of the 1970s. Those who do not have that intense interest, or who are easily distracted by reference notes, are invited to ignore them.

ACKNOWLEDGMENTS

I would like to thank the members of the staff at the Jimmy Carter Library who were most helpful during the many hours I spent reading the material deposited there. Martin Elzy, in particular, generously shared his expertise in guiding me through the maze of documents. The photographs that appear in the book are provided courtesy of the Carter Library. The staff at the library of the Georgia Institute of Technology was always responsive to my innumerable calls for materials and found for me in other libraries, or obscure places, books, articles, and film not readily available. The staff at the Brookings Institution library provided copies of materials from the Charles L. Schultze Papers and I am grateful. I thank particularly Stuart Eizenstat, who made available to me his unpublished manuscripts and granted me access to files in the Carter Library that are not yet available to the general public. Interviews with members of the Carter administration done at the White Burkett Miller Center of Public Affairs at the University of Virginia are available at the Carter Library and I have found them invaluable. Twenty-eight of these interviews were consulted in my work. Erwin Hargrove and Samuel Morley have published interviews with the chairmen of the Council of Economic Advisers from Truman through Carter, and I have used this rich resource. I am also grateful for having been given access to the interviews with Charles Schultze and Lyle Gramley that were done by Thomas Mayer and are now on deposit in the Special Collections at the library of the University of California at Davis.

    I appreciate the time given me for lengthy interviews by a number of people who served under President Carter in Washington or who were related to him in some other way. The list includes Michael Blumenthal and William Miller, both of whom served as secretary of the treasury, and Fred Bergsten, assistant secretary of the treasury; Charles Schultze, chairman of the Council of Economic Advisers, and Lyle Gramley, a member of the council; Bert Lance and James McIntyre, both of whom served as director of the Office of Management and Budget, and Van Doorn Ooms, economic adviser to McIntyre when he served as director; Stuart Eizenstat, assistant to the president for domestic policy; Alfred Kahn, adviser to the president on inflation; Alice Rivlin, director of the Congressional Budget Office during Carter's term in office; Thomas Stelson, assistant secretary of the Department of Energy; Lawrence Klein, head of Carter's economic task force during the 1976 campaign; and Henry Thomassen, economic adviser to Governor Carter. Finally, I am grateful to President Jimmy Carter for granting me time for an interview at the Carter Center.

I am grateful to those who read drafts of various chapters. Lyle Gramley was most helpful in checking the chapter on monetary policy for factual errors. I must thank, especially, Robert Hetzel, who read every line of the entire manuscript, gave me the gift of tough, honest criticism, and provided the perfect foil as I worked out in my mind the ideas in this book. I alone, of course, am responsible for the final result.

I must also thank John McLeod who worked out the technical details of the final arrangement of the manuscript. I also thank my son, Louis, who brought his computer talents to my rescue when my personal computer refused to do what I wanted.

JIMMY CARTER'S ECONOMY

CHAPTER 1 | **HOW IT ENDED**

THE 1980 CAMPAIGN

Jimmy Carter has said that there were three main reasons for his defeat in the presidential election of 1980.¹ Among those on his list was the fallout of the Iranian hostage ordeal, which Gary Sick, Carter's principal White House aide for Iranian affairs, has called "the most devastating diplomatic incident in modern U.S. history."² The part that the hostage crisis played in Jimmy Carter's loss to Ronald Reagan will never be known for certain. It obviously had an influence on the outcome. The taunting of Americans by a fanatical mob in the streets of Tehran added to the sense of loss of national prestige that had been building in the minds of voters since the ignominious escape by helicopter of the last Americans out of Vietnam. In addition to the hurt to the American psyche, there were more practical consequences of the Iranian crisis that tested the temper of the public; perhaps the most visible were a gasoline shortage and long lines of cars at gas stations caused by the cutoff of Iranian oil. Stuart Eizenstat, assistant to the president for domestic policy, remembers the tension of those days: "The cut-off of almost 6 million barrels of oil per day of Iranian production created gasoline lines throughout the nation. I personally felt the aggravation they caused motorists because I sat in several gasoline lines near my house for up to an hour so I could get to the White House to plan how to end them!"³

The lingering hostage crisis added to the image of administration ineptness formed in the minds of many voters—in President Carter's words, "the sense of impotence and incompetence that was generated from those hostages not being released."⁴ Television's power to capture public attention was demonstrated in the Vietnam War of the 1960s and the Watergate scandal of the 1970s. Its capacity to transmit information instantly and graphically exerts a powerful influence on the conduct of public affairs and can be devastating in defining in the minds of voters their perception of presidential performance. Stuart Eizenstat reminisced, after Carter's term ended, how "daily press attention given to the Iranian hostage crisis, with its glaring films of American hostages carried away in blindfolds against the backdrop of burning American flags, undercut President Carter's political standing."[5] With incredibly bad timing the first anniversary of the seizure of the hostages occurred on election day, November 4, 1980. On the day before going to the polls the public was again exposed on the evening news to the humiliating scenes captured by the television cameras a year before.

A second reason Carter gave for his defeat was the division within the Democratic Party, with liberal elements in opposition to the more conservative president. Long simmering, the conflict broke into the open with the challenge to the incumbent Democratic president by the candidacy of his fellow Democrat, Senator Ted Kennedy, in a divisive primary. The relationship between the two men is an interesting one. On many issues they were in agreement, with Kennedy playing an important role in the passage of some of Carter's legislative proposals. On the fundamental direction of the party, they were in conflict, with Kennedy, the heir of a proud political tradition, taking sharp issue with Carter's more conservative approach to national problems, an approach which the senator interpreted as abandonment of traditional Democratic principles. Kennedy prolonged the challenge long after it was apparent that he could not win, forcing the president to defend administration policies publicly in a political confrontation well into 1980 and to concentrate his energies on opposition within his own party rather than getting into position for his Republican adversary. "We have come out of this primary year and the unsuccessful Kennedy challenge not enhanced or strengthened by the contest, but damaged severely," Hamilton Jordan, Carter's chief political adviser, wrote to the president in a memorandum in late June.[6]

The third reason for defeat given by Carter is the condition of the economy at the time of the election. We come now to the economic issue and the focus of this book. Economic events of 1980 provided a major reason for Carter's defeat. There is compelling evidence that, in the end, people vote their pocketbooks.[7]

The Iranian crisis and the split in the Democratic Party were contributing factors in the electoral outcome, but the inflation that dogged the administration from its first days in office, and which crested in 1980, was probably the decisive reason for the defeat. Inflation was combined with unemployment in the last year of the Carter term. The economy fell into recession in the second quarter, the sharpest one-quarter drop in national output on record. If eleven presidential four-year terms, starting with Truman and ending with Bill Clinton, are compared, only in the Carter administration was the total output of the economy declining in the fourth year in office, the year critical for reelection. Reagan was not elected in 1980 because he was viewed as strong by the public in terms of solving the Iranian crisis. When respondents were asked to choose the candidate "best able to handle the Iranian situation" in a poll two months before the election, only 33 percent selected Carter, an unsurprising result; on the other hand, only 39 percent selected Reagan.[8] But the challenger hit a sensitive nerve when he asked voters during a campaign debate whether they were better off than they were four years before. It was not Iran but inflation and unemployment that were the uppermost concerns in the minds of voters. Asked in the same survey two months before the election to identify the "most important problem facing the nation," 61 percent named "the high cost of living," while only 15 percent chose "international problems." The intensity of public feeling two months before the election is illustrated by the fact that 52 percent took the surprisingly strong position of backing the imposition of wage and price controls.[9] The diagnosis frequently repeated in the 1992 Clinton campaign, identifying the critical issue in the contest—James Carville's "it's the economy, stupid"—could also be applied to the 1980 election.

Perhaps one cannot separate too sharply the effects of the Iran affair and the inflation on the campaign. Theodore White made the perceptive observation that in the Carter years, inflation and the hostage crisis were not unconnected in the minds of voters. The psychological effect on voters was similar; they both contributed to the same sense of helplessness. We couldn't free the hostages and we couldn't stop the inflation.[10]

THE ECONOMY IN 1980

Herbert Stein, chief economic adviser during the Nixon years, has written that when Reagan asked Americans in the 1980 campaign whether they were better off than they had been four years before, he could count on a negative response. But, Stein writes, "despite the inflation, and despite the slowdown in productivity growth, real per capita income after tax, probably the best simple measure of economic welfare, increased between 1976 and 1980. Indeed it increased just about as much in that period as in the four preceding years."¹¹ It could also be pointed out that the number of new civilian jobs created per year was greater during the Carter administration than for other presidents immediately before or after. But despite these positive outcomes, the Carter years were plagued with continuing economic crises, the worst of them concentrated in the final year in office.

The word that comes to mind in describing economic events in 1980 is "bizarre." The inflation rate soared to the highest level since the early 1950s. Charles Schultze, Carter's chief economic adviser, reported to the president that the inflation rate in January and February was in the 18 to 20 percent range.¹² Unemployment rose, cresting at just under 8 percent in midsummer and much higher in key industrial areas crucial in an election year. Of these two major ailments that afflict modern economies, inflation and unemployment, inflation is more subtle in its impact and more pervasive in terms of numbers affected.

The social damage from inflation traditionally cited is the redistributive effect on income and wealth. Redistribution of income is, in itself, not necessarily undesirable. Governments, from ancient times to the modern era, have redistributed income through the imposition of taxes that affect income recipients differently. But redistribution through taxation, while resented by the losers, at least takes place through a democratic political process. Redistribution through inflation lacks this legitimacy; it happens as though by the hand of fate, arbitrary in its selection of victims. Among the victims are creditors. Loans fixed in amount are paid off by debtors in cheaper dollars because of inflation. Those whose wages and salaries adjust sluggishly and rise more slowly than prices find their position in the wage and salary structure worsened. Those not protected by the automatic cost-of-living adjustments made for union wages and Social Security payments lose relative to those who are.

While inflation has undesirable social effects, the damage is usually exaggerated in the minds of the public. It has long been observed by those who do surveys of consumer sentiments that even those who benefit financially from inflation think of themselves as damaged. People have a limited sense of their net worth. The prices of houses rose more rapidly in the 1970s than the consumer price index, giving home owners generous capital gains. Housing was an excellent inflation hedge in the Carter years. The president's Council of Economic Advisers stated in its annual report in 1978 that the rise of new home prices was then "about 11 percent annually, or about five percentage points greater than the average increase of other prices."¹³ For the most part, home owners ignored this windfall in assessing the effect of inflation on their personal economic welfare.

For every loser in inflation there has to be a winner. Creditors are hurt, but debtors are helped as their indebtedness is reduced when adjusted for price changes. It is difficult to determine precisely who loses and who gains, but we know enough to suggest that widespread perceptions are probably incorrect. We tend to think of lower income families as the most vulnerable, but one careful study, published while inflation was raging in 1980, found that it was not the poor but the upper income classes that were hurt more by the inflation due to a drop in the value of their assets.[14]

While the social effects of general price increases are more modest than generally thought, the impact on the operation of the economy is substantial. Inflation increases the uncertainty associated with business strategies, uncertainty that affects both the amount and direction of investment decisions. Paul Volcker, appointed by Carter to be chairman of the Federal Reserve Board in mid-1979, pointed out in his first appearance before a committee of the House "that the uncertainty about future prospects associated with high and varying levels of inflation tends to concentrate the new investment that does take place in relative short, quick pay-out projects. Or firms may simply delay investment commitments until the pressures of demand on capacity are unambiguously compelling."[15]

In addition to the restraining effects of uncertainty on investment, the interaction of inflation and tax provisions may weaken incentives for capital accumulation. When inventories and fixed assets are valued at the original purchase price rather than at replacement cost, as they commonly were in the 1970s, costs are understated and profits overstated, an accounting practice that has the effect of increasing the tax liability. Volcker again pointed out in his first appearance before a House committee that "we can observe in these recent inflationary years a declining tendency in the profitability of investment. . . . One estimate indicates that the annual after-tax return on corporate net worth, measured as it reasonably should be, against the replacement cost of inventories and fixed assets, has averaged 3.8 percent during the 1970s, a period characterized by rapid inflation, as compared to 6.6 percent in the 1960s."[16]

INFLATION AND FINANCIAL MARKETS

While the fallout from inflation hung heavily on the country in 1980, the sense of crisis was signaled most dramatically by the behavior of financial markets. Interest rates rose in January to their highest level since World War II. Indeed, the yield on long-term Treasury securities moved above 11 percent for the first time in history. Rates even exceeded "the extreme levels set during the Civil War, when a viable market for long-term Treasuries simply didn't exist."[17]

The first effect of high interest rates is, of course, to stifle economic activity. Charles Schultze cited the powerful restraining effect in a memorandum to the president in early April. "A builder now starting a house must pay, typically, over 20 percent for a construction loan, and at the end find a buyer willing both to pay the extra price and to assume a 15 to 16 percent mortgage. The typical business firm . . . must pay 19 to 20 percent interest to carry inventories or to meet other working capital needs. Reg Jones [head of General Electric] told me that just in the past week, those GE dealers who must finance themselves (as opposed to getting GE financing) have virtually stopped ordering."[18]

There is another major effect of rising interest rates: a decrease in the net worth of wealth holders. The case of bonds provides us with a good example to make the point. The bond market is a major source of funds for the federal government and for American firms. Bonds represent a huge pool of accumulated wealth held by the public, with ownership constantly changing hands among the players—bankers, agents for life insurance companies and retirement funds, wealthy Americans, nonprofit institutions like universities, and, indirectly, the ordinary American who has bought shares in a mutual fund. The daily turnover in the secondary market for bonds is large in volume with prices changing continuously. The action is amplified by the movement of vast amounts of money across international borders with instantaneous transfer of funds through electronic means.

In the simple algebra of compound interest, the interest rate and the price of debt instruments are inversely related: as one goes up, the other goes down. Because of the nature of compound interest, it is at the long end of the market that swings in securities prices due to changes in interest rates are the greatest. Rising yields in early 1980 meant that the prices of long-term bonds and other fixed rate instruments fell dramatically with a large paper loss for holders of these securities. The *Wall Street Journal* reported in late February an estimate by Morgan Stanley and Company: "a staggering $400 billion in paper losses on bondholdings." The same late-February issue of the *Journal* also reported that a drop in the price of Treasury bonds maturing in the year 2009, "with a face value of $2 billion—in public hands—has saddled holders with $365 million in paper losses."[19] IBM long-term bonds issued in October 1979 had a capital loss of 25 percent by late February 1980. Al McDonald, White House deputy chief of staff, reported to Carter in early February on meetings he attended with groups of business leaders. "The bond market is 'near chaos' they claim. Major investment houses," he wrote to the president, "have been shifting heavily out of bonds over the last few weeks."[20] A *Wall Street Journal* reporter also gives some feeling for the mood of the market. "In the executive offices of most securities firms, the atmosphere of apprehension and gloom is as thick as the carpets. After asking his secretary to hold all telephone calls so he can chat without interruption with a reporter, a senior officer of a major bond-trading house manages to stay calm only about 30 minutes, then, tensing up, he bolts for the trading room. 'I have to see how much money we've lost while we were talking. The way things are going, it could easily be $2 million or $3 million.'"[21]

Before the inflation of the 1970s and 1980s, bonds had traditionally been a safe haven for money. While interest rates varied, they did so within a narrow range, and the prices of bonds, unlike the prices of common stocks, were relatively stable. Financial institutions—banks and insurance companies—sought security in portfolios heavily made up of bonds. The erratic behavior of the market in late 1979 and early 1980 had a thoroughly demoralizing effect on the buyers and sellers in this market. The respected British publication, the *Economist*, quoted a partner in Solomon Brothers as saying, "nobody knows where we are going, because we've never been here before."[22]

After reaching historic highs in early 1980, interest rates began to decline. By mid-year they had dropped substantially—short-term interest rates in June were about half of their March value—only to return toward the end of the year to the levels reached in the previous January and February. Interest rates moved up and down during Jimmy Carter's last year in office, oscillating around historically high levels. Henry Kaufman, respected economist for Solomon Brothers, called on the administration in a speech to the American Bankers Association in February "to declare a national state of emergency" to deal with inflation. If rates increase further, he is reported to have said, corporations and other issuers "will hesitate or will be unable to finance." His comments touched off a steep slide in the market.[23]

"In early 1980 things really fell apart," I commented in an interview with Charles Schultze a decade later. "Interest rates went through the ceiling, the bond market collapsed. It must have been scary." "It was," he said. "It was scary," but then he added, "we probably overreacted. Things would have settled some."[24] The damage to the president's image in the year of his run for reelection was massive. The financial crisis in late 1979 and early 1980 "put the final fatal imprint," Stuart Eizenstat has written, "on the Presidency of Jimmy Carter."[25]

CAUSES OF THE SURGE IN RATES

The surge in interest rates was due to a number of factors, two of which dominated events. The first was a tight money policy implemented by the Federal Reserve in October 1979, in an effort to contain the inflation, which was reaching epidemic proportions. I discuss this Fed initiative in detail at a later point. Consider for the moment the second, the immediate event that triggered the panic that overtook financial markets: the announcement in January of an upward revision in the budget deficit forecast for the fiscal year still in progress.

"I remember distinctly how it started," Stuart Eizenstat has written.

> I was in my West Wing office in December, 1979, when Bo Cutter, Deputy Director of OMB (Office of Management and Budget), came to tell me that the budget office had an updated forecast of what the deficit was likely to be for Fiscal Year 1980, the fiscal year that began in October 1979, and lasted through September 1980. Since OMB had consistently overstated the deficit in the president's budgets in the early years of the administration because agencies were not spending as fast as had been anticipated—a trend that began in the Ford years—I assumed once again we would have a smaller deficit than initially projected. I was shocked to learn from Bo that instead the deficit would be almost 50 percent higher than anticipated.... When the announcement was made public shortly before we submitted the budget for the next fiscal year, Fiscal Year 1981, in January, 1980, the financial community was equally shocked.[26]

The explanation for the change in the deficit forecast was reasonable enough. Most of the increase, as Bo Cutter was to explain later, "was caused by either drastically changed economic circumstances or defense increases that generally were approved of by the financial world. But the 1980 budget no longer seemed to represent a policy of restraint, rather it appeared symptomatic of the uncontrolled appetite of the federal monster."[27]

To set the stage for understanding in some depth the market's reaction to the budget announcement, one has to focus for a moment on the central role of interest rates. They perform, of course, a critical function in a market economy. The invention of debt and interest is not a breakthrough as momentous as the discovery of fire, but not too far behind.[28] Debt connects, like some financial time machine, the present and the future. It permits economic agents to command financial resources for use today based on expected future income. It makes it possible for people to distribute their consumption over the course of their lives in a more satisfying and optimal way—for instance, to buy cars and houses when they are young and their income and net wealth are low. Debt is crucial to corporations in assembling productive resources by borrowing on the basis of future profits. Financial markets provide the mechanism for this movement across time. The denizens of Wall Street work in time space, trading off the future for the present and the present for the future. The price of the trade-off is the interest rate.

The general level of interest rates, around which the rates on individual bond issues cluster, depends on a number of factors. A major influence, subtle but powerful, is people's expectations about the likelihood of inflation. If they anticipate a rise in prices, they build an inflation premium into the interest rate they demand for lending. Since the level of interest rates is heavily influenced by the inflationary expectations of financial markets, it is crucial to Washington policy makers to avoid setting off adverse psychological reactions. When expectations turn sour, they are difficult to reverse. The rates on instruments with longer maturities are the most sensitive to inflationary expectations. Since the long-term rates are more affected by inflationary psychology, they are more likely to get beyond the control of policy makers. Unfortunately, it is these long-term rates that are the more important for the operation of the economy because they apply to credit used for major spending decisions, such as investment in plants and equipment and the purchase of new homes.

The potential reaction of financial markets can severely constrain the policy options of presidents. Wall Street possesses, in effect, an implicit veto on presidential policy. The interaction of an administration and financial markets is further complicated by the fact that they operate in two different cultures. Wall Street doesn't understand—or more likely is simply indifferent to—the complexities of the political process, and Washington is not sensitized to the behavior of markets and interest rates. "While the two are only 45 minutes away by air," Stuart Eizenstat has written, "they are separated by light years of distrust and misunderstanding. But market realities have the last say-so. Wall Street votes with the upward or downward movement of stock and bond prices. Their reaction ultimately will make or break a President's program."[29]

No president is immune to the reaction of financial markets. George Bush entered the 1992 presidential race with an economic recovery from the 1990–91 recession too sluggish to create the new jobs necessary to reduce the unemployment rate. Stuart Eizenstat, now an outside observer, commented on Bush's predicament in a not unsympathetic way and perhaps with a touch of deja vu. A poorly performing economy weakens public perception about a president's leadership, he is reported as saying, and makes the White House "seem impotent . . . as if you're using a bucket to bail out a sinking ocean liner. You're inevitably diminished in stature in trying to deal with it."[30] The recovery in 1992 was complicated by the perceptions of financial markets. News reports on bond market behavior in Bush's last year in office echoed those of 1980. "A wave of unexpectedly strong economic news early yesterday startled inflation-wary traders and initially sent bond prices into a tail spin," reported the *Wall Street Journal* in early March 1992.[31]

Washington Post reporter Bob Woodward, of *All the President's Men* and Deep Throat fame, describes, in his book on Clinton's economic policy, a briefing of president-elect Bill Clinton in Little Rock by a group of economic advisers in 1992 shortly before the inauguration. They were discussing the effects of a reduction in the federal deficit, a priority of the new administration. Such a policy could be contractionary, they explained, because of the cuts in government outlays and the increased taxes necessary to move the budget in the direction of smaller deficits. But there would be a positive effect if fiscal discipline gave the administration credibility on Wall Street. Woodward describes Alan Blinder, soon to be a member of Clinton's Council of Economic Advisers and later to be appointed to membership on the Federal Reserve Board, as telling the soon-to-be president that with a cooperative Federal Reserve and bond market, deficit reduction could be relatively cost-less in terms of the effect on economic activity. "'But after ten years of fiscal shenanigans,' Blinder quickly pointed out . . . 'the bond market will not likely respond.' At the President-elect's end of the table, Clinton's face turned red with anger and disbelief. 'You mean to tell me that the success of the program and my reelection hinges on the Federal Reserve and a bunch of . . . bond traders?'"[32] Woodward reports that from around the table there was not a dissent. James Carville, chief strategist for the Clinton campaign, was later quoted by Woodward as saying: "I used to think if there was reincarnation, I wanted to come back as the president or the pope or a .400 baseball hitter. But now I want to come back as the bond market. You can intimidate everybody."[33]

Financial markets are relentless. They can be impulsive and shallow in the short term in their reaction to news from Washington. They also have a bias against a booming economy. The ideal state of business for a bond holder is an expansion timid enough to dampen inflation and prevent rising interest rates, and falling bond values, but not so weak as to trigger default on debt contracts. But over the longer pull, it should also be said, financial markets may be more objective in judging presidential economic policy performance than other outside critics.

The sharp increase in rates following the announcement by the Carter administration in early 1980 that the deficit in the budget would be higher than the earlier forecast was due to a mix of Wall Street concerns. The larger deficit would require financing and force the Treasury to go to the market in competition for funds. It was also viewed as adding to inflationary pressure. In any event, the chaos in financial markets left the impression of an administration out of control.

A FINAL NOTE

In early October during the 1980 presidential campaign, Jimmy Carter appeared at a town hall meeting—his most effective forum—in Nashville, Tennessee. A questioner arose and addressed the president. "Mr. President everyone makes mistakes. What do you think has been the greatest mistake you have made since you took office close to 4 years ago?" "If I had to do it over again," the President answered, "I'd put more emphasis on inflation."[34] He then went on to add that if he had known at the start of the administration of events to come, like the increase in oil prices by OPEC (Organization of Petroleum Exporting Countries), he would have acted differently. Over a decade later in an interview in his office at the Carter Center in Atlanta, I reminded him of this question and answer and asked if he still thought of inflation as his biggest mistake. "I think that was, on the domestic scene." And then he went on to add: "But there is no doubt that the entire world suffered from an unpredictable and massive inflation pressure from the uncontrollable price of oil. And I couldn't anticipate that."[35]

Carter was right in recognizing that forces were operating on his administration that were beyond his control. As Stuart Eizenstat was to say later, "in no other area of domestic affairs is a President so much at the mercy of external forces as in the critical area of economic policy. . . . It's just subject to a lot of external forces, the rain in Spain and whether you have a drought in Kansas and whether some Shiek wakes up on the right side of the bed."[36] Only Herbert Hoover, whose name is forever linked with the Great Depression of the 1930s, carried into an election economic problems as severe as those that burdened the thirty-ninth president. It was the judgment of the news media and other presidential observers of the day—and probably remains at least the vague impression of the members of the voting public who remember the Carter years—that Jimmy Carter's was a failed presidency. Revisionist historians have begun to challenge this judgment.[37] In this book I argue that Carter, like Herbert Hoover, was tested by economic forces over which he had limited control, forces that in the end brought down his presidency.[38]

Those who were of an age to vote remember only the lopsided victory of Ronald Reagan in the 1980 election: 51 percent of the popular vote versus 41 percent for Carter. John Anderson, a Republican congressman from Illinois who ran as an independent, received 7 percent of the ballots cast. What most have forgotten is that despite the almost overwhelming problems faced by Carter before the election, the race was close until the last week. Just before the single televised debate between Carter and Reagan on October 28, the president led the challenger in the Gallup poll approval rating, 45 to 42 percent. Following the debate the advantage shifted to Reagan—44 percent for Reagan and 43 percent for Carter. In the final poll, Reagan's advantage increased—47 percent to 44 percent. Gallup later reported that "Reagan's sweeping victory in the November election reflects one of the most dramatic shifts ever recorded in voter preferences in the last week of a presidential campaign."[39]

The debate hurt Carter. A televised debate poses risk for any candidate, particularly the incumbent who benefits less from the exposure than the less known challenger. Richard Nixon led John Kennedy in the polls before the first debate in the election of 1960. Following the debate he lost the lead never to regain it. Gerald Ford trailed Carter in early September of the 1976 campaign but caught up by the time of the second in a series of debates, a crucial one on foreign policy. Public reaction gave that debate to Carter, and Ford never regained the momentum.

The Carter-Reagan debate in 1980 was delayed by controversy over the issue of including John Anderson, the independent candidate. The League of Women Voters, which acted as sponsor—the league had arranged for the Ford-Carter debates in 1976—decided to invite any candidate with as much as a 15 percent approval rating. Anderson made the cutoff in September. Carter, however, refused to join in a three-way meeting. A Reagan-Anderson debate proceeded without him in late September. The league finally agreed to a two-way arrangement and Carter accepted the invitation to participate. Given the delay, the meeting of the candidates did not take place until a week before the election. Carter did not give a strong performance; the result was viewed by the public as more favorable to Reagan.

The debate was held too late for recovery; there were no second and third chances. It turned out to be a sudden death contest.

It is pointless to speculate whether Carter would have won if he had had the edge in the debate with Reagan. It is probable that an accumulation of factors had convinced the electorate that it was simply time for change. Hamilton Jordan, Carter's campaign manager, has said that "in retrospect, we never had a chance of winning that campaign. . . . It was only ultimately a nagging doubt about Ronald Reagan that kept that race close up until the final days."[40]

The physical transfer of the White House from one administration to another is swift and complete like the wiping of a slate. Lloyd Cutler, who had gone without sleep for two days to assist in the final negotiations for release of the Iranian hostages, recalls his last moments in the White House in a poignant account.

> After the President had gone with the Reagans up to the Hill and the actual inauguration ceremony had begun, I was still sitting on that telephone waiting for the final word on when the hostages' plane had actually taken off from Tehran. Then I began the process of clearing out my desk with Fred Fielding's people waiting outside the hall to get in. About one thirty, finally, with something under each arm and a couple of other people helping me carry things out, as I walked out of that West Wing basement, something caught my eye. Instead of the photographs that I was accustomed to looking at, the President and the Pope, meeting with Brezhnev in Vienna, and so on, there were photographs of Ronald Reagan and his dog. By one-thirty on January 20, the transition had happened, the new photos were up, everything was ready for the new President to return to his White House. And the only people who were going to carry on were the switchboard operators and those security guards.[41]

It had been a long road from where it had all begun, the election campaign of 1976.

CHAPTER 2 | **HOW IT BEGAN**

**THE
1976
CAMPAIGN**

In April 1974, a Gallup poll asked voters to select their first choice for the 1976 Democratic nomination from a list of seven names. Jimmy Carter was not on the list.[1] Two years later this little known governor was selected as the standard-bearer of the party, his "capture of the nomination," according to one political scientist, "arguably the greatest feat in the entire history of presidential nominating politics."[2] It would not have been possible for him to pull off this feat had it not been for changes in party nominating procedures. Modification in selection rules that enabled the outsider from Georgia to win the nomination were embodied in reforms adopted over the period 1968 to 1972.

The reforms were designed to open up the party to broad grassroots participation. Among other things they modified rules governing primaries. Before the reforms, those running for positions as delegates to the national convention could run without commitment to a specific candidate, a practice that left bargaining room for party leaders. Delegates were now required to be identified with a specific candidate, a rule that transmitted more precisely the preferences of party rank-and-file to the final nominating result. Rules governing caucuses and state conventions were also adopted. The opening up of participation in the nominating process was reinforced by legislated changes in election financing. Federal matching funds became available in 1976 for the first time in a presidential campaign.

In 1968, before the reforms, seventeen states had primaries for selection of delegates to the Democratic convention. By 1976 this number had increased to thirty. In 1968 three aspiring candidates ran in primaries. In 1976 thirteen candidates entered in an effort to get the nomination.[3] When Harry Truman, the incumbent president, was challenged in 1948 in the New Hampshire primary by Senator Estes Kefauver of Tennessee, Truman, who spoke his mind in earthy terms, had reacted by calling primaries "eyewash." For his day, Truman was basically right. "From the time of their introduction into American politics around the turn of the twentieth century, until well into the 1960s, primary elections were never the sole determinant of party presidential nominations."[4] After the reforms, primaries were no longer eyewash; they became the road to the presidency.

All politicians are ambitious and Carter was no exception. Early in his term as governor, even as he struggled with Georgia's problems, he was thinking ahead to the future. "I began considering a nation wide race in 1971 when I had only been in the governor's office a few months," he has said in an interview, "not distinguishing at that time between the vice-presidency—and the possibility of being on someone else's ticket—and being president."[5] Hamilton Jordan, a Carter aide then only twenty-seven years of age, produced a long memorandum, dated November 1972, which outlined the strategy for taking advantage of the new rules governing the nomination process and for getting Carter elected.[6] He followed this up with another lengthy memo two years later, four months before Carter publicly announced his candidacy, with a month-by-month outline of the campaign plan. If a museum honoring those who work in the boiler rooms of political campaigns is ever built, Jordan's two memos deserve a place among the memorabilia.[7]

Once the decision to run for the Democratic nomination was made in 1972, Carter quietly began to prepare for the campaign. He made trips to Latin America, to Europe, and to the Middle East, trips designed to promote Georgia business abroad, but that also helped to broaden his international experience. He had assistance on these junkets from Coca-Cola, which has its national headquarters in Atlanta. With offices all over the world and its resources and expertise, the soft drink firm resembles a private version of the state department.

Carter asked Robert Strauss, then chairman of the Democratic National Committee, if he could get involved in the 1974 congressional campaign. Strauss agreed and made him chairman of the 1974 Democratic campaign committee. In the process he met party activists and made contacts that would prove invaluable when he began his own run for the presidency. He arranged for Hamilton Jordan to move to Washington as executive director of the 1974 campaign committee, a position from which he could observe at close range the inner workings of the Democratic Party machinery. He collected names and data useful for the future. Staff members at the national headquarters good-naturedly referred to Jordan as "the Trojan peanut."[8]

Carter asked Stuart Eizenstat to help with preparing issue papers that could be used by the Democratic candidates running for office. Eizenstat was then practicing law in Atlanta. He had previously served as a volunteer issues coordinator in Carter's campaign for governor. In describing his role, Eizenstat has said that "during the course of the latter part of 1973 and through almost all of 1974, I was the chief drafter and editor of what turned out to be perhaps ten to twelve issue papers printed by the DNC [Democratic National Committee] which went to candidates critiquing the Nixon policies and proposing alternative Democratic policies to those that the Nixon administration was implementing. In the course of developing those papers ... I drew on many of the people who later came into the administration in minor and in major positions. People like Henry Owen, at Brookings, who became the coordinator for economic summits."[9]

A major learning experience came from Carter's membership on the Trilateral Commission. The commission was created in 1973, a group of three hundred private citizens from Europe, North America, and Japan who came together for annual plenary sessions to discuss issues of interest to the three areas.[10] It was a centrist, elitist group; one of its principal founders was David Rockefeller, head of the Chase Manhattan Bank. The commission had a broad membership, including such people as Walter Heller, chief economic adviser to John Kennedy; Arthur Burns, Alan Greenspan, and Paul McCracken, all economic advisers to Republican presidents; and Walter Mondale and George Bush. Zbigniew Brzezinski was the executive director. The American members represented a deep pool of talent. Over twenty members of the commission later served in the Carter administration, including Michael Blumenthal, secretary of the treasury, Harold Brown, secretary of defense, and Cyrus Vance, secretary of state. Brzezinski became the national security adviser.

Brzezinski has explained how Carter became a member by one of those coincidences with which life is replete. "We the organizers decided to have two governors on it: one Republican and one Democrat. We chose the Republican from the far West because of the Japanese and we were looking for a Democratic governor, and we thought it would not be interesting enough to have just a conventional Northeast Democrat, but to pick a bright Democrat from the South. I guess our first thought was Askew [of Florida] and then someone mentioned that there was a governor in Georgia who had opened up trade offices for the State of Georgia in Brussels and Tokyo. I remember saying, 'Well, he obviously is our man, he fits the Trilateral concept, let's invite him.' And we did, and then discovered that it was his predecessor who opened up the trade offices."[11] Jimmy Carter accepted the invitation in 1973 and attended the plenary session of the Trilateral Commission in Tokyo in 1975.

The commission produced a number of reports. They were centered mostly on economic issues; there were two major papers on the energy crisis, a subject in which Carter had a special interest. He read all of the papers carefully. Hamilton Jordan recalls his saying that "those Trilateral Commission meetings for me were like classes in foreign policy—reading papers produced on every conceivable subject, hearing experienced leaders debate international issues and problems and meeting the big names like Cy Vance and Harold Brown and Zbig."[12]

Stuart Eizenstat was asked to work on policy issues on a part-time basis shortly after the decision to run for president was made. He had prior political experience. He worked for the Lyndon Johnson White House in a junior staff position after graduating from law school and later served as Hubert Humphrey's research director in the 1968 campaign. He returned to Georgia, after Humphrey's defeat, to practice law. He has described those early days. "I spent long hours personally with the Governor in a downstairs study overlooking the lovely porch and veranda of the Mansion going over his positions on the national issues. Having never held a Federal position, he had no voting record or previous positions on the major issues of the day. I literally took issues alphabetically, from 'abortion' to 'Zaire,' and had him give his visceral reactions. I then dictated these and together we refined them over weeks and months preceding his announcement for the Presidency in late 1974, discussing their substantive and political implications."[13] Eizenstat added that "the positions were very much his [Carter's] and, despite bitter criticisms later in the press about the changeability of his positions, there was a remarkable consistency of views from those early days in 1974 to the last decisions in 1981 as President."[14]

THE PRIMARIES

With Hamilton Jordan working out the details for the campaign, Carter entered every primary but one, the only candidate to pursue a "run-everywhere" strategy. From the first contest in January till the convocation of the national Democratic convention in New York in July, Carter took on and eliminated other contenders for the nomination. The list is long with broad representation by veteran members of the party: Birch Bayh, senator from Indiana and described by Jules Witcover who covered the campaign for the *Washington Post* as "forty-six, a shrewd and ambitious politician with strong labor support and a deceptive veneer of country-boyish looks and backslapping cordiality;"[15] Lloyd Bentsen, freshman senator from Texas, later to be the 1988 running mate of Michael Dukakis, and still later, secretary of the treasury under President Clinton; Edmund Brown Jr., the mercurial governor of California; Frank Church, senator from Idaho, specialist in foreign policy; Fred Harris, former senator and populist from Oklahoma; Scoop Jackson, senator from Washington, specialist in national defense with thirty-five years experience in Congress; Terry Sanford, president of Duke University and former governor of North Carolina; Milton Shapp, governor of Pennsylvania; Sargent Shriver, Kennedy brother-in-law and George McGovern's running mate in the 1972 campaign; Morris Udall, the witty, likeable, and liberal congressman from Arizona; and Governor George Wallace of Alabama, the candidate with visceral appeal for middle and lower income white voters confused and embittered by rapid social and economic change. In addition to these active candidates, Hubert Humphrey was waiting in the wings should the primaries fail to produce a clear-cut winner. The large number of candidates is partly explained by the decision of Senator Ted Kennedy, who would have been a formidable contender, not to run for presidential office in 1976. The Kennedy abstention opened up the race.

The political pundits in late 1975 and early 1976 were divided in predicting the outcome of the Democratic contest. Robert Strauss ventured the opinion that a clear winner would not emerge from the primaries and that it would take two or three ballots at the national convention in New York to determine the nominee.[16] He was wrong. It is not surprising; the circumstances of the 1976 campaign were unprecedented. One by one other contenders dropped out of the race. By the time of the last primary in Ohio, the Carter victory was assured. It was an impressive victory—one is inclined to say, startling. It is doubtful that such a loner will ever be able to repeat the Carter success. He ran separate from the institutions of the Democratic Party. "When I was a candidate in 1976, almost all the leaders of the Democratic party from Bob Strauss on down were committed to other candidates," he said in an interview after he left office. "Either to Scoop Jackson or Hubert Humphrey or to Mo Udall. So I got the nomination without the help or support of the Democratic National Committee members or executive officers. And I won the nomination on that basis by taking my case directly to the people."[17] In defeating some of the best of the Democratic leadership, he would enter office as an outsider, a role that would plague him throughout his presidency. He was unique in many ways. He was, as one historian has written, "the first president to be elected from the Deep South since before the Civil War, the first to be elevated under the new presidential selection system of the 1970's, and the first true outsider—having no previous experience in Washington—to be elected since Woodrow Wilson."[18]

Confirmation of the result by the national convention of the party as it met in New York City in July was a formality. The role of the convention in the candidate selection process had been fundamentally changed by the election reforms of 1968 and 1972. "Instead of a body of delegates from the state parties meeting to ratify the results of a complex series of negotiations conducted by party leaders at the convention," one political analyst has written, "the convention is now a body dominated by candidate enthusiasts and interest group delegates who meet to ratify a choice made prior to the convention mostly through primary elections."[19]

Richard Reeves, who has written an account of the convention, has described how Jimmy Carter was taken to an office at the Marine Air Terminal located on the far side of La Guardia Airport when he arrived in New York in a chartered jet. From there he would leave for his first public appearance, a rally in front of the Americana Hotel where he would be staying. "In the office," Reeves writes, "Carter took off his shirt, and Secret Service agents helped him into a bulletproof vest for the rally. It was the first time the candidate had ever worn one."[20] It was a ghoulish symbol of the finality of his victory.

CARTER AND ECONOMIC ADVICE

Watching Carter gear up for a run for the presidency provides an interesting case study of the mechanics of presidential politics. Presidential incumbents have the full resources of the federal government available for advice. There are specialists on every subject on the White House staff and in the federal agencies available to brief them on every type of question that can come up during a campaign. There is a stable of speechwriters to prepare addresses and grind out position papers. Challengers begin with only a skeleton staff to develop the minimum number of policy positions necessary for someone running for office.

Even understanding this, one of the striking things about Jimmy Carter's campaign, during 1975 and a large part of 1976, is how small his resources were for developing the policies he needed to present to the electorate. Again Stuart Eizenstat has provided some details.

> An incredibly modest campaign organization was set up. Incredibly modest because he was unknown at the time, didn't have very many resources and was living from hand-to-mouth for a good while. And I worked as a sort of informal issues coordinator, working at nights and weekends with a group of volunteers. And we began to draft some things for him. . . . But the issues staff was really nonexistent except for the volunteers. There was no sort of on-going organization until some time, I suppose, in mid-1975 when Steve Stark came on board. Steve was in between college and law school. And Steve came on full time. . . . Subsequently a few people came on, kids in college who wanted to take a year or a semester off, but I don't think it was more than three people. One was even between high school and college. . . . And we sort of limped along like this for really the better part of the year.[21]

The staff working on policy issues remained small through most of the 1976 campaign. Eizenstat did not come on full time until after the Florida primary. Alfred Stern, professor on leave from Wayne State University, volunteered to help. He had worked with Eizenstat in the 1968 Humphrey campaign. A renaissance man who taught a course on the history of ideas at Wayne State University, Stern had taken a leave from his university post every four years since 1948 to work in a Democratic presidential campaign. Eizenstat and Stern and the handful of students were the issues staff until just before the nomination at the Democratic convention.

The limited size of the staff is one of the reasons for what came to be known as the "fuzziness issue"—the media charge that Carter was avoiding a discussion of substantive problems by refusing to be specific. The *Washington Post* commented on October 17, 1976 that "Carter has failed to project a clearly articulated vision of where he wants to lead the country. . . . An early October poll of registered voters by Yankelovich, Skelly and White Inc. found that 54 percent believed that Carter is fuzzy on the issues."[22] The need to provide details increased with his victories in the primaries. "As I got to be well known," Carter said later, "I became one of the focal points for the press and had to prepare myself much better to answer questions that were much more probing and that were engendered within the national press in Washington where they were much more knowledgeable about past history or current events."[23]

The pressure experienced by Carter to come up with answers about a wide variety of complicated issues is a common one shared by all presidential aspirants. "Unfortunately, the seriousness with which campaign promises are taken, and the degree to which they bind a candidate if he is elected president," to quote Eizenstat again, "is totally out of proportion to the degree of care and study which led to the promise. American presidential campaigns are inherently frenetic and disorganized."[24] Eizenstat went on to cite an example from the opposite side of the 1980 campaign. "There is little evidence that Ronald Reagan's fateful decision to endorse the Kemp-Roth three-year tax cut is based on anything like the type of systematic analysis presidents must have to assure sound policy making."[25] Eizenstat's instincts are close to the mark. Jack Kemp's endorsement in 1980 would have helped candidate Reagan in his primary contests with George Bush. Kemp was willing to give his support but, in time-honored tradition, for something in return: support of the Kemp-Roth proposal. The reaction of the Reagan camp seems, as told by insider Martin Anderson, somewhat casual. "When Reagan and his political advisers heard the terms of the deal," he writes, "they shrugged and essentially said, 'Why not?' Reagan had already indicated support for a series of annual tax rate reductions as a part of his comprehensive economic plan. Why not give Jack Kemp's political future a boost by endorsing the Kemp-Roth tax proposal?"[26]

Unsympathetic critics would say that in not providing more detail Carter was not being straightforward with the voters. More sympathetic observers might suggest that Carter's strategy was to run on a broad theme, returning credibility to government. A strong case can also be made that he was not more specific because he lacked the staff to work out the details; he sometimes could only state a general position on an issue. Jimmy Carter was a stickler for details; if he had not fully developed a policy, he said so.

An example of his refusal to be specific when he lacked the information for a detailed answer is found in an interview with editors of *Fortune* in May 1976. Carter was asked about his plan to revise the tax system. He had said repeatedly in speeches across the land that it was a national disgrace. "Do you favor taxing capital gains the same as other income?" a *Fortune* interviewer asked. Carter was specific in his answer about this major issue, an answer that surely cost him votes among the readers of *Fortune*: "Yes; I would tax all income the same." The questioner pressed for more detail.

Q: Would you tax accrued capital gains on inheritances?
Carter: That is a question I would rather not go into until I have examined it more closely.

Q: You have indicated you would eliminate many of the current deductions on the income tax. Can you say which ones you would eliminate?
Carter: No; that is something I want to avoid. I'm perfectly willing to accept the criticism about not being specific, but I don't know how to be specific yet. I would rather wait until I spend a considerable amount of time with a large number of advisers analyzing the entire tax structure, and then I want to propose it as one tax reform measure.[27]

After the Pennsylvania primary and shortly before the convention, at the point when it was clear that the nomination was locked up, the issues group was brought up to a respectable size. Stuart Eizenstat went to Washington in July to recruit staff. He interviewed a number of people on the Hill who had been prescreened by a source who had worked for the Kennedys and was familiar with the pool of Washington talent. Eizenstat hired a dozen people or so, none of whom he had ever met before, experts in every major area. They came almost entirely from congressional committee staffs or from the staffs of Democratic senators and congressmen. Most would join the Domestic Policy Staff, which Eizenstat directed after Carter was elected, or would serve in some branch of government.[28] "About the time before the convention was held in 1976," David Rubenstein, one of those hired by Eizenstat and eventually an Eizenstat deputy, later recalled, "Eizenstat had the authority to hire about fifteen young whippersnappers from Washington to come down to Atlanta to replace the couple of high school students who had up to then been doing all of Carter's issues work and probably better than the whippersnappers from Washington would later do."[29] The young student volunteers went back to school for the fall term, and a professional issues staff was left in their place. The group worked out of Atlanta. Among its members was Jerry Jasinowski, a trained economist who had worked for the Joint Economic Committee of Congress and who had responsibility for domestic economic policy. He would later serve in the administration as chief economist in the Department of Commerce. Robert Ginsburg, an attorney, who had served as a volunteer in the presidential campaign of George McGovern, worked on international economics.

In addition to the issues team who worked under Eizenstat, a transitions team was formed after the nomination under the direction of Jack Watson, a young Atlanta lawyer who later became White House chief of staff. This team dealt with policy issues, but with the intent of developing more indepth information on such matters as expiring legislation and expiring treaties to give Carter a running start should he be elected. The transitions team was housed in offices separate from the offices of the issues group—both in Atlanta—in order to isolate it from the excitement of the campaign. Bowman Cutter coordinated economic policy issues for the transition group. He later served in the Office of Management and Budget.[30]

Before the arrival of Rubenstein, Jasinowski, Ginsburg, and their cohorts, Carter had supplemented the work of his small issues staff by drawing on the expertise of his network of specialists around the country, which he and Eizenstat had carefully cultivated over several years. He drew on the advice of these outside specialists throughout the primaries and the general election campaign. Even after Eizenstat's staff was in place, its primary function was to coordinate the formulation of Carter's positions on issues by drawing on ideas and material gathered from outside advisers rather than to produce original analysis.[31] The arrangement was formalized through the creation of "task forces" to provide expertise on specific topics, an approach used by other presidential candidates. There were task forces on education, energy, foreign policy, housing, tax policy, and a half-dozen or so on other issues. There was also a task force formed to advise on economic policy.[32]

The leader of the economics task force was Lawrence Klein, professor of economics at the University of Pennsylvania, president-elect of the prestigious American Economic Association for 1976, and later, in 1980, winner of the Nobel prize in economics.[33] Klein was the first economist of national stature to advise the Georgia governor. Contacts develop during a politician's career through a combination of chance and deliberate search. The contact with Klein came through John Bowles, who was with Kidder Peabody and helped on occasion with the Carter campaign. Bowles, who had a masters in business administration from the Wharton School at the University of Pennsylvania, contacted the dean of the school looking for someone who could help Carter with economic policy. The dean approached Klein to see if he was interested. Klein met with Carter in New York in 1975 at the Conference Board, a respected research organization that provides businesses with data for tracking the economy's behavior and conducts conferences for management and other audiences.[34] The next contact came in early 1976 at the Atlanta airport. "We spent a day," Klein recalls, "and that was when I first met Stuart Eizenstat. I flew down from Philadelphia and there was a motel at the airport and I spent the day with Jimmy Carter and Stuart Eizenstat talking over economic issues."[35]

The task force that Klein agreed to form was an informal grouping, as were the other task forces helping with the campaign. The mix of attendees varied from meeting to meeting, as members were successful or not in fitting the sessions into already busy schedules. It included Carolyn Shaw Bell of Wellesley College, who had an interest in labor market analysis; Richard Cooper of Yale, specialist in international economics and later undersecretary of state under Carter; Albert Sommers, chief economist for the Conference Board; Lester Thurow, author of a number of best-selling books on economics and professor at MIT (Massachusetts Institute of Technology); and Michael Wachter, Klein's colleague from the University of Pennsylvania. Martin Feldstein, later to be chairman of the Council of Economic Advisers under President Reagan, attended some meetings, but at some point dissociated himself from the group.[36] Paul Samuelson, Nobel prize winner and informal adviser to President Kennedy, commented on the makeup of the task force: "Noteworthy is the eclectic spread of advisers over the ideological spectrum."[37] Klein recalls that "Jimmy Carter came to the university at the faculty club and we had a dinner meeting with him."[38] The most visible contribution of the task force was an economic position paper released in late April shortly before the Pennsylvania primary.[39] The actual drafting of the paper was done by Lawrence Klein and Stuart Eizenstat. "And then," Klein remembers, "it got worked over with the group."[40]

Klein continued to be an informal adviser to Carter through the transition period. Eizenstat recalls that he checked with Klein to see if he were interested in the chairmanship of the Council of Economic Advisers in the new administration.[41] He preferred to stay with his research at the university.[42]

BACKGROUND OF CARTER'S ADVISERS

Economists who advise presidents must live with the reality that their tools are imperfect. Economic theory lacks the predictive power of the physical sciences. The tentativeness of economic advice can be confusing to the uninitiated and frustrating to practical politicians who do not enjoy the luxury of the freewheeling and often inconclusive exchange of a graduate seminar. Presidents make hard decisions for which they must ultimately answer to the judgment of the voters. Harry Truman's remark in response to a staff economist's briefing, "on the one hand this" and "on the other hand that," is often cited: "What I need is a one-handed economist."

Because of the difficulty of providing conclusive proof for any given policy position, there is room for subjective judgment in economic advice and for the intrusion of political priorities. It would be hard to imagine an economist with liberal political beliefs serving as adviser to Barry Goldwater in the 1964 presidential campaign or a conservative economist advising Lyndon Johnson in the same contest.[43]

Economists are like fingerprints; no two are exactly alike. They defy simple classification. But it is accurate to say that Carter's economists were, for the most part, Keynesians. John Maynard Keynes's major work, *The General Theory of Employment, Interest and Money* was published in 1936 in the heart of the Great Depression. It is one of the most influential books on economics published in the twentieth century. At the risk of oversimplification, Keynes's central theme can be briefly explained. Mainstream economists prior to Keynes thought that a capitalistic economy has a capacity for self correction. Recessions do occur, but if prices and wages are free to adjust, the economy will, in the long-run, right itself. Keynes's retort that "in the long run we are all dead," is one of his more frequently quoted lines.

The most practical implication of Keynes's theory that the corrective capacity of the market is imperfect is that governments should act to supplement the market in times of unemployment. He particularly recommended an increase in government spending to stimulate a lagging economy or a cut in taxes to encourage consumer purchases. The most ambitious attempt to implement the ideas of the Keynesian revolution in the postwar period came during the Kennedy administration. A talented group of young economic advisers developed a proposal for a large tax cut to prod the economy. "By 1960," Herbert Stein has written, "the young economists who had been hypnotized by Keynes when they were graduate students in the late 1930s were mature enough to be the advisers to Presidents and pundits to the nation."[44]

Lawrence Klein was one of the early participants in the "Keynesian Revolution"—the title of a book based on his thesis research at the Massachusetts Institute of Technology while a graduate student in the 1940s. His predisposition was toward an activist stance on the part of government in dealing with unemployment, a predisposition shared by other Carter advisers. He was not only a part of the "revolution" in theory and policy insights that followed from Keynes's work; he was also a major participant in a second advance that took place alongside the innovations embodied in Keynesian analysis. This second development involved the building of large-scale econometric models, which combined economic theory and statistics to give empirical content to the new theory of the behavior of the national economy.[45] Such models are now used by both business and government.

It would seem that something as esoteric as econometric models would not be a topic of political debate in Washington, but their use for forecasting and policy planning became the subject of criticism during the Carter administration by some members of Congress. Supply-side economists on congressional staffs at the time of Carter's presidency, some of whom later served as advisers to President Ronald Reagan, were critical of certain features of these large-scale forecasting instruments, particularly their Keynesian slant. Their criticisms were injected into congressional debate by, among others, Senator Orrin Hatch of Utah, a member of the Joint Economic Committee and the Senate budget committee.[46]

It is doubtful that Jimmy Carter, or any other president, spent much time discussing Keynesian economics. Carter was interested in practical results and, in this, was like Franklin Roosevelt. Roosevelt actually met Keynes at the White House in 1934, a meeting set up by Felix Frankfurter. It was not a particularly satisfactory meeting for either side. Roosevelt commented to a cabinet member after the meeting, that "he left a whole rigmarole of figures. He must be a mathematician rather than a political economist."[47] Roosevelt, contrary to what one might think, was somewhat conservative in his basic fiscal beliefs. A thoroughly pragmatic man, he initiated a public works program probably less out of any commitment to Keynesian ideas than from the simple realization that you cannot let people starve.

When Carter looked for economic advisers, both during the campaign and later in the White House, he went to the pool of traditional Democratic economists. The priority given to full employment by the party and by Keynesians made them natural allies. The Carter program for stimulating the economy was, in some ways, a Kennedy rerun. Unfortunately the economic environment was quite different from that of the Kennedy years, as we will see. The real threat, it would later become clear, was not unemployment but inflation. Carter's advisers were not indifferent to the problem of inflation. Fiscal policy can be used both to stimulate the economy and also to tone it down in a period of rising prices. Nevertheless, the Keynesian bias for expansionary policies tilted administration policy, in the early years, in a direction less appropriate in an inflationary environment. Jimmy Carter was probably more sensitive than his advisers to the danger of over-stimulating the economy; he had the conservative instincts of a small businessman and lacked the intellectual commitment of his advisers to Keynesian doctrine.

THE 1976 CAMPAIGN AND THE ECONOMY

While election reforms made it possible for Carter to become president, two other factors played crucial roles, particularly in the general election campaign against President Gerald Ford. One was Watergate; the other was the state of the economy.

Watergate—the symbol of crimes in high places and the occasion for the first resignation of an American president in the two hundred years of our nation's history—traumatized the country's political consciousness. "Jimmy Carter did not create that mood," one historian, has written. "He was like a surfer who is in precisely the right position to catch the one wave of the day that will carry him all the way."[48] Jerry Ford, the incumbent, not only carried the burden of the Watergate scandal into the contest for the presidency, he also had the misfortune of having served during a severe recession.

The unofficial record keeper for recessions in the United States is the National Bureau of Economic Research. The bureau has traditionally described recessions in terms of their duration; their diffusion across the economy, as measured by the percentage of industries experiencing declining employment; and their depth. All of the recessions since World War II have been mild when compared to the Great Depression of the 1930s. But according to the indicators used by the National Bureau, the recession of the Nixon-Ford years was the most serious of the six declines in business activity up to that point in the postwar period. It lasted sixteen months, from November 1973 until March 1975, five months longer than any of its earlier counterparts. The drop in national output was larger than the decline in any previous postwar recession. The unemployment rate rose to 9.2 percent, over a percentage point above the previous postwar high.[49]

By the time of the 1976 campaign the economy was in a recovery mode. Total national output had begun its upward climb out of the trough of the business contraction. The perception of the typical voter, however, was that the economy was still in recession. Why public morale was low, even though economic revival was under way, requires a word of explanation.

Economists and the general public look at business cycle movements differently. When economists study business cycles they focus on a rather antiseptic, statistical analysis of the *direction* of movement. The economy is expanding or contracting. Economists are interested in understanding the underlying forces that provide forward momentum to an economy and in gaining insight into the imbalances that build up to halt expansion and send the system in a downward direction. It is a scholar's perspective, a search for understanding with which to predict the likely behavior of the economy in the future.

Voters are only dimly aware of the larger forces determining the behavior of the economy. For the most part, they are uninterested in the technical details. They react to slowdowns in the economy in a simple, straightforward way; they focus on the human cost of recessions. People are unemployed, paychecks stop, and workers and their families bear the burden of the failure of the economy to perform.

When a declining economy reaches a bottom and starts to recover, the recession is over in a statistical sense but not necessarily in human terms. The unemployment rate may not drop—it may even increase—even though an economic expansion is under way. One should think of our economy in a dynamic sense. Except for moderate interruptions during recessions, the economy continually expands. Population grows and new workers are constantly entering the labor force, most of them young, looking for jobs. The economy must grow simply to draw these new workers into employment.[50] If the nation in one year produces the same amount of output as it did in the last, the unemployment rate rises, since new jobs are not created to absorb new job applicants. The minimum growth necessary to reduce the unemployment rate to an acceptable level under Ford was not sustained in advance of the 1976 election. The rate at polling time in November stood at 7.8 percent. What economists saw as an expanding economy was seen by voters as an economy in recession.

The platforms of challengers in a presidential campaign are partly defined by the failures of the incumbent or, at least, by the failures for which he is blamed, fairly or unfairly, by the voters. In 1976, once one got beyond the Watergate affair, the key substantive issue was the recession. While Carter "addressed inflation during the campaign," Eizenstat has written, "he clearly made unemployment his number one enemy."[51] He made his appeal to a constituency of middle and lower income workers, the group most vulnerable to unemployment, the ones who must bear, as the candidate said in a major campaign speech, "the heartbreak and family disintegration that unemployment can bring."[52]

Carter chose to give the Labor Day speech, traditional for opening a Democratic campaign in the general election, at Warm Springs, Georgia, the beloved retreat to which the physically handicapped Franklin Roosevelt went for therapy and renewal and the place where he died. Carter was aware of the value of associating himself with the powerful symbolism of Warm Springs for his campaign kickoff. Standing on the hallowed grounds, the Democratic candidate linked himself with the spirit of Roosevelt and the traditions of the party. "When President Johnson went out of office," he said, "unemployment was less than 4 percent, and at the end of Truman's term less than 3 percent of our people were out of work. But the unemployment rate today is 7.9 percent. Under this Republican Administration the unemployment rate has been the highest since the Hoover depression."[53]

President Gerald Ford would plead during the campaign that the economy was on the road to recovery. "Since the depth of the recession," he said in the first debate that took place between the candidates, "we have added 4 million jobs." He went on to add: "I'd like to point out as well that the United States economic recovery from the recession of a year ago is well ahead of the economic recovery of any major free industrial nation in the world today. We are ahead of all of the Western European countries. We are ahead of Japan. The United States is leading the free world out of the recession that was serious a year and a half ago."[54] Despite the disclaimers, Jerry Ford carried into the campaign the heavy burden of unemployment.

CARTER'S CAMPAIGN ECONOMICS
In addition to the mass of news reports filed by members of the media who tracked the statements of the candidates on all areas of policy during the long and grueling contest, there is available for the record of the 1976 campaign a complete five-volume collection of the speeches, interviews, and press releases of the candidates, along with the transcripts of the three televised debates.[55] One of the things that is striking as you read through this massive amount of material is the degree to which a campaign is a learning process, not only for the public, but for those seeking office. It not only informs the voters on what a candidate stands for; it is also a process of self discovery for the one running for office as he is forced by the interchange with voters and the news media to refine his ideas, hone his positions on issues to greater precision, and become more proficient in mastery of technical details. Inconsistencies between positions adopted in the early phases of the campaign and modified later to reflect a growing command of the issues and to widen voter appeal must be justified somehow to a critical press. The problem of simply keeping track of what is said over a long campaign is shown by the effort required of Carter's staff to compile at his request a list of all the promises he made during the primaries and the general election. This summary of promises, along with a citation of the speeches or news releases in which they appeared, comes to 120 pages.[56]

In his statements on economic issues during the campaign, Carter was more detailed and specific about policies he would pursue if elected. "In at least one all-important area," *Time* magazine reported in June, "the accusation of fuzziness that has dogged Jimmy Carter throughout his 18-month campaign cannot fairly be sustained. In a stream of speeches, position papers and interviews, the Democratic front runner has expounded his ideas on all of the major, and some of the minor, questions of economic policy."[57]

Given highest priority among economic issues, as we have said, was the commitment to reduce unemployment. Carter's proposal submitted to the platform committee for inclusion in the Democratic platform appealed to the traditions of the party: "We Democrats still agree with Harry Truman that full employment is, and ought to be, a national policy and a national goal—and we ought to pursue that goal with all the determination and imagination we can muster."[58] On numerous occasions during the campaign, as in an interview with the editors of *U.S. News and World Report*, Carter is more specific in terms of his objective. "I would set a goal of bringing unemployment down to 3 percent among adults, 4 or 4½ percent for the whole labor force."[59] Why these percentages were selected requires a word of explanation.

Given the large number of workers in transition between jobs in an economy as mobile as ours, there are always people who are unemployed. If complete information about openings were readily available, movement from job to job would be rapid; but information on openings is limited, and search time is required for transition to new employment. There are other impediments to movement in the market, particularly when a shift to a new job requires a crossing of industrial, occupational, or geographical lines. Because of these frictions, it is impossible to reduce the unemployment rate to zero. The unemployment due to these constraints gives us the benchmark expressed in the somewhat contradictory phrase, "the full employment-unemployment rate." This number varies from nation to nation because of differences in barriers to physical movement, the customs and habits of the people, and the efficiency of public and private employment agencies. The precise amount for the United States is difficult to estimate and varies through time.

The Kennedy administration was the first to adopt a specific unemployment rate target, a step not without the possibility of political embarrassment. Announcing a precise numerical goal leaves an administration open to easy grading by the media. When national goals are stated in broad terms—"to get the country moving again"—a president's record is less vulnerable to scrutiny since the commitment is somewhat ambiguous. When a precise number is used as a goal, there is no ambiguity; it is obvious whether or not the administration has succeeded. The Kennedy Council of Economic Advisers set 4 percent as the full employment target, reflecting, as stated in the annual *Economic Report*, "a balancing of employment and production objectives with other considerations of national policy, within the limits set by the existing characteristics of the economy."[60] Carter accepted a target—4 or 4.5 percent—in the close vicinity of the Kennedy goal. An alternative way of expressing the objective came from the Humphrey-Hawkins bill then under consideration by Congress.[61]

The Humphrey-Hawkins bill provided one of the early signs of the tension between Carter and the more liberal wing of the Democratic Party that was to preoccupy the president over his four-year term. The bill was an attempt to broaden and make more binding the responsibility of the federal government to intervene to ensure economic prosperity, a responsibility laid out in vague terms in the Employment Act of 1946. This effort to legislate a higher level of activism was the product of the old-line Democratic liberal senator Hubert Humphrey and a member of the Black Caucus, Congressman August Hawkins. It reflected their frustration with the failure of the Nixon and Ford administrations to deal boldly, as they saw it, with the problem of unemployment.

One of the quirks of the bill was to state the full employment target in terms of adult workers rather than in terms of the total labor force, the conventional way in which the goal is expressed in policy discussions. The "3 percent unemployment for adult workers" phrasing of the Humphrey-Hawkins bill was thought by Carter economists to be equivalent to a 4 to 4.5 percent rate for the entire labor force. This simple number has major policy implications that would escape the average voter.

Statistical measures commonly reported in the daily news, and easily ignored or forgotten by the typical reader—the unemployment rate, factory capacity utilization rate, gross national product—convey crucial information about the performance of the economy and provide warning signals about problems that may be developing.[62] How an administration interprets the data is vitally important in terms of policy. If an administration plays the policy game cautiously in order to avoid the risk of inducing inflationary pressure, it sets the full-employment target at the top of the range of estimates considered acceptable by informed observers and runs the risk of tolerating excessive joblessness. If an administration is too aggressive and sets the full employment target too low, it runs the risk of setting off inflation. The appropriate target is a critical issue and a matter of continual concern. Democrats tended over the years before Carter to set the target rate a little lower than did Republicans, a practice that represents a bolder policy approach. Economists tend to reflect the political bias of the candidates they advise. As Paul Samuelson has said in speaking of economists: "The conservative will forecast high inflation dangers on the basis of the same data that lead the dogooder to warn against recession."[63]

The authors of the Humphrey-Hawkins bill were even more optimistic than the mainstream of the party about what could be accomplished in reducing unemployment. The early version of the bill set the full employment-unemployment rate below 4 percent in terms of the entire labor force—a clearly unrealistic rate during the Carter years—as a national goal. The bill had other provisions that were called into question by prudent observers. It displayed in its original wording a disturbing lack of concern for the danger of inflation. It also made the federal government the employer of last resort when the private sector failed to provide a sufficient number of jobs to employ all of those looking for work. Humphrey-Hawkins was the last hurrah of those whose mindsets took shape in the New Deal–Great Society policy era. It created a problem for Carter. Lawrence Klein was quoted in *Time* magazine in June as saying: "This bill could become an albatross, but no bill goes through Congress without amendments, and I can envision 10 amendments that would make this a good bill."[64]

During press conferences the news media repeatedly made the Humphrey-Hawkins bill a litmus test of Carter's Democratic credentials. When the first version of the bill was revised the target unemployment rate selected for the total labor force moved closer to a realistic number, 4 to 4.5 percent. Even this number was too low for some of Carter's advisers. Michael Wachter, Klein's colleague at the University of Pennsylvania and a member of Carter's economics task force, was reported as thinking the appropriate full employment-unemployment rate to be about 5.5 percent. Klein seems to have accepted the lower figure of 4 to 4.5 percent with the provision that an expansionary policy would be supported by an incomes policy to dampen inflationary pressure.

Carter gave the bill qualified endorsement. "I didn't approve of it the way it was originally written. With a mandatory total unemployment goal of 3 percent, taking in all age groups, most of my academic advisers thought that would mean double-digit inflation."[65] His conservative instincts made him less than totally comfortable with the ambitious goals of the Humphrey-Hawkins bill. His own common sense also made him recognize that the full employment target, however stated, is only an approximation and a rough sort of guideline. He reflected this in a press briefing at Plains in late July 1976.

Q: Governor, do you accept a definite goal—full employment means different things to different people. Do you use the Humphrey-Hawkins bill definition of 3 percent unemployment for people of 20 years or older?

A: I think that's a reasonable definition. You have to remember that when you are talking about the unemployment rate now, it's 7.5 percent or more. To start arguing about the exact definition of unemployment when it gets down to 3 percent is really an ideal exercise, but I think as a goal, that's a good one.[66]

A specific unemployment target was not included in Carter's proposals submitted to the Democratic Platform Committee, although the 3 percent adult rate was included in the platform adopted by the party.[67] In terms of timing, Carter set as his goal "full employment by 1979—before the end of the first term of my administration."[68] Not far into the administration Carter would have to face the Humphrey-Hawkins bill again as it wound its way through Congress and was finally passed in an amended version in 1978. We will see later that a too optimistic estimate of how low the unemployment rate could go before triggering inflation became the source of a major problem in the administration.

FISCAL POLICY AND MONETARY POLICY

To move the economy toward full employment, the April 1976 economic position paper stated that "we must have an expansionary fiscal and monetary policy for the coming fiscal year to stimulate demand and production."[69] The use of the budget to stabilize the economy was accepted as a matter of principle, but policy should aim for a balanced budget at full employment. "For the current fiscal year," the economic position paper continued, "an expansionary fiscal and monetary policy is necessary. Social needs and the need for economic stabilization may require from time to time unbalancing the budget. But we should strive toward budget balance, *within an environment of full employment*, over the long term. The surplus years should balance the deficits. *I therefore call for balanced budgets over the business cycle*. This can be achieved in 1979."[70]

Carter's fiscal policy stand, as stated in the economic position paper, is tilted toward the conservative. His balanced budget rule was similar in principle to the one pioneered by Herbert Stein in the 1940s and adopted by the Committee for Economic Development, an organization of business executives for which Stein was research director. The rule was accepted by

Richard Nixon when he was president.[71] In an interview fifteen years later Lawrence Klein elaborated on Carter's position: "You see, I think the prime point that we tried to make on this economic task force was that Jimmy Carter was fiscally conservative. Let us say fiscally prudent. He was not a big spender and he was not going to be reckless with the budget . . . and he would not simply use spending and fiscal policy as a weapon. He would have a balanced program. It would involve fiscal policy, but it would involve other things too. He was not in favor of budget deficits as a matter of principle."[72]

In a May 1976 interview with *Fortune*, Carter took the position, on the issue of monetary policy, that the money supply should be increasing more rapidly to stimulate the economy. For the longer term management of monetary policy, the April economic position paper argued for better coordination of central bank policy and fiscal policy. To foster coordination, the term of the chairman of the Board of Governors of the Federal Reserve should be made coterminous with that of the president. Under the provisions of the law—then and now—the term of the chairman overlaps that of the president. In the early years of an administration a new president must serve with a chair appointed by his predecessor. Allowing a president to appoint a new chair upon assuming office would ensure, presumably, greater compatibility between the two and a more unified national policy. This proposal was not a radical suggestion; it had long been supported by some observers of the Federal Reserve's operations. Paul Volcker made the same recommendation toward the end of his term as chairman of the Board of Governors in mid-1987.

Carter also argued during the campaign that the Federal Reserve should be required to report to Congress annually on its intentions. The inclusion of this position on the Fed among the campaign statements has to be explained partly in terms of the Humphrey-Hawkins bill, which also called for closer coordination of policy between the Federal Reserve and the office of the president. "You have to understand what was going on," Lawrence Klein responded to a question about Carter's views on monetary policy. "We had a lot of discussion, whether we could swallow Humphrey-Hawkins or not. I felt that aspects of it were naïve. . . . But Hawkins and we were very strong on the concept that the Federal Reserve should report to Congress on what their perspectives are, their plans for the coming period, and that has been a lasting part of that legislation."[73]

Carter proposed a jobs program to supplement fiscal and monetary policy, but the first emphasis should be on the private sector where the creation of jobs in our economy takes place. Beginning in the New Hampshire primary Carter showed a reluctance to have the public sector provide jobs directly except for certain cases, a position in contrast with that of other Democratic candidates who took a more aggressive stand.[74] According to studies cited by economic advisers, the cost of creating one government job, Carter said in an Associated Press interview, was $10,500.[75] It would be better to leverage government outlays by using the funds to encourage business to hire and train workers. A series of actions to stimulate private industry to hire the unemployed would be initiated: funding for the cost of on-the-job training by business, encouragement of employers to retain workers during cyclical downturns, public programs to train workers for jobs in the private sector, and incentives to encourage employers to hire young people.[76]

There are some cases in which government programs would be needed. "Young people, particularly minority groups, have an unemployment rate of 40 percent—a heavy contributing factor to the crime rate increase. There, I think, an investment in a program similar to the CCC [Civilian Conservation Corps] program that we experienced in the Great Depression would be beneficial to our country."[77] Specific initiatives were listed in the economic position paper: the provision of 800,000 summer youth jobs and doubling the Comprehensive Employment Training Act program from 300,000 to 600,000 training slots.[78]

INFLATION

If President Gerald Ford was vulnerable in the 1976 campaign because of high unemployment, he also had to bear the burden of a high inflation rate. Carter's problem was that in committing his administration to an aggressive full employment program he would, himself, run the risk of putting upward pressure on the price level.

Carter's answer during the campaign, to those who cited the danger of feeding inflation by an expansionary policy, was that the risk was minimal. "An expansionary policy," the economic position paper said, "can reduce unemployment without reigniting inflation, because our economy is presently performing so far under capacity."[79] In an interview with the editors of *Fortune* magazine, Carter said in response to a question: "I would proceed aggressively, with the first emphasis on jobs. My economic advisers and I agree that until you get the unemployment rate down below 5 percent, there's no real danger of escalating inflationary pressures."[80] In any event inflation should not be attacked at the expense of jobs. "There are far more humane and economically sound solutions to curbing inflation," he stated in his economic position paper, "than enforced recession, unemployment, monetary restrictions and high interest rates."[81] In a speech to the general board of the AFL-CIO (American Federation of Labor and Congress of Industrial Organizations), he became more partisan in his attack on Ford, as one might expect in an appearance before leaders of the labor movement: "We have an administration which uses the evil of unemployment to fight the evil of inflation—and succeeds only in having the highest combination of unemployment and inflation in the twentieth century."[82]

A set of measures to contain inflation is offered in the economic position paper. Most of them are long-term initiatives and addressed to the supply side of the economy: efforts to increase productivity "so that growth does not become overly inflationary"; reform of government regulations that increase costs and prices; and strict enforcement of anti-trust legislation.[83] Monetary policy is given a supply-side twist; the candidate supported "a monetary policy which encourages lower interest rates and the availability of investment capital at reasonable costs."[84]

In the context of the times, the possible use of wage and price controls as part of an anti-inflation strategy was an issue of public concern. In 1970 a Democratic Congress gave Richard Nixon discretionary authority to impose comprehensive wage and price controls, not expecting him to use them. Nixon did the unconventional thing for a Republican—and for one who had a direct and frustrating experience with controls while serving briefly during World War II at the Office of Price Administration.[85] He exercised the authority, imposing controls in a surprise move in August 1971. The initiative started with a ninety-day wage-price freeze and continued through a series of stages in which the controls were gradually relaxed. The experiment lasted till spring 1974, when all wage-price restraints were removed.[86]

Congress did not renew the standby authority for President Nixon when it expired. Whether Carter would ask for such discretionary authority became a matter of concern, particularly to the business community. He had committed himself in his April economic position paper as favoring standby controls.[87] He replied to a question during one interview with an answer repeated on a number of occasions: "I would like to have as a last resort, and if other economic policies can't prevail, some standby wage and price control authority. I don't think I would ever have to use it. But I would like that right as a source of persuasion."[88] The expectations of wage and price controls, which this campaign position raised, may have led to anticipatory price increases by some firms. *The Wall Street Journal* reported in early

December after the election that "a lot of talk has been going around that the recent flurries of price boosts are efforts by companies to beat the wage-and-price controls due to come back when Jimmy Carter takes over the White House."[89] *Newsweek* reported that businesses were raising list prices and then discounting them to customers. The tactic gave price setters the flexibility of maintaining prices at current levels in an environment of slack demand, while having the freedom to raise them and still be in conformity with price control regulations should they be imposed. "Part of the rise [in wholesale prices] is a paper increase only," *Newsweek* quoted Alan Greenspan, President Ford's chairman of the Council of Economic Advisers, as saying. "The basic industries are trying to buy themselves controls insurance with unreal list prices."[90] Jody Powell, newly appointed press secretary operating out of headquarters set up in Americus, Georgia, responded to what could be a serious problem by disputing "rumors that the President-elect is leaning toward wage-price controls."[91]

Powell's comment to the news media reflected a behind-the-scenes shift in the advice being given to the president-elect on the matter of controls. A group assembled in Plains on December 1 for a planning session on economic policy advised against a request for standby controls. "He was told there was enormous slack in the economy and that increased business and investment were a usual factor in any recovery and must be increased through predictable and consistent policies. . . . The view unanimously expressed was that confidence was the key to increased investment, and wage and price controls—even standby controls—would dampen that needed confidence . . . . Instead, voluntary restraint should be stressed."[92]

Carter accepted the advice and did not request standby authority for wage and price controls when he assumed the presidency. For all presidents, positions adopted at campaign stops are often modified when viewed from the Oval Office.

CHAPTER 3 | **THE NEW ADMINISTRATION**

THE PROCESS OF ECONOMIC ADVICE

After the voters had spoken on November 4, 1976, in what turned out to be a close election, the attention of the nation centered on Plains, Georgia. A stream of experts made the long trek to the tiny village where Jimmy Carter had grown up and still made his home. They came to consult with the president-elect and to advise him on the details of the new administration's policies. They also came to play their roles in a ritual enacted every four years—the ritual of selecting those who will fill the posts in the new administration.

They arrived from points around the country, first to the Atlanta airport and then by way of chartered bus for the three-hour trip to Plains. They came in groups—experts on national defense, on foreign affairs, and on economic policy—to Miss Lillian's Pond House, the modest home of Carter's mother just outside Plains near a small pond which gave it its name. Most of the sessions were held there, a setting that must have seemed strangely disorienting to those accustomed to the well-appointed offices of Washington and New York.

Early in December a group of leading economic figures gathered in Plains in a meeting I referred to earlier. Charles Schultze, soon to be chairman of the Council of Economic Advisers, was there as was Michael Blumenthal, the new secretary of the treasury. Two members of the Economics Task Force, Lawrence Klein and Richard Cooper, were there. Walter Heller, chief economic adviser to John Kennedy, and Arthur Okun, chairman of the Council of Economic Advisers under Johnson, represented continuity in the Democratic tradition of economic advice. A succession of meetings followed to iron out the details, with the mix of people in attendance changing somewhat from session to session. Juanita Kreps, the new secretary of commerce, and Jerry Jasinowski from the campaign issues team also came to Plains. Ray Marshall, selected to be the new secretary of labor, was there. Bert Lance, soon to be director of the Office of Management and Budget, was consulted.

The economists' task was to develop what came to be called the "stimulus package." The theme that was central to the campaign, getting the economy moving again, now had to be converted to specific programs and numbers. From Charles Schultze's account of the final drafting, one gets a feeling for the time pressure and the makeshift arrangements under which the staff of a president-elect works. "We had tentatively put together a package which included the tax cut and a little bit of public works," Schultze recalls. "The next day the congressmen were coming in and I recall flying from Plains to Bert Lance's mansion [in Atlanta] in Bert Lance's plane. Blumenthal, Lance and I were having dinner and at 12:00 o'clock when they went to bed I sat down and drafted the program. Bert Lance's young son got up at about 4:00 in the morning and typed it. I got up at six in the morning to correct it and the kid was just finishing typing it. We took it to the nearest state police barracks and they ran it off on the Xerox and that was the stimulus plan."[1]

Leading business figures led by Reginald Jones, chief executive officer of General Electric, came to Plains to be briefed on the contents of the package and to provide feedback on the mood of the business community. The president-elect met with representatives of the National League of Cities and the National Conference of Mayors to get their ideas. At the first gathering of the new cabinet shortly after Christmas at the Musgrove Plantation on Saint Simon's Island off the coast of Georgia, Schultze gave a rundown on the economic program. The content of the stimulus package is discussed in a later chapter. First I must explain the process for economic advice in the new administration.

THE ECONOMIC POLICY GROUP

As the time for the inauguration grew near, the advisory process became more formal and assumed its permanent shape. The economic advisory team after Carter took office was labeled the Economic Policy Group. At the core of this group was what had been called in the Kennedy administration, the Troika. The Troika, like the Russian sled pulled by three horses, had three key members: the secretary of the treasury, by tradition the official spokesman for an administration on matters of economic policy; the director of the Office of Management and Budget, the office which assists the president in preparation of the budget; and the chairman of the Council of Economic Advisers, the advisory group created by the Employment Act of 1946.[2]

Michael Blumenthal, prior to his appointment at Treasury, was chief executive officer at Bendix Corporation. Carter and Blumenthal could hardly have come from more different backgrounds. While Carter grew up in rural Georgia, Blumenthal had as a youth suffered the harrowing experience of escaping with his family from Germany and Nazi persecution.[3] He came to the United States by way of Shanghai, studied at Berkeley as an undergraduate, and went on to Princeton for graduate work in economics. Blumenthal served in the State Department during the Kennedy-Johnson years. Carter got to know him through the Trilateral Commission. Cyrus Vance, when appointed secretary of state, wanted him as his deputy. After talking to Blumenthal at Plains, Carter decided he would be better placed as secretary of the treasury.[4]

Bert Lance, Carter's first director of the Office of Management and Budget, had served as head of the highway department while Carter was governor. The only one of the Georgia group that came to Washington that was close to Carter's age, he had a unique peer relationship with the president. Lance lacked formal training in economics but brought to policy discussions a practical business sense and political savvy. He played an important role in decisions on economic policy in the early days of the administration because of his close relationship to Carter, but his role as an adviser was short lived.[5] Except for his tour with the Georgia highway department, Lance's career had been in banking. He resigned from the administration in the fall of 1977 due to controversy involving past banking practices. He was later cleared of any irregularities.[6] Lance was replaced as head of the Office of Management and Budget by his deputy James McIntyre. A lawyer by training, McIntyre served under Governor Carter as deputy state revenue commissioner and had worked closely with him in a reorganization effort involving a massive study of state government.[7] McIntyre served as head of the Office of Management and Budget for the remaining three and a half years.

The third member of the Troika was the chairman of the Council of Economic Advisers, Charles Schultze, who had spent his career in Washington either at the Brookings Institution or in government. In answer to a question of when he became involved with Carter, Schultze replied: "I didn't really get to know him or have much to do with his campaign until I don't know when, but it was after the nomination."[8] When asked how

Schultze's name surfaced for consideration for a position in the administration, Stuart Eizenstat replied: "How could Charlie Schultze's name not come up? Charlie was the preeminent Democratic economist. He had been the head of the budget bureau [under Johnson]; he was head of economic policy at Brookings and had written widely; very knowledgeable about government. If you wanted a main stream Democratic economist, you couldn't get anybody more preeminent than Charlie."[9] Schultze had a running start on the other members of the Troika. Lance lacked formal training in economics. Blumenthal, despite his doctoral degree in the subject, had not worked seriously in economics for a number of years. "Blumenthal," Schultze has said, "was a quick learner, but he came into this never having played in the macro policy game so he felt his way for a while."[10] Schultze was the chief strategist in forming Carter's first economic plan.

President Gerald Ford put into place a rather formal advisory process in the form of the Economic Policy Board. Its membership included selected cabinet members in addition to the members of the Troika. It met frequently—over 500 times during the two years of the Ford administration— and handled a wide range of domestic and foreign economic issues.[11] Gerald Ford was comfortable with the well-structured system of the Economic Policy Board and called it "the most important institutional innovation of my administration."[12] William Simon, secretary of the treasury, chaired the board, but William Seidman, assistant to the president, coordinated its work as executive director. A large part of the success of the Ford arrangement was due to Seidman who managed the paper flow going to the president and was accepted by the participants as an honest broker in handling the business of the board.

Schultze and Blumenthal in early January gave a memorandum to Carter on the organization of an Economic Policy Group for the new administration.[13] In a later memo in mid-February, Blumenthal and Schultze presented to the president their "final recommendations on proposed membership, basic structure and the process for formulating recommendations to you.... That a single cabinet level committee called the Economic Policy Group be created to help formulate and coordinate both domestic and foreign economic policy."[14] The February Blumenthal-Schultze memorandum provided further details. "The operation of the EPG [Economic Policy Group] should be less rigid than that of the Ford Administration's Economic Policy Board."[15] It would restrict itself to major issues and would meet weekly instead of four times a week like the Ford group. A small staff would manage the flow of reports and other paper.[16] "Actual policy analysis will be carried out by groups of staff members and senior deputies from the several agencies involved in the EPG. Most of these groups will be created ad hoc to deal with specific problems at they arise."[17] Under the plan the secretary of the treasury and the CEA (Council of Economic Advisers) chairman would serve as co-chairs of the Economic Policy Group and its executive committee.

Carter had decided, in his overall organization of the White House, not to have a chief of staff. He chose, as did John Kennedy, a "spokes-of-the-wheel" type of organization, with himself at the hub and with the spokes converging into his office giving direct access to cabinet members and selected staff. He would be his own chief of staff. He settled on this arrangement partly in reaction to the negative public image of the Nixon White House, an image of an embattled president encircled by a secretive staff who controlled access to the Oval Office.[18] Carter would have an open administration with cabinet government, where cabinet members played the key roles and had easy access to the president. As one of Carter's speech writers has said, "'cabinet government' became a good-government rallying cry."[19] The experience with this arrangement through various presidencies is that it doesn't work. Carter himself moved away somewhat from the experiment. The practice of weekly cabinet meetings did not last much beyond the first year, and he later appointed a chief of staff to provide more coordination to daily affairs. But in the beginning, cabinet government provided the pattern.[20]

The organization of the Economic Policy Group reflected this plan for cabinet involvement. In addition to the members of the Troika, an executive committee of the EPG consisted of the secretaries of state, commerce, labor, housing and urban development, and the national security adviser. The vice president and the assistant to the president for domestic affairs were ex officio members.

There were problems with the Economic Policy Group arrangement from the very beginning.[21] For one thing the number of people involved in the executive committee was too large. The original Blumenthal-Schultze memorandum to the president in early January proposed an executive committee consisting only of the members of the Troika and the secretary of state, but there was strong pressure to expand the membership. The secretary of commerce, Juanita Kreps, and the secretary of labor, Ray Marshall, both of whom had Ph.D.s in economics, pressed to be on the committee. Carter probably promised them at the time of their appointment that they would be involved in economic policy.[22] Membership for the HUD (Department of Housing and Urban Development) secretary arose for a different reason. The congressional Black Caucus pressed for representation by an African American. Patricia Harris, the HUD secretary, was added to the executive committee to satisfy this constituency.[23] With about ten members of the committee attending meetings, accompanied by two or three deputies or staff, attendance was sometimes as high as thirty or more people.[24] Schultze recalls that the President "walked into one meeting for the first time and he sits and looks around the room and, while I never heard him say it, I'm sure he was shocked by the huge attendance."[25]

To create a manageable arrangement, the Economic Policy Group was reorganized in July of the first year. The executive committee continued to exist, though it met at irregular and less frequent intervals. A smaller "steering committee" was created consisting of the Troika and a representative of the State Department for matters of international economic policy, and with the vice president and the assistant for domestic policy, Stuart Eizenstat, also in attendance at meetings. In the previous March, Schultze suggested to the president that he should step down as co-chairman of the EPG. "Mike and I work well together and had easily come to an agreement about division of responsibilities. But I cannot both play an independent role as your overall economic adviser and in some sense represent the EPG as co-Chairman." The president concurred.[26] The small staff created to schedule issues and to manage the flow of paperwork through the committee was lodged in the Treasury Department under Blumenthal, who remained as sole chairman.[27]

While these adjustments tightened up the advisory process, it continued to cause frustration for the president. Carter is reported as saying in the early months of the administration that he had lost confidence in the EPG. He thought seriously of dismantling it, stating that he had one group for foreign policy, one for domestic, "and did not want a third group for economics." He was dissuaded by Lance, who advised him that the president needed "economic advice from a visible entity."[28] To improve the process, it was decided that Eizenstat would assist in giving more structure to the paperwork going to the president.[29] Carter was never completely happy with the process of economic advice and was still tinkering with it as late as 1979.[30]

The main difficulty seems to have been that the steering committee did not sufficiently limit the paperwork and the options going to the president. In a May 1977 memorandum, Blumenthal commented on EPG procedures: "In accordance with the President's instructions I, as Chairman, will report to the President the results and recommendations of all EPG deliberations—

in the form of an agreed consensus or options reflecting the different viewpoints of EPG members. It is clear, however, that any Cabinet member who wishes to have his or her own position separately stated is free to do so. These papers will be attached as tabs to the basic EPG memorandum going to the President."[31] Stuart Eizenstat later recalled that "President Carter became increasingly frustrated with the operation of the interdepartmental Economic Policy Group, chaired by the Treasury Department, because its recommendations were often nothing more than the collection of differing agency recommendations, without adequate synthesis."[32]

The president himself was at least partly responsible for not enforcing restraints on the policy group or putting someone in charge who had the authority to act in his name. Schultze has said that "there was never enough discipline in the process so that on many issues, the president would get a 25-page memo broken into eight subsections, each with three options, so by the time you finished, you have 18 things to check off; and partly because Carter would never delegate to, say, Eizenstat, or to Blumenthal, or to anybody, the power to tell some cabinet secretary, no, there will not be option 18-B."[33]

Although Eizenstat was assigned the task of improving coordination, it was, as he would later comment, "without the capability to do it or the staff to do it and without the sort of clear mandate to do it. I mean it was just sort of 'help,' you know. Help me, let's somehow get this thing working better but without the directive that Bill Seidman would have and without the staff capacity."[34] No system works perfectly for any president and under Carter, as Eizenstat added, "one way or the other the issues got vetted. And people did end up having their debate but it was too messy. Much messier than it should have been."[35]

THE CAST OF CHARACTERS

Even if the process of economic advice had been more tightly organized, there still would have been a normal amount of friction because of differences in the political orientation of participants. Such differences are not unique to the Carter administration. John Kennedy brought in as chairman of the Council of Economic Advisers Walter Heller, whose views were in the liberal tradition. Due to the closeness of the 1960 presidential race, Kennedy sought balance in his administration and appointed Douglas Dillon, who had served in the Eisenhower administration, to head up the Treasury. "There's no question," Arthur Okun recalled later in an interview, "that from the outset Dillon and Heller were giving President Kennedy quite different advice."[36] The spread of Carter's game players across the political spectrum is a reflection of Carter's need to blend conservative and liberal claims throughout his presidency. "The range had Mondale and Eizenstat on one end," Charles Schultze recalls. "Jim McIntyre from OMB [Office of Management and Budget] might have been on the other. And I was toward the McIntyre end, but not fully."[37]

Schultze's position serves as a reference point for a comparison of the members of the group. As a Keynesian he was inclined toward demand management to keep the economy operating at a prosperous level; he was an activist on macroeconomic issues. On microeconomic issues he shared the basic respect for the power of the market to allocate resources efficiently that is ingrained in economists at an early age. Just before coming into the Carter administration, Schultze had written a book on the subject of economic regulation in which he proposed reducing the government's direct involvement in pollution control. In its place, he recommended injecting the discipline of the market into regulatory policy by internalizing for firms, through tax provisions, the cost of pollution. Such a policy would force firms to take account of the side effects of their operations on the environment.[38] Carter was aware of this book before meeting Schultze. Schultze later recalled: "I have a vague recollection early in the game. I don't know where this came from, but something that Bert Lance did or something else that was done of which I wasn't quite aware clearly indicated to me that either Carter had read or somebody had talked to him about that public interest book of mine. The basic idea came right through."[39]

Schultze's experience as head of the budget office under Johnson gave him firsthand exposure to the financial constraints that impose limits on policy decisions. The budget director understands from daily experience that resources available to government are limited and that tough choices have to be made in terms of total amount spent and the allocation of funds to specific purposes. Schultze also had a lot of "street smarts" about the ways of Washington. He had been through the fiery furnace with Lyndon Johnson.[40] Schultze's budget experience probably explains the reason for his surprising statement that he was closer to McIntyre than to some others on the political spectrum, despite the fact that McIntyre was the most conservative member of the Economic Policy Group. Their shared experience in the budget office is likely the reason why McIntyre, on his part, felt comfortable with Schultze. "I'd say Schultze and I were probably closer in our thinking about what ought to be done, particularly during the latter stages of the administration," McIntyre said in an interview. "Charlie Schultze is . . . one of the most reasonable, practical economists that you could ever

Carter and Charles Schultze, chief economic adviser, in the Oval Office. Courtesy of the Jimmy Carter Library.

deal with. He had a lot of political sense. He had worked for Johnson, he had been both in the economic area and the budget area; so he had a good grasp for economic policy making in government, how it should work, how it does work."[41]

When not in government Schultze's professional home has been at the Brookings Institution, one of the oldest of Washington think tanks. "Ask most think-tank directors outside America," the English publication the *Economist* reported a few years ago, "which institute they would most like to resemble and the odds are they will name the Brookings Institution."[42] Brookings has been a traditional source of talent for Democrats. The first economist to serve as head of the Council of Economic Advisers under Truman after passage of the Employment Act of 1946 was Edwin Nourse from Brookings.[43] A number of Carter appointees also came from there. In addition to Schultze there were, among others, Henry Aaron, who served under Joseph Califano in Health Education and Welfare; Fred Bergsten, assistant secretary in the Treasury; Barry Bosworth, director of the Council on Wage and Price Stability; and Henry Owen and William Quandt, who served on the National Security Council staff. Arthur Okun and Joseph

Carter and James McIntyre, director of the Office of Management and Budget, in the Oval Office. Courtesy of the Jimmy Carter Library.

Pechman, both Brookings fellows, were outside advisers to Jimmy Carter. Henry Owen once suggested to Carter in a memorandum that he might want to attend one of the regular Brookings Friday lunches at which senior staff, about twenty-five people, discuss the events of the preceding week.[44]

In addition to his role as head of the Council of Economic Advisers, Schultze also acted as personal adviser to the president. He saw Carter not only in group sessions but also privately. They originally met on a one-on-one basis twice a week. They both found they needed less time and settled into a pattern of meeting once a week and eventually every two weeks. Economic issues do not require the attention of a president on a daily basis. Schultze has observed that "quite literally if somebody gave me fifteen minutes or twenty minutes every morning to brief the President, I'd be at a loss. I wouldn't know what to say to him that would be worth his time every morning. Apparently there are in foreign policy. I guess it's the intelligence briefing, maybe that's all it is; for example, if you've got a Soviet trawler around. But in any event, that tremendous control of information every day in the operational area coming through one person is something you don't have in the economic area. It's just not operational."[45] While Schultze didn't see Carter as often as Brzezinski, his private contact with the president was substantial.[46]

Schultze has described his influence with Carter as about average for presidential economic advisers. "Greenspan was very close to Ford. I had less influence with Carter but apparently had more influence than Marty Feldstein had with Reagan; somewhere in between."[47] Carter, on his part, recalls being more comfortable with Schultze than with any other economic adviser. "Usually in the final stages," Carter said in an interview, "I turned to Charlie Schultze, with whom I felt compatible. Charlie would sit down with me in the Oval Office and just say in his inimitable way, 'you know, Mr. President, these are the practical things that I believe we can extract from all the various sources of advice and information and these are the options that you have,' and Charlie Schultze would pretty well narrow down the most advantageous policies."[48]

On the conservative side of Schultze were Blumenthal and Lance. At the liberal end of the spectrum of economic advice were Ray Marshall, the secretary of labor, Vice President Walter Mondale, and Stuart Eizenstat.

Marshall is a labor economist who came to the Carter administration from his faculty position at the University of Texas.[49] In the administration he was aggressive in pushing for a strong employment policy, as we will see later. He was a member of the Economic Policy Group but not its steering committee, which was at the core of the advisory process. He would send memoranda expressing his views directly to the president, bypassing the steering committee. What some participants in the policy action saw as an end run, Marshall saw as a legitimate exercise of his responsibilities as a member of the cabinet.[50] "I only called him when I thought it was terribly important, ordinarily when we had interdepartmental conflicts that we couldn't resolve, say with OMB or the Council of Economic Advisers, which I frequently had. We sometimes had to take these kinds of issues to the President."[51]

Walter Mondale played a role in the Carter administration that was unusual for vice presidents up to that time. Carter saw Mondale's Washington experience as complementing his own strengths.[52] "I had served in a fairly low level with Johnson," Eizenstat commented in an interview, "but enough of a level to know that the White House staff and the Vice President's staff barely talked. The White House staff rarely let the Vice President's staff in on anything important, if at all. And that was totally different with us due to President Carter. . . . The paper flow on any paper from our staff always went through Mondale and through Mondale's issues people. And we had regular staff meetings every Friday where all my staff would get together and Mondale's staff was always invited to come."[53]

Though an ex officio member of the steering committee of the Economic

Carter and some members of the economic policy group. *Clockwise from Carter's left*: Ray Marshall, Charles Schultze, Juanita Kreps, and Stuart Eizenstat. The person to Eizenstat's left is unidentified. Courtesy of the Jimmy Carter Library.

Policy Group, Mondale attended meetings infrequently. A young staffer who kept him abreast of committee developments came in his place.[54] Mondale met weekly with the president for a private lunch and actively participated at certain stages of the budget process, fighting for liberal programs. But Eizenstat is not sure, "on the broad issues in terms of the economic direction, that he pulled the President from where the President may otherwise have been. Maybe marginally."[55]

Eizenstat, also an ex officio member of the steering committee, had, as head of the Domestic Policy Staff, thirty or so professionals reporting to him. The development of domestic policy under Kennedy and Johnson was managed by a few presidential assistants. Policy making was institutionalized under Nixon with the creation of a Domestic Council made up of cabinet members with responsibility for domestic issues and supported by a large staff headed by John Ehrlichman. In practice, under Nixon, the staff dominated the process and the Domestic Council was relegated to a minor role.

Carter, with his emphasis on cabinet government, made clear at the start of the administration that the Domestic Policy Staff was to play a coordinating and supportive function for the policy development work of the agencies. "Eizenstat's conception of his own role and that of his staff," as one Carter scholar has written, "was similar to that of his predecessors in previous administrations. Clark Clifford, Theodore Sorensen, Joseph Califano and John Ehrlichman had been generalists and brokers between the president and program advocates and experts. The differences were in the degree of authority each had to arbitrate among contending parties and to decide disputes. On this scale the Eizenstat operation had the least initial authority of any of the White House domestic policy staffs since Johnson."[56] In time Eizenstat's role as coordinator strengthened as the reality set in that each agency has its own constituency with competing interests to be resolved and that nearly all policy issues cross departmental lines. A change giving the Domestic Policy Staff more power of coordination was formalized at a meeting of the cabinet at Camp David in April 1978.[57] Eizenstat also had as part of his role interacting with Congress to take the measure of the political limits of policy initiatives.[58] In this function he was sensitive to the needs of the liberal wing of the party and was, along with Mondale, the main conduit for ideas coming from the liberal constituency.

THE COUNCIL OF ECONOMIC ADVISERS

In addition to functioning as the president's personal consultant, Charles Schultze served in the major role of chairman of the Council of Economic Advisers. The council consists of three members, backed up by a modest professional and clerical staff. Agencies in the federal government generally have their traditional constituencies. The Treasury and Commerce Departments identify with business, the Labor Department with organized labor. The sole constituent of the Council of Economic Advisers is the president, and the council's task is to provide him with objective technical advice.

The council staff produces solid, analytical studies that provide the background for the memos that go to the president.[59] Since the council was created in 1946, it has been traditional to have turnover in both council and staff. Economists who serve typically come from their universities with leaves of absence shorter in length than presidential terms. Of the members of the Carter council, only Schultze, with a more generous arrangement with Brookings, served the entire four years of the Carter presidency.[60] Those who have served on the council or its staff think of the turnover as an advantage because of the continuing inflow of fresh ideas. There has traditionally been a nonpartisan flavor to the council staffing. Charles Schultze and Carter's inflation czar, Alfred Kahn, both served on the staff of the Eisenhower council under Arthur Burns. Lawrence Summers, chief economic adviser to Michael Dukakis in the 1984 campaign, served on the Reagan council staff under Martin Feldstein.

The chair of the Council of Economic Advisers is the spokesperson for the group, but Schultze consulted with the other two members on all memoranda sent to the president.[61] In the first set of Carter's council members, William Nordhaus, who came from Yale and has been coauthor for later editions of Paul Samuelson's famous introductory text, was responsible for microeconomics. Lyle Gramley, the third member, was in charge of the critical area of forecasting. Gramley came to the council from the Federal Reserve Board, where he served as director of the Division of Research and Statistics.

As mundane as it may seem, forecasting is filled with political implications. For obvious reasons administrations like to forecast good times ahead. The thrust of a president's program can be seriously constrained by a pessimistic economic outlook that lowers the estimate of future tax revenues for financing program initiatives. By choosing a forecast near the top of the range of growth rates accepted as credible by informed observers and financial markets, an administration can present an image of fiscal discipline when it submits its annual budget message to Congress. The Rosy Scenario forecast of the Reagan administration for 1981, which overestimated expected gross national product and understated the size of the budget deficit, is well known among economic projections.

The Council of Economic Advisers had the lead role in developing the forecast. Deputies of the other Troika members to whom the mechanics of the forecasting task was assigned, along with representatives from the Commerce and Labor Departments, also participated. The exercise was chaired by Lyle Gramley. Each of the participating agencies used a large-scale econometric model to arrive at a forecast, modified by judgmental adjustment when the straight computer run was not convincing.[62] A final forecast was then negotiated.

The Congressional Budget Office (CBO), created by the Budget Reform Act of 1974 and responsible for producing a forecast for congressional use, employed a somewhat similar technique. Alice Rivlin, director of the CBO during Carter's term, has described it as "consensus forecasting by using all the standard available models."[63] Until the creation of the Congressional Budget Office in 1974, with its staff of experts, the president had a monopoly on the economic forecast. The point may seem like a trivial one, but control of the numbers in Washington represents political power. In 1974 Congress became a player in the forecasting game.

One can get a feel for the importance of forecasting in the competitive interaction of the legislative and executive branches in an account of an incident described by Eizenstat.

> When we developed our welfare reform proposal in 1977, President Carter openly directed Secretary Califano and Secretary Marshall to assure that their proposal had not greater cost than the current welfare system.... Based on HEW [Department of Health, Education, and Welfare] calculations using 1978 dollars, the program's additional cost was estimated in the President's message at around $7 billion annually. CBO did its own estimate. I remember my shock and dismay at reading in the *Washington Post* that CBO, discounting the Administration's cost-savings in other programs and using 1982 dollars, calculated the price tag of this once "no additional cost" program at $17 billion a year! The program was dead as of that moment—and could never be resurrected after the CBO estimate. The President's figures, based on HEW estimates, were no more incorrect than CBO's. Both had legitimacy. But because the President's monopoly on cost estimates had been ended, he had lost significant power and control over his legislation.[64]

CARTER AND ECONOMICS

The discussion up to this point has been concerned with the group that advised the president and influenced the direction of his economic policy. We come now to the recipient of this advice and the way in which he received and reacted to professional counsel.

Carter did not have a formal course in economics in his undergraduate days, but he did not come to Washington completely unschooled in the subject.[65] His duties as governor brought him in contact with economic issues. The state of Georgia, like most states, has a constitutional requirement that the budget be balanced. It is the responsibility of the governor to provide an estimate of the tax revenues that will be available for the coming year before the legislature can begin the process of appropriating funds at its annual session. The revenue estimate requires an economic forecast so that income and sales tax receipts can be projected. During his term Carter created the office of economic adviser to the governor and brought in to fill the position Henry Thomassen, an economist on the faculty of Georgia State University in Atlanta.[66]

Carter learned from Thomassen. He asked him for books to read and they had discussions. As Thomassen remembers it, they did not sit down in a formal way; "we would talk over lunch sometimes. It was a lot easier to convey, of course, quantitative formulations to him [because of his training in engineering subjects]. If you were going to talk to him about the sales tax, or incidence of taxes, it was relatively easy then to develop a case where you could convey the interaction of two or three forces simultaneously, you know, the effect of income, price, and of the transaction which carried these things backward and forward. That could be done, whereas I suppose for someone who had never had any quantitative training that would not be an easy thing to do."[67]

In the state archives, there are memoranda to Carter from Thomassen on economic matters of national interest that are beyond the normal day-to-day concerns of a governor. For example, there is a memo with an analysis of the channels by which an increase in food and fuel prices exerts upward pressure on the general price level, a problem with which Carter, as president, would become intimately involved.[68] Another, entitled "Production, Prices, and Pass Through," has a twelve-page paper attached, prepared "in an effort to set into perspective for you issues surrounding prices, profits, and pass-through in the President's [Nixon's] recently announced Phase 4 policy." The memorandum begins with a description of the allocative efficiency of a capitalistic price system and explains how price controls distort the allocative process of the market.[69]

There were occasional letters from Thomassen to Carter after he became president.[70] One is particularly interesting. In it Thomassen questions the effectiveness of wage-price guidelines to control inflation unless something more substantive is done as part of an anti-inflation effort. A rather plaintive note is written in the margin by Carter, obviously frustrated by the complexity of the problem: "Hank, I understand from this what will not work. What will?"[71]

Those who worked with Carter describe him as quick to get the point of a line of analysis and to absorb input from advisers.[72] Given his training, he had sufficient background to feel comfortable, as Thomassen has noted, with the mathematical relationships that are central to economic logic. There is an interesting note from Carter to Stuart Eizenstat early in the administration: "Find out for me how many different econometric models we are using for international analysis and whether the CIA [Central Intelligence Agency] needs one."[73]

Schultze has commented on Carter's sharpness in grasping economic argument. "I remember one time he embarrassed me on a matter of all things, probability theory. Small anecdote; I went in one time and it had to do with set asides, production cut backs in agriculture. . . . I said you know we've had two good crops in a row, a third one will really be extraordinary. And he said: 'I thought those were independent probabilities.' I watched him invent in his own mind the concept of marginal opportunity cost. I mean he invented it and never had an economics course in his life. I just watched him think his way through it. He was just first class."[74] In the early days of dancing around to establish a relationship, Schultze began to send him material. "I fed him a steady diet of short memos on the latest statistics. . . . Every new important piece of data we would get the night before it was released, and then he would have a memorandum on his desk ranging anywhere from one paragraph to two pages explaining the number and usually a little bit about its significance and occasionally the dramatics of the development. . . . If you told him one thing one month and forgot and told him something different the next month, he would pick it up. That happened, occasionally, to my embarassment."[75]

Carter is remembered in his role as president for his involvement in details. This trait probably came not only from his engineering training but also from his experience as a naval officer on nuclear submarines where small mistakes can be disastrous and where, in the tradition of the Navy, a commanding officer is responsible for the actions of his subordinates.[76] "If anything," Gramley has commented, "Carter was more involved than he should have been with the details. He got briefed endlessly."[77]

Carter was more interested in microeconomic problems than macroeconomic ones, Schultze has said, though he adds that this was also true of Lyndon Johnson. Microeconomic problems, like the economics of energy, for example, are more focused than the broad macroeconomic issues involving the overall operation of the economy where the interplay of forces determining outcomes is not easy to track. "In domestic economic policy of a micro kind," Schultze has observed, "—win or lose—it's very easy to see an outcome to the struggle; you can do something, get a piece of legislation through or something like that. Macroeconomic policy is much more out of your control, in the sense that how often does the President get a chance to make macroeconomic policy? Not very often; when he does, his impact is relatively modest."[78]

His lack of interest in macroeconomics may also have been due in large part to his frustration in dealing with problems like inflation. "I think economics didn't grab his interest," Eizenstat has observed. "It's not something that fascinated him the same way foreign policy fascinated him. He tended over time to have a rather dim view of economists, because their forecasts always seemed to be wrong. I think he lost confidence in some of the economic advice he was getting. Conflicting advice, forecasts which didn't pan out. It was sort of a dark science for him."[79]

Schultze sent a memorandum to the president in late 1979 in which he reviewed the council's past forecasts "to see how well we have done in assessing developments that shape the course of the economy. Doing so keeps us humble, and helps to discipline our thinking about the future. I thought you might be amused by the result."[80] The forecast for the inflation rate for 1977, as measured by the consumer price index, was 5.3 percent. The actual rate was 6.8 percent. For 1978 the forecast was for 6.0 percent inflation. The actual rate was 9.0 percent. For 1979 the forecast was for a 7.5 percent inflation rate. The actual rate was 13.0 percent. Carter didn't say whether or not he was amused. He did pen in the margin a note: "Charlie, I hope your present forecasts [with dire predictions for 1980] are also wrong!" It should be said in defense of the council that all of the major forecasting models for the same time period had large underestimates of the inflation rate.[81]

Carter summarized his overall view of economic advice: "The problem was, and this is so patently well-known it is almost stupid to say it, you could talk to five economists about macroeconomic policy and they'd all give you a different version. Then you got down and said, well, ok what are we going to do about it? Should we raise or lower taxes, should we stimulate the economy or cool down the economy? . . . To me, that's what I had to deal with. I wasn't a theoretician sitting in an ivory tower just being absorbed with the excitement of discussing economics."[82]

In his frustration Carter probably did not differ from most presidents. We have already commented on Harry Truman's wish for a one-handed economist. He also said, in speaking of Edwin Nourse, his chief economic adviser, "he could never understand that the president of the United States has too many things to do to engage in long bull sessions on economics of the kind that take place at the Brookings Institution."[83]

CARTER'S POLICY PRIORITIES

A president's ability to understand the advice given by economic advisers is only part of the story of an administration's economic policy and not the most important. Every president brings to the Oval Office his own convictions about the goals of public policy. For forming his economic program, he brings with him a mind-set on the relative importance of employment opportunities and price stability, on the proper distribution of the nation's income, the protection of national resources, and the appropriate roles of the private sector and government in pursuing the country's economic interests. This set of priorities gives focus to an administration's economic policy and makes up what economists would call, in the lingo of the trade, a president's objective function.

This objection function is formed, in part, of course, by life experiences. Ronald Reagan had only a limited understanding of economics, but he had made movies in Hollywood and had bitter memories of the steeply progressive taxes applied in those days to earnings received beyond a certain level. He listened as his advisers explained the theory of the dampening effect on incentives of high marginal tax rates, but their technical arguments only served to reinforce his own beliefs. He knew from experience what they were talking about, and he made a large tax cut the centerpiece of his economic program.

To understand Jimmy Carter and his sense of values, one must go to Plains, the southwest Georgia town, population 600, where he was born. The main street, a row of stores along the railroad track, is almost unchanged from the time Carter was a child. You can relax on one of the worn bench seats in front of what was his brother Billy's gas station, where out-of-town reporters liked to hang out for the local color. As you sit there on a warm summer afternoon, you can hear the lazy sounds of insects, interrupted occasionally by the sound of a passing car, and as you relax in the quiet of this isolated spot, you can't help marveling at the fact that the head of the most powerful country in the world could come from this simple village.

Jimmy Carter wasn't actually reared in Plains. His childhood home was in Archery, an unincorporated community a few miles away. His father farmed the land that has long been in the Carter family. Earl Carter was enterprising and sold a variety of items produced on the farm, as well as the usual crops—cotton, peanuts, and watermelons. He ran a small general supply store. He later got into peanuts, buying the crops of local farmers and selling to the oil mill in wholesale quantities. He provided for his family but was not a wealthy man.

All of the members of the family had their assigned chores. They learned to contribute at an early age. Farming was back-breaking work in the 1930s in south Georgia, a labor-intensive and low-technology operation. Rural electrification came to Plains only when Carter was thirteen. "My life on the farm during the Great Depression more nearly resembled farm life of fully 2,000 years ago than farm life today," he has written. "I have reflected on it often since that time; social eras change at their own curious pace, depending on geography and technology and a host of other factors. It is incredible with what speed these changes have totally transformed both the farming methods and the very life-style I knew in my boyhood."[84]

Like Lyndon Johnson, born in the poverty of the Texas hill country, Carter saw firsthand that life is hard for many Americans. One of his favorite books is James Agee's *Let Us Now Praise Famous Men*, a piece done in collaboration with the photographer Walker Evans on southern tenant farmers during the Great Depression. The two of them went south, commissioned by *Fortune* to do "an article on cotton tenantry in the United States," according to Walker, "in the form of a photographic and verbal record of the daily living and environment of an average white family of tenant farmers."[85] They concentrated their attention on three families, following their activities from dawn to dusk over the period July and August in 1936. Jimmy Carter was not quite twelve years old when Agee and Evans carried out their project in northern Alabama. The result of their effort, a searing photographic and textual portrait of the harsh life and poverty of one-mule sharecroppers, was never published by *Fortune*, but later appeared as a book. *Let Us Now Praise Famous Men* sold less than six hundred copies and was out of print before Agee's death. It was reprinted and discovered in 1960.

A documentary on the highlights of Agee's life was done in 1978. Carter, then president, agreed to be interviewed in the film. "I don't know exactly why I like the book so much," he says in his cameo appearance on the screen. "One of the reasons is that the life he wrote about is almost exactly the life that I knew. We were not as poor, but my neighbors were, and his detailed description and his projection on a universal basis of the suffering and destitution of the people who were afflicted by poverty really touched my heart."[86] In his speech on the occasion of the dedication of the Kennedy Library in 1979, he quoted from a poem by James Agee.[87]

From his father he learned industry, thrift, and discipline. From his mother he absorbed a sense of social conscience. "Miss Lillian" was a registered nurse and she served the people of Archery. She was, in effect, the community doctor for nearby neighbors. She was the "liberal" in the community because of her moderate views on race. After the death of her husband and at the age of sixty-eight she joined the Peace Corps and served for two years in India.[88]

This contrast in parental influence helps to explain why it was difficult to place Carter as president on the political spectrum. He was not a conservative or a liberal; he was a mixture of the two. He inherited from his mother an instinctive feeling for those in need, from his father a sense of the limits of resources. He reconciled the two by a policy he labeled in a speech, while governor, "benevolent conservatism."[89]

Much has been made of his engineering mentality. A description of Jimmy Carter would be incomplete if one did not go on to say that the engineer is a part of the Carter personality, but not all. After he graduated from Annapolis, he applied for a Rhodes scholarship to study political science and history. He was a finalist but didn't receive the scholarship. He balanced his formal training in the physical sciences with extensive reading in history, literature, philosophy, and theology—that part of knowledge which is not emphasized at Annapolis.[90] He worked at it, much like a literature major might try to broaden himself or herself by reading one of the many books written to explain to the layman the mysteries of particle physics. He developed an intense interest in classical music. His love of classical music carried over into the White House, where pieces he selected were played each day in his office. "He was to an astonishing extent a self made man," Bert Carp, deputy to Stuart Eizenstat, has said. "I might conceivably order the great books but I wouldn't read them all. He's ordered them and read them and taught himself Spanish off a record."[91]

A FINAL NOTE

Carter won the Democratic nomination by defeating leading Democrats in the primaries. Once in office, his success as president would depend on his ability to heal and unite the party and to establish a relationship with congressional Democratic leaders. The part of him that was conservative was in constant conflict with the liberal wing of the Democratic Party. Eizenstat recalls "an early meeting we had with the Democratic leadership, a weekly congressional breakfast. Carter says to Tip O'Neill that one of the albatrosses around the Democratic Party's neck is the view that it's profligate in spending and we've got to tighten up. But Tip says, 'Mr. President, I've waited eight years for a Democratic president and this is what I'm hearing?'"[92]

Carter was asked in an interview with *Business Week* magazine during the campaign: "How would you categorize your brand of economics? Are you a Keynesian, monetarist, or what?" Carter answered: "How would you categorize me? I don't know."[93] It is clear that his conservative instincts left him uncomfortable with a budget deficit, which is usually thought of as a bias of Keynesian policy. He accepted the need for one early in the administration as part of his stimulus package, after advisers told him an expansionary fiscal policy was needed to reduce unemployment left over from the previous recession. But, he was a reluctant Keynesian, Charles Schultze has said.[94]

Carter's own inner conflicts between his conservative instincts and his urge toward compassion for the poor were amplified by the division of opinion within the administration. These conflicting pressures were first apparent in the design of the economic stimulus program.

CHAPTER 4 | **THE STIMULUS PACKAGE**

Less than a week after the inauguration the key members of the Troika, Michael Blumenthal, Bert Lance, and Charles Schultze, began their appearances before committees of Congress to explain the content of the stimulus package that had been developed during the transition planning sessions at the Pond House in Plains.[1] The package had two parts. The first involved tax cuts that could be implemented in the first year to give the economy an extra boost. A jobs program, which would take time to initiate, would follow in the second year as the effect of the tax cut was starting to subside. Schultze recalls that there "was negotiation among all parties back and forth about how big each one was, partly before inauguration and partly after."[2]

The tax cut part of the program was directed toward both individuals and business. In the original formulation the business part made up about a fifth of the total tax reduction.[3] Businesses would be given a choice between two options: a refundable 4 percent credit against income tax based upon social security payroll taxes; or an increase from 10 percent to 12 percent in the investment tax credit, a credit arrangement first sponsored by President Kennedy in 1962. The employer income tax credit was chosen among a number of options, a transition briefing paper indicates, because "a study by the staff of the Senate Budget Committee indicates that a tax change of this type would have a significantly more powerful employment effect per dollar of revenue loss than other types of tax changes examined."[4] It also had the happy characteristic of being anti-inflationary because it reduced labor cost.

It was expected that labor intensive firms would pick the first choice and capital intensive firms the second.[5]

Schultze's recollection of how the two business tax cut options came about provides an interesting example of how policy is negotiated among a large number of presidential advisers.

> Some people, and I am fairly sure I was one of them, wanted a modest improvement in depreciation allowances for some investment incentives. Then along came the idea we had to do something for small business and there was a countervailing proposal which was a very small credit on employer taxes for the employer's share of the payroll tax. There was a small amount, around a billion. We couldn't get agreement on it, and I finally came up with the suggestion to give people an option, and the small businessman with less capital could take the payroll tax deduction and the others could take depreciation, and it will cost you a little bit more, but not a lot more unless we get an argument about it.[6]

There was also a state and local government benefit in the stimulus package, an increase in a counter-cyclical revenue sharing program already in existence. The amount involved was increased from $1.25 billion to $2.25 billion starting from mid-year. The counter-cyclical program, which existed in addition to general revenue sharing, was linked to the unemployment rate. When national unemployment fell to 6 percent, this sharing program automatically turned off. One-third was distributed to state governments and two-thirds to local governmental units.

The consumer portion of the tax cut consisted of a $50 rebate on 1976 income taxes to be distributed in April, May, and June through a reduction in 1977 withholding from pay checks. An additional tax cut for individuals included a "tax simplification and reform" feature that would raise the standard deduction and would also replace a complex set of standard deduction provisions. The increase in the deduction was, for couples, from $2,100 to $2,800. The benefit to taxpayers would apply to 1977 taxes and would begin with a reduction in withholding from payrolls beginning a month after the passage of the bill.

The decision was made that the rebate would be issued to all citizens. Fifty dollars per exemption would be given to those with a tax liability; fifty dollars per person would be given to those who had no tax liability but had filed for the earned income tax credit; and fifty dollars would be extended to social security recipients and those receiving supplemental security income payments. It was estimated that after these individuals were included, another eight million people would be left out: low-income non-aged singles or childless couples not eligible for the earned income credit, or persons eligible for the credit but who failed to file to receive it. At the first meeting of the Economic Policy Group, Secretary Blumenthal expressed concern about this final group; those who most needed the rebate would not get it.[7] In an analysis of this problem, it was estimated that about $200 million to $300 million in rebates were involved in these categories. It was also estimated that the cost of locating the excluded individuals was $100 million. "With differing degrees of reluctance," a memorandum to the president reported, "all members of the Economic Policy Group agree that the gains are not worth the costs."[8]

The largest part of the tax cut was the rebate. One of the first matters to be addressed by staff was a technical question involving the effectiveness of a one-shot cut in taxes in stimulating the economy. The University of Chicago economist Milton Friedman had argued in a famous piece of research that people do not tend to spend increases in income that they view as transitory. They only increase consumption spending when the increase in income is viewed as permanent.[9] If the so-called "permanent income hypothesis" were correct, then a one-time increase in disposable income due to a one-time cut in taxes would not lead to an increase in consumption and would not be effective in stimulating the economy. The question of the impact on spending of a one-time tax change came up in connection with a fiscal action taken in 1968 by the Johnson administration in an attempt to slow down the economy during the Vietnam War. In that case a one-time tax surcharge had been imposed in order to reduce consumer spending. Some argued that the surcharge would not have the intended retarding effect on consumption. There was considerable after-the-fact analysis of the effectiveness of the 1968 surcharge.[10]

In defense of a one-time tax cut, Carter's advisers appealed to the impact of a tax rebate passed in 1975 during the Ford administration. In the latter part of 1974, shortly after Gerald Ford succeeded Richard Nixon, it became clear that a recession was under way. Ford's response was to include in his state of the union message in January 1975, a proposal for stimulative tax cuts, including a rebate on 1974 individual income taxes worth about $12 billion.[11] Ford faced the same issue of the effectiveness of a one-time tax cut, a question raised not only by outsiders but in internal administration debate. "A rebate," these inside economists argued, according to one report, "tends to be perceived as a bonus, which workers may decide to save instead of spend. If that is the case, then the tax cut is less of an economic stimulus than it otherwise might be."[12] In the end, Congress not only passed the Ford stimulus package, it increased the amount.[13] The view that a temporary tax cut stimulates the economy continues to be accepted by politicians. A one-time tax rebate was proposed by George W. Bush—and passed by Congress—in the first year of his presidency to stimulate the economy.

Carter advisers used the Ford rebate to show that a fiscal initiative of this type does have a stimulative impact. In congressional testimony in January, Charles Schultze cited the case of the Ford tax cut. The rebate "will immediately add to consumer income and, on the basis of experience with the 1975 rebate, will shortly begin boosting sales of consumer goods. Let me point out, Mr. Chairman, that the 1975 rebate did work. In the first year of economic recovery from early 1975 to early 1976, after that rebate was passed, the gross national product jumped by a very large 7.3 percent. Consumption jumped in that first year by 6 percent. Economic studies of how that rebate worked indicated that people did spend, not immediately, but over a period of one, two, three quarters, most of that rebate on consumer goods."[14]

Carter's advisers chose a temporary tax cut, rather than a permanent one, in order to save future revenues for balancing the budget, an objective which Carter proposed to achieve by end of his first term. This reason for the choice of the rebate was pushed hard by Charles Schultze, a former budget director who understood well the dynamics of public financing. He argued further that a tax reform bill to be presented later—also a key part of the Carter program—would probably require a tax cut as a sweetener for gaining congressional acceptance. Tax reform is traditionally combined with a tax cut to make the reforms palatable. "The tax rebate route preserves our options for the future," Schultze wrote in a memorandum to the president. "A large permanent across-the-board tax cut now would be an effective substitute for the rebate in terms of its effects on consumer spending. But by mortgaging future revenues, it would seriously impair the probability of being able to achieve meaningful tax reform later on while balancing the budget by 1981."[15] Carter emphasized the fact that a large portion of the entire stimulus package was designed to limit permanent budget costs. In his message to Congress forwarding the stimulus package, Carter noted that "because we are committed to a balanced Federal Budget for the fiscal year 1981, we want to hold down the size of permanent spending increases or tax reductions. The tax rebate and many of the spending programs are temporary, and will end as the economy recovers."[16]

CARTER AND THE GROWTH OF GOVERNMENT

As a former governor, Carter had an instinctive feel for the need to match governmental outlays with revenues. Because most of the states of the union are required by constitutional arrangement to balance their budgets, governors are disciplined by a legal requirement to avoid deficit spending. "Carter was, in the long run, a fiscal conservative," Charles Schultze replied in response to a question about Carter's position on the stimulus package. "My impression was that he realized that he was the leader of the Democratic Party, and they all told him he had to do these things which meant a bigger deficit. He wasn't sure he liked that. He would go along with it. . . . He turned with more conviction to austerity during his last two or two and one-half years, even though it was much messier. Even though it was a lot tougher politically, it suited his own inherent views better."[17]

The mind-set about government financing that Carter brought to the presidency was reinforced by a general uneasiness in the country with the increase in government spending and budget deficits. This concern was growing not only in the United States but also in the other industrialized nations. The 1960s and the 1970s were decades of expansion of government in all of the member countries of the Organization for Economic Cooperation and Development (OECD), a group whose membership includes most of the industrialized nations. During this time period, the average size of national and local government outlays in the OECD rose, in relation to the gross national product, by over 20 percentage points to a level of 47 percent. The American increase was smaller than in most of the other major industrialized nations, but, even so, the upward movement of government outlays was large and became a subject of intense political debate.[18]

Prior to the 1930s, total expenditures, other than for defense or delayed payment for past wars, never exceeded 1 percent of the gross national product (GNP) by a significant amount. In the 1930s, New Deal programs increased this ratio to 5 percent. There was a further small increase during the early postwar period through the Eisenhower administration. Over the 1960s and 1970s, prior to Carter's presidency, domestic spending grew from 7 percent of the GNP in 1955 to a little under 15 percent in 1977. Total outlays for all purposes, domestic and defense, did not increase that much—from 18.2 percent of GNP in 1955 to 20.1 percent in the year of Carter's election—but there was a sharp change in the composition of total outlays. Spending for national defense fell steadily, from 11.2 percent of GNP in 1955 to 5.4 percent in 1977, while domestic spending rose sharply. The fact that voters permitted this shift from defense to domestic outlays is related to what has been called a "framing effect." "The central implication of this view for the politics of budgetary choice," Schultze has written in a survey of the historic behavior of the budget, "is that a tax increase—that is, an out-of-pocket loss of after-tax income—is viewed more negatively by voters than would be an agreement to forgo a tax cut of equal magnitude. Voters are very loath to support a general tax increase to raise federal civilian spending; but they will forgo a tax cut when defense spending declines as a way of reallocating the resources to civilian programs."[19]

That this trade-off between defense and domestic spending had it limits was recognized by Schultze in a Brookings Institution study written in the year before Carter came to office. "During the past twenty years," Charles Schultze observed, "the fall in the defense share has made it possible to start and then rapidly expand a large number of new domestic programs with only a small rise in the portion of national income taken in federal taxes. Whatever the course of defense spending may be in the next decade, it is virtually certain that its share of GNP cannot continue to shrink at the same pace. As a consequence, constraints on domestic programs will be more severe than they were in the previous decades unless the overall share of federal spending in GNP rises significantly above 20 percent."[20]

The growth of government spending that had taken place gradually after World War II, and then intensified in the 1960s, was part of a long historic movement. An OECD report in the mid-1980s pointed out that "writing a century ago, the German economist Adolph Wagner argued that the demand for increases in the scope of public sector activity would be a natural consequence of the higher living standards which accompany economic industrialization. A number of factors," the report continued, "were advanced in support of this view, including the increased complexity of industrialized economies which would necessitate higher state expenditure on law and order, transport and communication (both seen as 'natural monopolies' best controlled by the state), coupled with extension of various forms of regulator activity."[21]

In the 1960s government growth took place with a general consensus in many countries that the public sector was below its optimum size. It was possible to get support for increasing public outlays in that decade because public sector expansion took place in an environment of strong economic growth. Growth brought with it an increase in government revenues, which made it possible to finance new programs without raising taxes. Carter came to the presidency in the 1970s just as the growth of government began to be questioned. "During most of the 1960s, the prevalent belief was that some kind of federal budgetary program could be designed to deal with almost any social problem," Charles Schultze wrote in his Brookings article. "This conventional wisdom of a few years ago seems now to have been replaced by its polar opposite: most federal programs do not work well and consist principally in 'throwing money' at problems.'"[22]

This disaffection with increased government activity was reinforced by several bothersome developments. The first was the exposure of taxpayers to the phenomenon of "bracket creep." Because of the inflation of the late 1960s and the 1970s, tax payers with inflated incomes moved up to higher percentage income tax brackets, even though earnings adjusted for the inflation did not increase or rose by very little. A second factor that intensified the debate was the increasing share going to the provision of transfer payments—outlays directed toward individuals—which had redistribution as a dominant objective. These transfer payments also created entitlements that reduced the flexibility in managing the nation's finances and ensured future growth in the size of these transfers due to demographic changes in the population. By the time of Carter's inauguration, transfer payments, along with interest payments on the public debt, made up two-fifths of the 20 percent of GNP devoted to federal programs.

The third and major reason for the second thoughts about the increase of government outlays was the slowdown in the rapid economic growth rate. Personal disposable income adjusted for inflation rose about 50 percent from 1957 to 1967, but only about 32 percent from 1967 to 1977. Higher taxes and less generous increases in income were a powerful combination in creating frustration on the part of voters. A tax revolt was evident in legislative enactments in New Jersey and Colorado in 1976 and 1977 to limit government spending. Taxpayer frustration was perhaps best symbolized by the passage of Proposition 13 in California in 1978. The momentum created by the passage of this California proposition carried on to the national scene in the legislative proposal, referred to earlier, sponsored by Congressman Jack Kemp and Senator William Roth that would reduce federal income taxes by one-third over a three-year period. Carter would have to deal with this initiative later in his administration.

During the Kennedy administration, staff economists emphasized the existence of a "fiscal drag," a sluggishness imposed on the economy by rapid growth of federal revenues. The solution proposed was a tax cut to return spending power to the private sector. This tax cut was enacted in 1964 under Lyndon Johnson. By the time Carter came into office, the problem had reversed itself. "Developments have radically altered the nature of the budgetary problem," Charles Schultze had written, "and have transformed the historical problem of fiscal drag into its opposite, the problem of fiscal squeeze."[23]

Upon entering office, Carter was faced with a problem with which traditional Democrats of the postwar period had not had to deal. During the 1976 campaign he had committed himself to an effort to control expansion of the public sector. Looking back in his memoirs Carter reflected that "I had inherited the largest deficit in history—more that $66 billion—and it was important to me to stop the constantly escalating federal expenditures that tended to drive up interest rates and were one of the root causes of inflation and unemployment."[24] In reply to a question during the 1976 campaign, "what should be the approximate balance between government and private shares of the GNP?" Carter affirmed his wishes to contain the growth of the public sector, but with a realistic sense of the difficulty of breaking the momentum of two decades of government growth. "Well, the government share has been steadily growing," he replied. "My inclination would be to attenuate the growth, at least. My hope would be that we could hold down or reduce the government proportion of the GNP compared to what it would have been if I wasn't in the White House. I can't promise you that I'll stop it or reverse it, but I'll do what I can to hold it down."[25] The average annual growth rate of federal outlays adjusted for inflation during the Carter years turned out to be 3.5 percent. During the Reagan years, when control of government spending was given top priority, the average annual growth rate was a little lower, 2.9 percent, "and well in excess of the 1.1 percent rate that the administration had projected in 1981."[26]

Part of Carter's strategy to contain government was to use the zero-based budgeting technique he had introduced when governor of Georgia. In implementing this procedure all agencies were required, when formulating their yearly budget proposals, to look at the separate components of the existing program and evaluate each as if it were a new initiative. An informed decision was to be made in terms of cost-benefit either to continue or discontinue the various programs. Under this scheme of budgeting, each fiscal year started, in theory, from ground zero.

In an effort to get a better hold on the budget, Lyndon Johnson had also attempted to force more disciplined budget decisions with a technique borrowed from McNamara's whiz kids at the Defense Department, a procedure known as "Planning, Programming, and Budgeting" (PPB). Charles Schultze was involved in the attempt to implement PPB while budget director under Johnson. Before he met Carter, he had written a book on the Johnson procedure.[27]

It is not surprising that presidents would find attractive a formalized routine for gaining control of the huge amount of outlays allocated among a host of federal agencies. The problem is to find a technique that actually works. Carter's zero-based budgeting had limited success, as did the Johnson effort. When asked about Carter's record with this budget approach, James McIntyre, who was closely involved in the attempt to introduce it, both in Georgia and Washington, replied: "I think it depends upon your definition of success. At the federal level, in particular, the expectations with what you could do with zero-based budgeting were just overwhelming and you could never have achieved those expectations. I think there was too much unnecessary paper work. And in that sense, it wasn't very useful. There were some successes. For example, in the CIA and Agriculture, I found they used zero-based budgeting very effectively to set their own priorities."[28]

Alice Rivlin, who watched the whole attempt from her position as director of the Congressional Budget Office, has reflected on the episode. "I was skeptical about it. I was a veteran of PPB and then there had been another approach in the Ford administration, Ford or Nixon, called management by objective, and then Carter came along with zero-based budgeting. It seemed to me a lot of paper work that wasn't accomplishing very much. Each administration had to have a new name and a new set of forms and this was the Carter one."[29]

NEED FOR THE STIMULUS

The purpose of the stimulus program was to give more momentum to the recovery from the 1974–75 recession. "The chances that the recovery will 'spontaneously' begin doing better than the projections are not high," a transition memo reported in late December 1976. "Economic growth slowed considerably in the last six months. Real GNP growth for the third quarter ran at a 3.9 percent annual rate. Preliminary estimates for the fourth quarter of 1976 show a further reduction in real growth to 3 to 3½ percent. As a result, all forecasts for 1977 have been revised down substantially to between 4 and 5 percent, if no new actions are taken by the government. Such rates of growth will not reduce unemployment significantly, leaving the unemployment rate well over 7 percent next year."[30] In testimony before the House budget committee in February, Charles Schultze reported that the average percent change in the GNP seven quarters after the trough of recession in previous postwar recoveries was 7.7 percent. In the seven quarters of the 1975–76 recovery, the GNP increased less than half of that rate, 3.1 percent.[31] As a result of the slower growth, Schultze further testified, by the start of 1977 industrial production barely recovered to its 1973 level. Business investment in plant and equipment was still well below the 1973 level.[32]

The stimulus provided for in the bill finally submitted to Congress amounted to $15.5 billion in both 1977 and 1978. The administration considered the size of the stimulus to be moderate. In testimony before the House Committee on the Budget, Charles Schultze commented that "as in any case with any economic policy, there are uncertainties in the outlook, that could make a stimulative policy too weak or, conversely, too large. This package has been designed to tread prudently between the twin risks of over and understimulation."[33] In the same appearance before Congress, Schultze gave his forecast for the impact of the stimulus: "The growth of real gross national product from the fourth quarter of 1976 to the fourth quarter of 1977 would be in the range of 5¾ percent to 6 percent. Without added stimulus, that growth rate would probably be only 4½ to 4¾ percent."[34] He raised the possibility of additional stimulus at a later point: "If business investment and exports pick up nicely in late 1977 and in 1978, the decline in stimulus now planned after mid-1978 will be quite appropriate in order to avoid excessive prodding of a healthy economy. If, on the other hand, private demand does not respond sharply enough to the stimulus package, and the self-sustaining expansion we envision does not come up to expectations, additional measures can be taken. It is far easier to add more stimulus later in 1978, should that be needed, than to retract excessive stimulus once committed."[35]

The package was not large by historic standards. The size of the program was estimated during the transition period to be considerably less than both the Kennedy/Johnson cut in 1964 and the 1975 program enacted during the Ford administration. The Carter stimulus was thought to be less than 1 percent of the GNP for 1977, whereas the Kennedy package was 1.7 percent and the Ford package 1.5 percent of GNP.

Expert advice, other than that coming from within the administration, agreed that stimulus was needed. A report prepared by the Congressional Budget Office staff and included for the record by Rivlin in her testimony before the House Committee on the Budget in January 1977, estimated that "in the absence of policy changes, the economy now seems headed for a relatively modest 3.5 to 5.0 percent growth during 1977, with no acceleration in sight for 1978. Growth in this range is likely to keep the unemployment rate above 7 percent during all of 1977 and above 6.5 percent during 1978."[36] The report simulated the effect of a number of fiscal options, options not significantly different from those in the Carter proposal, to determine the impact. The inflationary effect of the options was estimated to be fairly small.[37] Rivlin testified in mid-April 1977, that "if consumer spending rates are high and private investment is vigorous, a healthy rate of economic growth can be maintained with minimal stimulus from the Federal budget. On the other hand, if consumer spending rates are weak and private investment is sluggish, continuing Federal stimulus will be necessary to keep the economy growing."[38]

Otto Eckstein, president of the widely used forecasting firm Data Resources, testified that "the need for fiscal stimulus is apparent in the economy depicted without stimulus. The unemployment rate remains above 7 percent throughout 1977. President Carter's fiscal stimulus program for 1977 and 1978 recognizes that the economy requires mildly expansionary fiscal policies over the next 2 years."[39] He thought a larger boost would not be appropriate since it would be harder to get a larger program going in an orderly way and "while we are in no danger of widespread bottlenecks or demand-pull inflation this year or next, the risk becomes greater for 1979 and 1980."[40]

A group of businessmen, led by Reginald Jones of General Electric, met with Carter in Plains in December before the inauguration. They thought a stimulus was necessary to increase business investment. In February Jones testified before the House Ways and Means Committee. "Economic stimulus we feel is in order. The real questions are the size and the make up of the program. Now as to size, when you have a $1.7 trillion economy it takes a fairly sizable program, something over one percent, to have any impact at all on the direction."[41] Jones went on to argue, though, for a permanent, rather than a temporary, tax cut. His first reason was the need to restore to the taxpayer revenues that resulted from inflation, which pushed people into higher income tax brackets. He also testified that the one-time tax cut for individuals would not have as much of a quantitative effect as a permanent cut. Like Charles Schultze, he appealed to the example of the 1975 tax cut under President Ford, but with a different interpretation. "The tax rebate of 1975 was instructive. A substantial portion of that went into paying off debts and building up savings. . . . Our records show that that rebate did not really flow into spending until the early part of 1976."[42]

The liberal side of the Democratic Party thought the stimulus too moderate. Eizenstat has reported that Carter's "1977 fiscal stimulus package was bitterly criticized by the AFL-CIO [American Federation of Labor and Congress of Industrial Organizations] as too paltry to lift the nation from recession."[43] In December 1976, Carter met in Plains with the National League of Cities and the National Conference of Mayors. "Here," Eizenstat reports, "he got a very clear indication that basic elements in the Party wanted a much larger stimulus package."[44] Walter Heller, who had been chairman of the Council of Economic Advisers under President Kennedy and one of the architects of the 1964 tax cut, thought the stimulus too weak to achieve its purpose.

> Given the poor performance of U.S. economic recovery in 1976 and the great distance the economy still has to go to achieve reasonable levels of employment and output, the 1977 portions of the Carter program, though well designed, is unduly modest in size. The modesty of the Carter program for 1977, at $15.5 billion of stimulus, is quickly seen by comparing it with projected GNP of $1,875 billion. This stimulus of less than 1 percent contrasts sharply with the tax cut approved by your committee in 1964. At $14 billion it was close to 2% of that year's $636 billion GNP. By this time next year, our annual rate of output will have crossed the $2 trillion mark.

Then, in a play on the title of a widely discussed book of the time, he added, "in devising fiscal programs for an economy of that size, small is not beautiful."[45]

THE JOBS PROGRAM

The second part of the stimulus package was the jobs program. Essentially it was an extension of already existing programs put in place through the Comprehensive Employment Training Act (CETA), enacted in late 1973 to replace a patchwork of employment and training programs.[46] There were three main features in the Carter jobs program. Public service employment was increased from a level of 310,000 workers, which it had reached under President Gerald Ford, to 600,000 in fiscal year 1977 under Carter and to 725,000 in fiscal year 1978. It was an ambitious effort. Public service employment peaked in 1978 and gradually declined as Carter moved in the direction of more budget discipline. The other parts of the jobs program included a youth and training program under CETA, which was increased by 208,000 slots in fiscal year 1978, and a provision for an increase in public works programs.

The issue of the size of the jobs program was debated right up to the inauguration. A staff member pointed out in a briefing for Carter in early December 1976, that "the government had not had experience with such a large public service job program and it might be hard to cut back in later years."[47] The aggressive advocate for jobs programs as part of the stimulus package was the new secretary of labor, Ray Marshall. At a dinner at the Treasury attended by the leading advisers in early January, Marshall argued, according to notes taken by Eizenstat, "for as much direct job creation and as little tax reduction as possible." Charles Schultze was Marshall's chief protagonist, arguing for a smaller program than Marshall wanted and "stating that a tax cut was necessary to create long-term growth in the private sector where 5 out of every 6 jobs existed. He pointed out that public service jobs were counter-cyclical and not permanent in nature."[48] At a meeting with the president-elect and the vice president-elect the following day in Plains, the face off between Marshall and Schultze continued.[49]

Schultze opposed a large volume of public works for several reasons. He did not think they were cost-effective. The public service employment and the local public works features of the stimulus program were basically grants to state and local governments. Programs were administered by "prime sponsors," cities and counties of 100,000 or more in population and combinations of cities and counties. States were prime sponsors for the remaining communities. Ongoing federal supervision had to be administered for 450 communities. When the federal government relies on the state and local governments to do the stimulating job, one economist argued at the time, "it is placing its own stabilization policy at the mercy of the behavior of state and local governments."[50] There was a good likelihood, Schultze argued, that funds provided for public employment would merely substitute for other funds that state and local governments would have spent on projects they would have undertaken anyway. The net stimulation would be smaller than the outlay on the jobs program because of this substitution effect.[51]

The Office of Management and Budget pointed out in an issues paper that the Public Service Employment law forbade substituting federal funds and workers for regular funds and workers, but that such substitution did, in fact, take place. There have been econometric studies and anecdotal evidence, the report read, "but there is no consensus on the precise magnitude of the [substitution] problem. Estimates range from 40 percent to 100 percent, with general agreement that the longer (beyond a year) the program stays in place, the more likely it is that the higher end of the range is reached."[52] In the end, the public service employment program may have been more successful than the study cited by OMB suggests. It is a difficult assignment to measure the precise amount of substitution. A careful study done during 1977 and 1978 concluded that because of certain changes made in the implementation of the public service program, the substitution rate was kept to a relatively low number, 15 percent.[53]

Schultze was, in any event, fighting a losing battle. Direct job creation has an intuitive appeal for politicians who can point specifically to new jobs caused by the federal program, whereas the effect of a tax reduction on unemployment is more indirect and diffused through complicated channels. The congressional attitude was embodied in a statement by the chairman of the House Subcommittee on Manpower, Compensation, Health and Safety, that "public service employment is the most effective emergency solution because it is direct. It hires people."[54] The Democratic members of Congress had also invested a lot of political energy in passing temporary jobs programs before Carter's arrival in Washington, particularly in response to higher unemployment rates in the early 1970s and the recession of 1974–75.

What mattered most were the positions adopted by the congressional leadership. House Speaker Tip O'Neill took the position "that the Administration should forget the rebates and put the money directly into job creations."[55] Senate majority leader Robert Byrd also preferred the jobs over the rebate.

Carter himself found the jobs programs appealing, according to Schultze. "He immediately liked the idea of the employment programs. It would get people back to work in a way you could see concretely.... You could see his eyes light up when Ray [Marshall] would go into all this stuff about putting people to work and training them, and giving them work skills and all these marvelous things you could do."[56] In a later interview Schultze added,

> I was very skeptical of the possibility of doing the employment programs. I thought I had the President convinced of this, until he did some mental arithmetic—he was very quick at arithmetic—and all of a sudden he divided the population of Plains into the population of the U.S. and found out that among the million-and-a-half, let's say, employees who would have been hired under this public employment program, there would only have to be two in Plains, or one, whatever, and he could himself visualize the kind of the work that person could do, and I lost the argument. All of a sudden, Mondale who had grown up in some little town in Minnesota, did the same thing, and he said, yes, I know where I could put three people to work. I said, "what about Abraham Beam, Mr.

President, he's got 150,000 in New York City to put to work." In any event Carter had concretized that employment thing in his own head.[57]

MOVEMENT OF THE STIMULUS PACKAGE THROUGH CONGRESS

A major change in Carter's business tax proposal came from the House Ways and Means Committee under the chairmanship of Congressman Al Ullman. There was little support on the committee for the choices the administration package gave to businesses. Ways and Means, which initiated all tax bills, had a long record of experience with the investment tax credit, going back to the days of the Kennedy administration. "The committee showed little enthusiasm," according to one account, "for increasing the investment tax credit. It had jiggled the credit up and down or on or off just too many times, and members expressed growing skepticism about its effectiveness in stimulating investment."[58] Charles Schultze argued strongly in a briefing paper for the president that he should defend the investment tax credit in an upcoming meeting with congressional leaders. "Investment is the most laggard sector in the economy," Schultze wrote. "At the end of 1976 total national output (GNP) was 3 percent above the 1973 pre-recession peak, business investment was 12 percent below its pre-recession peak."[59] The argument did not convince the committee. The committee also rejected the income tax credit feature presented by Carter as part of the stimulus package. Members thought it too small to be effective. It would reduce payroll costs by less than one-fourth of 1 percent, a number obtained by multiplying the 4 percent credit times the social security payroll tax of 5.85 percent.

In place of the president's business tax cuts, it substituted a tax credit for companies who hired additional employees, an arrangement labeled "an incremental employment tax credit." The original committee proposal would allow a credit of 40 percent of wages up to $4,200 a year for new workers. The maximum an employer could receive each year would be $40,000. Even though the amount was increased to $100,000 in the final version, the low ceiling would limit interest in the credit to small employers. The tax credit proposal was due, in part, to a general mood in Congress to bring the private sector into the program. The record of the public employment program was, in part, unsatisfactory. Over the course of its history CETA was not without its controversies. Although Ways and Means changed the form of the business tax cut, the amount of taxpayer savings was close to the president's proposal. The bill reduced federal revenues by an amount just below the administration's original estimate.

Administration advisers were critical of the substitute for business tax cuts. It had, they felt, a number of problems.[60] The credit was incremental in the sense that it would apply only to increases in employment. The committee was insistent on this provision because it did not want to provide a windfall for firms that did not provide additional jobs. The incremental feature would give more bang for the buck. The Treasury Department, under both Republicans and Democrats, was not comfortable with incremental tax subsidies. Obtaining data to measure employment increases that did not impose additional data collection costs on firms was a problem. Among other things, it was difficult to distinguish from existing accounting records between part-time and full-time employees. The credit would encourage substitution of part-time for full-time workers. It would also reward firms that were growing for reasons having nothing to do with the credit. Some members of Congress were concerned that growing parts of the country would benefit compared to more economically stagnant regions. Secretary of the Treasury Blumenthal pointed out, in a memorandum to the president, the bias in the tax credit benefit in favor of expanding companies. "The Ullman tax credits would go only to growing companies, not to those stabilizing or reducing payrolls through new labor-saving measures. This is bad policy. The government should not discourage implementation of labor-saving devices." The bill also, Blumenthal continued, complicated the tax laws.[61]

In a letter to Congressman Ullman, Carter pointed out that a disadvantage of the tax credit was its procyclical nature. The proposal would give a tax benefit to businesses when the economy is expanding and withdraw it when the economy contracts. It would also be arbitrary in its effects on industry, "since in the recovery phase of a business cycle durable goods firms expand rapidly and would receive much of the credit, while trade and services firms, where many of the disadvantaged are hired, would be less favorably treated." The credit would also promote a reduction in productivity because it would encourage labor-intensive production methods. By way of handling Ullman delicately, he suggested the possibility of compromise. "I have directed my top economic advisers to consider a variation of your proposal for grants or credits to be targeted to the number of disadvantaged or long-term unemployed hired by industry."[62]

Ullman was not receptive to administration arguments or willing to compromise. He had made an early commitment to the employment tax credit. He first presented his idea for this form of a business tax cut at the meeting in Plains in early January when Carter formally presented for the first time his stimulus package to the leaders of Congress.[63] "I have had a long discussion with Al Ullman on the stimulus package," Blumenthal reported to the president. "He is dead set on substituting his incremental employment tax credit proposal for our business tax reduction alternatives. We will have our work cut out for ourselves to get him off this. While it makes no economic sense at all, it clearly sounds superficially plausible and has broad political appeal to many House members. Recommendation: We should state our opposition to Ullman's proposal clearly, but in a relatively low key way. If we lose in the House, there is still a very good chance that his proposal will be knocked out in the Senate or fail in conference."[64] At a congressional leadership breakfast on March 8, 1977 to discuss the stimulus program, Ullman's jobs credit was a main issue.[65] The debate over the business tax was fundamentally changed when Carter announced his decision on April 14, 1977 to drop both the rebate and the business tax cut parts of the stimulus package. Nevertheless the Ullman proposal continued its movement through Congress and was passed into law, with modifications, by both houses. An analysis based on a survey of firms in 1978 indicated that the impact of the credit on jobs was slight. A high percentage of firms were not aware of the credit. Firms that did know increased employment only 3 percent more than firms that were ignorant of the program. "A simple examination of the descriptive statistics indicates that even if the tax credit substantially affected some firms, most firms either did not know of the program or were not influenced by it."[66] The job credit had a short life. It ended when Carter failed to recommend its extension beyond 1978. Carter did propose in its place a targeted jobs credit that was limited to the hiring of disadvantaged young people and the handicapped.

Carter's decision to drop the rebate came after he concluded that it was no longer needed. The rebate was not a popular idea. As the legislative decision process dragged on, Blumenthal told the president that he had met with business leaders, and they urged him to drop the rebate.[67] In Congress the jobs program was popular, but the rebate was not. Schultze has said that "all the Congress hated it. For some reason it struck them as immoral. You just hand a fifty dollar check to people That's terrible! It was intriguing. I think the only person in town who liked the rebate was Charlie Schultze."[68] Carter, himself, had never been really comfortable with the rebate idea. Schultze has said that "I think he was talked into that by me, his macroeconomist, more than anything else."[69] Eizenstat has reported that at a breakfast meeting with members of the House Ways and Means Committee, in mid-February, "surprisingly, the President stated that he himself had philosophical problems with the $50 rebate, but that it was necessary to avoid out-year expenditures."[70]

With the delay in the passage of the rebate, economic conditions had changed. The economy was rebounding more strongly than had been anticipated. Blumenthal and Lance were both urging the president to drop the rebate. Lance had misgivings about it from the beginning. "By April 13," according to an account by a reporter given special access to the White House in the early days of the administration, "he had raised enough doubts about the proposal so that the President called him and his other top advisers together to hash the matter out."[71] Charlie Schultze continued to defend the rebate.

Carter was fast moving toward Blumenthal's and Lance's position. He noted that in early April retail sales were up strongly. He indicated to Eizenstat that "he would not have been in the position of proposing it [the rebate] if economic conditions were as they are now."[72] In a summary of events, Stuart Eizenstat has written that "on April 13, 1977, the President stated at a meeting with the Vice President that he had decided to drop the rebate."[73]

The discussion about the rebate reflected the liberal and conservative division among Carter's advisers. Carter commented on this in an interview after he left Washington.

> Bert, Mike Blumenthal, and I were more conservative than anybody else among my advisors. We were more conservative than Charlie Schultze or Stu Eizenstat, more conservative by far than Fritz Mondale. The test came with the fifty dollar rebate. When we went into office, there was a unanimous commitment to an immediate creation of jobs and we had anticipated that the fifty dollar tax rebate could be implemented by April. We were going to pass it in February and March and it was going to be an immediate thing. Well it didn't happen that way. It went through the House quickly without any delay. It got to the Senate, and a lot of opposition was being aroused to it because the economy seemed to be stimulated more than we anticipated on its own. Bert and Mike Blumenthal and I felt that the fifty dollar tax rebate should not be implemented and we had a squabble among our economic advisors, an inevitable squabble, but not anything ugly. We finally prevailed, and we just aborted it.[74]

Carter had a sharp sense of the danger of inflation from the very beginning. He was also more optimistic about a spontaneous recovery from unemployment than some of his advisers. Reflecting on the course of events later in an interview, Lawrence Klein commented that "the unemployment that we were seeing after the first oil shock was our first serious bout with very high unemployment after the Second World War. The transition team was very skeptical about how fast that could be brought down, and Carter, himself, was very bullish, optimistic, and in the end he was right. It came down fast. We were surprised at how closely the unemployment rate fitted in with his view and the way things worked out rather than their view."[75]

Another strong reason why Carter withdrew the rebate proposal is that it was having a difficult time in the Senate.

DELETION OF THE WATER PROJECTS

A major cause of the tax rebate's trouble in the Senate was Carter's somewhat dramatic action to delete a number of proposed water projects from the budget under consideration when he entered office. One of the ironies of the federal budget ritual is that an outgoing president whose term ends on January 20 must submit to Congress, just two weeks prior to his departure from office, a budget for the coming fiscal year. Budgets are dated by the year in which they end. The dating procedure can be confusing to the uninitiated. The 1977 fiscal year budget, already in effect when Carter assumed office, had begun in October 1976 and would not end until almost nine months after his inauguration. The 1978 budget proposed by Ford in early January 1977, would begin in October 1977, and end in September 1978. If, upon entering office, a president does not present revisions of his predecessor's budget, he has no input into budgetary decisions for the first two years of his administration. It was essential that Carter act to modify the budget according to his own priorities.

These changes had to be prepared during the busy transition period and in the earliest days of the new administration. Stuart Eizenstat has described the pressure. "You have to develop the budget revision while you're still appointing people. You don't have assistant secretaries and the departments on board able to give their input. . . . You don't have any program people that you can talk with except the permanent bureaucracy. It's an enormously difficult thing to do in a transition period. And by February 8 or 10 you're expected to come up with an alternative budget."[76]

President Ford had included in his budget a number of water projects of interest to Congress and they caught Carter's attention. He had looked at public works proposals with a critical eye while governor of Georgia. "He had a long time bias about water projects," Bert Lance observed after the administration left office. "He had been there before. A major controversy in Georgia was the Squirrel Bluff dam project on the Flint River which runs down the western side of Georgia. He came down on the side of cancellation. It was not unexpected that when we got to Washington, one of the first things we'd do would be to look at all the water projects because he felt that the federal government had made the wrong decision in that one, and that they needed to be saved from making any further wrong decisions. . . . The water projects decision was just as predictable as anything could be. I knew when we got to that item in the budget what was going to happen."[77] The staff of the Office of Management and Budget had long questioned the cost-effectiveness of various water projects, reinforcing Carter's beliefs. Carter zeroed in on this item.

In his budget revision presented to Congress on February 22, he eliminated nineteen projects affecting seventeen states. The projects were taken out of the budget to be examined further for environmental impact or cost-effectiveness. A second hit list of additional projects involved six more states.[78] Not only were a large number of rank-and-file members of Congress affected by the decision. Chairs of major committees had projects in which they had a personal interest, including Senator Russell Long of Louisiana, whose state had five of the projects marked for deletion. Long was chairman of the powerful Senate Finance Committee, through which the rebate legislation had to go. Due partly to the pressure of time, there was no advanced consultation. The deletions hit Congress like a bombshell.

In his letter to Congress explaining the removal of the funds for the water projects, Carter listed a number of problems: "one project would be built in an earthquake zone, potentially jeopardizing the lives of thousands of people; one project appears to be in violation of an international treaty, and Canada has repeatedly asked the U.S. to suspend construction; and one project would have resulted in a federal investment of $1.4 million for each individual landowner benefitting from the project, and only about 60 landowners would be benefitted."[79] Haynes Johnson of the *Washington Post* has written that "you didn't have to follow Washington politics for decades, as I had, to know that Carter was right in calling many of these water projects wasteful and largely unnecessary. . . . The way Carter acted, and why, went to the heart of his idea of how he should function as a president."[80] The decision may not have caused such a backlash if it had been handled in a more politically sensitive way.

Development projects are a favorite benefit for members of Congress to provide for constituents. As Carter would write later, "scores of these plans were in progress, from original conception to the final construction state. Some of the more senior members had been waiting many years for their particular proposals to get to the top of the list. The projects represented major political plums for each district, tangible symbols of the representative's influence in Washington."[81] Those not directly involved in the cancellation of a project sympathized with those who were, since proposals they might wish to submit later could also be vulnerable in a more questioning climate. Carter pointed out in his memoir that he made clear in the campaign that he would look carefully at proposals. "I had repeatedly emphasized the need to eliminate waste and pork-barrel projects in the federal government," he wrote. "Some of the people had heard and understood what I was saying. The members of congress had not."[82] Despite the forewarning, the deletions still came as a surprise.

In terms of the cold realities he may have been right, but the episode soured relations with Congress for some time. Carter has written that "the issue of the water projects was the one that caused the deepest breach between me and the Democratic leadership."[83] His popularity in the West never recovered. One of the immediate victims of the episode was the tax rebate. According to one reporter, after the water project decision, Russell Long, "whose vigorous support was vital to the passage of any tax measure, now publicly spoke of the rebate with studied detachment."[84] In an account of the discussion at a congressional leadership breakfast, Eizenstat quotes the majority leader, Senator Robert Byrd, as saying that there were only forty votes for the rebate. "He stated," Eizenstat reports, "that prospects for the rebate had been damaged by the 'hit list' of water projects. It was a terrible list. . . . He said he could not overestimate the damage done by the water project issue."[85]

In looking back at the episode, Eizenstat has written that it is important "for the President not to dissipate his honeymoon period on quixotic efforts at marginal activities."[86] Carter compounded his problem with Congress by agreeing in a telephone conversation with House Speaker O'Neill to a one-sided compromise on the projects. It was a compromise that angered members of Congress who supported him on environmental grounds and who constituted a number large enough to block override of a veto if Carter decided to exercise it. Carter himself has said that "this compromise bill should have been vetoed because, despite some attractive features, it still included wasteful items which my congressional supporters and I had opposed. . . . Signing this act was accurately interpreted as a sign of weakness on my part, and I regretted it as much as any budget decision I made as President."[87]

Given his own doubts about the need for the rebate and the uncertainty of the measure's chances of passing in the senate, Carter withdrew the proposal. The way in which the canceling of the rebate was handled is another example of the difficulties with Congress the administration experienced in its early days. Some supporters in Congress, like Senator Muskie, chairman of the Senate Budget Committee, had put their names on the line in behalf of the temporary tax cut. Representative Ullman had supported the measure in the House. They were not informed of the decision to drop the rebate prior to the announcement. There was hard feeling. President Carter said later that "I almost lost a friend in that episode with Ed Muskie."[88] Muskie was quoted as saying, "if economic conditions in April justify this abandonment of the course we set two months ago, Congress has a right to know why those conditions were misjudged in February when the program was proposed."[89] The abruptness of the decision raised questions about the president's sureness in handling policy issues. There was loss of credibility. At a later point the administration became good at forming task forces for handling major issues and became more effective in dealing with Congress. But first impressions are hard to overcome. Most presidents are granted a certain grace period. One presidential observer has said that "no president had experienced as difficult a first year with congress as did Jimmy Carter."[90] Carter entitled a chapter in his memoir, "My One-Week Honeymoon with Congress."

The final stimulus bill that Carter signed included the tax reduction for individuals in the form of the increased standard deduction, the incremental tax credit for employers, and the counter-cyclical assistance for state and local governments, all in addition to the jobs programs. Although the bill was different from the administration's original proposals, the president was advised that "the Office of Management and Budget concurs in the recommendation of the Treasury Department that on balance the enrolled bill warrants approval. The other concerned agencies likewise recommend approval or have no objection."[91] The memorandum reported that the revenue differences in the administration proposal—excluding the rebate and the business tax cut—and the final bill were modest, estimated at a little over $12 billion over six fiscal years. Carter's original proposal called for a total stimulus of a little over $15 billion in both 1977 and 1978. The final numbers turned out to be $6 billion for 1977 and $17 billion for 1978.[92] The minutes of the executive committee of the Economic Policy Group for May 18, 1977 reported that "there was broad agreement that despite the withdrawal of the rebate we still expect to achieve growth in 1977 toward the lower end of the 5.5–6.0 percent range," the interval in the original administration forecast, which included the rebate.[93] The Economic Policy Group was correct. The 1977 GNP did settle at the lower end of the range.

THE INFLATION THREAT

The high priority given to a full employment policy at the start of the administration is shown by the fact that the stimulus package was the only major Carter initiative ready by the time of the inauguration.[94] In the end it was not unemployment that would be their major concern. The real demon with which they would have to wrestle was inflation.

The 1930s was the decade of the Great Depression. The 1970s would be the decade of the Great Inflation, the worst peacetime inflation in the United States in a century. The Great Depression left its mark on the national psyche for the next three decades. From the end of World War II, a high priority of government was preventing serious unemployment from ever occurring again. This is the tradition Carter inherited. The Great Inflation left its own mark on the public consciousness. Price stability became a major policy objective for the United States and for most of the industrialized nations. Now, over two decades later, the financial market, a sensitive barometer of private sector thinking, reacts strongly to any signs of inflation.

The inflation during the Carter administration was the last of three major surges in the general price level. The first occurred in the latter part of the 1960s during the administration of Lyndon Johnson. John Kennedy had proposed to Congress in the early part of the decade an expansionary tax cut, one of the first explicit attempts to implement a Keynesian fiscal policy. Kennedy's advisers thought the economy had underperformed during the Eisenhower years. The expansionary fiscal action—proposed by Kennedy, implemented by Lyndon Johnson in 1964, and designed to "get the country moving again"—is usually judged as having been successful. The unemployment rate fell and without setting off inflationary pressure. The subject of *Time*'s cover story for the last issue of 1965 was John Maynard Keynes. *Time* was almost euphoric in its description of the results of the Keynesian experiment. "In Washington," the article said, "the men who formulate the nation's economic policies have used Keynesian principles not only to avoid the violent cycles of prewar days but to produce a phenomenal economic growth and to achieve remarkably stable prices."[95]

The economic Camelot came to an end in the latter part of the 1960s. The shift from a balanced performance to an economy with strong inflationary pressures was due, in large part, to a major policy error—the financing of the Vietnam War. A massive increase in military expenditures, without a compensating reduction in domestic spending or a tax increase, was added to the expansionary programs of the New Frontier and Great Society. "The recent inflationary period has its distant origins," Schultze would later explain to Carter in a memorandum tracking the history of anti-inflation policy, "in the inflationary means used to finance the Vietnam War. The result was a classic case of excess demand inflation."[96] As one commentator has written, "at a somewhat deeper level, the United States had a burst of inflation in the 1970s because economic policymakers during the 1960s dealt their successors a very bad hand."[97]

The second wave came during the administration of Richard Nixon. Nixon first adopted a contractionary policy to dampen the inflation he had inherited. The Federal Reserve also assumed a restrictive monetary stance. As Schultze reported to Carter in the history of inflation memorandum, "the shift in monetary policy was particularly harsh. The annual growth rate of M1 [a measure of the money supply] dropped from 8 percent in the second half of 1968 to less than 3 percent in the last half of 1969."[98] The recession of 1970–71 followed. Nixon changed his position as the 1972 election approached. He had long thought that his loss to John Kennedy in the 1960 presidential election was due to the failure of the Eisenhower administration to initiate an expansionary policy prior to the campaign. He intended to avoid the same mistake in 1972. The American economy expanded rapidly in the election year, in response to expansionary monetary and fiscal policy. A 6 percent growth in the GNP caused a drop in unemployment to 5.1 percent at the end of 1972 from 6 percent a year earlier. The inflationary pressures inherited from Johnson reappeared.

A combination of other factors caused the increase in the inflation rate that followed Nixon's expansionary policy to accelerate even further. The closing of the gold window in 1971—an action discussed in the next chapter—was followed by an explosion of international liquidity, a buildup of dollar holdings in foreign banks that made inflation a common experience of the major economies. A synchronized expansion by the industrialized nations led to an above-average demand that created major scarcities in critical materials, a demand which coincided on the supply side with a worldwide crop shortage. Food prices accelerated in the second half of 1972, rising at an annual rate of 10 percent. Additional pressure on American prices came from unusually large purchases of United States grain by Russia, China, and India. American food exports increased more than 17 percent in 1972.[99] Mandatory wage and price controls, introduced by Nixon in 1971, put a temporary lid on prices but caused a buildup of inflationary pressures, which were released in a price bulge when controls were largely ended in early 1973. The disruption of oil shipments and the quadrupling of petroleum prices by Organization of Petroleum Exporting Countries in 1973 and 1974 added further to the rise in prices. "An incipient inflation," as Paul Volcker has described the period, "that, amplified by repeated rises in world oil prices, soon reached an intensity beyond any seen in the life of the American republic."[100] An American inflation rate of 2.4 percent in the 1960s grew to 9.6 percent in the period 1973–75. The inflation rate in the other major industrial nations was even higher, with the exception of West Germany.

President Gerald Ford inherited an inflation that was not only alarmingly high but had also built up a momentum of its own. Despite the recession of 1974–75—the deepest recession in the postwar period up to that point—inflation failed to abate. We had entered a period of "stagflation" in which both severe unemployment and large increases in the price level existed side by side. When Carter entered office, the inflation rate was just below 6 percent, despite an unemployment rate in excess of 7 percent.

CARTER AND THE INFLATION

Carter's advisers were not, of course, unaware of the inflation problem when they came into office, but they thought it manageable. The theme emphasized in the 1976 campaign was repeated in the early days of the administration. At a meeting at Plains prior to the inauguration, "the President-elect was advised," according to Eizenstat's notes, "that he could have real growth of 8 percent in 1977 and reduce unemployment from 8 percent to 6¼ percent with only a 0.2 percent increase in inflation."[101]

It should be said that inflation was not a major concern in general discussions of economic policy in the election year. Commenting on the 1976 campaign in an interview two years after he left office, Carter recalled that "we had about a 7½ percent unemployment rate during 1976 when I was running. . . . I never had a question, I don't believe, in the entire campaign for president about inflation. When I met with individual groups or college professors or anybody else, nobody ever brought up the question of inflation. It was not a burning issue. The only thing was, what are we going to do about jobs. When I met with the congressional leaders at the Pond House immediately after the election, the only thing we discussed economically was jobs."[102]

Economic advisers to congressional committees gave advice similar to what Carter was getting: that unemployment was the problem, and that the danger of adding to inflation through stimulative policies was minimal. Alice Rivlin, director of the Congressional Budget Office, reminded the members of the Senate Budget Committee in testimony a week before Carter's inauguration, that the committee had stated in a report the previous September, that "Congress should monitor the recovery in the immediate future with particular care and stand ready to provide additional stimulus if future weakness in the private sector requires it." Rivlin went on to say that "data during the last few months have confirmed fears of a disappointing recovery. Growth of GNP in dollars of constant purchasing power has fallen to approximately a 4 percent annual rate instead of the 5.5 to 6.0 percent path expected in framing the second concurrent [budget] resolution."[103] Rivlin then presented to the committee fiscal options that included a tax rebate and four other spending and tax cut proposals, a package roughly of the same size as the measures Carter would propose.

> The inflation effects of these spending options are estimated as fairly small. The rebate, because it is only a one-time payment, is estimated to have virtually no effect on the rate of inflation. Each of the other options has an inflation effect which builds gradually to an estimated 0.1 to 0.2 percentage points by 1980. In other words, if inflation under current policy were 4.5 percent in 1980, enactment of one of the last four options would raise it to an estimated 4.6 to 4.7 percent. These estimates reflect the view that expansionary policies at a time of substantial unemployment and excess capacity are much less inflationary than these same policies would be in a high-employment economy.[104]

Paul McCracken, chairman of the Council of Economic Advisers under President Nixon, was more cautious in his statements about the inflationary impact of a stimulus package in testimony before the same committee. He noted basic strengths in the economy, pointing out that "the economy does now seem to be moving upward at a somewhat faster clip," but concluded that, "nonetheless, in my judgment, a program of fiscal stimulus is now in order."[105] In response to a question whether fiscal stimulus could be implemented "without serious inflationary after-effects," McCracken responded: "I think so. Here we have to recognize that our ability to forecast has been rather limited generally, but particularly in this area of what is going to happen to the price level.... We do have to recognize that there is some risk here, but I think it an acceptable risk. The fact is that we can maintain a fairly strong rate of expansion in the economy and, at the same time, not put pressure either on the price level or the cost level."[106]

A leading business figure, Reginald Jones, head of General Electric, said in testimony on the stimulus package before the House Ways and Means Committee, that "there is so much slack in the economy right now that we believe a fairly sizable program of permanent tax cuts and job oriented action programs would not cause unmanageable inflation or deficits, rather would strengthen the economy against future inflation and future deficits."[107]

The forecasts in the early part of Carter's term were not the first in the history of presidential policy to underestimate the danger of inflation. At the beginning of 1973, the Nixon administration was optimistic about the economy's capacity to expand without setting off inflationary pressure. "The CEA's [Council of Economic Advisers'] forecast for the year would, in retrospect, seem fantastic," a student of the Nixon economy has written. "Output would advance briskly through the first half of calendar 1973, the CEA said, then gently ease as full employment loomed into view. Inflation would fall from a 3.5 percent rate in 1972 to 2.5 percent in 1973."[108] A Federal Reserve report that industry was operating at 83 percent of capacity in the first part of 1973, compared to a high of 92 percent in 1966, suggested there was room for expansion without excess pressure. In fact, the second wave in the Great Inflation was already underway.

The inflation rate, as measured by the Consumer Price Index, should be thought of in two different ways. There is, first of all, the overall rate periodically announced by the Department of Labor and reported by the news media. The reported rate can be distorted by the behavior of certain prices included in the index, like the prices of food and energy. Poor weather causes food prices to rise sharply, an increase which passes through to the overall price index. The "underlying rate" is computed by eliminating the price effect of random events like the weather, events that are not expected to continue. The reported consumer price index in the last year of the Ford administration was around 5 percent. Good growing conditions in that year lowered food prices and, in turn, the overall inflation rate. The underlying rate was about a percentage point higher than the overall rate. The reported rate understated the inflation problem in early 1977.

When Carter came into office, we know in hindsight, he walked into an economic trap. Even if the underlying rate held steady at about 6 percent, adverse changes in the weather, or other events, could easily cause the overall rate to rise above the underlying rate to a level that would be politically unacceptable. The president's economic advisers were not unaware of the danger. At a meeting in the Pond House in early January before the inauguration, "it was pointed out," according to Eisenstat's notes, "that the inflation rate might jump even without a stimulus." The advisers recognized that the underlying rate was around 6.5 percent and that if food prices and mortgage rates changed, "inflation would jump."[109]

ARTHUR BURNS AND THE FEDERAL RESERVE

The president of the United States does not directly control either fiscal policy or monetary policy, the two tools available for stabilizing the nation's economy. The chief executive recommends a budget to Congress and has influence over the outcome, but in the end, Congress makes the decisions on taxes and spending. The Federal Reserve (or "Fed") controls monetary policy with minimum interference from the president. The Fed was created by Congress and reports to that body. Having been given certain powers to act, it operates as an independent government agency. The seven-member Board of Governors, along with the presidents of the twelve district Federal Reserve banks, make up the controlling body of the system. Key decisions are made by the Federal Open Market Committee, which is made up of the Board of Governors plus five presidents of the district banks. The chairman of the Board is the dominant figure in Fed policies.

The chairman's four-year term in office overlaps the presidential four-year term. After a president is inaugurated he must interact with a chairman appointed by the previous president. Jimmy Carter inherited Arthur Burns, who had another year to serve. In an earlier Washington career he was chairman of the Council of Economic Advisers under President Eisenhower. While serving in that role, he also briefed Vice President Richard Nixon. When Nixon became president in 1969, he appointed Burns as his in-house economic adviser. When the term of the sitting Board chairman expired, Nixon appointed Burns to the post. He continued to serve under President Gerald Ford. He was an unusually forceful chairman. "His colleagues on the Board and the Federal Open Market Committee exerted little influence on monetary policy," a senior staff member at the Board during Burns's tenure has written.[110]

Board chairmen usually deal with an administration at arm's length. Burns, while maintaining his independence, was, nevertheless, closely involved with the Ford administration. Serious consideration was given to making Burns a member of Ford's Economic Policy Board, the predecessor to Carter's Economic Policy Group. "Legally, Burns could not be a member of the EPB," Alan Greenspan, who was chairman of the Council of Economic Advisers under Ford, later recalled. "In fact, they had originally thought of putting him on, and I said, 'you cannot do that.' Why don't we put him on as an unofficial member who is invited to the meetings? So he was invited. . . . Burns was at virtually every meeting that we had with the President."[111] While President Carter showed Burns the courtesies one would expect, the two were not close.[112]

There is occasional tension between presidents and the Federal Reserve. Presidents dislike tight money, which slows the economy, reduces job opportunities, and causes political backlash. The Federal Reserve has a concern about unemployment, but it also has as a major responsibility, preventing the economy from overheating and generating inflationary pressures. The frequently repeated saying of William McChesney Martin, who preceded Burns as chairman of the Fed Board, is worth repeating here: that it is the duty of the Fed to take away the punchbowl just when the party gets going.

Carter's economic advisers, who designed the stimulus program "to get the country moving again," were continually concerned that the Federal Reserve would offset the fiscal stimulus with monetary restraint. Charles Schultze was asked in an interview conducted after the administration left office, "What did Burns think of the stimulus package?" Schultze's response was short: "not enthusiastic."[113] In a memorandum to the president in early March, Schultze briefed Carter in preparation for a discussion with Burns:

> Arthur Burns has waged a life-long fight against big government, deficit spending and inflation. He regards budget deficits as the principal source of inflation, and his views on budget deficits are as much a matter of moral conviction as they are of analytic reasoning. There would be little point in trying to convince Burns that the stimulus package was needed. He does not think so, and he is an intellectually stubborn man. . . . His repeated assertions that the large deficits in prospect may push up interest rates sharply are particularly damaging. Participants in financial markets know that he, as Chairman of the Federal Reserve Board, is in a unique position to make that prophecy come true. While he insists that monetary policy will not offset the stimulative effects of the fiscal package, his statements about the probable impact of the fiscal program on interest

rates seem to imply the contrary—at least to participants in financial markets. As recovery proceeds some moderate rise in short-term interest rates is inevitable. But it need not and should not be large.[114]

It has been the custom for most of the presidents since John Kennedy to meet about every six weeks with what came to be called the Quadriad. At the Quadriad session the president and his three key advisers—the secretary of the treasury, the chairman of the Council of Economic Advisers, and the director of the Office of Management and Budget—meet with the chairman of the Federal Reserve Board. The purpose of the meeting is to share concerns with the hope of a smoother coordination of policy. Apparently these meetings have a limited usefulness. "You sit down once every six weeks with the President and the chairman of the Fed," Schultze said in a later interview. "During periods in which there was any kind of inflationary problem, with a Democratic President, it is always a little bit like two dogs sniffing around each other. Most of them knowing that the other's got a different constituency and a different problem. Both of them in all cases respecting each other. And I just didn't find it very useful. . . . The President looks at his calendar, maybe the night before he's read a briefing paper, and says, 'Oh, I've got to talk to the Fed Chairman today.' "[115]

The president was briefed before each meeting on topics for discussion, and the briefings reflected advisers' concerns about possible Fed actions. "The pace of economic growth has quickened markedly since the start of this year and the end of the cold weather," Schultze wrote the President in May 1977, just before the first meeting of the Quadriad. "Economic growth at this pace will require a continued strength in residential construction and an acceleration of business investment particularly in structures. You may want to raise the question as to whether conditions in financial markets are expected to be favorable to this investment growth. (An indirect way to probe Burns about interest rate and credit market developments. Burns is sensitive to being probed about the future course of interest rates—he doesn't like it done directly.)"[116]

In preparation for a meeting of the Quadriad in July, Schultze reported to the president that "the exchange value of the dollar has weakened recently. . . . Chairman Burns is concerned about the depreciation of the dollar, partly because he fears it may accentuate inflationary pressures. He may use this as a reason for tightening on monetary policy. (Higher interest rates in the U.S. would attract capital from abroad and strengthen the dollar in foreign exchange markets.) . . . You may wish to convey to Burns that

First meeting of the Quadriad. *Left to right*: Charles Schultze, Arthur Burns, Michael Blumenthal, Carter, and Bert Lance. Courtesy of the Jimmy Carter Library.

the Administration would be concerned if interest rates began to increase significantly during a period of widespread fears of another pause in the expansion."[117]

For the September meeting Schultze wrote to the president that "businesses are in a very cautious and uncertain mood, and maintenance of a satisfactory rate of economic growth over the rest of this year, and particularly into 1978, is by no means assured. . . . Recent monetary developments continue to be dominated by Federal Reserve efforts to slow the growth rate of the money supply. The Federal Reserve's long-range target for growth of the narrowly defined money supply (M-1) is 4 to 6½ percent. Since April, M-1 has been growing erratically, but relentlessly, at a pace far above the target range. . . . The Federal Reserve has responded by raising the interest rate it controls gradually, but steadily, from 5⅜ percent in May to about 6¼ percent presently."[118]

Schultze was well aware that excessive growth in money can induce inflation, and respected the Fed's legitimate concern over the rapid increase in money, but in his memorandum to the president, he raised a technical problem—the behavior of the velocity, or turnover rate of money. The total amount of spending depends not only on the amount of money available to the public, but also on the number of times that money is used. Arthur Burns once called the velocity "money's second dimension."

"We are concerned," Schultze wrote, "that the rate of increase in money velocity is slowing down from the rapid pace of the past two years. If this is true, the Fed's current targets for money growth could be inconsistent with continued healthy expansion. . . . During the first two years of the recovery, the velocity of M-1 rose at an annual rate of 6½ percent. . . . During the last two quarters, however, the rise in velocity of M-1 has slowed to less than a 2 percent annual rate. If that slow rate of increase continues, efforts by the Fed to hold growth of M-1 to within its target range could seriously damage the recovery."[119]

While the administration was concerned with what it viewed as a danger of excessive monetary tightness in 1977, hindsight suggests that the Fed was less restrictive than it should have been, given the level of the inflation rate and the acceleration of price increases that would come in 1978. Short-term interest rates did rise about 2 percentage points over the course of 1977, and longer term rates grew about half that amount.[120] Part of this increase is normal in the recovery period of the business cycle as a larger demand for funds in a more prosperous economy puts pressure on credit rates. Modest Fed restraint imposed as an anti-inflationary measure nudged rates up further.[121] While the nominal rate went up in response to Federal Reserve action, the "real" rate of interest—the nominal rate adjusted for inflation—was quite low and, on occasion, negative. The year 1977 was not a period of tight money.

As the time for Burns's term to expire—January 1978—approached, Michael Blumenthal and Charles Schultze recommended against reappointment. "While Arthur Burns is not completely inflexible in the short run," they wrote in a memorandum to Carter, "he is fundamentally unsympathetic towards giving joint priority to reducing unemployment and inflation; he will not hesitate to frustrate the unemployment goal if he thinks there is the slightest risk for the inflation goal. A Fed chairman forceful enough to dominate the Board has the independent economic power to enforce his own priorities on the nation. . . . Arthur Burns has stirred up opposition to many of your policies, and will continue to do so. He is not committed to the same fundamental goals as the Administration, and positively relishes in leading the opposition when he thinks it important."[122]

Carter didn't need much encouragement to replace Burns. "I didn't get along very well with Chairman Burns," he said in an interview after he left office. Then he cited his belief that Burns had turned to an expansionary policy to assist Nixon in his campaign for the presidency in 1972. "He's the one who, when Nixon was facing reelection, was the most eager or willing to use the Fed policy to help Nixon with a stimulus for the economy, an action which I don't think was good for the country."[123] It is clear that the Federal Reserve overstimulated the economy prior to the 1972 election. Whether the reason for the action was to assist Nixon is a controversial issue that has been discussed at length in news columns and periodicals. A number of observers have the same interpretation as Carter's.

CHAPTER 5 | **THE MONDALE MISSION AND THE LONDON SUMMIT**

Two days after his inauguration, President Carter dispatched a team led by Vice President Mondale to visit Tokyo and the major capitals of Europe. The president's instructions were to give top priority to economic issues in the discussions with foreign leaders.[1] Mondale was accompanied on the trip by Richard Cooper, Yale economist appointed undersecretary of state for economic affairs in the new government, and Fred Bergsten, an economist well known in Washington circles who had been named assistant secretary of the treasury for international economic affairs. These two, along with Anthony Solomon, undersecretary of the treasury for monetary affairs, not along on the trip, made up the main core of advisers at the subcabinet level on international economic problems.

The thrust of the Mondale mission was to give Carter's domestic stimulus program an international dimension by pressing West Germany and Japan to follow the United States in a joint expansion effort. In congressional appearances in the first weeks of the administration, officials explicitly linked the domestic stimulus program and the international initiative for economic coordination. Testifying before a House committee, Treasury Secretary Michael Blumenthal, for example, emphasized the "international economic context in which this [stimulus] program should be viewed. . . . It is important that those stronger countries, like the United States, Germany, and Japan, work together to expand as rapidly as is consistent with sustained growth and the control of inflation. By adopting this stimulus program, the United States will be asserting leadership and providing a better international economic climate. We will then ask the stronger countries abroad to follow suit. This program itself implicitly calls on them to undertake stimulus efforts of proportionately similar amounts to ours."[2] The Mondale team was charged with selling this idea.

The proposal for economic coordination pressed on West Germany and Japan was a natural part of the thinking of those who participated in early policy discussions at Plains before the inauguration. It was based on what came to be called the "locomotive strategy," an idea pushed by the Trilateral Commission, to which, as stated earlier, a large number of the members of the new administration had belonged. These included, in addition to the president himself and Vice President Mondale, members of the administration with direct interest in international economic affairs like Blumenthal and Cooper.

The basic argument for this strategy is that nations had become increasingly interdependent due to the rapid postwar growth of world trade, and a joint expansion would have spillover effects, with benefits to the international community larger than those secured when nations act alone. One of the first formal treatments of the advantages of cooperation was done in a book by Richard Cooper in 1968.[3] Since international trade was dominated by the United States, West Germany, and Japan, the strategy centered on these three major economies. By their own vigorous growth, they would pull along the other industrialized nations and the developing countries.

The idea was not completely new to American policy thinking. The United States, acting alone, could and did provide the economic thrust for worldwide expansion in the first decade-and-a-half following World War II. American dominance made it possible for it to fulfill this role. By 1960 it was clear that the United States was no longer in this hegemonic position, that the nations of Europe and Japan were making strong recoveries from the devastations of war, and that leadership in worldwide expansion would now have to be shared. The Kennedy administration advanced a "dumbell theory" to describe the relationship of the United States and Europe, an analogy suggesting two strong economic powers joined by common interest and mutual dependence. "The metaphor was meant to conjure up weight-lifting," one commentator has whimsically observed, "not cynical thoughts about the intelligence of policy makers."[4] "Between 1959 and 1964," the same commentator goes on to add, "American policy no longer attempted, virtually single handedly, to lead the world toward prosperity; this was now to be accomplished by moving arm in arm with Europe (with Japan, still a junior partner, tagging along behind)."[5] By 1977 Japan was no longer a junior partner.

The United States was not the only voice urging expansion by the three large economic powers. The Organization for Economic Cooperation and Development (OECD), representing twenty-four nations from Europe, North America, and Japan, had been pressing for greater macroeconomic coordination since the early part of the 1960s. Just before Carter's inauguration, in its December 1976 *Economic Outlook*, the OECD's secretariat argued that "under present circumstances, it is clearly desirable for [the United States, Germany, and Japan] to ensure that their domestic demand is on a path which progressively reduces unemployment and provides the setting in which other countries can proceed toward export-led growth."[6] The OECD was not convinced that Germany and Japan were on a growth path consistent with their potential. The OECD's forecast of economic activity in Germany for 1977 challenged optimistic German growth projections and also estimated that the margin of unutilized resources in Japan was likely to remain substantial.[7] Pressure on the Germans also came from within the European Community.[8]

A report issued by sixteen economists from the European Community, North America, and Japan meeting at the Brookings Institution in November 1976, stated as their basic conclusion that "Germany, Japan, and the United States should now adopt domestic economic policies geared to stimulating economic activity. Stronger economic expansion in the three countries, each of which has recently experienced a lull, need not intensify inflation problems but should reduce domestic unemployment and provide benefits to other countries. . . . Germany, Japan, and the United States were singled out as the appropriate engines of world economic recovery because of their weight in the international economy."[9] The United States was represented on the committee by Paul McCracken, chairman of the Council of Economic Advisers under Richard Nixon, and Arthur Okun, chairman of the council under President Johnson.

The quadrupling of petroleum prices in 1974 by the Organization of Petroleum Exporting Countries (OPEC) resulted in large surpluses in their international accounts, an increase not matched by an equal increase in spending for imports. The counterpart of OPEC surpluses were the deficits of the oil importing countries. The oil price increase of 1974, Richard Cooper has written, "was a dramatic event, probably the largest shock per unit time the world economy has ever seen. In a mere three months, over 12 percent of the value of world exports were sharply redirected."[10] World sentiment leaned toward sharing the adjustment to the trade imbalance. Criticism of German and Japanese surpluses during this period of international disequilibrium was strong in various international forums. The final *Economic Report* of the Ford administration cited the shift in the American current-account balance, from surplus in the second half of 1975 to a deficit in the second half of 1976, as contributing to the international adjustment process by helping to offset the large OPEC surpluses. The report also noted that "no such support to better international equilibrium was apparent in the shifts in the current account positions of the other two major industrial countries."[11]

Prime Minister Callaghan of Great Britain had raised, without success, the issue of a joint expansion by the big three in a summit meeting in 1975. He visited Washington in early 1977. A memorandum for President Carter from the Council of Economic Advisers briefed the president on conditions in Britain at the time of the visit, pointing out that "the British economy over the past several years has suffered from slow economic growth coupled with high inflation rates relative to other industrial countries. . . . Unemployment remains high. As a consequence, the outlook for adequate growth of world trade is of particular importance to the British authorities."[12] Callaghan had an ally in the Carter administration, which took the position that a joint economic expansion of their domestic economies by the United States, Germany, and Japan would provide a market for the exports of the rest of the nations and contribute to the correction of the payments imbalance.[13]

The state of the world economy at the time of Carter's inauguration added a sense of urgency. The 1974–75 recession, with record unemployment for most countries, was the worst downturn in the postwar period. It also brought with it the first drop in world trade since World War II.[14] The recovery was less rapid than in previous recessions, when allowing for the depth of the decline, and by the fall of 1976 it was faltering. The economic growth rate for the seven largest countries, a healthy 6.9 percent in the first half of 1976, had fallen to 3.4 percent in the second half.

RECEPTION IN GERMANY

The Germans reacted to the outside pressure to adopt an expansionary policy with resentment and were skeptical about the wisdom of such a move. Helmut Schmidt's reception of the American delegation in Bonn was frosty. Even before the arrival of the delegation, Schmidt had adopted a harsh attitude, saying, according to the *New York Times*, that officials of the Carter administration who were recommending that Germany should adopt a stimulative policy should "please better shut their mouths."[15] The German economic record on unemployment and inflation was better, he asserted, than that of the United States and he needed no lessons on how to manage German economic policy. During one session with the Mondale team he made a point of praising William Simon, the conservative secretary of the treasury under Gerald Ford. "We owe a lot to Bill Simon," he is reported to have said. "We owe Bill Simon everything," Mondale bantered back; "without him we wouldn't have won the election."[16]

Schmidt was concerned about the continuing danger of inflation and asked the Americans about the expected effect of the Carter stimulus package on the inflation rate in the United States. When Bergsten replied it was expected to raise the inflation rate by only 0.3 percent, he is reported to have been "incredulous."[17] Schmidt shared in general the German opinion that on issues of economic policy Americans are unreliable. After the delegation departed from Bonn, he is said to have expressed resentment at being lectured to by the two inexperienced academics, Cooper and Bergsten.

In his memoirs Helmut Schmidt recalls the Mondale trip: "Only a few days after taking office in January 1977 Carter, speaking through vice president, Walter ('Fritz') Mondale, urged us to entertain an expansive monetary and financial policy. . . . Pointing out that worldwide inflation would be the inevitable result, we rejected the proposal."[18] Schmidt's characterization of his reaction, we will see later, was not as final or absolute as his account suggests.

In a sense the meeting of the Mondale group and Schmidt was a clash of two cultures. The Americans were preoccupied with the unemployment problem, due in part to the traditional sympathies of the Democratic Party, but also due to the concerns shared by many Americans still haunted by the ghost of the Great Depression. The Germans, on the other hand, have an historic fear of inflation, an aversion burned into the German psyche by experiences central to their history. Germany had been through two major inflations in the twentieth century. The German hyperinflation of 1923 is the standard textbook case of runaway prices. In that episode prices rose so rapidly that workers contracted for a wage on a daily basis. They were paid twice a day. At the lunch hour workers would bring their first pay envelope of the day to the factory gate to give to one of the children in the family. The child would run to a store where the mother waited in a queue to spend the money before it lost its value. At the inflation's peak, prices were rising at close to a 30,000 percent annual rate, just over 20 percent a day. At that rate the price level doubles in less than four days.[19] As prices rise and the value of money falls, people holding assets fixed in terms of money, debt instruments like bonds and mortgages, see their wealth disappear. As the value of the mark fell in terms of domestic purchasing power, its value relative to other currencies also dropped. At the height of the German hyperinflation, the entire mortgage debt of Germany could be purchased for one American penny. John Kenneth Galbraith observed that "the larger effect of the inflation was the liquidation and transfer of wealth rivaling that in Russia in the same year."[20]

World War II was also followed by an inflation shock, and these episodes sensitized political leaders to the obligation to defend the integrity of the nation's currency. "The spectre of inflation has haunted Germany ever since," another observer has noted, "and after 1949 successive German governments have made control of inflation their number one priority."[21] Ludwig Erhard, West German minister of economics in 1958, lectured President Eisenhower: "Whereas the Germans, because of their history, always worried about inflation, the Americans, because of their history, always worried about depression. The resulting danger was that America would overrespond to threats of recession and cause serious inflation in the long run."[22]

The fear of inflation was institutionalized in the country's financial control system. "Safeguarding the currency" was the preeminent role assigned to the Bundesbank, the German central bank, by its 1957 charter. With the introduction of the Euro in 1999, the authority of the Bundesbank, and other European central banks, was replaced by the creation of the European Central Bank. But during the Carter administration, the Bundesbank exercised total control in Germany. "The bank's abiding nightmare . . . remains the hyperinflation of 1923," one student of German monetary policy observed.[23] The priority given price stability by the Bundesbank continued a long German tradition. In 1939 all the members of the board of the Bundesbank's prewar predecessor, the Reichbank, signed a letter to Adolph Hitler. "The letter complains in a very harsh, and, given the circumstances, courageous tone about the excessive increase in military expenditure, which was endangering price stability."[24] In line with its legislated charge, the Bundesbank delivered one of the lowest and most stable rates of inflation among the industrialized nations. Despite the slowdown in the recovery from the 1974–75 recession, inflation remained at the 8 percent annual rate in the seven largest industrial nations, but only half that in Germany.

In the European Monetary System, prior to the introduction of the Euro in 1999, other countries imported the credibility of the Bundesbank by tying their currencies to the German mark. At the time of Carter's election, the mark was second only to the dollar as a reserve currency held by other countries. One of the fears about the introduction of a single European currency and a single European central bank is that the new bank may not have the Bundesbank's commitment to price stability. The Bundesbank was, as the central bank of Germany, one of the most independent of central banks and wielded enormous power.[25]

If the German price performance was better than that of its major trade rivals at the time of the Mondale visit, its record for output of goods and services was beginning to be less impressive. The recovery of the German economy from the destruction of World War II is rightfully described as the "German miracle." It can be dated from the currency reforms and decontrol of prices engineered by Ludwig Erhard in 1948, steps which allowed free markets to operate. Economic growth in the first two years of the market economy was above 15 percent on an annual basis, a performance exceptional by any standard, but partly due to starting from such a low base. As the economy completed the start-up stage, the growth rate returned to a more normal level. Still the economy grew during the 1950s at a vigorous rate of a little over 8 percent annually. Only Japan grew at a faster pace, and then only marginally so. Only once in the decade, in the 1958 slowdown, did the expansion pace dip below 6 percent.[26]

In the 1960s and early 1970s the growth rate dropped somewhat dramatically to almost half the average rate of the 1950s—still a healthy 4.5 percent, but exceeded by France, Italy, and Japan.[27] The year 1973—a year identified with the oil embargo triggered by the Yom Kippur war, followed shortly by the first major oil price increase of the 1970s—represents, for Germany as for other industrialized countries, a marker dividing the golden age of the 1960s and early 1970s from the troubled times of the next two decades. For the rest of the 1970s the German economy grew at the low rate of a little over 2 percent. The slower growth continued into the Reagan years. There was not only a decline in historical terms but a relative decline by international standards as well. German growth in the 1980s trailed that of the European powers—France, Italy, and the United Kingdom—as well as the United States and Japan.[28] Schmidt, who served as chancellor from mid-1974 to October 1982, headed a country that was past the crest of its striking achievement. Even in the face of a declining growth rate, the Germans continued to give high priority to price stability.

RECEPTION IN JAPAN

The reception the Mondale team received in Japan was warmer than their reception in Bonn. Carter had talked to Prime Minister Takeo Fukuda on the telephone before the inauguration asking for cooperation in leading the world expansion. Fukuda's reaction to Mondale's overtures was basically positive.[29] But there was in Japan, as elsewhere, a sense of caution. In 1977, a cautious attitude was appropriate. Japan, which imports a high percentage of its oil needs, had been hit hard by the oil shock of 1973–74. The consumer price index rose by 24 percent in 1974. The inflation rate was still high, 9.4 percent, in 1976.

Even before the Mondale mission arrived the government had initiated, however, an expansionary policy. Fukuda had only been chosen as premier by the Liberal Democratic Party the day before Christmas 1976. As he assumed office he promised fiscal stimulus. A supplementary budget was presented shortly before the arrival of the Mondale team with a fiscal boost predicted to produce a growth rate of 6.7 percent and to increase domestic demand by enough to eliminate the current-account surplus. A number of Japanese economists thought the amount of the expansionary effort inadequate for achieving these goals. The Americans were also skeptical.

The idea of an expansionary policy was not as inherently unacceptable to the Japanese as it was to the Germans. The Japanese were, in fact, pioneers in the 1930s in using fiscal policy to stimulate business activity. The idea of state intervention was not an alien one in Japan since, by the 1930s, the government had had a close relationship to the economy for over half a century. A prominent Japanese economist gave a seminar on Keynes's famous treatise, *The General Theory*, at Hitotsubashi University only two months after its publication in 1936.[30] Even before Keynes's book arrived on the scene, the Japanese had experimented with expansionary policy. As an antidote to recession that began in 1930, the government initiated stimulative fiscal and monetary policies. Deficit financing averaged 30 percent of government expenditures over the period 1931–36. Large military outlays associated with Japan's military adventures were a substantial part of the deficit, and the expansionary fiscal policy lent encouragement to the warlords. Nevertheless, one Japanese observer has described this fiscal policy initiative as "a grand experiment anticipating Keynesian economics."[31]

In the years immediately following the war, inflation was rampant in Japan, as it was in Germany, and the policy focus was quite different from that of the prewar period. With Japan still under occupation, President Harry Truman dispatched Joseph Dodge, a conservative banker, to deal with the inflation problem. Dodge imposed a policy of tight finance. Government would grow only as the total economy grew; outlays would expand within the limits of the increase in tax revenues. As a result the Japanese had two decades of balanced budgets. There was little pressure on government from the academic economists to introduce expansionary policies. In the postwar period Keynesian ideas were weak in the universities because of the dominance of Marxian thinking.[32] In any event, the policy concern was not short-run stabilization of the economy but long-term export-led economic growth, with government guiding investment into high value-added industries. It was a policy that succeeded. Japan had its own economic miracle.

The year 1965 is a fiscal landmark in Japan, with government for the first time using deficit financing to supplement tax revenues. Part of the reason for the deficit and those that followed was the growth of social transfer programs and the increased outlays required to deal with environmental concerns. But the deficits were kept to a modest level. This was the case even in the recession of 1974, the first year of negative output growth in the postwar period. A 24 percent inflation rate caused by the first oil price shock was the dominant concern. "It was not until . . . 1975 under strong international pressure that deficit financing became a major policy tool."[33] Even though Japan had reasons to expand in 1977 because of the sluggish recovery from the recession of 1974–75, it was still cautious about the Mondale proposal. It reluctantly joined in because of U.S. coercion.

A particularly sensitive issue for the American team was an undervalued yen. The American position was that the Japanese were intervening in foreign exchange markets to keep the value of the yen low, a step designed to make Japanese goods and services more attractive to trading partners and, at the same time, make others' products less appealing to the home market. Both Cooper and Bergsten thought that the Japanese had been intervening unfairly to manipulate the value of the yen. In order to see the issue at stake—and to better understand the vulnerability to volatile exchange rates that plagued Carter through most of his administration—it is helpful to make a brief comment on the international monetary system as it existed at the time of his inauguration.

INTERNATIONAL MONETARY SYSTEM

The gold standard serves well as a prototype against which other global monetary arrangements can be compared. In its purest form it governed international monetary affairs from the 1870s to 1914 and with a brief revival in the 1920s. Under a gold standard currencies are defined in terms of gold, which automatically means that they are defined in terms of one another. The stability of exchange rates resulting from the linkage to gold is one of the attractive features of the gold standard. It reduces for market participants the uncertainty in moving from one currency to another.

The gold standard had another important feature: it imposed discipline on trading nations. If a nation experienced inflation, its goods became less desirable and so also its currency. As its currency fell in value, trading partners demanded gold in payment. The loss of gold on which the domestic money system was based caused a decrease in the money supply. The decrease in the money supply, in turn, would force the economy into a recession, which would release the inflationary pressure. The original imbalance was resolved, as they said at the time, by "going through the wringer of deflation."

The essential feature of this monetary regime was its automatic adjustment mechanism. Stability of exchange rates took priority over domestic concerns. Remnants of the gold standard that survived the First World War came apart during the Great Depression as nations struggled with severe unemployment problems and the discipline of the gold standard became politically unacceptable.

The regime put into place after World War II was created at a meeting of forty-four nations at the Mount Washington Hotel in Bretton Woods, New Hampshire, in 1944. In the new system the United States set the price of gold at $35 an ounce. Other currencies were defined in terms of gold or the dollar and were, therefore, defined in terms of one another. Only the United States agreed to exchange its currency for gold at the official price, a commitment that made the dollar and gold equivalent. It was a pledge with credibility since the United States at the end of the war controlled about three-fourths of the world's monetary gold and produced 40 percent of the world's economic output. Because other countries no longer redeemed their currencies for gold, movements in the precious metal could no longer serve as a constraint on variations in exchange rates as they did under the gold standard. Other nations agreed to maintain the value of their currencies within 1 percent on either side of the official rate by intervening in foreign exchange markets, buying or selling their currencies in order to maintain the official value. The foreign reserves used for purchasing currencies consisted, for the most part, of gold and the dollar.

The Bretton Woods arrangement differed from the gold standard in that it gave a nation some breathing room. If a nation experienced inflationary pressure and its currency's value tended to fall outside the agreed limits, it could delay imposing a tight money policy to stifle the inflation—or impose a more moderate one—by using its reserves to support the currency. If reserves became scarce, it could borrow from the International Monetary Fund, an institution created at Bretton Wood to administer the articles of agreement and to lend to nations in trouble. The additional reserves permitted a more gradual and less painful adjustment in the nation's external balance.[34]

The Bretton Woods regime had a relatively long run, lasting until the 1970s. There were periodic changes in par values by the member nations to adjust to changing conditions in competitiveness, as allowed by the system. But, in general, stability of exchange rates was maintained, a condition that contributed, along with an American-led multinational reduction in tariffs, to the rapid postwar growth of international trade. "By common consensus," one observer has said, "the period from 1950 to 1973 was Western capitalism's most successful age. Trade expansion was the engine of remarkable economic growth and, at least until the late 1960s, domestic price levels were anchored by the exchange rate regime."[35]

The United States played a crucial role in the international monetary arrangements of the postwar period. Its balance of payments deficits, whereby it sent more dollars abroad than it received back in exchange, provided the liquidity needed for growing world trade. The American deficits were, in the beginning, less a matter of concern than a sign of the recovery of Europe and Japan. Part of the dollars accumulated in foreign hands were converted into gold at the American treasury. But the larger part of accumulated dollars was held as working reserves.[36] In effect, the dollar served as an international money.

The benevolent hegemonic role played by the United States was key to the success of Bretton Woods in the first decade and a half after the war, but the arrangement had a basic flaw that contributed to its final demise. A domestic currency like the dollar was never intended to serve as an international money, and its use for this purpose involved an inherent instability.[37] As the United States, through its payments deficits, supplied the dollars needed to finance the increase in world trade, increasingly larger amounts of dollars accumulated in foreign hands, all redeemable, in principle, in gold.

During the last two years of the Eisenhower administration there was mounting concern over the American position, and in the closing months of his presidency something of a crisis developed over private speculation in the private London gold market.[38] When President Kennedy took office, he is reported to have told his advisers that the two things that concerned him most were nuclear war and the international balance of payments.[39]

There was another potential problem that aggravated the contradictions in the system arising from the use of the dollar as the currency of international trade. Bretton Woods was a lopsided world. The obligations assumed by the participating nations were not symmetrical. If the dollar weakened on foreign exchange markets due to deficits in its balance of payments, other nations were forced to intervene as their currencies became more valuable relative to the dollar. The United States' trading partners were required to support the value of the American currency. Put in another way, the United States stood in a position of being able to cover its debts abroad by simply creating money. The success of Bretton Woods depended, in large part, on America's not abusing what de Gaulle called the dollar's "exorbitant privilege."

Until 1965 the United States basically fulfilled this requirement. It had the best record for long-run price stability of any major country. Its deficits in its overall balance of payments were elevated in the 1950s and 1960s beyond what was necessary to supply the needs of world liquidity, not because of a deficit in its trade in goods and services, but rather because of the military spending seen as necessary to defend the Western Alliance and because of foreign aid programs and direct investment by American corporations, particularly in Europe. In 1965 American policies became destabilizing. The deficit financing of the Vietnam War set off domestic inflationary pressures that placed the dollar in a precarious position over and above the strains created by its use as an international money. By the start of the 1970s a state of crisis existed. The problem that had become a matter for concern in the last year of the Eisenhower administration crested during the presidency of Richard Nixon.

An obvious solution was to negotiate a change in the relationship of the dollar, now clearly overvalued, to other currencies. The Nixon administration cautiously approached key trading partners to test their willingness to accept such an adjustment. The overture did not meet with success.[40] Faced with a situation approaching a state of crisis, the administration devalued unilaterally. After meeting with his advisers at Camp David, Nixon announced in a speech on August 15, 1971 the closing of the gold window; the United States would no longer redeem dollars presented to it for the precious metal.[41] Since the dollar was no longer anchored in gold, its value began to float in response to supply and demand pressures.

In closing the gold window, President Nixon presented our trading partners with an accomplished fact. Committed to an historic tradition of fixed exchange rates, the participating nations attempted, at a conference at the Smithsonian, to reconstruct the system by redefining the par values of the currencies to more truly reflect relative competitiveness—including a formal devaluation of the dollar—and allowing a wider range of variation in their worth on the open market. It was, in its own way, a remarkably ambitious attempt, since agreement had to be reached not only on the new value of the dollar but on a whole new grid of exchange rates involving a large number of currencies. Private dealers found the adjustments unconvincing, and the Smithsonian parities came under market pressure almost as soon as they were established. After a succession of speculative attacks on various currencies, the arrangement was abandoned. In 1973 the world moved by default to a system of floating rates in which the value of currencies fluctuate on a daily basis in response to changes in supply and demand.

The floating arrangement was formalized by an amendment of the Articles of Agreement of the International Monetary Fund a year before Carter's inauguration.[42] A number of economists, including Nobel prize winner Milton Friedman, welcomed a regime of flexible exchange rates.[43] Under a system of flexible rates, a nation would not have to act, either to support its currency through intervention in the market or to introduce tight monetary and fiscal policies to restore competitiveness. Disequilibrium in international balances would be resolved by continuing adjustments in rates as the market judged, on a daily basis, the strengths and weaknesses of the trading nations and the relative worth of their currencies. Fluctuations in exchange rates, it was argued, would be modest as the actions of speculators would smooth the oscillations, a continuing minuet of mini-devaluations and revaluations in response to shifting events. What has actually occurred is an unexpected volatility of exchange rates, a volatility due mainly to the huge increase in the mobility of capital.

The Carter administration took office shortly after this global monetary crisis. Paul Volcker, who negotiated the Smithsonian devaluation of the dollar and who was later appointed by Jimmy Carter to head the Federal Reserve, has said that "the two years after the Smithsonian agreement were the most economically turbulent of the postwar period up to that point."[44] Carter inherited a new system, only recently in place, with a vulnerability to volatile foreign exchange markets and with the rules of the game not yet fully understood.

We are now in a position to understand the objections that the Mondale team raised to an alleged Japanese "dirty float." The 1976 amendment to Article IV of the Articles of Agreement of the International Monetary Fund provided that nations can legitimately intervene in foreign exchange markets—buying and selling currencies—to prevent "disorderly market conditions." Nations are not permitted to intervene to lower the value of their currency simply to gain a trade advantage. American officials were convinced that the Japanese were manipulating the value of the yen for their own purposes. A debate had taken place in 1976 over the issue. In congressional testimony in June 1976, Fred Bergsten, soon to join the Carter administration, "accused Japanese authorities of maintaining an inappropriately competitive rate and disguising the true extent of their operations by depositing the dollar proceeds in private banks."[45] Three months before the election, the issue of Japanese activity in the foreign exchange market was discussed in an all-day session with economic advisers at Plains.[46] On the Mondale trip, Bergsten was authorized by the president and the secretary of the treasury to admonish the Japanese in the strongest terms to refrain from such intervention. "We knew exactly what they were doing and wanted them to stop." The Japanese were taken aback, Bergsten has reported, but apparently his protests had effect. The yen rose after the Mondale visit.[47]

Part of the pressure exerted by the Mondale group on both the Germans and the Japanese was related to the expected behavior of exchange rates in the event Germany and Japan refused to join in an expansionary action. The American position was that the United States would engage in a stimulus program regardless of whether the two trading partners followed or not. If the United States expanded alone, a worsening of the American trade deficit would follow and Germany and Japan could expect a depreciation of the dollar against their currencies. The higher value of their currencies would make their goods more expensive on international markets. To offset the decline in exports they would have to stimulate domestic spending, arriving, finally, at the position initially urged by the Americans. The more efficient policy would be to join the United States in an expansionary program from the beginning. The dollar did indeed depreciate in 1977, and the United States did not take action to support it in order to keep pressure on West Germany and Japan to expand.[48]

The January Mondale mission was followed in the ensuing months with contacts by subcabinet officials with counterparts abroad working toward an agreement on a locomotive strategy. Negotiations among the top leaders—Carter of the United States, Schmidt of West Germany, and Fukuda of Japan—began at the May London summit of the seven major world powers in 1977 and continued at the Bonn summit in 1978.

THE LONDON ECONOMIC SUMMIT

The economic summit held in May 1977 provided Jimmy Carter with his first opportunity to meet the leaders of the other major powers and to press in person his argument for implementing a locomotive strategy. The London summit was the third such gathering held for the purpose of discussing economic issues of mutual interest. The first was initiated by the French president, Giscard d'Estaing, and held at Rambouillet a few miles outside Paris in late 1975. More traditional channels for exchange of economic information among governments were in place at the time of the Rambouillet summit. The Organization for Economic Cooperation and Development reported on the monetary and fiscal policies of its members. The OECD's Economic Policy Committee, attended by economics and finance ministers, provided for an exchange of views on macroeconomic policy. The International Monetary Fund also sponsored multilateral consultations on macroeconomic issues, and the heads of the central banks met regularly at the Bank for International Settlement in Basel, Switzerland. It was the view of Giscard and Chancellor Helmut Schmidt of Germany, with whom Giscard maintained close contact, that something else was needed, given the problems of the 1970s—the collapse of Bretton Woods, the oil crisis of 1973–74, and the deep recession that followed. None of the existing committees "were suited to generating the political momentum the economic problems of the post-oil-shock period required. What was needed was a new series of consultations at the highest level."[49]

It was Giscard's intent that the meeting would be informal, with the principals unencumbered by a retinue of ministers and aides. It would be a small group with close personal contact, a setting in which confidence could develop among the leaders. The model for the economic summits was the Library Group, so called because it first met in the library of the White House in early 1973. The initial session was attended by the finance ministers of the United States, France, Germany, Japan, and the United Kingdom, who, in an informal and private setting, were able to speak with a candor not possible at other international meetings. Giscard and Schmidt, both finance ministers at the time, were part of the Library Group. When Giscard became president of France and Schmidt became chancellor of West Germany, both in 1974, they sought to reproduce the informal setting of the Library Group at the highest level, a forum for national leaders to discuss openly major economic issues.

The Rambouillet conference was attended by the heads of six nations: France, Germany, Italy, Japan, the United Kingdom, and the United States.

Before accepting the invitation to participate, President Ford sent George Shultz, who had recently resigned as secretary of the treasury under Richard Nixon, to go to Europe to confer with Giscard, Schmidt, and Harold Wilson of Britain and determine the likelihood of a successful outcome from such a meeting. Schulz, who had been the American member of the Library Group and knew these leaders well, reported favorably to Ford who then accepted the invitation.[50]

There were three days of meetings at Rambouillet, the fourteenth-century chateau where Napoleon spent his last night before exile to St. Helena. The topics discussed at this first economic summit became the focus of the summits that followed: macroeconomic policy, trade, East-West relations, energy, and North-South relations.[51] More important than the topics covered was the simple fact that the meeting took place. "Never before had presidents and prime ministers met multilaterally to discuss economic matters."[52] The second summit was hosted the next year by Gerald Ford at Puerto Rico. It was not as ambitious in scope as Rambouillet. The notice for the Puerto Rico summit was given only one month in advance. Representatives of the participants had time for only one meeting to prepare the agenda prior to the session. The meeting had one distinction. Ford invited Trudeau of Canada, not represented at Rambouillet, to attend. Thereafter Canada rounded out what became a Group of Seven. A powerful seven. Anthony Solomon, undersecretary of the treasury, noted in a memorandum to Secretary Blumenthal, "they produce 85% of the total output of the developed world and can virtually determine the course of the world economy."[53]

When Carter came into office he strongly supported the idea of an economic summit, as did his advisers. "The key positions in the new administration were staffed by alumni, not of the Library Group, but of the Trilateral Commission."[54] Members of the commission were dedicated to the idea of cooperation among the major powers in an interdependent world. Carter's strong commitment to the idea of an economic summit, over his four years in office, contributed to making this annual meeting a permanent feature of international dialogue.

Preparatory work for the sessions was done by designees who came to be called "sherpas," the guides who led the principals to the summit. The American sherpa under Ford was George Shultz. Under Carter it was Henry Owen. Because of his key position in preparing for the summits, Owen played an important role in coordinating policy on international economic issues.

Gerald Ford had two economic advisory committees. In addition to the Economic Policy Board, primarily concerned with domestic issues, there was the Council on International Economic Policy (CIEP), first established by Congress in 1972 during the Nixon administration. Carter decided not to seek renewal of the CIEP, whose expiration date was approaching. Eizenstat recalled in an interview that members of Carter's transition staff talked to a number of people in the Ford administration who felt that the council was not a useful arrangement.[55]

Under Carter the Economic Policy Group (EPG) handled both domestic and international policy. Michael Blumenthal, who, as secretary of the treasury, was concerned with both domestic and international issues, chaired the EPG. Further input on international policy came from Richard Cooper, who represented the State Department and was a member of the Economic Policy Group, and from Henry Owen, who attended meetings as appropriate. A deputies group for international economic issues was formed at the assistant secretary level in early 1978. Representatives from the State Department, the Treasury Department, and the National Security Council attended the deputies' meetings, along with representatives from the Council of Economic Advisers, the Office of Management and Budget, and the Domestic Policy Staff. Included among their responsibilities was "forwarding to the Steering Committee [of the Economic Policy Group] a concise weekly report on the status/progress of inter-agency work throughout the Executive Branch on major international economic issues."[56] Fred Bergsten, assistant secretary of the treasury for international economics, has said that policies were well coordinated. "The international economic policy people were appointed as a team. They all knew each other. They belonged together rather than being thought of as vertically separated in the individual agencies."[57]

Henry Owen has been described by Madeleine Albright, who served on the National Security Council under Brzezinski, as playing an ad hoc role in policy formation.[58] He had served in the State Department under Lyndon Johnson as chairman of the department's Policy Planning Council. From the State Department he went to Brookings as director of foreign policy studies. He was appointed by Carter as special representative to the president to prepare for the London summit. After the summit was over, Owen returned to his position at Brookings. He came back to the administration full-time in 1978 as the president's special summit representative, "with responsibilities for economic summits and for international economic policy."[59] At Carter's insistence the summits became somewhat more formalized. The sherpas met three times for preparatory work prior to the meeting of the leaders, with a follow-up six months after the summit to review the results. The summits became a year-round process, and Owen was an integral part of the arrangements.[60]

The results of the London summit were disappointing in terms of commitment to a joint expansion on the part of the three major industrial powers. Since the year was almost half over by the meeting date, the timing was not favorable for introducing new initiatives for 1977. The Germans and the Japanese resisted adopting specific growth targets, simply pointing to forecasts, already announced earlier in the year, of a strong performance for their economies in 1977. The official predictions were a 5 percent growth rate for the German economy and 6.7 percent for Japan. Carter had weakened his case for joint expansion by dropping, only a month before the London summit, the proposal for the tax rebate submitted to Congress at the beginning of the year. The cutback in his stimulus package, due partly to inflation concerns, gave Helmut Schmidt opportunity for an "I told you so" reaction. Further, Schmidt succeeded in getting into the final communiqué a statement reflecting the German priority of price stability, an indirect way of expressing discomfort with the locomotive strategy.[61]

Even though the Germans and the Japanese resisted setting a specific growth target at London, the forecasts they brought to the table had the effect of an implied commitment, as economic forecasts often do at both the domestic and international levels. Actual performance of the German and Japanese economies fell short of the predictions for 1977. German data released soon after the conference showed only 1.2 percent growth for the second quarter of 1977, measured at an annual rate. For the whole of 1977, economic growth was 2.6 percent for Germany, about half of the predicted value. The Japanese came closer, but below the forecast by more than a percentage point. Both countries initiated expansionary measures in the fall of 1977, but with minimal effect for the year. In documents submitted for a meeting of the representatives of the Group of Seven in late September 1977, Germany conceded that the 1977 gross national product growth would fall below the forecast reported at the London summit. Japan, with its better record, cited the economic measure taken in early September and stated that it had "pursued those policies which are necessary to fulfill the summit growth pledge."[62] Only the United States achieved its growth target. The target was 5.8 percent; actual growth was 5.5 percent.

The difference in economic expansion rates among the major powers led to an increase in the American current-account deficit and a depreciation of the dollar, as predicted by American officials in the event that the United States expanded alone.

THE TRADE DEFICIT AND THE DOLLAR

In 1977 the United States ran the nation's largest merchandise trade deficit. The deficit, while sizable, was not in itself an aberration. It was simply a continuation of a recent shift from past historical experience. For the first seven decades of the 1900s, the American trade balance was in surplus: we sold more goods abroad than we bought from other nations. In 1971 we recorded our first trade deficit of the century. There was a temporary reprieve in 1975, in the form of a large surplus. A decline in American economic activity in that year—a drop larger than that of our trading partners—resulted in fewer foreign imports. In addition the aftereffects of the dollar devaluations in 1971 and 1973, which made our exports cheaper and our imports more expensive, finally set in. In 1976 and 1977 a trend of deficits in our trade balance continued. The 1977 merchandise trade deficit was $31 billion, three times the deficit of 1976. It was offset, in part, by a surplus in the "invisibles"—travel, transportation, and income from investments abroad—which, along with merchandise trade, make up the so-called current account. But the 1977 trade deficit was still a matter of serious concern.

Assistant Secretary of the Treasury Fred Bergsten testified in a congressional hearing that "the swing in the trade balance is due almost entirely to two factors: (1) the growing U.S. dependence on foreign oil and (2) the fact that our major trading partners have achieved less than we by way of sustained economic expansion."[63] The increase in the value of oil imports was dramatic, from $8 billion in 1973 to $28 billion in 1975 to $47 billion in 1977. The increase in 1977 accounted for almost half of the increase of the trade deficit in that year. The larger imports of oil were caused by a drop in the domestic production of crude oil and an increase in domestic demand. The decline in American production, which averaged 3.5 percent a year since 1972, was due, in part, to disincentives associated with the price controls imposed on oil in 1971. (I discuss the price controls in detail later.) Demand rose almost 7 percent in 1976 and 6 percent in 1977, causing increases of 20.5 percent and 19.5 percent in the import of oil volumes in the two years.[64] The OPEC nations used part of their oil revenues to buy American goods, purchases which partially offset in the current account American outlays for imported oil. According to one contemporary estimate, however, they spent only sixteen cents on American goods for every dollar spent by the United States on OPEC oil.[65]

Memoranda circulated within the administration emphasized, as did the second point in Bergsten's testimony, the differences in the rate of economic expansion in the United States, Europe, and Japan as a major cause of the trade deficit. A weakening of the competitive position was rejected as a contributing factor. "On the basis of relative prices (U.S. versus foreign) adjusted to exchange rate changes," a briefing paper for Secretary Blumenthal argued, "U.S. price competitiveness has remained essentially unchanged since mid-1975, the record trade surplus year. The trade deficit increases cannot be explained in terms of relative price performance; the IMF agrees."[66] The negative effect of the more rapid United States expansion on the American trade position was aggravated by the fact that Americans spend a larger proportion of an increase in income on imports than is the case with Europeans. At the same time that the United States began to incur substantial current-account deficits, the Germans and Japanese began to accumulate large surpluses. Between 1976 and 1978 the German current-account surplus more than doubled and the Japanese surplus increased fourfold, in both cases a reflection of the country's sluggish domestic economy.

The American trade deficit was closely connected with another problem: the rapid depreciation of the dollar in the first two years of the administration. Following the introduction of flexible exchange rates at the end of 1973, the dollar was relatively stable in foreign exchange markets until the latter part of 1977, when it began to depreciate rapidly.[67] From September through December 1977, the dollar fell more than 5 percent relative to a bundle of major currencies. It would continue to fall until October 1978, when the drop became precipitous. As the dollar declined, the German mark and the Japanese yen rose in value. Over the period from the fall of 1977 to the fall of 1978, the German mark appreciated by 11 percent in terms of the dollar and the yen by almost 29 percent. The appreciation of these foreign currencies increased the prices of American imports, adding another problem for domestic inflation control. To follow the dance of the dollar over the first two years of the administration requires a brief aside.

The somewhat volatile behavior of rates, following the initiation of the floating system, caused renewed interest in what determines the level at which exchange rates settle. These rates are partly determined by trade patterns. If a nation's goods are in heavy demand, so also is the demand for its currency, which tends to appreciate. Exchange rates depend, however, not only on transactions in goods and services but also on trade in financial assets. If foreigners choose to invest in America bonds, they must first obtain dollars to complete the transaction. The additional demand for dollars leads to its appreciation.

The appeal of American financial instruments depends on differences in interest rates in the United States and abroad. Higher rates in the United States than in Germany should attract German funds. Interest rate differentials, however, are not enough, by themselves, to cause capital movements. A German citizen who purchases an American bond has to repatriate interest payments, and eventually the principle, by converting dollars into marks. If Germans expect the dollar to lose value relative to the mark in the future, they will not purchase American bonds unless the difference in interest rates is sufficient to compensate for the expected loss incurred by dollar depreciation. In an age in which dramatic improvements in information technology have taken place, vast amounts of funds are transferred daily across international borders. Since such financial movements depend heavily on exchange rate expectations, a psychological element is involved and rates behave in ways difficult for economists to model. We know that in the longer run, exchange rates move toward levels reflecting relative purchasing power over goods and services. We also know that in the short run, rates are determined mainly by the actions of asset holders. What we don't know is whether, at any given moment, the current rate is below or above the long-term value. In 1977 and 1978 undershooting of the rate appropriate in terms of long-term fundamentals seems to have taken place. In the first part of the Reagan administration, the rapid appreciation of the dollar was a case of overshooting, and the differential was so large as to constitute a speculative bubble. We have at the moment no theory for short-run exchange rate movements with strong predictive power.

The 1977 depreciation of the dollar, due to the current-account deficit, could have been offset by foreign purchases of American financial instruments. "Although U.S. interest rates rose in 1977–78—by almost 3 percentage points on short-term securities—while they fell in Germany, Japan, and Switzerland," one observer has pointed out, "the resulting differential in interest yields was not nearly sufficient to offset the market's expectations of further movements in exchange rates. Those expectations had their roots in the substantial current-account imbalances, the apparent inability of the Carter administration to do anything about oil imports, and the tendency for the rate of inflation to rise in the United States while it fell in Germany, Japan, and Switzerland."[68]

The decline of the dollar, and the increase in the value of the mark and yen, were viewed quite differently in the United States and in Europe. American officials looked upon the changes in currency values as a way of correcting for U.S. current-account deficits and German and Japanese surpluses. "Carter's men contemplated the prospect of Deutschmark appreciation with equanimity, since it represented an alternative, though more circuitous, path to their goals of faster Western growth and reduced payments imbalances. Given German export dependence, they believed, the prospect of a stronger Deutschmark would encourage the Germans to adopt more stimulative measures."[69] The Americans did not intend to lessen pressure on Germany and Japan to expand their economies by intervening in support of the dollar in foreign exchange markets.

American trading partners reacted to the decline of the dollar with a considerable amount of acrimony, particularly in Europe. They saw the dollar's depreciation as giving American goods an unfair advantage on international markets. The depreciation was also viewed as endangering the stability of their economies. In order to prevent the dollar from falling too drastically—and the mark from rising to too high a level—the Germans felt it necessary to support the U.S. currency by purchases on foreign exchange markets. The purchase of dollars with marks added to the number of marks in circulation. It would be possible to "sterilize" the impact of a payments imbalance on the monetary base with offsetting moves by the central bank. Japan was able to neutralize much of the effect on the monetary base of the inflow of dollars. Since the Germans were not successful in doing so, the behavior of the German money supply was determined in large part by these dollar inflows.[70] The United States, in effect, partially controlled the German money supply, which increased more rapidly than the American money stock both in 1977 and 1978.[71] The German central bank reportedly exceeded its money growth target by 100 percent in the last quarter of 1977. The monetary expansion raised concerns about the danger of inflation. The Bundesbank complained repeatedly about being forced to support the dollar unilaterally.

The problem of dollar-induced inflationary pressure was not new to the Germans. They had dealt with it periodically for two decades prior to the arrival of the Carter administration. "Since the mid-1950's, German stabilization policy has repeatedly been undermined by influences originating abroad," wrote Otmar Emminger, president of the Bundesbank, in a survey of postwar German monetary experience. "The struggle against imported inflation has dominated German monetary policy, and indeed German stabilization policy generally, over much of the last twenty years."[72] The most recent unsettling experience before Carter arrived in Washington occurred in the days of transition from the pegged rate system of Bretton Woods. Starting in 1971 with the closing of the American gold window, to the official beginning of the floating system in 1973, "the size of United States payments deficit," according to an OECD-sponsored study, "effectively removed balance-of-payments constraints in the OECD countries and facilitated a massive expansion of money supplies."[73] On March 1 1973, as the days of Bretton Woods were finally coming to an end, "the Bundesbank absorbed $2.7 billion—the most money any central bank had ever bought or sold in a single day."[74] There were domestic reasons for taking expansionary action in many of the OECD countries in the transition period. Yet it is clear that as a result of large American external deficits, "more expansionary action was taken than would otherwise have been the case and, especially, more of this action took the form of monetary expansion."[75] Jimmy Carter inherited from recent American policies a residue of lost confidence in our ability to act with restraint. The problem of Germany's support of the dollar also continued beyond 1977 and 1978. In his memoirs, Helmut Schmidt refers to Washington pressure on the Bundesbank to intervene in support of the dollar in the summer of 1979: "But we could meet the request only to a limited degree because we took the risk of inflation in our own country seriously; every mark spent in support of the dollar bloated the German money supply."[76]

The depreciation of the dollar also had implications for Middle Eastern countries. Since oil is denominated in dollars, the fall in the dollar's value meant that the real price of oil declined. During Carter's trip to the Middle East in December 1977, he met with King Khalid of Saudi Arabia to discuss, among other things, Saudi concern over the drop in the value of the dollar. The depreciation that took place during the Nixon administration contributed to the decision by OPEC to raise prices in 1973. The possibility that OPEC might raise the price of oil again to compensate for the decline in the dollar in 1977 and 1978 was a matter of concern. The depreciation contributed to a correction in the U.S. trade balance by lowering the cost of exports to foreigners, but it also created conditions where a rise in the cost of oil imports could partially offset this trade advantage.

European irritation with the United States over the matter of dollar depreciation was increased by the perception, widely reported in the European press, that Secretary of the Treasury Michael Blumenthal, was deliberately "talking down the dollar" in order to improve the American trade position relative to that of its major trading partners. Particularly cited were remarks Blumenthal made at a press conference in Paris in June 1977, after a meeting of OECD ministers, which were interpreted as encouraging a decline in the value of the dollar. Blumenthal has stated repeatedly that he had no such intent.[77]

Blumenthal's assertion that he was not attempting to depress the dollar's value, beyond what fundamental conditions in the United States and Europe would suggest as appropriate, is credible despite widespread press reports to the contrary.[78] The floating exchange rate system was intended as a mechanism for correction of disequilibrium in international balances by automatic depreciations or appreciations of the national currencies. This is the position taken by the Carter administration in its 1978 *Economic Report*.

> The Administration's policy toward dollar exchange rates has been to let market forces determine them but intervene when necessary to counter disorderly market conditions. This approach is based on the view that it is better to give market forces continuous influence on rates, rather than to have a period of officially determined rates followed by a sharp and disruptive adjustment. The historical experience with attempts to fix exchange rates is not an enviable one. . . . While exchange rate fluctuations sometimes have been undesirably large and are often unpleasant reminders about unsatisfactory aspects of underlying economic conditions, the evolution of the system of market-determined exchange rates has been a major achievement of this decade.[79]

The administration also argued that currency adjustment was a two-way process, with currencies of deficit countries depreciating while those of surplus countries increased in value. This is the point made by Blumenthal in formal remarks at the ministerial meeting of the OECD: "We face interrelated problems in an interdependent world. We cannot solve one problem at the expense of the others. Nor can any nation expect to be an island of prosperity in a sea of economic troubles. Our problems must be solved together and cooperatively. . . . We can meet this challenge; we can succeed in achieving sustained non-inflationary growth . . . if both surplus and deficit countries allow exchange rates to play their appropriate role in the adjustment process."[80] It has been pointed out that Arthur Burns, chairman of the Federal Reserve Board, had stated two months earlier in a lecture at Columbia University that countries with significant and persistent current-account surpluses "should not actively resist tendencies toward appreciation in the value of their currencies in foreign exchange markets." Burns's remarks were not followed by the same type of reaction that Blumenthal's received. "Blumenthal learned the hard way," commented one close observer of events, "that Finance Ministers must avoid such statements even when the objective economic facts justify them."[81]

Internal documents circulated within the administration are consistent with Blumenthal's public statements. "U.S. exchange rate policy remains unchanged," Undersecretary Solomon advised the secretary in July 1977. "The dollar should be allowed to reflect underlying economic and financial conditions, and we intervene only to counter disorderly exchange market conditions."[82] In briefing materials prepared for an upcoming press conference, President Carter was advised to respond to a question about the dollar along similar lines.[83]

According to a memorandum in which Blumenthal reported to President Carter on the results of a trip to Paris in early August 1977, German officials were less troubled by the fall of the dollar than the European press was. "The meeting with the Germans on the exchange rate issue went extremely well," the secretary wrote. "The German press had made a major issue of recent rate movements, claiming that the U.S. was acting irresponsibly, 'manipulating' the exchange rate. . . . The German official reaction to the rate movement had been much more restrained, though there was suspicion that the press comments were stimulated by government spokesmen."[84]

While the administration's position was to let market forces operate, there was, at the same time, an awareness that the dollar's decline could get out of hand. Should that happen, intervention to support it in foreign exchange markets would be necessary. Secretary Blumenthal reported to the cabinet in late July 1977, that "the U.S. economy is stronger than most others and is developing faster than most others. Of course, we need to watch for any precipitous decline [in the dollar] and the speculation and 'snowballing' effect that could be associated with it."[85] At a cabinet meeting in early November, Commerce Secretary Juanita Kreps asked Blumenthal what he had learned about the stability of the dollar on a recent trip to Europe and the Middle East. "He responded that the situation is not as bad as it may appear here and that, in his view, the worst thing to do would be to spend billions of dollars in an effort to 'support' the dollar."[86] The time was fast approaching, however, when some type of American action would become necessary. Markets were beginning to be "disorderly."

In December 1977 and January 1978, memoranda in the Carter files take on a tone of increased concern. Carter himself is troubled. "I would like to be informed and involved," he writes to Blumenthal and Schultze in early January, "in the preparation of plans to deal with the dollar problem should further difficulties arise."[87] "We are growing faster than most other industrial nations and this, in combination with large oil imports, has tended to put downward pressure on the dollar," Blumenthal and Schultze explain in the memorandum replying to Carter's request. "We don't need to worry about a modest and orderly depreciation. If our trade balance doesn't improve over the next two years, gradual exchange rate adjustment would be appropriate. We would be in serious trouble, however, if there should occur a massive capital flight from the dollar and a sharp depreciation of its value in foreign exchange markets."[88] The consequences of such a fall in the dollar's value are spelled out in detail. Such a development would "create major disturbances in money, capital and commodity markets that could threaten the stability of the domestic and international financial systems, detract from U.S. ability to exercise leadership in world affairs, exacerbate inflationary pressures in the United States by increasing import prices, increase protectionist pressures and lead OPEC to raise oil prices."[89]

In December 1977 and January 1978, the United States acted. On December 21, Carter publicly announced that America would intervene if necessary to counter disorderly conditions.[90] An existing currency swap arrangement between the Federal Reserve and the Bundesbank was increased in amount, a change that augmented American holdings of German marks to be used for intervening on behalf of the dollar. To make American financial instruments, and the dollar, more attractive, the Federal Reserve exerted upward pressure on interest rates by raising the rate it charges to banks for borrowing by half a percentage point. The action was described by Charles Schultze in a memorandum to the president as "a step publicly identified as intended to support the faltering international exchange value of the dollar. This resulted in 0.2 to 0.3 percentage point increases in interest rates across the board."[91] When the dollar fell to a symbolic low in early March 1978—below two Deutschmarks to the dollar—the United States, in the face of international criticism, acted again. It doubled its swap lines with Germany and agreed to draw on its borrowing rights with the International Monetary Fund if necessary to defend the dollar. "The Bundesbank hailed this as a watershed," one account of the episode reports, "because it was the first time since the switch to floating rates that the United States has expressed its willingness to use its own foreign exchange reserves to defend the dollar."[92]

From March 1978 until the summit meeting at Bonn in mid-July the dollar remained fairly stable.

I will return later to the 1978 Bonn summit that followed the London meeting. For the moment we turn our attention to the domestic inflation problem and the administration's strategy for preventing prices from rising while adding stimulus to the economy.

CHAPTER 6 | **STRATEGY FOR INFLATION**

Every administration comes into office with a high degree of optimism, sees itself as elected by the people to solve the nation's problems, and is anxious to get on with it. The Keynesian beliefs that most of Carter's advisers brought with them reinforced the natural optimism of a new team of policy makers and gave them the assurance that they could steer the economy in the right direction. Here I examine their confidence in the context of what came to be called the Phillips curve, a line drawn in a graph that visually describes the hypothesis advanced by the economist A. W. Phillips.

While a young lecturer at the London School of Economics in the 1950s, Phillips did research utilizing historical wage and unemployment data. His statistical analysis, published in 1958, showed that over the period 1861–1957, money wages rose as unemployment fell. Money wages are closely related to the prices of goods that workers produce. Other economists, in their follow-up to Phillips's work, emphasized the price-unemployment connection rather than wage-unemployment. Plotted on a graph, the Phillips curve describes the relationship of the inflation rate and the rate of unemployment. The interpretation of the curve is that as the economy expands and the unemployment rate drops, the rate of inflation begins to increase. The Phillips curve rapidly became embodied in the Keynesian model. Phillips had a relatively short career and produced a modest number of professional papers, but the paper in which he reported on his wage-unemployment research is one of the most frequently cited articles in the postwar period.[1] As I have written elsewhere, "there are not many examples of economic research with such immediate impact. Samuelson included the Phillips curve in the fifth edition of his famous textbook published in 1961. Within three years of the publication of Phillips's original paper, his curve became part of the standard economic model."[2]

The uninitiated might wonder why Phillips's finding had such an impact. Common observation would seem to suggest that as the labor market begins to tighten in an economic expansion, upward pressure on the wage and price level begins to develop. When Keynes was writing in the 1930s, the unemployment rate was so high that it was generally assumed that the economy could expand without fear of inflation. Keynes himself had the subtlety of mind to realize that inflation could set in before the economy was fully employed.[3] But the conventional treatment simplified the matter by assuming that prices would be stable until full employment was reached. Doubts about this accepted approach were raised during the 1950s when prices rose even though there was unemployment generally viewed as excessive. Phillips's timely research formally addressed the matter of the relationship between inflation and unemployment. His empirical data showed that as the economy expanded, historically, and the unemployment rate fell, prices would tend to rise even before full capacity was reached. He also provided numerical estimates of the trade-off between price stability and full employment.

There was bad news and good news in the Phillips story. The bad news was that price stability and full employment are incompatible. If full employment were the policy goal, one would have to tolerate some level of inflation. If price stability were the prime target, one would have to expect a higher level of unemployment. The good news was that a trade-off between the two fell within acceptable bounds. A year after Phillips's work was published, Paul Samuelson and Robert Solow, both of the Massachusetts Institute of Technology, fitted a Phillips curve to U.S. data and reported their findings at a meeting of the American Economic Association. Their analysis showed that the unemployment rate could fall as low as 4 percent without the inflation rate rising above 3 percent. There was an exploitable trade-off between full employment and price stability.[4] The finding played a central role in the thinking of Kennedy's economic advisers, a group which included Samuelson, who acted as an outside expert, and Solow, who was on the staff of the Council of Economic Advisers. The 4 percent unemployment rate target selected by the Kennedy administration as its full employment-unemployment rate was based on the Samuelson-Solow analysis. The Kennedy-Johnson expansionary fiscal experiment of 1964 seemed to confirm the Phillips findings. Unemployment fell to a low level without setting off a surge in the inflation rate.

Carter's advisers brought to the administration, in the Phillips curve tradition, confidence that both full employment and reasonable price stability were possible. A transition paper prepared in late December 1976 pointed out that "economic growth has slowed considerably in the last six months. As a result, all forecasts for 1977 have been revised down substantially to between 4 and 5 percent, if no new actions are taken by government. . . . Such rates of growth will not reduce unemployment significantly, leaving the unemployment rate well over 7 percent next year. . . . The chances that the economy will 'spontaneously' begin doing better than the projections are not high. There have been few spontaneous recoveries in the years since World War II." Seven different tax and spending combinations, ranging from $12 billion to $20 billion, were analyzed using the Wharton and Data Resources econometric models to determine the economic impact. The paper reported that "the various proposals had a minimum impact on the rate of increase in the Consumer Price Index. The rate of increase was enlarged by 0.1 to 0.3 percentage points."[5] The higher value of this range, 0.3 percent, was the estimate given by Assistant Secretary of the Treasury Fred Bergsten when questioned by Helmut Schmidt about the inflationary effect of the stimulus program during the Mondale mission to Germany in the first week of the administration. As mentioned in the previous chapter, Schmidt is reported to have been "incredulous."

Carter intended to repeat the Kennedy initiative to "get the country moving again," but, as hindsight makes clear, a degree of caution would have been prudent. The economic environment for Carter was quite different from that enjoyed by his Democratic predecessor. Kennedy came into office following a period of stable prices under the Eisenhower administration.[6] Carter came into office following the historically high prices reached under Richard Nixon, and when inflation had already built up a strong momentum and the price outcome of policy initiatives was less predictable.

By the time Carter became president, the Phillips curve thesis that full employment could be reached while maintaining a stable inflation rate had already come into question. The record of high levels of both inflation and unemployment in the late 1960s and early 1970s provided the empirical evidence that the affordable trade-off of the relationship shown by Phillips's research and the Samuelson-Solow paper perhaps no longer existed.

Why the trade-off had disappeared became a matter of intense debate. Keynesians pointed to the massive external shocks of the early 1970s—

materials shortages and the oil price increase—as a reason for the breakdown of the Phillips curve. The implication was that after the shock effects had worn themselves out, the affordable trade-off numbers would return. Milton Friedman, leader of the "Monetarist" school, argued that the trade-off was an illusion from the beginning, and that a decrease in the unemployment rate under conditions of a mild inflation was based on a deception. When money wages rise during a period of inflation, workers see themselves as better off and have an incentive to supply more labor. The unemployment rate drops. But what really matters for workers is not the money wage but the "real" wage, the wage defined in terms of what it can buy at the supermarket. When workers eventually realize, in a period of rising money wages, that prices have also risen and that their "real" wage has not changed, they withdraw their labor and the unemployment rate returns to its original level, but at a now higher level of prices. Unless the inflation rate increases in repeated steps—unless the inflation rate begins to accelerate—unemployment cannot be permanently reduced. Friedman pointed to the levels of inflation of the 1960s and 1970s as proof of his argument.[7]

A second stage in Friedman's type of analysis came with the contributions of the "rational expectations" school led by Robert Lucas. In Friedman's theory, workers recognize the erosion of their real wage with a time delay, so that a trade-off can exist for a short period. Lucas and his associates argued that workers in inflationary times recognize rapidly that the real wage has not risen—indeed they learn to anticipate inflation—so that the trade-off does not exist, even in the short run. The practical implication of Lucas's argument is the "policy ineffectiveness" theorem, which denies that government has any ability to affect the level of employment.[8] The Keynesian optimism, Lucas argued, was "fundamentally flawed." It was Carter's misfortune to come into office just as the consensus on macroeconomic policy was becoming badly fragmented. It was possible for two Nobel-prize-winning economists to give a president diametrically opposed advice in 1977. At a conference in June 1978, Frank Morris, then president of the Federal Reserve Bank of Boston, summarized the status of policy thinking by saying that "it is probably fair to say that economic policy is now being made in at least a partial vacuum of economic theory."[9]

A memorandum from Charles Schultze to the president in early 1977, providing a background on inflation, presented the view accepted by Keynesians, and the one that underlay Carter's anti-inflation policy. Schultze listed two forces that initiate an increase in the price level. The classic cause of inflation is excess demand. "From 1965 through 1969, the economy was operating continuously with real output above the nation's productive potential. The result was a classic case of excess demand inflation." Schultze went on to explain the second cause. "A larger part of the 1973–74 acceleration of inflation, however, stemmed from supply shocks. The special factors that influenced prices in those two years were of unprecedented severity for a peacetime period."[10]

A pattern in the more recent inflationary periods, Schultze's background memorandum to Carter continued, is that

> removal of the initiating forces of inflation does not, unfortunately, mean that inflation comes to an end. Once underway, an inflationary process becomes deeply embedded in the structure of wage, cost, and price increases, and develops a momentum of its own. Unwinding from a prolonged inflation is extremely difficult. If monetary and fiscal policies since 1975 had been less expansive, aggregate demand would have grown more slowly. . . . Perhaps some modest decline in the inflation rate would have occurred had unemployment been kept at a 7 or 7½ percent rate. The principal result, however, would have been to constrain the growth of output and employment rather than to reduce the rate of inflation. Inflation has continued at around a 6 to 6½ percent rate not because aggregate demand has grown too rapidly, but because the momentum of inflation is so strong.[11]

The basic intent of the Carter anti-inflation strategy was to break the momentum.

CARTER'S ANTI-INFLATION PLAN

In mid-February 1977, Charles Schultze sent to the president a progress report on the work of the Council of Economic Advisers, which took the lead in preparing a comprehensive anti-inflation policy. The proposal would be sent to the Economic Policy Group (EPG) for discussion at the beginning of March, Schultze said, and a presentation would be made to the president as soon as the EPG finalized the details. On March 24 a forty-page draft of the deflation policy was completed and circulated within the administration. A shorter summary was sent to the president.[12]

The goal of reducing inflation is important in its own right, the summary stated, but also for reaching other goals. Measures to expand the economy would be discredited if inflation accelerates. The Federal Reserve would not provide the money for even the current rate of inflation, much less a higher rate. The inflation is affecting the attitudes of consumers and businessmen regarding their buying plans. The inflation target given in the summary was ambitious. "A reasonable goal for dampening the basic inflation rate should aim at a reduction somewhat in excess of one-half percent annually over the next several years. More specifically the average rate of increase in the non-food, non-energy component of the consumer price index should be brought down to 5 to 5½ percent a year from now and to about 4 percent by the end of 1979."[13]

Among the options for attacking the inflation, the choice that is specifically rejected in the report is that of using unemployment to reduce pressure on prices. The cost of this approach would be unacceptable. Arthur Okun, a fellow at the Brookings Institution and a strong influence on Schultze and other members of the administration who had come from Brookings, reported in a speech an estimate of the cost in terms of lost national output. "To save one point on the basic inflation rate through policies that restrain total spending, we lose more than 5 points—easily $100 billion—of our annual real GNP [gross national product]."[14]

A copy of Okun's speech can be found in the files of the Jimmy Carter Library. An unidentified staff member penned a note attached to the speech: "Send to the President." Carter returned the copy to Eizenstat with only the notation: "Stu, Information, J."[15] Whether the president read the material or not is unclear. He certainly heard from his economic advisers the same argument found in the Okun speech. "The human and social costs of this approach [restrictive monetary and fiscal policy] are prohibitive," the summary of the inflation problem drafted for Carter says. It adopted Okun's $100 billion output loss estimate. "The inflation process must be explained clearly to undo the nonsense that emanated out of Washington in recent years which tried to sell high unemployment (achieved by hawkish fiscal-monetary policies) as the panacea for inflation."[16] In view of the cost of reducing inflation through monetary and fiscal tools, the administration proposed an alternative approach, one that would break through the momentum of a wage-price spiral by direct intervention in the wage and price decision process.[17]

There were several ways in which this intervention could be implemented. At one of the meetings in Plains before the inauguration, Carter was told, according to Eizenstat's notes, "that his options included: (a) mandatory wage and price controls; (b) guideposts with voluntary compliance; (c) a deal with labor and management, which the president-elect was told would not work because neither side could deliver; and (d) private messages of restraint."[18] The most aggressive option, a formal set of mandatory wage and price controls, such as those imposed by President Nixon, was eliminated as a possibility in the discussion at Plains. It was also rejected in the summary of an anti-inflationary policy drafted for the president. "They cannot be fairly administered; the longer they are in force the greater the inefficiencies they impose; and the depressing effect on investment and risk-taking is likely to be severe."[19]

The second option, wage and price guidelines, had been used by the Kennedy administration. A "voluntary" program was introduced in which wage and price decisions were to be governed by a specific set of guidelines provided by the government. Critically important was wage behavior. We spoke earlier of the underlying inflation rate as the rate obtained when the price effect of random events like the weather is eliminated. The underlying rate can be looked at in another way. Prices tend to move with domestic costs. Since labor costs contributed about 70 percent of production costs in the 1970s, the underlying rate can also be thought of as measured by labor costs. Labor costs remain unchanged if wage increases are offset by improvements in output per worker. The broad rule for wage increases in the Kennedy program was based, therefore, on improvements in worker efficiency. "The guide for noninflationary wage behavior," the 1962 *Economic Report of the President* said, "is that the rate of increase in wage rates (including fringe benefits) in each industry be equal to the trend rate of over-all productivity increase."[20] Wage increases following this rule would not result in an increase in labor cost and need not be followed by price increases to protect profit margins.[21]

Getting compliance with the Kennedy program was left, for the most part, to the prestige of the presidential office and the public support that this office can rally. Precise numerical guidelines were developed to provide the public with a basis for judging whether a particular wage-price decision was in the national interest. "Jawboning" by government officials was used to pressure unions and firms to adhere to the guidelines. The most dramatic episode in implementing the policy was an open confrontation between President Kennedy and United States Steel over a decision by the corporation to raise its price. The administration felt the corporation had done so even though labor had moderated its wage claims in contract negotiations; United States Steel had not kept its side of the bargain. Kennedy vented his anger in a presidential press conference that was widely reported. When the president leaned heavily on the firm, including threats of possible antitrust action, United States Steel and other steel companies that had followed along with increases of their own rescinded the price rise. A residue of bitterness remained, both for the administration and for the business community.[22]

Precise numerical wage and price guidelines, such as were adopted by the Kennedy administration, were also rejected in the draft summary of a Carter anti-inflation program. "While a general statement about the average relationship between prices, wages, and productivity growth needed to achieve any given inflation target has significant education value, it cannot be used as a rule in specific cases. Especially in view of the sharp changes in wages, prices and productivity since 1973, numerical guidelines are not the answer to the current situation." The alternative chosen by the administration included the weakest option presented at the Plains meeting: simple persuasion to convince labor and business to cooperate voluntarily in moderating price and cost increases without specific guidelines. The Council on Wage and Price Stability created to administer the wage and price controls under Nixon, with authority due to expire in 1977, should be renewed for two years. The basic role of the council would be to provide information. The council should prepare "for internal use only" a review of major upcoming wage settlements. In the case of inflationary increases, "government representatives should seek informal discussions with both parties to discuss alternative, less inflationary approaches." The council should issue a final public report on the settlement agreed to by both sides. The structure of the review for pricing decisions would parallel that for wages. In the one part of the proposal that had bite, the Council on Wage and Price Stability "would notify individual firms of a request for prior notice of price changes." There then follows a statement of the fundamental belief of the economic advisers. "This program is the beginning of a continuing effort to demonstrate that lower unemployment and lower inflation can be simultaneously and consistently pursued by the Carter Administration."[23]

Copies of the draft were circulated within the administration. Carter sent a handwritten note to Schultze reflecting his conservative fiscal position: "There is nothing in your inflation memo involving government spending restraints—future impact of initiating new programs—balancing the federal budget, etc. Why?"[24] Ray Marshall, who, like most labor secretaries, was sympathetic to labor concerns, stated in a memorandum to the Economic Policy Group his opposition to government pressure on unions and business.[25] A copy of the summary was sent to Arthur Burns, chairman of the Federal Reserve Board. Burns talked to the president by phone and sent over a follow-up memo containing twenty proposals to reduce inflation.[26]

Burns, who had been in favor of the wage and price controls of the Nixon administration, argued for tough action by the Council on Wage and Price Stability. "Have cowps be vigilant and have public hearings when public interest is involved."

Schultze took a position opposite to that of Marshall. "I guess I was always leaning, in the direction of doing more by way of guidelines, specific guidelines," he recalled in an interview after the administration left office. "I would say the Treasury people and Bert Lance, initially anyway, were much more reluctant. Marshall and the labor interests were adamantly against it.... That's one of the cases where it was very hard to do much because our major constituency was fighting you like mad."[27]

Carter's relationship with labor was a mixture of mutual suspicion and occasional collaboration. At the beginning of the administration, labor leaders approached Carter, one student of the period has written, "in the context of their historical experience with previous Democratic presidents.... Their enthusiasm sprang from the aspiration to return to the unfinished agenda of the Kennedy and Johnson years."[28] Labor came out of the New Deal with an enhanced role in Democratic circles and with the expectation that its views would command attention at the highest level. But economic conditions did not allow Carter the same degree of freedom enjoyed by his predecessors to accommodate labor demands. Inflation and the slowdown in the rate of growth of output per worker imposed on Carter constraints that his Democratic predecessors did not have to face. The problem of limits affected Carter's relationship with all groups in the liberal wing of the party. Labor was one of the more demanding.

Coming from the rural south Carter lacked the exposure to the union movement that Democratic leaders from the Northeast and Midwest industrial regions had experienced. He also thought of himself as representative of all the people. "Carter saw unions as just another interest group," Eizenstat has been quoted as saying. "They did not have a special call on his heartstrings."[29]

Carter came into conflict with the AFL-CIO (American Federation of Labor and Congress of Industrial Organizations) early in the administration. His proposal for an increase in the minimum wage—a point to which I will return later—was viewed by the unions as unsatisfactory. There were also two major legislative defeats. A common situs picketing bill and labor reform legislation failed to pass, though an analysis of the outcome suggests that labor, rather than Carter, was more responsible for the failure of the proposals.[30] After an acrimonious meeting with George Meany and his

Carter and his advisers at a meeting with George Meany. *Left to right*: Meany, Carter, Ray Marshall, Walter Mondale, and Stuart Eizenstat. Courtesy of the Jimmy Carter Library.

AFL-CIO executive council in April of his first year in office, Carter held his contacts with labor to a minimum. Mondale became the main administration point man with labor.[31] The dilemma Carter faced was that he needed labor's cooperation in an anti-inflation program, and union resistance to the use of even voluntary guidelines prevented anything more that mild persuasion from being part of the president's first anti-inflation statement.

The announcement of the Carter program was released on April 15, 1977, followed by a press conference attended by the president and his economic advisers.[32] A discussion of the causes of the inflation was included at the suggestion of the president. "We are all in agreement," Schultze had written to the president, "in line with your statements to the Economic Policy Group, that the full statement should have a section which attempts to educate the public to the causes of inflation, both those that the government can control and those such as weather which it cannot control."[33] The statement continues with a pledge of fiscal discipline. "By any objective measure, the economy has ample room to expand without running into excess demand. Yet many people fear that current budgetary policies will lead to renewed inflationary pressures. I want to address those fears directly. Inadequate tax revenues from a stagnant economy—not legitimate Federal spending programs—are the principal source of the deficits. As the recovery proceeds, the deficits must shrink and eventually disappear. . . . I have made a firm commitment to have a balanced budget in a normal economy by Fiscal Year 1981, and I intend to do everything I can to honor that commitment." In line with Carter's suggestion to Schultze that he include a statement on containing government outlays, the announcement promised "to discipline the growth of Federal spending in the years ahead. The budgets that I will submit will contain responsible expenditure ceilings." This statement on budgets is the reason the more liberal Joseph Califano, secretary of health, education, and welfare, commented at a meeting of the Economic Policy Group that "the tone of the anti-inflation statement appears conservative and outside the mainstream of the Democratic Party."[34]

The document listed eleven specific actions to be taken by government. Carter formally asked Congress to extend for two years the statutory authority of the Council on Wage and Price Stability, which was set to expire on September 30. The administration stated its intention to work toward eliminating the regulation of certain industries like the airlines. Increased competition would have the effect of lowering prices. Regulations pertaining to the environment that increase costs for firms would be modified. The government would support free international trade, "an effective means of improving efficiency and maintaining competition within American industry." Antitrust laws would be enforced vigorously.

A number of the anti-inflation steps listed in the statement, such as deregulation and the prosecution of the antitrust laws, would contribute to price stability in varying degrees but would have effect mostly in the long run. The policy addressing the more immediate problem of momentum inflation, intervention in the wage-price decision process, was timid. The president simply called for the cooperation of management and labor. "This joint effort must be voluntary and cooperative and not be based on coercive or self-defeating controls. Accordingly I have asked the president of the AFL-CIO and the chairman of the General Electric Company to help to coordinate this new cooperation between labor, management, and the Government."[35] Within the administration Secretary Marshall had pushed the idea for a labor-management committee. "The President agreed," Eizenstat has reported, "that it was a good idea and would be a good way to 'avoid guidelines.'"[36]

Since the administration rejected tight fiscal and monetary policy as an option for dampening the inflation, the only alternative with a chance to succeed was a strong wage-price intervention program. The administration chose a weak version of government involvement. Eric Sevareid commented on the CBS "Evening News" on April 8, presumably with leaked information on the forthcoming release of the president's program, that "there are no signs the government will take any direct action on inflation. Its anti-inflation program about to be announced apparently will call only for talk—and polite talk, not even government jawboning—between industry, labor, and government—and on a now-and-then basis."[37] Schultze agreed later that the anti-inflation plan was not a strong one. In an interview after the administration left office, he was negative in his assessment. "We had an anti-inflation program, so-called, in April, 1977, which had all kinds of bits and pieces in it, none of which meant anything."[38]

OUTCOME OF THE ANTI-INFLATION INITIATIVE
In mid-1977 Blumenthal announced the formation of an EPG deputies group to monitor the progress of the anti-inflation program.[39] The picture was not encouraging. In the first half of the year prices rose rapidly; the consumer price index went up at an annual rate of 9 percent. Schultze reported in a memorandum to Carter that the increase was due mainly to a large increase in food prices. Farm prices had fallen sharply over most of the 1950s and then remained stable until 1965. Food inflation became a problem in the latter part of the 1960s. Disruptions in food supplies continued in the 1970s. In earlier decades disruptions had less effect on prices because of large grain inventories and idle capacity. By the 1970s inventories were lower and unused acreage had been brought into production, primarily because of historically high world demand for American agricultural exports in the early part of the decade.

It is the fate of the presidency that those who occupy the office receive credit or blame for economic events over which they have little or no control. Over the first half of the 1960s during the Kennedy-Johnson administrations, a period when price increases were at an historic low, shock inflation was virtually absent. In 1976 President Ford benefited from a decrease in farm prices to bring the inflation rate below the underlying rate. Carter had the opposite experience in 1977—an increase in food prices in the first half of the year of almost 14 percent.

In early 1978 the jump in food prices was repeated. The consumer price index rose at an annual rate of 9.3 percent, a substantial acceleration from the 6.8 percent inflation rate of 1977. "Nearly all of the surge can be attributed to price developments outside of the industrial sector of the economy," a press release of the Council on Wage and Price Stability reported. Food prices rose at an annual rate of 16.4 percent. "The sharp rise in food prices has been the single most dramatic change in the inflation outlook during the first quarter.... [It] has been largely the result of a 41.1 percent annual rate of increase in meat prices."[40] The striking increase in meat prices was due to a peculiarity in livestock production. "The cattle cycle," Alfred Kahn and Robert Bergland, the secretary of agriculture, reported to Carter in early 1979, "is just entering the recovery phase after a four-year liquidation resulting in the largest percentage decline in cattle numbers since the early 1900s."[41] Low beef inventories in the late 1970s were due, in part, to a cutback in beef production because of poor harvests and high feed prices in 1973–74.[42] The administration hoped an increase in pork and fowl would dampen the impact of the decline in beef production. But "the extra-cold winter," *Time* magazine reported in early 1979, "has dulled the sex drive of sows. Because they have not produced as many piglets as usual, the price of pork chops is going up."[43] Walter Heller, President Kennedy's economic adviser, commented that "we seem to have an accident-prone inflation."[44] In the first half of 1978, the consumer price index rose to 9.8 percent.

Carter's advisers were concerned that the food price shocks of early 1977 and 1978 might not be isolated events. "We have to worry," Schultze wrote the president in mid-May of 1977, "that some part of the recent increase in food and energy prices will ultimately get reflected in higher wage gains; there is a growing possibility of some acceleration in the underlying rate of inflation."[45] There was reason for concern. The inflation rate with food and other uncontrollable items excluded—the underlying rate—increased from 6.1 percent in 1977 to 7.2 percent in the first six months of 1978. The increase in average hourly earnings in 1977 was up slightly compared to the previous year. There was a larger jump in earnings in the first quarter of 1978.

While money wage rates increased somewhat in 1977, and more rapidly in the first quarter of 1978, a different picture emerges when the increases are adjusted for inflation. In 1977 "real" hourly earnings, earnings adjusted for inflation, rose only 1.4 percent—considerably less than in the previous year—because of the increase in prices. In the first quarter of 1978 the increase in average hourly earnings adjusted for inflation was zero. The danger in the real wage slowdown was that it would increase union resistance to wage restraint. In 1977 the major collective bargaining settlements averaged, for the life of the contract, less than in 1976 and a percentage point less than the average of the previous decade. The increase jumped significantly in the first quarter of 1978 due mainly to an expensive new contract in the coal industry. The challenge to the administration was to keep new contract settlements from imitating the settlement in coal.

The need to hold wage increases down was accentuated by a decline in the growth rate of output per worker. Little noted in the news media, and too technical an issue for discussion in political debate, the fall in productivity was a defining event in the Carter administration. It was also a problem for Presidents Nixon and Ford. It continued to plague the administrations that followed the Carter presidency, and remained a problem for economic policy until the latter part of the 1990s, when productivity gains began to show improvement. Later, I will discuss in detail the impact of declining productivity growth rates on Carter's economy. I simply point out here that the effect of pay raises on labor costs depends critically on productivity behavior. If output per worker is rising, increases in wages are partly offset by this increase in efficiency. Higher wages need not lead to an increase in labor cost nor be a reason for an increase in prices. Wage increases consistent with productivity growth are the way by which workers share in increased prosperity. Under Carter, productivity gains had fallen too low to compensate for wage increases. "Labor productivity has slowed significantly over the past four quarters," the Council on Wage and Price Stability reported in May 1978. "As a result of this slowed productivity growth, unit labor cost increases have escalated dramatically. Labor costs, which had been increasing at an annual rate of 6.0 percent, rose 8.2 percent over the past four quarters."[46]

The effort to get industry and labor cooperation in a program to moderate price and wage increases, a central part of the anti-inflation strategy announced in April 1977, showed little results. In August 1977, the president met with the economists who had served on the 1976 campaign task force. Charles Schultze prepared briefing material for the meeting. "Discussion with the Labor-Management Committee on ways to secure moderation in private wage and price decisions," he wrote, "are proceeding slowly. They have not broken down, but they have not yet produced anything."[47]

THE DECELERATION PROPOSAL

In reaction to the lack of progress on inflation, a number of memoranda circulated within the administration in early 1978. Michael Blumenthal and Charles Schultze wrote the president that "the price outlook is deteriorating. Weather influences contributed to some of the sharp rise in consumer goods prices in January. But a more fundamental worsening of the outlook also appears to be underway. In light of these price developments and potential consequences, we believe that it is imperative that you act decisively to focus greater attention on the anti-inflation program."[48] The advisers' concern was reinforced by public reaction. Richard Moe, aide to Vice President

Mondale, reported in a memorandum that "the attached Harris poll indicates that the percentage of people who give the President a favorable rating on his handling of the economy has gone from 47 percent ten months ago to 24 percent now.... Moreover, other recent polls show a dramatic shift in public concern over inflation as opposed to unemployment."[49]

Charles Schultze recommended going to stage two in the administration's effort to get wage-price restraint. His proposal stopped short of formal guidelines with specific percentage limits on wage-price increases. But it recommended something beyond a vague exhortation for labor-management restraint. First suggested by Barry Bosworth, director of the Council on Wage and Price Stability, the proposal called for a deceleration in future increases in wages and prices. Schultze later described the idea as "a somewhat more concrete incomes policy.... It was a fairly clever way of trying to have guidelines without a specific number."[50]

Carter's reaction to the proposal was lukewarm at best. He may, by this time, have become frustrated by the failure of inflation to respond to administration efforts. But he was willing to try. He wrote in the margin of Schultze's January memorandum: "Charlie—The program seems (inevitably, I guess) very general in nature and mostly wishful thinking. However, I'll do all I can to help make it successful. J. C."[51]

The deceleration strategy was outlined in late January in the 1978 *Economic Report of the President*. It was a key part of the president's second major anti-inflation initiative, announced in a speech before the American Society of Newspaper Editors in April 1978. "Two months ago," the president said, "I proposed that in each industry and each sector of our economy that wage and price increases this year be voluntarily held substantially below the average wage increases of the last 2 years. I'm determined," he went on to say, "to take the lead in breaking the wage and price spiral by holding Federal pay increases down. Last year Federal white collar salaries rose by more than 7 percent. I intend to propose a limit of about 5½ percent this year, thereby setting the example for labor and industry to moderate price and wage increases."[52]

The speech included a litany of anti-inflationary actions. "We must work to reduce the budget deficit," the president said, and to reduce regulatory costs. Perhaps the most substantive action announced was the intention to use government purchasing as a sanction to enforce the deceleration policy. "All executive branch agencies will avoid or reduce the purchase of goods or services whose prices are rapidly rising, unless by so doing we would seriously jeopardize our national security or create serious unemployment."[53]

He also announced the appointment of Robert Strauss, already serving as special trade representative, as his counselor on inflation. Strauss was well known for his acceptance by Congress and the business community, and for his special talent for persuasion. Strauss would be Carter's official jaw-boner.

"I do believe," Strauss wrote to the president less than a month after the anti-inflation speech, "we will be successful in getting a substantial number of leading business firms to endorse the effort to conform."[54] Firms from the automobile, aluminum, and steel industries announced in April through June their intentions to comply, along with American Telephone and Telegraph and the National Association of Home Builders.[55] Labor's reaction was not as positive. "I had my second meeting with Messrs. Meany and Kirkland yesterday," Strauss continued, "this one very blunt with little or no progress." Prior to a meeting of the president and his staff with officials of the AFL-CIO and the heads of the individual unions in early May, Ray Marshall and Robert Strauss briefed Carter on the results of a meeting they had had with Meany and other labor leaders. "It is clear," they wrote, "that the unions are skeptical of the potential effectiveness of the Administration's anti-inflation policy. The unions, moreover, are unwilling to practice wage deceleration prior to any indication of a slowdown in price inflation."[56]

Unions' reluctance to go along with deceleration was disappointing but understood. "Any wage and price program puts the AFL-CIO in a very difficult institutional bind," a briefing paper for the president said. "A union is an elected, contractual agent in the advisory proceeding of collective bargaining; asking a union to pull its punches in wage negotiations is like asking a defense attorney to do less than his best for his client."[57] There is another factor. Firms can modify their pricing policy quickly should the pace of inflation make a deceleration pledge untenable. Labor unions engage in multiyear contracts, and those without a cost-of-living adjustment clause are bound to a wage settlement over an extended period regardless of the behavior of prices. The record of presidential efforts to initiate effective anti-inflationary policies—under Carter, as well as Nixon and Ford before him—created in the minds of union leaders an understandable amount of skepticism.

A meeting of the president and his staff with officials of the AFL-CIO and the heads of the individual unions took place in early May 1978. Carter did not attend the entire meeting, and staff members carried on the dialogue with labor leaders. In his remarks at the session Carter said that he understood that business is better able to take the initial step, but he asked labor leaders for a deceleration pledge. According to Eizenstat's notes of the meeting, Carter appealed to their mutual interests. He said that there would be a negative reaction from Congress regarding "things we've joined in as partners if they oppose deceleration."[58] Meany said that he wanted to support an effort to fight inflation. He didn't believe Carter was the primary cause of inflation as the business community does, he said in a somewhat biting aside. But he couldn't pledge to do what he couldn't deliver. He said that the AFL-CIO doesn't control local bargaining. Sol Chaiken, president of the International Ladies' Garment Workers Union, said—again according to Eizenstat's notes—that his union "will cooperate only when the Consumer Price Index is dropping."[59]

There was a basic, fundamental reality that plagued the effort of the administration to temper wage demands. Events were conspiring to reduce the real wage, the purchasing power of workers. The decline in productivity meant that there was less increased output for Americans to share. The increase in food prices meant that workers in manufacturing and services had to surrender more of their production to the agricultural sector to maintain their food consumption. When oil prices rose in late 1978 and through 1979, the United States had to give more of its output to the OPEC nations to maintain the level of their use of oil. There were less goods left for Americans to share. For workers, this meant that their real wage, the purchasing power of the pay envelope, would have to decline. The hard fact had to be faced: there was less pie to go around. If workers refused to recognize this inability of the economy to provide the same increases in the standard of living as in the past by demanding higher nominal wages, inflation was inevitable. Schultze and Bosworth made this point in a memorandum to the president. "There have been very small gains in the average worker's real income over the last decade," they conceded. But it was not due to an increase in employer profits. "The labor share (including fringe benefits) of total income has actually increased slightly over the last decade. Thus, the problem is a lack of growth in the size of the pie rather than a deterioration in any one group's share."[60]

The inflationary momentum did not slacken in response to the deceleration program. Schultze later evaluated the program's effectiveness. "It was too vague. We preached and promoted and jumped up and down, but with little effect."[61] Strauss reported to the president on his activities in a memorandum toward the end of July. "We are talking with Schultze, Bosworth and others about possible additional steps: incomes policy, productivity programs, and the next move with labor."[62]

FEDERAL RESERVE POLICY

While the executive branch struggled with the problem of inflation, the Federal Reserve was engaged in its own independent strategy. After the decision was made not to reappoint Arthur Burns as head of the Federal Reserve when his term expired in early 1978, a number of possible candidates to replace him were discussed within the administration. The choice finally fell on William Miller. Miller was not an economist, nor did he come from the financial world. He was at the time of his appointment chairman of Textron, a diversified company headquartered in Rhode Island, with 180 plants and facilities in the United States and in several foreign countries. The company employed 65,000 people and had sales in 1976 of $2.6 billion. Miller was a graduate of the Coast Guard Academy, which had the same basic curriculum as the Naval Academy when Carter was a student. Miller later received a law degree. He and Carter were the same age and the president felt comfortable with him. He was probably recommended by people associated with the Boston Federal Reserve Bank, where he was respected for his service as a director. Carter's advisers approved of Miller. "Miller shares your basic goals and views," they wrote the president. "He would be an independent Chairman, but he would also be cooperative and easy to work with."[63] Miller assumed office in March 1978. He would serve in that post until August 1979.

Even though Miller was considered by Carter's advisers as a team player, a normal amount of tension between the administration—still in an expansionary mode—and the Federal Reserve continued. In preparation for the first Quadriad meeting with Miller in April, Schultze wrote the president that "I expect that he will be somewhat more forthcoming in discussion of current issues relating to the interaction of monetary and fiscal policies than Chairman Burns was. This is based, in part, on his interest in discussing with us, in advance, the agenda that we might propose to you for these meetings." In the same memorandum, Schultze suggests that Carter emphasize the administration's anti-inflation program—the speech outlining the wage and price deceleration plan would be delivered a few days later—to make Miller feel monetary restraint was less necessary.[64] A month later, in May 1978, Schultze briefed Carter on monetary developments. "Economic growth in the current quarter," he wrote, "is very large—in the range of 8 to 10 percent annual rate. This is combined with very large food price increases. The combined growth in output and prices is, in turn, leading to a very high growth of the money supply (M-1), above the Fed's target range. The Fed has already raised interest rates by ½ percent in the past two weeks. Even if Bill Miller would be willing to live with monetary growth rates above target for a while, the other members of the Federal Open Market Committee are not likely to."[65]

In preparation for the June 1978 Quadriad meeting, Schultze wrote to Carter that disturbing inflation developments and the Federal Reserve's response "are causing concern that the economy could slow excessively later this year and in 1979. Some slowing appears to us to be both likely and desirable. But the coordination of monetary and fiscal policy can make a critical difference between desirable moderation and slowing down at least to the point of a 'growth recession.'"[66] Carter's advisers were concerned enough to take the unusual step of requesting a meeting with the Federal Reserve Board "to assess their views." While the advisers thought of the chairman as not indifferent to their concerns, they knew there were inflation hawks among the other members of the Board who would push for a more restrictive policy. Treasury Secretary Blumenthal and Charles Schultze, accompanied by the two other members of the Council of Economic Advisers, attended the meeting in late June. Schultze passed on his assessment of the meeting to the president. The Board, he reported, is very concerned about inflation. "Some members of the Board appear to be prepared to tighten monetary conditions still further. With perhaps one exception, the members of the Board do not see even a growth recession as desirable to combat inflation. But they seem willing to run some risks with tight money because of their inflation worries. Chairman Miller is under considerable pressure from some of the more vocal and articulate inflation fighters on the Board. He himself is very sensitive to the danger of overdoing monetary restraint."[67]

Lyle Gramley, who was the Federal Reserve senior staff economist before joining the Council of Economic Advisers and who had deep respect for the traditions and jealously guarded independence of the central bank, later recalled the meeting with the Board. "The one effort that the Council of Economic Advisers made in trying to influence monetary policy was so abortive. We went over as a Council to talk to the Board about our concern about tight money and its effect on the economy. I had some notion before we went that this was not the appropriate thing to do. It would be quite unproductive. And it was. If anything it may well have been counter productive."[68] Chairman Miller's recollection of the meeting suggests that the contact did not have a big impact. "Well, yes, there was a meeting at the request of Charlie Schultze. We met one afternoon in our lounge for him to just give us a briefing on some of the things he thought were going on, and it was probably unusual, but just communication. And at that time I think from his vantage point, he saw certain directions and things happening and we were interested, as we always were, in communicating and learning, but we then had the responsibilities and carried them out as we thought we should."[69]

If the administration was concerned that monetary policy would be too restrictive, some outside observers took another view. *Fortune* magazine, for example, published an article in late 1978 entitled, "Bill Miller Is a Fainthearted Inflation Fighter."[70] To explain the basis for judging when Fed policy is too tight or too loose, a brief aside is necessary. The quantity of money and interest rates are, of course, related. If interest rates are high, one would ordinarily conclude that the Fed is restraining growth in the quantity of money. The rate that the Fed manages on a day-by-day basis is the federal funds rate, the rate banks charge one another for overnight loans. The Fed does not set this rate administratively, but it can determine the rate through its role as the supplier of bank reserves. It controls reserves by buying and selling federal securities in the open market. If it sells, money to pay for the purchase is drawn from banks and their cash reserves are lowered. If reserves are reduced because of Fed sales, banks are forced into the federal funds market to augment reserves. The increased demand, interacting with a Fed-controlled supply, forces the funds rate to rise.

During 1978, interest rates were indeed high. The federal funds rate rose to almost 10 percent, a 3.5 percentage point increase over the rate in 1977. The discount rate, the rate the Fed charges banks for loans and, at the time of the Carter administration, a more explicit indicator of Fed intentions, was raised in steps, from 7.25 percent in August 1978 to 9.5 percent in November. The November increase was a full point, an unusually large jump. It was included in a package assembled by the Treasury to support a declining dollar. When the federal funds rate and the discount rate go up, interest rates to firms and consumers in the retail market also increase. The prime rate, the rate used for corporate loans, rose from 8 percent in March 1978 to 11.5 percent in early December. At the same time that interest rates were rising, however, the money supply was increasing at a rapid pace. The Federal Reserve had set a target range of 4 to 6.5 percent for increases in the money supply. First quarter growth was at a rate slightly above the top of the range. In the second quarter the most closely watched measure of money rose a little over 9 percent. In the third quarter it rose by 8 percent. If one looked at these increases in the money supply instead of the interest rate, one would conclude that money was not tight but easy.

The difficulty faced by the Fed is reflected in an interview with William

Miller after the administration left office. "In 1978," the interviewer said, "it was a struggle because M-1 was tending to grow and you are constantly having to increase the federal funds rate in order to contain it." "Yes," Miller replied, "we were leaning against it and we actually did M-2 [a broader measure] pretty well. Over the year-and-a-half that I was there, we were almost constantly in a tightening mode."[71] But interest rates would have had to increase even more to contain the growth of money. Nominal rates were high but, given the inflation rate, real rates were actually low. This contradiction in signals is the point made in the *Fortune* article. "The open-market committee has been steadily raising its target for the federal funds rate since last spring, but it is clear that the target has consistently been too low. Though nominal rates have been high, real rates have been negative much of the time."[72]

As 1978 progressed, it was evident, as mentioned earlier, that the inflation rate was accelerating and that there was not as much slack in the economy as advisers had previously thought. By early 1979 the advisers had shifted into an anti-inflation mode. With this change in position, they began to urge caution on the Fed. Efforts to persuade the central bank through normal channels to shift its strategy failed. The advisers felt strongly enough to resort to a different tactic. Blumenthal and Schultze leaked to the press their view that the Fed needed to tighten. "If you look at the actual numbers," Schultze said in a later interview, "and if you ask yourself, during the Carter years, was there a period in which the economy was straining too hard, and I'd say there was pretty clear evidence it was, for a short period of time, in late 1978 and the first half of 1979. Then it slowed down. But that's precisely the time [when we thought tighter money policy was appropriate.]"[73] The leak by Carter's advisers is an unusual happening. It may be the only time in the history of the United States that an administration has pressed the central bank to move into a more restrained posture.

There is another interesting facet to the story, one that gives insight into Carter's way of thinking. Schultze reported to the president in mid-April 1979, that the Federal Reserve would likely act soon to tighten monetary conditions. "The steps will probably be moderate ones. You also know that your economic advisers, realizing the risks, believe such steps are nevertheless necessary." He attached a proposed statement to be released by the administration if and when the Fed acted. From the wording of the memorandum, Carter seems to have accepted the idea of firmer Fed control, but he objected to the method that Blumenthal and Schultze used. In the margin of the memorandum, Carter wrote: "To Mike and Charlie. I think the little 2-week news media crusade to force Fed action is unnecessary and improper. In the future, remain silent on what the Fed might do unless I specifically approve any so-called leaks. J. C."[74] "I didn't realize I had written that," Carter said in an interview after he left office. "But I think that describes about as lucidly as I possibly could, my concern about violating what I considered to be the prerogatives of the Fed."[75]

It is easy to critique the Fed in hindsight for the conduct of policy in 1978 and into 1979, but at the time of its decisions the future behavior of the economy was not entirely clear. Miller recognized the problem of the rapidly expanding money, but was also alert to the consensus among both public and private forecasters that a recession in 1979 was imminent. Leonard Silk, a *New York Times* reporter, has written that "in mid-April, 1979, Miller told me an economic slowdown was in progress and he had no intention of tightening monetary policy further. He said he didn't think the inflation, which had gone back up to double-digit rates in the first quarter, reflected excessive demand for goods."[76] Whatever the Fed's intentions, the money supply continued to advance at a rapid clip in the second quarter of 1979.

The next stage of the administration's inflation strategy will be taken up at a later point. The Bonn summit, held in mid-1978, three months after the deceleration program was announced, must be discussed first. At Bonn the inflation rate in the United States would become a matter for discussion.

CHAPTER 7 | **THE BONN SUMMIT**

The London summit had been disappointing in terms of results—a failure to get a formal commitment by the Germans and Japanese to an expansionary policy. As the Bonn summit, to be held in 1978, approached, the president and his advisers were still committed to the need for expansionary policies. The administration pressed hard to ensure that the Bonn meeting did not end in the same way as the London summit.

Japan's performance in 1977 was a concern to Washington, not only because it did not reach the growth rate that had been predicted, but also because of its large trade surplus. Instead of a projected Japanese deficit of $700 million, the actual number turned out to be a surplus over $10 billion. To deal with this problem, the United States proposed subcabinet-level discussions to be held in Tokyo in September 1977. Fred Bergsten from the Treasury and Richard Cooper from the State Department led the American delegation. "Bergsten leaves tomorrow for the first round of Sub-Cabinet meetings with the Japanese," Anthony Solomon reported to Secretary Blumenthal. "He and Cooper plan to structure the group discussions in terms of Japan's global responsibilities and to hit them very hard during the counterpart talks on three items: meeting their GNP [gross national product] growth target in 1977 and achieving at least as rapid growth in 1978, moving the current account into deficit as quickly as possible, and starting a long-term effort to alter Japan's structural external surplus."[1] The results of the meetings were not wholly satisfactory to the Americans. The Japanese were not seen as specific enough on the matter of growth policy.[2] International criticism of Japan's failure to act more vigorously also became more vocal, particularly at an International Monetary Fund meeting held in September 1977, and at a session of the Economic Policy Committee of the Organization for Economic Cooperation and Development in November.

For reasons not explored here, the leading role on the part of the Americans shifted from the Treasury and State Departments to the office of the special trade representative, Robert Strauss. Henry Owen felt strongly that the United States should press Japan for a commitment to a specific growth target in the range of 7–8 percent for 1978. He urged Strauss to make a growth target a part of trade concessions. Negotiations to bring this about were carried on by Strauss's deputies. As a result of these negotiations, the Japanese agreed in mid-December to expansionist policies for 1978 designed to achieve a 7 percent growth target.[3]

Since the Japanese made an early and substantial commitment for 1978, the pressure for stimulative action centered on Germany as the Bonn meeting date approached. In response to the invitation from Schmidt in January to attend the 1978 summit in Germany, Carter indicated interest but delayed acceptance until firm pre-summit commitments were in place. "I agree that we should plan for another Summit in mid-July," the president wrote in a letter to the German chancellor. "The final decision should await a review of our personal representatives' preparatory work—including their assessment of economic policy and prospects in the Summit countries, since we want to be sure that another Summit can be followed by useful results."[4]

In a memorandum for the vice president in preparation for a Washington meeting in early February 1978 with German economics minister Lambsdorff, Henry Owen reminded Mondale that "the chief leverage we have is to threaten implicitly not to hold a mid-July Summit in Bonn, as Schmidt plans, unless German growth improves. I spoke along these lines to Lambsdorff Wednesday," Owen continued, "pointing out that the Japanese growth target is now 7 percent and U.S. growth projections for 1978 are fairly good, so that Germany is the main uncertainty. He said that the German Government was taking the line publicly that it would introduce no more stimulus measures but that, in fact, it would review the situation this spring and, if growth prospects were not encouraging, it would announce new stimulus measures at or before the Summit."[5]

Michael Blumenthal visited Bonn in mid-February and raised the threat that the United States would not attend the Bonn summit unless the Germans made an advanced commitment on their growth plans. "We don't need a new economic summit," he was quoted as saying, "that would only send empty platitudes floating down the Rhine."[6] Henry Owen, commenting in a memorandum to the president on Blumenthal's report on his trip to Bonn, wrote that "Schmidt understands the message we gave Lambsdorff—that we will only make a final decision about Summit timing in light of our review of the Summit Preparatory Group's work this spring, and that this review will take special account of economic prospects in Germany. Schmidt stressed to Mike how important a Summit was, for political as well as economic reasons, and how much he was looking forward to it. It's evident that he wants the Bonn Summit; it is also evident that he understands what our price is."[7] Satisfied that Schmidt would take action on the growth issue—though the commitment was somewhat vague—the administration announced on March 12 that the United States would attend the summit.

In mid-March 1978, British prime minister Callaghan visited both Washington and Bonn, acting as a broker to work out a package of concessions agreeable to the various parties. Carter sent letters to Fukuda of Japan, Giscard of France, and Schmidt of Germany as a follow-up to the Callaghan visit.[8] The basic agreement that developed is outlined in a memorandum from Henry Owen to President Carter reporting on a lengthy meeting with Schmidt in Bonn in early April. "When I saw him last week, the Chancellor told me that he accepts the notion of a package approach suggested in your letter to him." The United States' part of the package included a commitment to undertake actions to deal with the dual problems of inflation and energy usage. The United States' inflation performance for the fifteen months since Carter's inauguration, a rate higher than that abroad, was beginning to be a concern for our allies. The large amount of oil imported by the United States also created problems for the other industrialized nations. A part of the solution for oil would involve allowing oil prices in the United States to rise to world levels with the goal of dampening domestic use. "The Chancellor stressed the need for effective U.S. anti-inflationary action to strengthen the dollar; he said he realized from his own experience both how painful such measures were bound to be politically in the U.S., and how necessary it was to stick with them, year in and year out, if inflation was to be brought under control." With regard to energy, the chancellor "made clear that nothing would do so much to enhance European confidence in U.S. leadership as effective action to limit oil imports."[9] As far as the German commitment is concerned, Owen reported, the chancellor

> said the German government would introduce a stimulus package if the FRG could not achieve its 3.5% 1978 growth target. He warned that he could not say so publicly, until and unless the time came to act. He was un-

clear about the timing. . . . The Chancellor wanted you to know how hard he had worked to achieve a tax cut last year when he realized that German growth was falling below target; he asked me to tell you that he was confident that he could get parliamentary approval this time if it proved necessary. . . . The discussion gave us most of what we wanted: German agreement to a package approach, and a commitment to stimulus measures, if needed. It did not settle the important problem of stimulus timing. I suspect, as you have indicated, that the Chancellor will eventually agree to action at the Summit, since he wants a successful Summit.[10]

Charles Schultze chaired a committee of representatives from the summit countries with the task of preparing a paper on macroeconomic issues, a paper finalized in Washington in mid-May. The results were presented to the summit sherpas at the end of the month. "The paths that our economies are likely to follow through 1979 *if current policies are maintained* would be unsatisfactory in several respects," the report said. "Unemployment is unlikely to come down significantly and may continue rising in Europe. Excess capacity would remain substantial. . . . The development of a common strategy for more growth and employment must be regarded as a chief task of international economic policy."[11] Schultze's own proposal was for a German stimulus package equal to 1 percent of gross national product. In a summary of the discussion at the meeting of the sherpas, Henry Owen reported that the German representatives hedged on what commitment Schmidt would make. The Germans said that the Federal Republic of Germany would take stimulative action if it appeared that the growth rate would be inadequate,

> but added that it will take time for Chancellor Schmidt to form a domestic consensus around this action. They suggested that the Summit might discuss general directions of policy, rather than specific commitments; the Group felt this kind of Summit would be greeted skeptically, in the media and the financial community. German representatives then said that at a Summit where other nations pledged needed actions (i.e., the U.S. on energy and inflation and other countries on trade) the Chancellor might say that he recognizes the need for additional expansion and will consult with German political parties about how to meet it—making, in effect, a "best efforts" pledge.[12]

Domestic policy adviser Stuart Eizenstat, who had serious concerns about the domestic implications of a U.S. commitment on oil, particularly an increase in oil prices, wrote a comment in the margin of the Owen memorandum: "Henry: If all we get is a 'best efforts' pledge from Schmidt we should not make a specific pledge on oil prices—with all the attendant dangers."[13]

Schmidt played a waiting game, unwilling to tip his hand until sure of internal political support. The chancellor had to deal with a whole range of domestic interests—the Bundesbank, economic experts, unions, and business. The central bank, the most critical player in the game, opposed a stimulative fiscal policy. Otmar Emminger, the president of the Bundesbank, said publicly in mid-June 1978, that the pace of German recovery had stepped up and that Germany should not commit itself to expansionary actions at the coming Bonn summit. Arthur Burns, former chairman of the Federal Reserve, later reported that Emminger urged him to dissuade Schmidt from implementing a stimulus package then under active consideration.[14] An important segment of German expert opinion was generally skeptical about the wisdom of a demand management approach to economic policy. One member of the German Council of Economic Experts, a committee created by Conrad Adenauer in 1963 to advise the West German government, commented on the supply, rather than demand, orientation of many German economists. The role of government, in this view, is not to use policy to propel the total economy forward by a large injection of fiscal stimulus, but to remove distortions in economic incentives that affect the supply of goods coming to market. "Development through competition may be compared with a millipede. Locomotion is ensured by a large number of small cogs functioning on an all-wheel-drive principle. The concept beloved by international Keynesians of a 'locomotive' as the draught horse of dynamic development is erroneous."[15]

Schmidt, himself, shifted his views about demand management policies over the course of his career, reflecting a policy maker's need for flexibility in adapting to changing conditions. As minister of finance, a position he held before becoming chancellor in 1974, he favored expansionist policies. In 1972 he made an oft-quoted statement that it is better to have 5 percent inflation than 5 percent unemployment. His comment caused controversy in Germany where it went against accepted views. His belief in such a Keynesian trade-off was dampened by the inflation that accompanied the oil price increase of the early 1970s. The need to maintain Germany's export advantage impressed him with the importance of price stability. As the recession of 1974–75 made itself felt, Schmidt, as chancellor, shifted positions and undertook stimulative fiscal actions. He also pressed the United

States to expand in order to increase German exports. When Ford told Schmidt in a meeting in Washington in late 1974 that he expected the United States economy to start its recovery in the summer of 1975, Schmidt urged Ford to turn the American economy around sooner. "Compared with the later controversy about reflation in 1977–78, the German and American positions in 1974–76, were reversed," according to one account. "In the earlier period German Chancellor Helmut Schmidt was a vocal advocate of macroeconomic coordination programs of various sorts, whereas President Gerald Ford, unlike his successor, was at best lukewarm toward international coordination."[16]

Shortly after he left office as chancellor in 1982, Schmidt was again in an expansionary mood. In a lengthy position paper, printed simultaneously in a number of publications in early 1983, he urged the seven major powers to take joint action at the upcoming Williamsburg summit to deal with the severe recession of 1981–82. "It is time for a joint economic policy offensive if governments mean to live up to their responsibility to tackle unemployment," he wrote. "The western industrial countries must take the lead, with the United States at the helm. What is needed is close coordination of individual economic policy measures in the major countries. . . . At the economic summit in Williamsburg in May, concerted action by the seven summit participants . . . must be the central theme."[17] At the time of the Bonn summit in 1978, he publicly resisted American pressure to adopt an expansionary policy in respect for the traditional German suspicion of exercises in demand management, while privately moving toward reluctant acceptance of a need to stimulate a lagging economy.

External sources other than the United States were pressuring Germany as they were also pressuring Japan. The heads of government of the European Community called for "concerted action" to accelerate European recovery at the regular meeting of the European Council three months before the Bonn summit. Schmidt used this external pressure to his advantage in the domestic debate. Even if outside demands had not been there, Helmut Schmidt had almost certainly decided for domestic reasons that the moment had come for stimulative action. The unions, which had close ties to Schmidt's Social Democratic Party (SPD) and contributed a large share of the party's income, were pressing for an expansionary policy, as were the more left-wing members of the SPD. Partly because of the mark's appreciation against the dollar, the inflation rate in Germany was low, a condition which reduced the risk from stimulative fiscal action. The high unemployment rate provided a reason for a policy initiative to maintain the economic upswing. Slower growth in Germany in the 1960s and early 1970s could be explained as a supply-side problem due to a labor shortage. The lethargy of the later 1970s had all the marks of a lack of sufficient demand, high unemployment, and a low rate of capital utilization—a condition amenable to fiscal stimulation.[18] One informed report of events in Germany at the time indicates that "in effect, those closest to Schmidt confide, the chancellor 'let himself be pushed' into a policy that he probably favored on domestic grounds but would have found costly and perhaps impossible to pursue without the 'tail wind' provided by the summit."[19] Americans were aware that this was the case.[20]

Schmidt had the delicate task of dealing with internal opposition to expanding and external pressures to do so. As he himself said in a speech to the Bundestag in January 1978: "We are trying you might say to steer a golden, middle course between the demands of the opposition here . . . and the insistence of some abroad that we should increase our deficit."[21] As part of the internal political maneuvering, a letter to Chancellor Schmidt from the minister of economics was leaked to the press a few days before the beginning of the Bonn meeting. The letter stated that the time had come for an expansionary program on domestic grounds. Schmidt played it very close to the vest right up to the end, delaying a firm commitment to a precise growth target until the second day of the summit meeting.[22] The waiting game paid off. By the time of his decision to agree at Bonn to an expansionary policy, a consensus that stimulative fiscal action was appropriate had developed among political, business, and labor leaders.

The position of the Bundesbank was the final critical connection. One of the interesting things about the summit meetings is an absence of discussion of monetary policy. Since the independence of the central banks meant that leaders of the Group of Seven could not make commitments for monetary expansion, their decisions were limited to budget policy over which they had some influence. The successful implementation of fiscal actions depended heavily, however, on whether or not the central banks would offset the fiscal stimulus by monetary restraint. Recognizing that Schmidt intended to commit himself to stimulative fiscal action at the Bonn summit and that such an initiative had public endorsement, the Bundesbank agreed to support the fiscal action to the degree of preventing government borrowing from exerting upward pressure on interest rates.

The formal communiqué issued at the end of the Bonn summit included the statement that "as a contribution to avert the world-wide disturbances of economic equilibrium the German Delegation has indicated that by the end of August it will propose to the legislative bodies additional and quantitatively substantial measures up to 1% of GNP, designed to achieve a significant strengthening of demand at a higher rate of growth."[23]

AMERICAN COMMITMENT ON OIL

It was recognized at Bonn that the United States economy was moving at a fast pace and needed no further stimulation. The American part of the package—a commitment to steps to dampen the inflation rate, and to a reduction in oil imports—was included in the final agreement. According to the official communiqué, "the President of the United States stated that reducing inflation is essential to maintaining a healthy U.S. economy.... He identified the major actions that have been taken and are being taken to counter inflation in the United States."[24] Expressing his intention at Bonn to act on the matter was not a difficult commitment. As already said, domestic prices did not behave over 1977 and the first part of 1978 as expected by Carter's advisers, and were becoming a major concern for the president. The commitment on oil was the more difficult one for the administration to make. One informed account of the summit reported that "as the U.S. party departed for Bonn, they were privately more worried about their own part of the package deal than about the contributions of the other summiteers."[25]

By the beginning of the 1970s the historic independence that America enjoyed in providing for its own needs for oil had disappeared. The United States' dominance in manufacturing before World War II was based in large part on the plentiful endowment in industrial materials and fuels.[26] In 1913 the United States produced two-thirds of the world's petroleum. Even through the 1950s and 1960s, its surplus capacity enabled it to help other nations when shortages of oil appeared in international markets. By the 1970s this was no longer the case. "In the earlier crises the United States could (from the perspective of oil-consuming countries) be 'part of the solution'; by 1973, it was 'part of the problem.'"[27] American demand for petroleum exerted upward pressure on world oil prices—the United States consumed at the time one-third of the world's energy—and strengthened the hand of the Organization of Petroleum Exporting Countries (OPEC). The *Washington Post* commented in an editorial at the end of 1977, "the carefree, eat-drink-and-be-merry American attitude toward oil is increasingly regarded as a menace by the people abroad whose cooperation this country needs most—the oil producers who favor price restraint, the political moderates in OPEC, the democracies against whom the United States is bidding for limited supplies."[28]

Bonn summit. *Left to right*: Takeo Fukuda, prime minister of Japan; Guilio Andreotti, prime minister of Italy; Carter; Helmut Schmidt, chancellor of Germany; and Valery Giscard d'Estaing, president of France. Courtesy of the Jimmy Carter Library.

At the time of the Bonn summit, international complaints about American oil imports were as unanimous as was the resentment of the Germans and Japanese for their trade surpluses. The pressure on the Americans was increased by a pledge of the nine European Community member nations, at a meeting at Bremen ten days prior to the Bonn summit, to cut their consumption of oil by half over the next seven years. Carter recalls in his memoirs that "energy shortages and price surges were causing widespread unemployment and inflation in all our countries, as well as serious imbalances in world trade. Our nation's inability to deal with so crucial a question was becoming an international embarrassment."[29] As his part of the Bonn agreement, Carter promised to allow the price of domestically produced oil, which had been kept at artificially low levels through regulation, to rise to the world level in order to discourage consumption.

The removal of oil price ceilings would allow price to play its critical role in the efficient allocation of resources. When the price of oil was kept artificially low, the automobile industry received the signal that fuel efficiency need not be a consideration in automotive design. For their part, consumers received the false message that oil is an abundant product to be consumed freely. In Europe the pricing mechanism was allowed to function in the market for oil. Prices rose in response to OPEC actions. Given the dominance of the United States as a consumer of petroleum, the international market was affected by American pricing policy with adverse consequences for our trading partners. The ultimate solution was to allow the price to rise to reflect the relative scarcity of petroleum. Henry Owen did not exaggerate when he observed that the United States' decision to decontrol oil prices is "arguably the single most important step taken by the industrial countries to address the world energy problem."[30] Exactly how this Bonn commitment was to be implemented was a matter of debate within the administration for the following eighteen months.

Oil was included in the general wage-price controls imposed by President Nixon in response to the inflation of the early 1970s under authority conferred by a Democratic Congress. A two-tier system was put in place. Oil resources already developed were made subject to price control. Newly developed oil was exempted from price restraints. Holding the line on "old" oil prevented large windfall profits from accruing to the industry. Allowing "new" oil to rise in price encouraged production at the margin. Presidential price control authority expired in 1974. A two-tier system continued, however, formally embodied in legislation passed by Congress in 1975. The two-tier arrangement created a problem of equity due to differences in refineries' access to controlled, low-priced oil. Because of the difference in access, two gas stations in the same area in the same city were selling gas at prices that differed as much as 12 cents a gallon.[31] To eliminate inequities a policy was adopted entitling refiners to buy price-controlled oil in proportion to refinery capacity. These entitlements equalized crude oil acquisition costs between refiners who had access to domestic price-controlled oil and those who relied on "new" oil and the higher priced imported crude. The entitlements kept American oil below world prices. The result was to encourage domestic demand, and, in effect, subsidize imported oil.

Even before the Middle East oil embargo, informed observers recognized that an energy problem was developing. The first initiative of the Nixon administration was appointment of a cabinet task force on oil import control in early 1969.[32] In June 1971, Nixon sent a comprehensive energy message to Congress. His proposal included creation of a Department of Natural Resources, a nuclear power program, and research into synthetic fuels. In an announcement of a four-point program for dealing with the nation's energy problems in June 1973, Nixon warned that "unless we act swiftly and effectively we could face a genuine energy crisis in the foreseeable future." In a major televised address to the nation, he announced "Project Independence." Among other things he asked Congress to establish a 50-mile-per-hour speed limit. Efforts by the administration to develop an energy policy got lost in the distractions of Watergate. Events, however, kept the energy issue on the public agenda. The oil embargo of 1973 and the quadrupling of petroleum prices by OPEC in 1974 dramatized the immediacy of the energy issue. The shortage of gasoline and heating oil in parts of the country in the winter of 1973–74 heightened the attention of the general public.

Shortly after assuming office in August 1974, Gerald Ford created an energy board to deal with the energy problem.[33] He submitted to Congress in January his Energy Independence Act of 1975. The bill was a comprehensive piece of legislation. It included provisions for development of petroleum reserves, proposals to increase energy efficiency in buildings and homes, and a requirement that the automobile industry improve gas mileage. The president also promised to act to decontrol the price of domestically produced oil.[34] In December 1975, Congress finally passed a watered down version of Ford's submission in the form of the Energy Policy and Conservation Act. Oil price deregulation was not part of the package.

The fundamentals of the energy problem were reasonably well understood by those involved in the energy debate in the early 1970s. The various proposals for solving the problem concentrated on conservation and the development of new energy sources. Coal and nuclear energy are the main alternatives to oil. American coal reserves are sufficient to satisfy the country's energy needs for several centuries. Nuclear power offers the possibility of unlimited energy resources. The Ford package contained a request for authority to require power plants to convert to coal usage. But coal and nuclear power have serious problems; they are dirty and dangerous. Those who searched for an answer to the energy problem in the early 1970s understood that oil would be the main source of energy for the foreseeable future. At the time of Carter's inauguration, oil and its associated product, natural gas, supplied 75 percent of the nation's energy, even though they made up only 8 percent of the nation's energy reserves.

Reducing imports by allowing the price of oil to rise to world levels involved severe political problems, starting with consumer indignation over higher prices at the gas pump and higher monthly bills for oil used for home heating. Letting prices rise to a level necessary to adapt to supply and demand would also allow American oil companies to share in windfall profits arising from the artificially high prices imposed by the OPEC cartel. Voter sentiments against the oil companies were intense. Polls showed that the public had strong doubts about whether or not a true energy shortage really existed or had been imposed by a conspiracy among oil producers. The prevailing sentiment in the Ford administration was to impose a market solution to the problem, but public suspicion of the oil companies forced the administration to develop proposals with a mixture of government controls and the free market.

Designing an energy program with enough public acceptance to be adopted by Congress must also take into account the conflicting interests in the country. Energy policy does not have a natural constituency. Higher prices are applauded by oil producers and fought by organizations representing consumers. Sectional differences pitting oil producers in the western part of the country against consumers in the east created intense resistance in Congress to various policy solutions. "It is extremely difficult to write an energy bill," Speaker of the House Tip O'Neill commented as he dealt with energy legislation in Congress. "This, perhaps, has been the most parochial issue that could ever hit the floor."[35]

The problem of developing a comprehensive energy program was further complicated during the Ford and Carter administrations by changes in congressional procedures originating in the organizational reforms of the early 1970s. According to one estimate, there were twenty committees and thirty-eight subcommittees in Congress with significant energy jurisdiction during Carter's administration.[36] There was also a "cozy triangle" of interlocking interests among the executive and legislative branches of government and outside parties. In a dramatic act of frustration soon to be experienced by Jimmy Carter, Ford ripped pages from a calendar in a television address to the nation in May 1975 to demonstrate how long Congress had been sitting on his energy proposals. Jimmy Carter would have to face the same type of conundrum. "The energy legislation," he was to say, "was tedious, like chewing on a rock that lasted the whole four years."[37] The long, drawn-out process in a Congress dominated by members of his own party contributed to the weakening of his image as a national leader.

THE CARTER PLAN

Energy was not a major issue in the 1976 campaign.[38] Both contenders advanced proposals, but the matter died due to lack of voter interest. Carter did promise to seek creation of a cabinet-level Department of Energy and to produce an energy package early in his administration if elected. He also made a commitment during the campaign to deregulate the price of natural gas over a five-year period—a pledge he would later regret. Stuart Eizenstat has described how the promise was made in the heat of the campaign. "At a critical juncture late in the 1976 campaign, Governors Boren of Oklahoma and Briscoe of Texas called me in the Carter Presidential campaign office to urge that the candidate put in writing his willingness to decontrol natural gas prices over a five-year period so they could use it to campaign for Carter in their States and obtain votes from their oil interests. With my energy aide, Kitty Schirmer, I drafted a letter which I forwarded to the candidate on 'Peanut One.' He quickly approved it between campaign stops. His pledge was a factor in Carter's narrow win in Texas." According to Eizenstat's account of events, Carter later felt compelled to continue controls due to powerful arguments advanced by advisers.[39] Eizenstat has called the decision to abandon the campaign pledge "perhaps the most fateful domestic decision made by President Carter. . . . It weakened his western support irreparably, and tied up the energy bill for 18 months on the Hill because of the impasses over this issue."[40]

Leading the task force that designed the energy program after the inauguration was James Schlesinger, who first served as an assistant to Carter and was later appointed as the first secretary of the newly created energy department. Schlesinger had previously seen service in a number of positions under Republican administrations: chairman of the Atomic Energy Commission, head of the CIA (Central Intelligence Agency), and secretary of defense. From their first meeting in Plains, Carter and Schlesinger developed a rapport and the president gave him a lot of leeway. He also gave him a ninety-day deadline. Schlesinger produced on schedule the National Energy Plan in April 1977.[41] Critics have questioned how well the development of the package was handled. Both the president and the new energy czar gave more emphasis to the technical details than to developing consensus. Carter had directed Schlesinger's group to work in secret, lest leaks about proposals under consideration cause a buildup of resistance even before the final package was announced. There was little of the interagency review usually given to legislative proposals. Even the Treasury and the Council of Economic Advisers were not kept apace of the group's progress until the later stages when both Blumenthal and Schultze insisted on being briefed on the plan. While the secrecy thwarted premature opposition to the final proposal, it also precluded the development of support within Congress as work on the package progressed.

Carter launched his energy program with a nationwide fireside chat, wearing a sweater for symbolic effect in a White House where the thermometers had been set back to conserve energy. He presented his plan in his first postinaugural address to a joint session of Congress. It contained familiar provisions, but while it built on previous efforts of Presidents Nixon and Ford and various congressional committees, it was more ambitious in scope, a sweeping and comprehensive proposal. Carter explained the strategy of presenting a comprehensive package. "If we put forward one part of the energy program, it's going to be shot down because on its face it would be unfair to some major groups in our country. . . . We need to put the whole thing together in a comprehensive ball of wax that I could understand and so could the American people. So that they could say, well, I lost something on this issue but I gained my compensatory advantage here."[42] The energy program, which had received only passing discussion in the campaign, became a centerpiece of the administration's domestic agenda. As said before, Carter labeled the undertaking "the moral equivalent of war," borrowing a phrase from William James at the suggestion of his old navy mentor, Admiral Hyman Rickover.[43]

The final proposal had a large number of provisions—113 in all—ranging from measures to develop new sources of energy to initiatives for energy conservation.[44] Carter thought of the program as preparing for the transition to a time fast approaching when domestic and foreign sources of energy would no longer be abundant. The plan had a frame of reference extending over several decades, but the working benchmark was 1985. The measure of success was the reduction in the number of barrels of oil imported per day. The bill called for a cut in gasoline consumption of 10 percent below existing levels by 1985. At the time of the legislative proposal, transportation absorbed over 25 percent of American energy uses and automobiles half of that. The 1975 Energy Policy and Conservation Act, passed under Gerald Ford's presidency, mandated auto fuel efficiency standards. Carter's plan added an incentive scheme.[45] It called for a tax on cars performing below prescribed efficiency standards and a rebate for those above. The initiative set a goal of a two-thirds increase in coal production, and for bringing American homes and all new buildings up to minimum standards of fuel efficiency. It also included a proposal for continuation of the Ford program for creating a strategic oil reserve.

DECONTROL OF OIL PRICES

The key provision of the National Energy Plan—and the critical part of the Bonn commitment—was decontrol of oil prices. "Old" oil, that discovered before 1975, would be kept under price controls, though the price would be allowed to rise at the general rate of inflation. "New" oil, that discovered after 1975, would rise to the world price level over a three-year period. The gradual phasing in of the higher prices would reduce the burden on consumers of adjusting to the increased cost. A second part of the price decontrol plan was the imposition of a "crude oil equalization tax," to be applied in three stages starting in January 1978. The tax would equal the difference between the control price and the world price and thus bring the cost of oil to American consumers up to the world level. It would achieve the effects of a free market on the demand side and reduce consumption. The revenues resulting from the tax on excess profits would be distributed to the American people in the form of tax rebates, with direct payments to Americans with no tax liability. The rebate and direct payment provisions would offset the impact on middle and low income families of the inflationary pressure caused by decontrol. The bill had a liberal cast. It was tilted toward conservation and consumer protection but with less concern for producers' incentives.

Speaker Tip O'Neill cleared the path for rapid passage of the Carter energy package. To prevent the delays that would have been inevitable if the legislative proposal were broken up in separate parts and distributed to a number of committees and subcommittees, O'Neill short-circuited the system by creating a super committee. He appointed to the Ad Hoc Select Committee on Energy members loyal to him and charged them with responsibility for moving the National Energy Plan through the legislative process. The plan was passed by the House almost intact three months after it was sent to Congress. The House performance was not matched in the Senate. The president reported at an April cabinet meeting "that Senate Majority Leader Byrd is concerned about the procedure the House has adopted to consider the omnibus energy bill. Senator Byrd does not believe that such a procedure will work in the Senate."[46] The energy bill met particular resistance from Senator Russell Long, chairman of the Senate Finance Committee. By the spring of 1978, after a year's struggle with Congress and with the Bonn summit coming up shortly, the energy legislation was caught in gridlock. The crude oil equalization tax, in particular, was in serious trouble. Since oil price deregulation was made contingent in the Carter plan on the passage of the tax, the plan to allow American oil prices to rise to the world level was also put on hold. If Congress had passed the Carter energy proposal as submitted, the matter of oil deregulation would not have been on the agenda of the Bonn summit.

In late June 1978, Carter met with the energy leaders in the House and Senate to urge passage of his program. To put pressure on Congress he threatened to impose a $5–$6 import fee per barrel of crude oil if Congress failed to act. Senator Robert Dole reacted strongly by introducing an amendment in the Senate prohibiting the president from imposing an import fee. Carter pointed out at a leadership breakfast shortly before leaving for Bonn that the Dole amendment had put him in an embarrassing position with European leaders. To counteract the effect of the Dole amendment, Carter asked Senate majority leader Byrd to visit Europe and assure the leadership there that Congress would pass energy legislation. Byrd reported back at a leadership breakfast on July 11, 1978, according to notes taken by Eizenstat, that Helmut Schmidt and other European leaders "were concerned with the inability of the United States to come to grips with the energy problem and were under the impression that congress is doing nothing. Byrd thought that he had changed their minds, assuring them that an energy bill would be on his desk before adjournment."[47] On the preceding day the majority leader had reported to the cabinet that the European leaders were primarily preoccupied with the passage of the equalization tax.[48] The president stated at a meeting with the congressional leaders in late June that if Congress failed to pass the tax proposal he would need to act administratively.[49]

Apparently what Carter intended to promise at Bonn was not completely decided at the time he departed from Washington.[50] There was sharp disagreement among his advisers about the American commitment. Some aides were concerned that the president would be embarrassed by making a promise he couldn't keep—a concern that focused on the possibility that Congress would not only fail to pass the equalization tax but would act to constrain his administrative options. Stuart Eizenstat and Vice President Mondale, both attuned to the concerns of the liberal wing of the Democratic Party, worried about the effect of an increase in price on Carter's political support among the party's "basic constituency, labor, blacks, Hispanics, low-income" who are "viscerally unable to bring themselves to accept it, or certainly to applaud it."[51] Alienation of this basic group would make it even more difficult to get their acceptance of the stringency of the 1980 budget that would be proposed to Congress in January 1979, as part of the anti-inflation program. Michael Blumenthal, Anthony Solomon, Richard Cooper, and Henry Owen, whose primary focus was international policy and who were preoccupied with the fate of the dollar and trade deficits, strongly supported a commitment by Carter to decontrol price. Charles

Schultze, as a professional economist, had a natural predisposition to a free price system. He was, nevertheless, concerned about the effect of a rise in the cost of oil on the domestic inflation rate.

The inflationary implications of the energy program were recognized from the earliest days of the administration. Carter was asked at a press conference in mid-April 1977, whether the energy program "coming in a few more days" would be inflationary. The president responded that "we hope to be able within the energy policy that I present to hold down the impact on inflation to less than one-half percent by emphasizing wherever possible voluntary conservation."[52] Carter's statement was based on an estimate of the Data Resources econometric model provided by Schultze.[53] A year later, as the Bonn summit was approaching, Schultze and Blumenthal were becoming deeply concerned about the accelerating inflation. They sent a strong memorandum to the president in mid-March. "The price outlook is deteriorating," they wrote. "Weather influences contributed to some of the sharp rise in consumer good prices in January. But a more fundamental worsening of the outlook also appears to be underway."[54]

As Bonn approached, Schultze's central concern was whether or not the Germans would commit to a reflationary policy. A decision by the United States on the subject of oil, which could have inflationary implications, should be governed by what the Germans were willing to promise. "No one knows," Schultze wrote to the president, "what Schmidt's negotiating tactics for the Summit are."[55] The central problem, in Schultze's mind, was still the difference in expansion rates in the United States and abroad. "Through 1977, increasing oil imports were the major, but not the only element increasing our deficit," Schultze advised Carter a few days before the Bonn meeting. "Over the past year, oil imports have fallen. Manufactured imports have grown very sharply, while manufactured exports have risen very little. . . . Faster growth in the United States than in our major trading partners continues to be a fundamental explanation for the rapid relative growth of U.S. manufactured imports in comparison with the growth of U.S. exports."[56] In a separate memorandum he outlined the economic consequences of alternative outcomes at Bonn. There are basically two options, he wrote:

> Either you can commit to take administrative actions (e.g., impose a fee) if COET [crude oil equalization tax] fails to pass; or you can state that you will weigh alternative courses of action but not make a commitment at this time. . . . Summing up the benefits and the risks, I conclude that in the absence of major gains at the Bonn Summit, I would recommend not

committing to administrative actions at this time. The risks for the economy, the increased inflationary pressures, and the political expression of Congress on this subject argue against the wisdom of this commitment at this time, unless there is an offsetting *quid pro quo*.[57]

In the end the leaders of the summit nations came to an agreement at Bonn stated in precise quantitative terms. Schmidt committed his nation to a stimulus package of up to 1 percent of the German gross national product. The president reported to congressional leaders after his return that both the German and the Japanese stimulus would take the form of tax cuts to increase domestic demand, rather than steps to raise exports and pump up the two economies at the expense of their trading partners.[58] For his part, Carter made a specific commitment on oil, a pledge to raise the average level of domestic oil prices to world prices by the end of 1980. The views of the group primarily concerned with international policy prevailed. Domestic policy staff was, apparently, not aware that such a specific commitment would be made. According to one interview, Eizenstat "was surprised and dismayed by the announcement at Bonn. Eizenstat faulted the foreign policy side of the administration for not being 'sensitive to domestic considerations.' No decision memorandum had been prepared prior to the summit, and the domestic implications of the pledge had not been discussed."[59] Over the next months an intense debate took place within the administration about the way the commitment would be carried out.

CHAPTER 8 | **BONN AND OIL**

**THE
INTERNAL
DEBATE**

In a briefing memorandum drafted a few days after Bonn for Michael Blumenthal, who was scheduled to appear on the popular Sunday program "Meet the Press," Undersecretary Anthony Solomon wrote that "the President made no commitments on the exact ways in which he would achieve the 1980 objective. . . . He is free, therefore, to continue the difficult problem of working out with the Congress the necessary measures to achieve this objective and/or take administrative action."[1] Before Bonn the administrative options most frequently discussed in inner councils were import fees or quotas, approaches that had become less acceptable given the congressional resistance demonstrated by the Dole amendment. A more promising option was price decontrol by direct presidential decision.[2] On the basis of the 1975 Energy Policy and Conservation Act, oil price controls would end in mid-1979. The president would then have discretionary authority to continue controls, abolish them, or phase them out. By the same 1975 legislation, all controls would automatically expire in October 1981, unless Congress extended the legislation. Carter had a window of time extending from mid-1979 to late 1981 to act without congressional approval. What he would need from Congress, if he chose to decontrol oil prices through administrative action, was the windfall profits tax. On this matter Congress had been stubbornly resistant. In November 1978, Congress finally passed an energy bill, eighteen months after it was first submitted. About half of the president's proposals were not enacted, including the equalization tax. This omission left the petroleum pricing strategy still to be worked out.

A lengthy memorandum jointly authored by eight policy advisers was sent to the president in early January 1979. "This memorandum discusses, for your information, several options which are open to you on domestic crude oil pricing policy. It also analyzes the relationship of the various options to economic and inflation policies, energy policy, international commitments, and to the Administration's agenda for the coming Congress. While we are not seeking a decision at this time, we did feel it important to provide you with the basic information which we have developed thus far.... The choices which you will face in deciding this issue are not easy and your advisers have widely divergent recommendations."[3] The lineup among the participants in the debate was the same as before the summit, but the argument became more focused after the Bonn commitment was an established fact. Advisers primarily concerned with international policy continued to press for decontrol. Domestic advisers opposed it. Charles Schultze stood somewhere in the middle.

The dilemma facing the administration was that the two commitments made at Bonn—to raise the price of oil in the United States and to give priority to reducing inflation in policy decisions—were at least, in part, incompatible. If the Bonn pledge on oil were kept, the inflation rate could be expected to rise.

The inflation problem at the turn of the year had become alarming. The consumer price index registered an inflation rate of 9 percent for 1978. In the first few months of 1979 the price outlook was worsening. Lyle Gramley, chief forecaster for the Council of Economic Advisers, reported to the president in March the Bureau of Labor Statistics' estimate of the change of consumer prices in February. "The news is grim indeed," Gramley wrote. "The total of all items in the CPI [consumer price index] went up 1.2 percent in February—an annual rate of increase of 15 percent, the largest increase since September 1974."[4]

As we will see later, the administration initiated in late 1978, a few months after the Bonn summit, a stronger anti-inflation program that included formal standards for wage and price increases. The inflation buildup in 1978 and into 1979 threatened the anti-inflation strategy, which was based, in part, on getting unions to exercise restraint in wage demands. If the cost of living continued to rise at a rapid rate, discipline on the part of the unions could not be expected. "The anti-inflation program is likely to collapse" Schultze wrote, "if some price deceleration is not achieved soon."[5]

The year 1979 was particularly critical since a number of key labor contracts were up for renewal. Of particular concern was the negotiation under way with the teamsters union, which was reported to be asking for wage and benefit increases of 13 to 14 percent the first year and 30 to 35 percent over three years. Information available to the administration suggested a reasonable chance that the negotiations would produce a lower wage settlement.[6] But if the teamsters succeeded in obtaining gains in excess of administration policy, other unions were likely to attempt to match the teamsters' settlement. In such a sensitive situation, the matter of oil price decontrol took on an added dimension. "Many of the important 1979 wage negotiations involve three year contracts," the interagency memo of January 3 said. "In these cases, the 1980 and 1981 inflationary effects of [a decontrol decision] take on far greater significance. It will be very difficult to urge the unions to restrain demands, when, at the same time, the Administration is pursuing an oil pricing policy which will add 0.8 percent to the CPI over three years."[7] Alfred Kahn, who came to the White House to assume the role of inflation czar after the Bonn summit and while the oil deregulation debate was in progress, has described how Doug Fraser, the union leader, came into his office and said: "If you people deregulate crude oil, you can kiss your standards goodbye. If you make my workers pay a dollar for gasoline then I'm not going to stick to the wage standards."[8] The machinists union would openly break with Carter over the issue. The dilemma could not be ignored. If the administration took steps to raise oil prices, inflationary pressure would come not only from the direct impact that higher oil prices would have on the consumer price index, but also from the indirect effect of abandonment of wage restraint by the unions.

THE DOLLAR AND DECONTROL OF OIL

The inflationary effect of decontrol of oil prices was a main concern of Carter's domestic advisers. The potential impact that a failure to decontrol would have on the dollar was the primary concern of those responsible for international policy. In a joint memorandum sent to the president in late March, Secretary of State Cyrus Vance, Treasury Secretary Michael Blumenthal, Energy Secretary James Schlesinger, Commerce Secretary Juanita Kreps, and Henry Owen pressed Carter to phase out controls "by no later than October, 1981."[9] In addition to stressing the importance of keeping our commitments, the memorandum argued that if decontrol did not take place, "we would risk speculative attacks on the dollar."

The problems of the dollar from the latter part of 1977 into 1978 provide the monetary backdrop for the Bonn summit and the deliberations that took place within the administration on the oil decontrol decision through the early months of 1979. The weakness of the dollar in foreign exchange markets in the winter of 1977–78 left the Europeans and the Japanese with a general uneasiness about American foreign exchange rate policy.[10] Helmut Schmidt, uncertain as to how firm was the American commitment to dollar support, and provoked by what he interpreted as a failure of United States leadership, worked behind the scenes to bring about monetary integration in Europe as a way to dilute the disturbing effect of dollar movements on the German mark.

Germany and the other countries of Europe had a stake in creating a zone of exchange rate stability. Over half of the total trade of European Community countries was conducted with other European Community nations. In addition, the countries of Europe are more open than the United States is in terms of trade. Exports were 23 percent of the German gross national product in 1978, compared to less than 7 percent for the United States. This high degree of openness makes the German economy, and the other European economies, more vulnerable to variations in the exchange rate. A depreciation of any nation's currency has an inflationary effect due to the increased cost of imports. But a depreciation of the mark has a bigger impact on the inflation rate in Germany than a similar depreciation of the dollar would have in the United States. The European Monetary System, first proposed by Britain's Roy Jenkins in late 1977, while serving as president of the European Commission, was given life by the energies of Helmut Schmidt shortly before the Bonn summit.

The idea of monetary integration in Europe was not a new one. The earliest attempt to bring about monetary stability in Europe, following the collapse of Bretton Woods, was the "snake in the tunnel." After the closing of the gold window by the United States in 1971, the member nations of the International Monetary Fund attempted to preserve some form of a pegged rate system. One part of this abortive attempt was to allow a wider range of currency fluctuations than had been permitted under the original Bretton Woods agreement. Instead of a permissible band of 1 percent on either side of the official rate, fluctuations up to 4.5 percent were now allowed.[11] The Europeans followed the Smithsonian accord with an arrangement of their own. The six original members of the Common Market, joined by the United Kingdom, Ireland, Denmark, and Norway, agreed to narrower limits of variation in their own currencies within the larger band now applying to all members of the International Monetary Fund (IMF). Hence the description, the "snake in the tunnel." The snake's band of 2.25 percent within the larger IMF band was to be maintained by Europeans buying and selling their currencies among themselves. The arrangement amounted, in effect, to a regional Bretton Woods. The snake got into trouble early when some of its members were forced to drop out because of their inability to remain competitive. The tunnel itself was lost in March 1973, when the attempt to hold together the revised version of Bretton Woods fell apart. As the Bonn summit was approaching, the only thing left was the snake, a European monetary zone with only a handful of nations—Belgium, Denmark, Germany, and the Netherlands—still adhering to the snake's provisions.

The European Monetary System proposed by Schmidt was an extension of the snake. It provided for a set of fixed parities, defined in terms of the European Currency Unit, the ECU, a theoretical unit of account derived from a basket of currencies, with each weighted according to its importance in European trade. This "exchange rate mechanism" used the same band as the snake for the acceptable range of currency fluctuation, but it had additional features that were absent from its predecessor monetary arrangement. It provided, for example, for a credit facility—a fund for assistance to nations whose currencies came under pressure. It also incorporated a "divergence indicator," which signaled when a currency had reached 75 percent of the maximum spread. When this level was reached, a nation was expected to act in support of its exchange rate. It was said that "the new system was not a snake but a rattlesnake, since it embodied a 'divergence indicator' that emitted signals."[12]

To prevent premature opposition, Schmidt and President Giscard d'Estaing, who joined him in the initiative, proceeded in secret, keeping even members of their own governments uninformed. They unveiled their proposal for "a zone of monetary stability in Europe" at a meeting of the European Council in Copenhagen in April 1978. The new European Monetary System (EMS) was endorsed by the heads of government at a second meeting of the council at Bremen ten days before the Bonn summit. It was an arrangement that would enjoy a high level of success from 1979 to 1992 and would set the stage for the introduction of the common currency, the Euro, at the turn of the century.[13]

Schmidt reported at a press conference following the Bremen meeting that both he and Giscard had talked to Carter about the EMS several weeks before and that Carter had given "his political agreement in principle."[14] Anthony Solomon commented in a press interview that "we have always supported the concept of full European economic integration, and I think it's a decision for the Europeans themselves. It's perfectly compatible with the broad international monetary system as we know it today . . . and we would have no problem with it."[15] Despite these public statements, the reaction within the administration was somewhat ambivalent. Treasury officials were concerned that the European Monetary System might pose a threat to American interests. Quite clearly one of the reasons for the creation of the EMS was to reduce European dependence on the dollar. A document is reported to have been prepared by Assistant Secretary of the Treasury C. Fred Bergsten "which allegedly detailed all the problems that the EMS might pose for the United States, and the continuing concern of officials in the Treasury."[16]

Acceptance of the European Monetary System by the United States was, in Schmidt's mind, a quid pro quo for his agreement to stimulate the German economy. This was recognized by the Americans. A briefing paper for the president recommends that he say at Bonn: "We welcome or endorse the European Community decision to explore increased monetary cooperation. . . . We will be happy to cooperate with the European Community in studying aspects of the proposed arrangements." In the briefing paper is a side note to the President: "It seems increasingly clear that Schmidt and Giscard have strong feelings on this subject; how positive you sound in saying the above will have a lot to do with how they react to your statements on other matters."[17]

The European Monetary System was, in the end, not formally endorsed in the final communiqué at Bonn. In place of an endorsement was the rather bland statement that "the representatives of the European Community informed the meeting of the decisions of the European Council at Bremen on 6/7 July to consider a scheme for close monetary cooperation. They welcomed the report and noted that the Community would keep the other participants informed."[18]

The behavior of the dollar was also a matter of discussion at Bonn. Other members again criticized the United States for what they saw as neglect of its currency, a charge they had made repeatedly in the past. Carter restated the American position, minimizing the need for direct intervention in foreign exchange markets and stating that real stability could only be achieved by attacking fundamental causes.[19] While Carter's point was given recognition in the final communiqué, the need for intervention by central banks was also asserted. "The erratic fluctuations in exchange markets in recent months have had a damaging effect on confidence, investment and growth throughout the world. . . . Although exchange rates need to respond to changes in underlying economic and financial conditions among nations, our monetary authorities will continue to intervene to the extent necessary to counter disorderly conditions in the exchange markets."[20]

Shortly after the Bonn summit the dollar went into a serious decline. In the middle of August 1978, there was a series of tense meetings over the state of the dollar. The Swiss franc appreciated a record 5 percent against the dollar in one day; the German mark 2.5 percent. Blumenthal said at a meeting on August 15 with Schultze, Miller, and Eizenstat that there was danger of an international crisis.[21] The fall of the dollar could cause a drop in the stock market, torpedo business confidence, cause inflationary pressures, and lead other countries to retaliate. Miller agreed; an international panic was possible. He was pessimistic about the success of direct intervention in exchange markets. "The market would eat up $5 billion." At a second meeting on the same day, thirteen advisers met with the president, the size of the meeting emphasizing the state of alarm. The dollar had taken another slide during the day. The attendees included, among others, the vice president, Cyrus Vance, Michael Blumenthal, Security Adviser Brzezinski, who seldom attended sessions with the economic advisers, William Miller, Charles Schultze, and Henry Owen. In the general discussion there was agreement that the slide was unwarranted, the reaction psychological, and that it constituted a semi-panic not truly reflective of the underlying situation. Miller said, nevertheless, that they had a clear and present danger. The crisis could take all off the summit hook.[22]

From the beginning of August 1978 to the end of October, the dollar fell 18 percent against the German mark. The final blow came with the market's reaction to a speech delivered by Carter on October 24, 1978. The speech outlined new steps in the administration's continuing anti-inflation program. The initiative promised more budget control, cuts in federal hiring, and a reduction in regulatory costs. It also announced the imposition of new wage/price standards. This speech will be discussed in detail later. Even before it was delivered, the market, reacting to news leaks, judged the program ineffective.[23] The president's instincts in this case were better than that of his advisers. Eizenstat's notes of Carter's meeting with Vice President Mondale, Charles Schultze, and political adviser Hamilton Jordan, five days before the anti-inflation speech, provide a fascinating view of a president deeply concerned about the pressing problems of inflation and the fate of the dollar, and skeptical about the policy steps his advisers have been planning. According to Eizenstat, "he feels there is nothing in the speech [to be delivered on October 24] and we'll be laughed at."[24] Carter was right about the reaction. Following the speech the dollar dropped precipitously. The administration was faced with a major emergency.

In response to the crisis Carter assembled key aides four days later for a dramatic late Saturday night session.[25] The president had left the White House in the early morning for a day of scheduled meetings with Democratic candidates in New York and New England and to attend the annual Jefferson-Jackson Day Dinner. He returned to the White House shortly before his emergency meeting with advisers in the Map Room at 10 o'clock. Blumenthal, Kahn, Miller, Schultze, and Solomon attended the meeting.[26] Eizenstat was out of town for the weekend, but was kept informed by telephone.[27] Blumenthal pushed aggressively for forceful action. He drew on a package prepared by Solomon at his direction some weeks earlier. According to one report, Carter asked pertinent questions for an hour. He was impressed by the argument that a further fall in the dollar, a decline that would increase the cost of American imports, would undermine his anti-inflation program.[28]

The package chosen for defense of the dollar, and announced on Monday November 1, provided for action that was qualitatively different from the interventions of the previous winter. The first component in the package was implementation of a tighter monetary policy to dampen domestic inflationary pressure and to attract foreign investors to the dollar by higher interest rates. The Federal Reserve had already edged up the discount rate, the rate it charges for bank loans, in a series of moves earlier in the year to stabilize the dollar. In the November 1 package, the rate was raised a full percentage point to an historic high, 9.5 percent, the largest increase in the rate since 1933. The package also provided for amassing a large amount of funds for direct intervention in foreign exchange market. A further component provided for the sale of "Carter bonds," instruments reminiscent of the "Roosa bonds," named after Robert Roosa, undersecretary of the treasury under President Kennedy.[29] The Carter bonds, Treasury securities denominated in foreign currencies, would have a market appeal to foreigners who viewed other currencies as safer than the dollar, and the sale of these instruments would absorb dollars in foreign hands. Heavy foreign exchange market intervention took place on November 1. The effect was immediate, with the dollar gaining 10 percent against the German mark.

In December 1977, Undersecretary of the Treasury Solomon had submitted, in his role as acting secretary, a series of recommendations for Carter, who was about to embark on a trip to Europe and the Middle East. The memorandum said that Carter should not agree during the trip "to 'coordinated' or large-scale intervention, to increase domestic interest rates or to curb domestic growth to strengthen the dollar."[30] Over the course of the year things had changed in a dramatic way. In the November 1 initiative, Carter did all three.

The tighter money policy, which was central to the November 1 initiative, further widened the gap between Carter and party liberals, for whom higher interest rates were anathema. Eizenstat has reported that "the Vice President expressed to me his deep concerns that such action would lead to recession and would reverse the progress we had made in reducing unemployment." In his account, Eizenstat goes on to add that "few decisions were more difficult for the President. Following a path of high interest rates was inimical to his background as a small businessman and to his economic policy. But the President agreed to the action, convinced it was necessary to avoid a collapse of the currency."[31] Uncertainty over the dollar continued over the following year, particularly in the summer and early fall of 1979, but the intervention basically ended the crisis that began in the first half of 1977 and continued through 1978. When the oil decontrol debate became more active in early 1979, the fate of the dollar was still a major preoccupation of advisers directly involved in international policy.

THE DECISION FOR PHASED DECONTROL

The January 1979 interagency memorandum, which was referred to earlier, set the stage for the internal debate on oil decontrol and raised the possibility of delaying the decontrol decision, given the disturbing acceleration in inflation. "The options presented below engage one fundamental issue. Should our energy policies and international commitments on energy be deferred or delayed in their implementation so as to minimize the near term inflation effects which an increase in U.S. prices to world levels would entail?" Two options were presented. In option one, "designed to minimize near-term direct inflation effects," decontrol would be stretched out to 1985. In the interim, the price of new oil would gradually rise to world level by October 1, 1981, the date of the expiration of presidential authority. Old oil would remain under controls until January 1985, a provision that would require an extension of the chief executive's power to act. The controls on old oil would remain to minimize the inflationary effects of price increases "since old oil prices [now artificially low] would have to increase by about $10 per barrel to reach current world levels. It is from increases in this oil category that the majority of the inflationary effects of decontrol derive."[32] Under the second option, prices would be allowed to rise to close two-thirds of the gap between the overall average U.S. price and the world price by September 30, 1981, the last date of presidential authority. On October 1, 1981, when controls expired, the balance of the gap would be closed. "It is important to note," the January 3 memorandum continued, "that this approach 'back loads' the price increases resulting from decontrol so that much of the inflationary and other macroeconomic effects are put off until 1980 and 1981."[33] Under option one, the inflationary effect would be inconsequential in 1979 and add only 0.1 percent to the consumer price index in 1980 and 1981. Option two, on the other hand, would add 0.1 percent in 1979, 0.3 percent in 1980, and 0.4 percent in 1981.[34]

Neither of the decontrol options fulfilled the Bonn pledge in a technical sense. The first option, stretching out decontrol to 1985, fell well short of Carter's summit commitment. The second option, a phased decontrol beginning in mid-1979 and ending with decontrol completed on October 1, 1981, came close to complying, falling only nine months short of meeting the promise to let prices rise to the world level by the end of 1980. It was thought that this short a delay would not be a problem for the summit partners. "Your advisors now believe the other Summit participants will accept slippage of the date for reaching world price levels from December 1980, to October, 1981."[35]

Jimmy Carter scheduled an all-day meeting at Camp David on March 19, 1979, for the purpose of firming up a decision. Three days before the meeting Stuart Eizenstat and his assistant for energy issues, Kitty Schirmer, outlined in more detail for the president the key options as they had been honed in the discussions among advisers in the preceding months. "The process of developing the basic crude oil pricing options and the macroeconomic analysis of these approaches has proved more difficult than originally expected."[36] Four choices would be presented for discussion at the Camp David meeting. Option one was full decontrol on June 1, 1979, "the first date upon which you have authority to alter the heretofore Congressionally mandated price schedule." Option two was a phase-out of controls by September 30, 1981, "the date on which existing price control authority expires under the Energy Policy and Conservation Act of 1975." Option three provided for elimination of controls by 1984 through gradual price increases. It also allowed regulatory changes to encourage new production, actions including relief for marginal wells, deep strippers designed to retrieve the last remnants of oil from a well, and those geared to enhanced recovery. The fourth option involved no changes in existing arrangements until inflation abated, an option that implied extension of controls by Congress to 1985.

The first option, outright decontrol, was pushed hard by Secretary of the Treasury Blumenthal. "Immediate decontrol may strike you as an extreme approach, but I think it deserves your serious consideration," he wrote to Carter in a memorandum just before the Camp David meeting.[37] "The decontrol decision offers you an opportunity" he continued, "to take complete charge of a major problem, which has been locked in political stalemate for 8 years, and to resolve it in the national interest with a single, bold stroke. . . . By contrast, all 'phased' decontrol plans involve complex half-measures on pricing that would invite complaints from all sides and could lead to frequent confusing revisions by the bureaucracy or the Congress." He makes a persuasive argument for his recommendation. "Immediate decontrol would deal a major blow to those now pushing up world oil prices . . . and would put you in a position of commanding leadership among our industrial allies." It would boost energy conservation and production and shrink the trade deficit and strengthen the dollar. He was not convinced that immediate decontrol would be unduly inflationary. "It is very important to understand that the inflation estimates for all the decontrol options are extremely uncertain, and that the differences in inflation impact among the options are smaller than the margin of error in the estimates. . . . It would be very imprudent to base this fundamental policy decision on estimates involving several tenths of a percent on the CPI—those estimates are simply not reliable enough." At the Camp David meeting Blumenthal pressed his case, arguing that Carter had the same chance to be bold here as he had been in the Camp David Middle East episode with Begin and Sadat.[38] Blumenthal did not succeed in enlisting supporters for total decontrol, possibly because others thought the step too bold to gain political acceptance. Eizenstat warned the president that full decontrol "would probably provoke serious Congressional attempts to overrule your decision."[39] In a meeting ten days after the Camp David session, Blumenthal continued to press his position. At this meeting Carter specifically rejected the proposal "as too much all at once."[40]

The last option, doing nothing at all, was never really considered as realistic. With total decontrol and the stand-pat option eliminated, the president was left with the choices of phased decontrol by September 30, 1981, or delaying the phase-out until 1984.

Thirteen people attended the Camp David meeting, including the president, the vice president, Chairman Miller from the Federal Reserve Board, and the major principals involved in the decontrol decision.[41] They assembled in Laurel Lodge, which had been used at the Camp David peace talks with Begin and Sadat. The meeting began with a lengthy survey of economic conditions by Charles Schultze. He concentrated his remarks on existing inflationary pressure, which oil price decontrol would intensify. This was an oral presentation of a written report contained in a memorandum sent to the president a few days before the Camp David session.[42] Eizenstat's sketchy notes record the discussion as it turned to the main point of the meeting, oil decontrol.[43] James McIntyre supports the second option, decontrol by October 1, 1981. Alfred Kahn, whose primary responsibility is for the anti-inflation policy, is ambivalent. His basic instinct is to allow free markets to work—in his first assignment in the administration as head of the Civil Aeronautics Board, he decontrolled the airlines—but he is concerned about the effect of higher oil prices on union decisions. "Some part of him favors decontrol," Eizenstat's notes report, "but without a social compact he is against options for immediate decontrol or phased decontrol by October, 1981. Our [anti-inflation] program depends on belief in fairness and equity, he continued. How can we take this to the workers?" Schultze is also worried about losing union support for the wage guidelines. "There is a short chance of wage compliance, he argues, if they deregulate oil prices without some offsets." In addition to some type of assistance for the poor, he seems to have had in mind a cut in the gasoline tax or a postponement of an increase in the Social Security tax to compensate for the effect of the oil price increase. He also had the inflation concern. He had argued at a previous meeting of the Economic Policy Group that they should stretch out the oil pricing schedule as far as they could go despite the Bonn pledge, or do it by September 1981, but end-load the increase in price. Vice president Mondale is strong in his opposition to decontrol. He argues, first of all, that consumer demand is inelastic; consumers are not sensitive to price. The increase in oil prices will have only a small dampening effect on demand, a benefit gained at a high cost.[44] The increase would be very inflationary. It would "blow every fuse in the economy and lead to an increase in inflation at a time of incredible profits." Carter was not unsympathetic to the feelings of his vice president, a man who had labored over his career within the Democratic Party for liberal policies in the tradition of Franklin Roosevelt. "My heart goes out to Fritz," Carter is quoted as saying in Eizenstat's meeting notes.

An important part of the final decision involved the issue of whether or not decontrol should be made contingent on passage of the excess profits tax. International advisers who took a strong position on decontrol also argued forcefully that the decision to decontrol should not be contingent on the passage of a tax. In a joint memorandum to the president in late March, Vance, Blumenthal, and others argued that

> by making decontrol contingent on tax measures, we would achieve neither decontrol nor the tax measures; both liberals and conservatives would have strong reasons to resist the legislation.[45] We would merely create a prolonged and embarrassing congressional stalemate on energy policy—a replay of the last two years of debate on COET [Crude Oil Equalization Tax].... Most importantly, the approach would be seen as an abdication of Presidential leadership. The 1974 controls legislation (enacted by a Democratic congress) vested full pricing authority in the Executive after June 1, 1979 precisely because it was clear to all factions that Congress lacks the political ability to address this matter coherently. Our experience with the COET bill confirms this. To return the decision now to the Congress, during a world oil crisis, would be seen as an evasion of Executive responsibility.[46]

While some advisers, like Vice President Mondale, thought decontrol should be conditional on passage of an excess profits tax, the majority took the opposite position. "Virtually everyone agrees," Eizenstat wrote to the president, "that if you decontrol, it should not be made contingent upon a tax."[47]

While the president and his advisers debated among themselves the course to follow, they also engaged in consultations with governmental agencies and with members of Congress. This interaction was in sharp contrast to the secrecy in which the original energy bill had been developed in the early months of 1977. "We learned something in two years," a White House senior staff member is quoted by the press as saying. "An energy plan didn't have to come down as tablets from Mount Sinai."[48] Eizenstat, who was assigned responsibility for coordinating the discussions, recalls that "for months, every evening for two hours, I convened a large interagency group of top-level policymakers representing almost every agency in government."[49] The consultations with members of Congress were reported to the president in memoranda prepared by Eizenstat and Frank Moore, Carter's congressional liaison. There was a variety of opinion among the legislators, as would be expected. Senate majority leader Byrd supported phased decontrol ending in 1981. "He would also support an excess profits tax—a portion of which would go to the poor and the rest to energy research." Senator Ted Kennedy "will oppose any decontrol phased or immediate." Congressman Al Ullman, chairman of the crucial House Ways and Means Committee, thought the "administration should phase out controls by 1981. The public already expects energy prices to go up," he continued, "so decontrol won't hurt the anti-inflation fight that much. A tax will help on the politics."[50] Moore reported on a separate meeting with senators. "The discussion that ensued was predictable with the senators pushing their local concerns.... There was some consensus, however. The main consensus was that we could get no energy tax passed if decontrol is contingent on adoption of the tax." Senator Long, chairman of the pivotal Senate Finance Committee, said "he had gotten a bad reaction to a pass-the-tax-first plan. It will not work; count him out. Feels it will fail for the same reason COET failed." Senator Frank Church "says it is a dilemma—that if the president goes on TV he will be blamed for prices which are going up anyway."[51]

As the discussions continued, Carter himself had doubts about his pledge at Bonn. These second thoughts are described in Eizenstat's notes taken at a series of meetings. "J. C. says he'd like to try to convince Schmidt and Giscard that the need to control inflation is the most important. He did not know how the Bonn pledge occurred but all of a sudden everyone was pushing him for it. The worse political thing is rising inflation and rising energy prices in 1980. He will try to convince Schmidt."[52] In a meeting with the vice president, McIntyre, Schlesinger, and Schultze, he said that "he has to defend taking $17 billion from consumers [in increased oil payments] and it hangs on his mind. He can't see how to defend the decision in townhall meetings."[53] He must deal, he says at another meeting, "with the albatross of energy and inflation. The Bonn commitment bothers him."[54]

The president was playing a two-level game—one with his international counterparts and one with Congress. Because of Bonn, decontrol of oil became an international as well as a domestic decision. If he decontrolled there would be harsh criticism from domestic players; if he did not decontrol, other nations would react sharply. A memo from Richard Cooper, undersecretary of state for economic affairs, to Eizenstat expresses the need to keep the Bonn pledge: "failure by the United States to honor this commitment . . . may be used by others, especially West Germany, as an excuse to back away from some of their own already-implemented commitments. Our failure would also have an adverse effect on U.S. credibility regarding future commitments."[55] "We would be violating both the letter and the spirit of your Bonn Summit commitment," a joint memorandum to the president from State and Treasury reads. "This course would undermine the credibility of our economic and security policies generally in Europe, Japan, and the Middle East."[56]

In the end, the international commitment dominated the decision. On April 5, 1979, in a nationwide television address, Carter announced that "a phased decontrol of oil prices will begin on June 1 and continue at a fairly uniform rate over the next twenty-eight months." He also asked Congress to pass a windfall profits tax of 50 percent to be levied "on producer revenues attributable to decontrol or to future price increases by OPEC [Organization of Petroleum Exporting Countries]." Proceeds from the tax would go to an "energy security fund" to help low income families pay for fuel and to provide subsidies for mass transit and energy investments. The decontrol program began on schedule on June 1, 1979.[57] It was not contingent on passage of the windfall profits tax. In the end the tax fared better in Congress than expected. Faced with the responsibility of explaining enormous industry profits to the voters if it did not act—particularly those arising from the OPEC price increases—Congress eventually passed a version of the excess profits tax. Carter signed the bill early in April 1980.[58] Also passed, close to the time of the tax legislation, were the final elements of Carter's energy program, a synthetic fuels program, a standby gasoline rationing plan, and a solar energy initiative.

"Although it grievously hurt him with major elements of the Party," Eizenstat was to write later, "it was one of his most courageous and most important decisions, and broke the Gordian knot which had prevented a sound energy policy."[59] Carter was aware of the political damage that would follow the decision, a damage Congress refused to share. "Sixty-eight percent of the public," he said in one of his meetings, "thinks government is misleading them on energy."[60] For unrelated reasons, the beginning of the rise in petroleum prices coincided with a period of gasoline shortage. Voters were particularly incensed by the gas lines which started in California in the spring of 1979, and rapidly spread to the eastern part of the country. They lacked the patience to take time to understand the complex decontrol procedures for various categories of oil as outlined in Carter's decision. They did understand the inconvenience of waiting in long lines for gasoline. The administration had difficulty in explaining the shortage to the public, the reasons for which were not entirely clear. It seems to have been due to such factors as a delayed impact of the cutback in exports from Iran and to low inventories of American refineries. Voters attributed it to a government-industry conspiracy. Eizenstat briefed the president on events surrounding the gasoline shortage in an often cited memorandum forwarded to Japan, where Carter was attending the 1979 economic summit. "Nothing which has occurred in the Administration to date . . . has added so much water to our ship. Nothing else has so frustrated, confused, angered the American people—or so targeted their distress at you personally, as opposed to your advisors, or Congress."[61]

THE BONN SUMMIT, EPILOGUE

The Bonn summit occupies a unique place among the summits that have taken place since the first one at Rambouillet. Bonn represents the high-water mark of a Keynesian type of demand management. The commitments were basically met by all participating nations.[62] The most lasting effect of the summit was the deregulation of oil. The impact of the expansionary macroeconomic policies is more open to debate. Most observers would agree with one assessment that "the agreement reached at Bonn stands as a striking example of the use of the summit process to promote the coordination of economic policies. Unfortunately," the commentary continues, "the merits of the program were rapidly overshadowed by external events. Six months after the summit, the Shah was overthrown by revolution in Iran, and the world economy thrown into disarray by the second major oil shock in five years. Trade deficits deepened and inflation accelerated in all of the non-oil-producing economies of the free world. Germany itself experienced in 1979 its first current account deficit since 1965 and saw its inflation rate rise above 5 percent"[63]

Critics of the Bonn summit cite the aftermath of the conference as an example of the futility of attempting international macroeconomic coordination. A prevalent opinion in Germany was that surrender to American pressure to engage in a fine-tuning exercise in stimulative fiscal policy was responsible for German inflation problems in 1979. The evidence for this position is not strong.[64] Stimulative fiscal policy was not without precedent in Germany in the 1970s. Budget decisions were taken to offset "fiscal drag," the tendency of tax receipts to increase more rapidly in an expansion than the nation's income. "The summit was apparently a factor in determining the timing of tax cuts," says one close observer of the German economy in the Bonn period. "That is a far cry, however, from the claim that the German government reluctantly but altruistically agreed to something at the summit that was contrary to their own interests."[65] As Bonn approached, Schmidt's advisers were urging him to adopt expansionary action. Fiscal stimulus would most likely have been initiated even if the Bonn summit had not taken place. As I pointed out earlier, American pressure was useful for Schmidt's purposes in the internal German political debate. "The oil price shock was clearly the major inflationary burden for the German economy," Undersecretary of the Treasury Anthony Solomon has argued, "not the Bonn summit agreement."[66]

In any event, the fiscal actions that followed the Bonn commitment were offset, in part, by steps taken by the Bundesbank in 1979.[67] A tighter monetary policy was imposed, not to offset the fiscal measures, but rather in reaction to the inflationary pressures that followed the oil shock. The November 1978 action by the United States in support of the dollar gave the Germans more freedom to conduct an independent monetary policy, to reverse the excessive increase in money due to dollar support actions in 1978.[68] When the restrictive monetary policy was combined with the expansive fiscal action, the effect on the inflation rate in Germany of the Bonn commitments was modest. Richard Cooper, in answer to the criticism that Bonn contributed to subsequent inflation, has pointed out that "in fact, the rise in the GNP [gross national product] deflator in Germany remained unchanged from 1978 to 1979 and actually fell in Japan from 4.0 percent in 1978 to 2.0 percent in 1979."[69]

It is interesting to note Helmut Schmidt's later thoughts about Bonn. One student of the summits reports that "in an interview with the author in February, 1983, Chancellor Schmidt, who had for several years after the second oil shock been a critic of the Bonn agreements, returned to his original support for the program: 'The Bonn summit was successful because all the participants had a real desire to achieve concrete results. That required give-and-take. Any negotiation does, whether it be with the Soviet Union or domestically between different political groups. At Bonn, as host, I made sure that each government contributed to the total package.'"[70]

The interpretation of the effects of the Bonn summit was more positive in Japan. The Industrial Bank of Japan commented that "in line with President Carter's locomotive theory, fiscal policy was used to stimulate domestic demand, while overseas, America's expansionary economic policy encouraged the recycling of oil money into developing countries to create a development investment boom, which in turn helped to increase exports of Japanese industrial goods. Thus the Japanese economy was helped tremendously by Carter's 'locomotive theory' and by the development investment boom in the developing countries."[71]

Going beyond the matter of how the Bonn summit should be rated, there is a broader issue to be considered—the issue of whether or not, in general, international cooperation on macroeconomic policy is effective. The reasons for coordination's appeal are straightforward. Technology has reduced economic distances. In the 1950s someone wishing to trade in foreign exchange markets could do so only in the conventional business hours of their own time zone. Today they can buy and sell around the clock. Barriers to trade in goods and services have been reduced dramatically through a series of multilateral trade negotiations over the postwar period. We live in a world of global markets. Even though this argument has strong intuitive appeal, a large number of economists, probably the majority, are skeptical about the benefits of macroeconomic cooperation.

Most of the concerns revolve around the uncertainty associated with joint action.[72] There is, first of all, uncertainty about the initial conditions of the economies entering into agreement. Economic data published by governments are subject to frequent revisions so that at any given moment policy makers are unsure of the reliability of important indicators. When Gerald Ford assumed the presidency, the critical challenge seemed to be inflation. The president assembled a national conference of specialists to dramatize the problem. WIN buttons—a call to action ("Whip Inflation Now")—were produced and distributed. We know in retrospect that at the time of this call for fiscal discipline and consumer spending restraint, the recession of 1974–75, the worst since World War II, had already begun. The administration had to abruptly reverse course. At the time Carter launched his stimulus program, the president's advisers and outside experts underestimated the strength of the inflationary momentum already building in the economy. The problem of incorrectly gauging the condition of an economy is magnified when more than one nation is involved.

Even more important than the uncertainty surrounding the initial conditions is the uncertainty about the analytical model underlying policy makers' decisions. There are various interpretations among experts about the effect that policy measures have on employment, price stability, and long-term growth. Economists tell different stories about "how the world works." There are sharp differences about the values of the policy "multipliers" that measure the impact that changes in the money supply or the government's budget have on policy targets. The size of these multipliers varies considerably in competing schools of thought. This uncertainty is magnified when several nations are involved. To put the matter in terms that reflect a decent amount of humility, decision makers are "uncertain which of the competing models represents the least inadequate approximation of the 'true' model (the actual relationships that will in reality determine the consequences of policy actions).... This analytical uncertainty is the single greatest impediment to sound policymaking within national governments and to successful international cooperation for macroeconomic policies."[73]

Added to these technical difficulties is the fact that social objectives differ among nations. In the early Carter years the administration was concerned about inflation, but gave higher priority to full employment. The Germans took the opposite position. Differences in objectives call for different types of policy actions. Even if countries have the same objective functions, the precise measurement of these objectives is often in doubt. The statistical definition of full employment was, as discussed earlier, a subject of debate during the Carter administration, with estimates of the full employment-unemployment rate ranging from 4 to 6 percent. One is never sure how close to full employment an economy is at any given moment. "The most enduring disagreement in OECD [Organization for Economic Cooperation and Development] policy making," one economist has observed, "is the perception by other countries that there is room for demand expansion in the German economy (and often in the Japanese economy as well), in contrast to the perception by the responsible policymakers in those countries that there is not."[74]

Even if countries have the same priorities, there is political uncertainty about the ability of leaders to deliver on commitments. Carter struggled with domestic interests to fulfill his Bonn commitments, as did Helmut Schmidt in Germany.

A number of studies have attempted to measure the benefits of coordination. At a Brookings conference in the latter part of the 1980s, twelve leading econometric models were used to simulate the results of various policy actions assumed to be taken by the United States and its trading partners.[75] There was considerable disagreement among the models. A later study, which drew on the Brookings simulations, found that coordination was beneficial to the United States and to other countries in only a little over half of the cases. Coordination could just as easily leave the countries worse off as better off.[76] Other economists do not take as pessimistic a view, but even in the more optimistic accounts, the size of benefits are not estimated to be large.[77] "It has become conventional wisdom, based on the empirical studies," reports one researcher, "to say that the incremental gains from coordination of the largest economies in the OECD are small or at most modest in size."[78] Benefits may be, in part, a matter of timing. One economist argues that gains in a period of crisis can be large. "The uncertainty in these periods," he argues, "is precisely what provides the incentive to coordinate, rather than being an obstacle to coordination."[79]

Regardless of the skepticism among professional economists about the benefits of international cooperation, policy makers continue to attempt improvement in their mutual welfare through cooperation, though in an episodic way and with efforts concentrated in periods of crisis. In President Reagan's first term the administration adopted, under the leadership of Treasury Secretary Donald Regan, a laissez-faire policy on international economic relations. The administration refrained from initiating coordination proposals and from intervening in foreign exchange markets on behalf of the dollar. In the second term, George Baker replaced Regan as secretary and reawakened interest in policy coordination. Foreign exchange coordination aimed at depreciating an overvalued dollar became a priority. The change in policy can be dated to a meeting of the major nations at the Plaza Hotel in New York in early fall 1985, where an agreement was reached to lower the dollar's value. Accusations that Baker was "talking down the dollar" were rampant. Initiatives for intervention in the foreign exchange market were combined with multilateral surveillance of economic policies—surveillance authorized by the Group of Seven at the Tokyo Economic Summit in 1986. At the same time the United States pushed the Germans and the Japanese to stimulate their economies to reduce their trade surpluses and the American trade deficit. In a bilateral agreement with the United States, the Japanese agreed to stimulative monetary and fiscal actions. The whole episode is reminiscent of actions in the Carter administration.[80] An attempt at coordination was repeated in the Clinton administration when the United States, along with other nations, pressed the Japanese to cut taxes and raise spending to stimulate their economy and to act as a regional locomotive during the Asian crisis of 1998.

In his final and personal evaluation of the Bonn summit, Anthony Solomon said the following:

> [T]here is a good argument that the major lost opportunity of the Bonn summit agreement was that not enough pressure was put on the United States to face squarely its inflation problem and take stronger measures early enough to bring inflation under control. To be sure, there was some language in the Bonn communiqué reaffirming a commitment by the United States to several modest anti-inflationary measures. But a more specific program of action, mirroring the quantitative undertaking of the

countries that agreed to stimulate demand, should have been proposed. And it might very well have gone through. The result would have been to have speeded the adjustment of U.S. inflation, and perhaps to have avoided some of the disturbances that subsequently plagued the financial markets.[81]

The problem of inflation in the post-Bonn years is the subject of the next chapter.

CHAPTER 9 | **THE WORSENING INFLATION**

The deceleration program announced in April 1978, discussed in an earlier chapter, was designed to slow the momentum of the inflation by asking employers and labor to limit their increases in prices and wages below the average of the previous two years. If the rate of increase of wages and prices could be reduced, inflation could eventually be brought under control. It was evident toward the end of the year that the program was not working. The president's economic advisers went back to the drawing board. The result of their discussions was a proposal for a tougher incomes policy: formal wage and price guidelines with specific quantitative constraints.

The resistance of labor had been, from the beginning, a stumbling block to initiating formal wage-price guidelines. Secretary Marshall, a voice for labor within the administration, had earlier opposed attempts to force unions to abide by strict wage restraints. Reacting to the disturbing increase in inflationary momentum, he shifted his position. Schultze described the event in a post-presidency interview. "There was a strange incident that occurred before we actually did get into the guidelines. It was a memo from Marshall, that surprised everybody, including himself, I think, that led to an opening for guidelines. When I first read the memo, I couldn't believe that it was coming from Marshall, and we said let's seize it and run with it."[1]

Eizenstat reported to the president on a meeting with Strauss, Bosworth, Schultze, and Marshall. There was a consensus among the group that "our current inflation program is not succeeding and has no 'teeth.'" More work is needed on Marshall's proposal, but "its general thrust is important in moving us into the next—and tougher 'phase' of our anti-inflation program—namely a phase which would have much more explicit 'standards' (guideposts) tied together with specific teeth in the form of government action taken toward those industries and unions which fail to follow the standards."[2]

In mid-September 1978, two months after the Bonn summit, Blumenthal, acting as chairman of the Economic Policy Group, sent a lengthy memorandum to the president outlining the new anti-inflation policy.[3] A wage standard for 1979 would require a 7 percent limit on annual increases in wages plus private fringe benefits. The price standard for 1979 "would continue to be one of deceleration based on a target for economy-wide price increases, consistent with the 7 percent wage standard, of 5¾ percent." Blumenthal's 5.75 percent price rule was the result of adjusting the 7 percent wage increase for an estimated increase in productivity, which would permit the wage increase without a change in labor cost.[4] A lowering of the wage standard by 1 percentage point annually results in a price forecast for 1981 of a little over 4 percent. The Council on Wage and Price Stability would monitor industry performance. With the introduction of formal guidelines, the anti-inflation program would begin to resemble the Kennedy incomes policy of the 1960s. Alfred Kahn was persuaded to move from the Civil Aeronautics Board to be head of the Council on Wage and Price Stability and be the president's personal inflation adviser.

The idea of a federal procurement policy, which had been advanced earlier, was revived. Firms that do business with the government would be required to certify compliance with the standards for wage and price increases on their total line of business.[5] Most of Carter's advisers supported the idea of the procurement sanction. The Office of Management and Budget opposed it because, OMB stated, "the minimal impact of such an enforcement would not be worth the substantial (and as yet incompletely planned) administration effort that would be required. Legally the program is far from a sure thing."[6] The president decided to include the procurement sanction in his speech on October 24, 1978.[7]

Another major feature of the policy initiative was a pledge of budget restraint. Charles Schultze recalled in a post-presidency interview that "the gut of the speech was the guidelines. But at the same time, there were elements in there that recognized the fact that you can't do it just by guidelines, we also have to lean on the economy a little harder by way of fiscal policy."[8] In the speech, the president made a specific budget commitment:

Alfred Kahn, Carter's inflation fighter, with Stuart Eizenstat to his right and John Wright, deputy director of the Office of Management and Budget, to his left. Courtesy of the Jimmy Carter Library.

"Next year, with tough restraints on Federal spending and moderate economic growth in prospect, I plan to reduce the budget deficit to less than one-half what it was when I ran for office—to $30 billion or less."[9]

The wording of the budget component of the new anti-inflation program was a matter of disagreement within the administration. Eizenstat wanted to avoid too precise a deficit reduction number in the speech. He wrote to the president that "some members of the EPG [Economic Policy Group] suggest that any inflation statement announce either a specific number or a narrow range of numbers . . . for the deficit we will propose for the Fiscal Year 1980 budget [the budget that would be proposed to Congress in January 1979]. In my view that would be a serious mistake. We should wait till late this year, when a forecast of the economy is available."[10] In a memorandum to Carter, Schultze described Secretary Blumenthal as taking a tough position, believing "that the anti-inflation program will be neither effective nor credible unless the Fiscal Year 1980 budget deficit is cut below $30 billion, which he believes is feasible if we are willing to eliminate some programs and show extraordinary restraint in spending generally."[11] Mondale advised the president not to propose "any specific numbers before January when you know more."[12] Schultze was uncomfortable with making a precise numerical pledge when the final results of the budget then in force were not yet known.

The decision to include the deficit pledge in the speech went right down to the wire. Carter's first inclination, as revealed in the option selected in a decision memo, was simply to announce a significant deficit reduction. In the final speech he chose the tougher statement recommended by Blumenthal. Occasionally there is drama in politics. Schultze tells the story about the final decision on the budget statement:

> I do recall at the last minute, just before the speech was literally being typed for the teleprompter, the President had a meeting with Henry Belman and Muskie and other members of the Budget Committee. Whether the House members were there, I don't know. I guess the members of the budget committees were there, and they strongly urged him to make such a pledge. I remember his calling McIntyre and me into a little side room and asking, "Should I?" I remember it was one of those things where you've got two minutes to make up your mind. I was for it on the grounds, "well it would strengthen the commitment he makes in the speech on the one hand, but before you know what all the numbers are going to be, what are you getting yourself into." Finally I said, "OK, go ahead." Mcintyre had always been for it, and I remember Eizenstat being mad as hell that this was made when he wasn't there. Literally, they changed it on the teleprompter, so he could include that thirty billion dollar budget deficit commitment.[13]

THE TAX INCENTIVE PLAN

The key problem in getting the cooperation of labor was, as our earlier discussion suggested, the possibility that the increase in prices would be larger than the increase in wages mandated by the wage standard. "I do not believe it is reasonable to expect a voluntary program to survive," Labor Secretary Marshall wrote in a memorandum to the president in early 1979, "if the volunteers feel they will lose ground to inflation."[14] "What we had been telling them (not thinking about oil prices)," Schultze was to say later, "was play ball and you won't lose. Now we're telling them play ball with us, and by the way, if there is a price increase, don't get it back in your wages. And that becomes a much tougher game."[15] Charles Schultze recommended a bold tactic to solve this problem: "real wage insurance" or the "Tax Incentive Plan" (TIP). Under this plan, if the inflation rate rose above 7 percent—the limit on wage increases allowed by the wage standard—workers who observed the standard would receive a tax rebate to compensate. "The real wage insurance program can allow us," Schultze explained, "to assure any groups of workers who cooperate with the program that even with bad breaks they won't lose by their cooperation. . . . In the public's mind this proposal would remove one of organized labor's major *substantive* arguments against the wage standard."[16]

The story of how this suggestion got included in the president's speech is told by Schultze in a post-presidency interview. The idea for an incentive plan to get labor's acceptance of a wage standard had been discussed in economic literature by Arthur Okun and others. Barry Bosworth brought it up for discussion within the administration. At first it was not well received. "The staff," Schultze recalled,

> came up with what I would say was, on balance, a very lukewarm to negative attitude on the TIP; they didn't come up with a flat recommendation. . . . By staff I mean Council members and staff—same thing in Budget and Treasury. . . . I presented that report to the assembled Economic Policy Group. This was a fairly large group including Bob Strauss and Fred Kahn and the Budget Director, some White House staff and everybody. And the TIP idea was presented, and all of a sudden Bob Strauss' eyes started flowing and all the politicians in the room and everybody else got all excited. "Great idea; we've got something new. Don't drop it. It's the only new thing we have, and everything else in the package has been leaked, but this is a marvelous idea. We have a new Carter initiative." They brushed aside all the technical objections. Mind you, I was for it, so I'm not objecting. But I was for it with a lot of questions. But all of sudden it just swept the room.[17]

The president announced in his speech on October 24, 1978, that he would "ask the congress next January to enact a program that workers who observe the standards would be eligible for a tax rebate if the inflation rate is more than 7 percent."[18] The proposal had a frosty reception in Congress. The administration was probably lucky that it died a quiet death, for the cost would have been high. An interesting part of the Schultze memorandum describing the plan to the president is the estimate of the risk in terms of payout if price increases were to exceed wage increases. For an unacceptable

Carter at his desk in the Oval Office awaiting the start of his October 24, 1978, inflation speech. Courtesy of the Jimmy Carter Library.

amount, according to Schultze's computations, a number of unlikely bad breaks would have had to occur.[19] Schultze later recalled:

> [What] embarrassed the economic advisers was a probability run that we did. The key thing on the TIP was what are the probabilities of inflation going high enough above our threshold that you really have a big fiscal payout. For that to happen you had to get a fairly sizable growth in prices relative to wages. A large drop in real wages had to happen, the way we had rigged it. I remember we had run the numbers, and we went to the President with this probability distribution which had been run off the past data. We said, "Mr. President, the chances are one in a hundred that you'd ever have to pay off as much as X. You'd have to have another oil price increase as big as the last one, and we all know that's not going to happen." It [the 1973–74 oil shock] was one case, nothing else in history like that. It would never happen.[20]

Unfortunately it did.

The October 1978 initiative did not go well. The unions did not agree to go along. In addition, an AFL-CIO (American Federation of Labor and Congress of Industrial Organizations) suit to have the procurement sanction declared unconstitutional hindered imposition of the one sanction the administration possessed. A district court ruled against the administration. Stuart Eizenstat and Alfred Kahn wrote to the president in early June 1979, that the court decision "is a potentially fatal setback not just because the major threat behind the guidelines has now been removed, but because the entire anti-inflation program is now almost universally seen as all but officially dead."[21] The ruling was probably not that important in retrospect. An appeals court overruled the district court, but the General Accounting Office later reported that there were "no known instances where a violator has been denied a government contract."[22]

THE INFLATION OF THE LAST TWO YEARS

The inflation record during Carter's term can be divided into two equal parts. In 1977 the consumer price index rose 6.5 percent, slightly above the rate the president inherited from the previous administration. In 1978 the inflation rate rose to 7.7 percent. The acceleration of inflation in 1978 made it clear that the economy was entering a new phase. The administration's reaction was embodied in the anti-inflation plan announced in October.

The last half of the Carter term saw an inflation explosion. Prices reached a double-digit range in 1979 and 1980. In mid-March 1979, five months after the guidelines program was announced, Schultze presented a discouraging picture in a lengthy paper to the Economic Policy Group. "Since our economic policy for 1979–80 was formulated late last year, a number of developments have occurred that immediately threaten the success of the anti-inflation program. While we expected high inflation to continue in the first part of 1979, before the anti-inflation program had time to bite, price increases in the last several months have actually accelerated."[23] Lyle Gramley and Daniel Brill reported that the consumer price index increased to a 13 percent rate for the first four months of 1979.[24]

Despite labor's hostile reception of the wage-price guidelines, the early surge in inflation was not due to increases in wages. What killed the October 1978 anti-inflation program, almost before it came into effect, was a series of external supply shocks. Food prices continued to be a problem as they had in 1977 and 1978. In June 1979, Charles Schultze reported to the Steering Committee of the Economic Policy Group that agriculture prices rose at a 15 percent annual rate from the fourth quarter of 1978 to April 1979. He expected agricultural prices to rise another 10 percent from the fourth quarter of 1978 to the fourth quarter of 1979 and continue at an 11 percent rate over 1980.[25]

Carter at an inflation breakfast. *Left to right*: Charles Schultze, Michael Blumenthal, Alfred Kahn, Carter, Walter Mondale, and Barry Bosworth. Courtesy of the Jimmy Carter Library.

The increased cost of home ownership, a component of the consumer price index, plagued the administration over the length of the presidential term. Between 1977 and 1980 ownership costs rose at an average annual rate of 13 percent. Inflation in housing was real enough. It reflected, in part, increases in interest rates due to the effort of lenders to compensate for inflation. But the increase in home ownership cost was seriously overstated in official reports due to incorrect measurement of housing costs in the index. Prior to 1983 the Bureau of Labor Statistics, which prepares the consumer price index, measured housing costs using current prices of new houses and current mortgage rates. Obviously, most owners are not living in new homes or paying the current mortgage rate. The bureau now uses revised methods of calculation to eliminate this incorrect measurement. If one looks at the period 1978 to 1998, the biggest distortion of the measured cost of living occurred between 1978 and 1982.[26] A dramatic example can be found in the first quarter of 1980, when the consumer price index showed the inflation rate as close to 18 percent. An alternative deflator used for personal consumption expenditures by the Department of Commerce—a deflator with a more accurate method for measuring housing costs—reported an inflation rate of 12.3 percent for the same quarter.[27] Not only was the cost of housing overstated in the consumer price index, but the distortion was automatically passed on as an increase in wages for union contracts with a cost-of-living adjustment provision (COLA). In 1980, 60 percent of the major unions had the cost adjustment included in their negotiated agreement.[28]

The supply shock that caused the most damage was the increase in crude oil prices by the Organization of Petroleum Exporting Countries (OPEC) in early 1979, only three months after the introduction of wage-price standards the previous October. The twofold increase in oil prices over the course of the year was smaller, in terms of percentage, than the increase in 1973–74 when prices quadrupled, but the economic effect was as great because of the increase in oil imports following the Nixon years. The impact of this second oil shock of the 1970s was amplified by the deregulation of domestic oil prices in a series of steps that began in June 1979—a move designed, as I discussed earlier, to bring the price of domestically produced oil in line with world prices. The first phase of the deregulation added only marginally to the price of oil in the remainder of 1979, but administration economists thought decontrol would have a larger effect in 1980.[29] Whatever the impact of deregulation, Lyle Gramley and Daniel Brill reported in mid-1979 that the energy component of the consumer price index rose in the first four months of 1979 at an annual rate of 32 percent.[30] After the oil shock, Eizenstat said later, "Economic Policy Group meetings became studies in frustration and damage control."[31]

The increase in oil prices intensified the rate of inflation, but it did more. It worsened the terms of trade relative to OPEC nations. The United States had to give more goods and services to the oil producing countries to obtain oil. Put in another way, paying more for oil meant that consumers had less for other purchases. The effect was to dampen domestic demand and production. "During the next 12 to 18 months," Gramley and Brill wrote to the Economic Policy Group's Steering Committee in May of 1979, "our economy will experience both slow economic growth and high inflation." Stuart Eizenstat underlined this sentence in his copy of the memorandum and wrote in the margin, "political disaster."[32]

The administration estimated that about 50 percent of the consumer price index—food, housing costs, and energy—was not covered by the wage-price guidelines. Even if the incomes policy had been 100 percent effective in restraining wages, prices would have gone up at a disturbing pace. In the face of historically high inflation rates, wages did rise. Because of workers' attempts to maintain real income, Treasury Secretary Miller reported in congressional testimony in mid-1980, compensation per hour (wages plus fringes) had been boosted to the 9 to 10 percent range.[33]

The second-year wage-price standards were due to be announced in October 1979. They would have to be presented for public comment in August. A decision was made to set up a series of consultations with business, unions, and members of Congress. In preparation for these meetings, the Steering Committee of the Economic Policy Group asked the president for guidance as to his wishes.[34] Included among the ideas floated by the president—with both pros and cons presented—was a request for legislation authorizing fines for violations, and to bar firms or state and local governments that violated the guidelines from various federal benefits. Also included was a proposal for legislation requiring firms to prenotify the Council on Wage and Price Stability of desired price and wage increases, and empowering the council to suspend the increases for a period—for example, 60–90 days. None of these proposals were acted on, and their somewhat unrealistic quality, when viewed in hindsight, illustrates the truth behind the statement, made by one economist, that "controls or incomes policies are policies of desperation."[35]

At the end of September 1979, just before the second-year standards were to be announced, the administration and the leaders of the labor movement reached a "National Accord."[36] At the center of the accord was a Tripartite Pay Advisory Committee, appointed by the president. With equal representation from labor, business, and the general public, the committee was charged with advising the Council on Wage and Price Stability. The pay standard for the second year would not be announced until the committee had made its recommendation. When the committee made its decision, it recommended a 7.5 to 9.5 percent range of allowable pay increases. Carter's advisers felt that a 9.5 percent ceiling on wage increases was like imposing no restraint at all. There was tension between the Advisory Committee, the Council on Wage and Price Stability, and the Economic Policy Group.[37] In a major inflation speech in mid-March 1980, the president accepted the committee's pay increase range.[38] Presumably, a concession on the pay allowance was necessary to get labor's cooperation. With the inflation rate running at 13 percent, Carter was lucky to get a 9.5 percent ceiling. He pressed, however, for a more intense monitoring of the agreed upon guidelines. In his inflation speech he announced a tripling of the Council on Wage and Price Stability's staff. The council worked throughout the administration with limited personnel. Even with this increase, the staff was only one-tenth of the staff that enforced the wage and price controls under Nixon.[39]

The attempt to maintain a credible incomes policy was a futile exercise.

Alfred Kahn addresses the cabinet. Seated to Carter's right is Secretary of State Cyrus Vance and to his left is Secretary of Defense Harold Brown. Courtesy of the Jimmy Carter Library.

Alfred Kahn reported to the Economic Policy Group in June 1980 that "the pay standard is being quite widely ignored." As an example, he noted that in the first quarter 53 contracts in the construction industry, out of a total of 135, were in a range between 10 and 20 percent.[40] The Council on Wage and Price Stability wrote to the Economic Policy Group in mid-June that some advisers had discussed "the desirability of simply extending the pay (and possibly the price) standard through end of calendar-year 1980," instead of announcing a revised standard on schedule on October 1.[41] Treasury Secretary Miller wrote to the president at the end of July that "trying to extend them, with minor modifications, into a third year will probably be fruitless."[42]

Through the last half of 1980, the wage and price standards had little effect. The death knell of the program came after the November 4 election, when the Pay Advisory Committee urged that the standards program be abandoned. "The present voluntary program has lost its capacity to command effective support," the committee said. "Inflation has been too high and enduring and the regulations too complex and artificial."[43]

The General Accounting Office (GAO) published in December 1980 a study of the effectiveness of the wage-price guidelines pursued by the Carter administration.[44] "The main question we try to answer," said the report, "is how effective have the Council's wage and price standards been in restraining inflation? This is a difficult question. In the end, however, we could find no convincing evidence that the standards have had any effect on the rate of inflation. In our judgment, inflation would have been no worse during the past two years without the standards."[45] Administration economists disagreed sharply with the Accounting Office's conclusion. They particularly objected to one of the criteria used by the GAO in determining the success of the standards: a simple question of whether or not inflation declined during the program. The Council on Wage and Price Stability insisted that the standards covered only half of the prices in the economy. They were not designed to restrain cattle prices, crude oil prices, or housing costs, and to judge them on the basis of the overall inflation rate was unfair. The General Accounting Office report found no restraint even on prices and wages covered by the standards. Again, the administration economists disagreed. Prices and wages rose in the covered sectors, they argued, but not as much as they would have without standards. Both sides marshaled econometric results to defend their point of view. The 1981 *Economic Report of the President* issued just before the administration left office stated that "studies by the Council on Wage and Price Stability and the Council of Economic Advisers have estimated that annual wage increases were 1 to 1½ percentage points lower during 1979 than they would have been without the standards. The consequent reduction in labor costs also appears to have been passed on to consumers through lower price increases. A more recent evaluation of the pay and price standards by CWPS suggests that the program continued to have a moderating effect in the second year."[46]

A fair conclusion seems to be that the effect of the guidelines was marginal at best. Schultze agreed in an interview done after the administration left office. "We put the guidelines in in late 1978 for the year 1979," Schultze said. "The key thing on the guidelines is the wage part of it. And immediately, almost, you start getting these big oil price increases, because the Saudis announced their first stage runup in December, 1978. So from the beginning, I think they helped a little bit, not much, the first year. At any rate we were always behind the curve. Always reluctant to really alienate the labor allies. I'm not going to suggest that you could have done a lot with the guidelines anyway, but we were too little and too late."[47] Lyle Gramley, who served on the Council of Economic Advisers with Schultze, has taken the position that the effects of the guidelines were even less than marginal. When asked his opinion of the incomes policy in a later interview, Gramley replied: "I told Charlie, at the time, this is largely a waste of time. The effects of this are going to be so marginal that we shouldn't be spending our time on it, unless we are willing to engineer, develop and implement a much more effective anti-inflation policy."[48]

FAILURE OF THE ANTI-INFLATION POLICY

Three decades after the Great Inflation of the 1970s, economists still disagree about the causes of the historic acceleration of prices. There are two interpretations of events. One emphasizes the severe supply shocks of the decade. The other argues that excessive demand was the main cause.

The administration began, as we have said, with a Keynesian slant and with the conviction that a stimulus policy was needed to move the economy toward full employment. Excess capacity would allow an expansion without exciting inflation. Inflationary pressure that developed could be handled through an incomes policy. The breakdown of the strategy, Schultze and other advisers would argue, was due to supply shocks. The most thorough examination of this thesis has been done by Alan Blinder of Princeton.[49] After detailed analysis of the effect of the external shocks that took place—not only during the Carter administration, but also in 1973–75 under Nixon—Blinder concluded that these shocks were the main reason for the Great Inflation of the 1970s. "Despite the cacophony of complaints about 'ruinous' budget deficits and 'excessive' monetary growth, the headline-grabbing double-digit inflations of 1974 and 1979–80 were mainly of the special-factor variety."[50]

Other economists have emphasized excess demand as the fundamental cause of the inflation.[51] External shocks of the 1970s, they argue, provide a partial explanation, but the effect was temporary. Had a proper amount of demand restraint been applied, the damage would have been less. The Carter years were only one part of the epoch of the Great Inflation. The period began with the excessive demand initiated by the Johnson administration in the late 1960s and continued under Nixon in the early 1970s. Strong public support for the priority of a full employment policy led the various administrations to adopt an expansionary policy when unemployment threatened, putting the nation in a vulnerable position when external disturbances occurred. The baseline inflation was some 5 percent a year in the early 1970s before there were severe supply shocks.[52] When the shocks did occur, there was a reluctance to adopt a highly restrictive monetary and fiscal policy that would put the economy into a severe recession. Richard Nixon chose mandatory wage and price controls to contain high inflation rates rather than adopt stringent demand restraint.

When Carter introduced his stimulus policy after assuming office, he was not out of line with the history of the previous decade. In the face of rising unemployment, President Ford succeeded in getting a tax rebate of $8 billion along with other tax credits in 1975.[53] Given the most severe recession since the Great Depression, he could hardly stand passive. Ford chose a temporary tax cut in order not to complicate future efforts to balance the budget at a later date. Carter chose a tax rebate for the same reason.[54] Carter's 1977 stimulus package turned out in the end to be relatively mild. When the rebate and an optional tax credit for business were eliminated from the original proposal, the size of the package was reduced by about $14 billion. Joseph Pechman of the Brookings Institution, one of the leading scholars on budget matters at the time, concluded that "ironically, in view of the positions of the candidates on the economic issues during the 1976 campaign, President Carter's fiscal 1977 budget turned out to be somewhat less stimulative than President Ford's."[55] Alan Greenspan, chairman of the Council of Economic Advisers under Ford, reflected the same type of opinion. "I thought the campaign rhetoric implied a very significant policy change, one that would be a mistake and re-ignite inflationary forces. As it turned out, for the first nine months of the Carter administration, policies were not really very different from those that Ford probably would have followed."[56]

The same cannot be said for the tax cut proposal submitted to Congress in January 1978. From the transition days following the 1977 election through the first two years of the administration, Carter's economists were aggressive in policy strategy. Charles Schultze wrote in a memorandum to Secretary Blumenthal in mid-1977, that "our latest economic forecast . . . results in a GNP [gross national product] growth of only 4¾ percent from fourth quarter 1977 to fourth quarter 1978. I believe we ought to start thinking very soon about what we do if economic events between now and year-end confirm this outlook. In particular, how do we plan for what may be a needed tax cut in 1978?"[57] Later in 1977, the deputies' forecasting team confirmed Schultze's concerns. It wrote to the Economic Policy Group in October that "we now expect real GNP growth over the 4 quarters of 1978 to be just over 4 percent . . . with the rate of growth tapering off to 3½ percent during the latter half of the year."[58]

The group's forecast was based, in part, on incorrect information. The incident is a good example of the problem that all presidential advisers must face. Recommendations are made in real time; they are based on currently available data. The first estimates of economic performance published by government agencies go through a number of revisions, sometimes large, before they enter into the historic record in final form. Gramley reported to the Steering Committee of the Economic Policy Group in late October 1977, that "the pace of economic expansion was disappointingly slow in the third quarter. Real GNP increased at an annual rate of 3.9 percent, with more than half of that growth occurring in government purchases."[59] Three months later, in January 1978, the *Economic Report* raised the estimate of third-quarter performance to 5.1 percent. The 1979 estimate was 5.7 percent, and the 1980 *Economic Report* raised it further to 7.0 percent.[60] The administration, it should be said, was not alone in its forecast, which was roughly consistent with the broad consensus of private forecasters. It was this outlook that led to the 1978 cut in taxes.

Tax reform was an important part of Carter's campaign for the presidency. He had called the tax system, in a bit of campaign rhetoric, a "disgrace to the human race." Both Senator Russell Long and Congressman Al Ullman, chairs of the finance committees of Congress, pressed Carter not to send a reform bill in 1978.[61] Congress had just passed tax reform in 1976 and was not interested in taking up controversial legislation in a congressional election year. Carter chose to follow through on his campaign commitment and forward tax legislation.[62] The bill contained a tax cut provision aimed to give relief to lower income families, but also proposed reforms to close "loopholes" benefiting upper income groups.

In January 1978, Stuart Eizenstat and Charles Schultze sent a memorandum to Carter to brief him on an upcoming meeting with Congressman Al Ullman, chair of the House Ways and Means Committee, by which new tax legislation is initiated. The reform bill included in its net effect a $25 billion tax reduction. The Treasury Department had argued for a lower number, $20 billion, but the number proposed by Schultze prevailed.[63] Ullman, Eizenstat and Schultze pointed out, favored a smaller tax reduction. They urged the president to press Ullman for a larger cut. "Unless tax reductions are enacted . . . the growth of the economy will slow later in 1978 or in 1979. The decline in the unemployment rate will cease, and unemployment would begin to rise. . . . We see no sign that inflation is heating up again, or is likely to do so over the next two years."[64]

The final bill passed by both houses and sent to Carter for his signature contained only a modest amount of reform. It did include a tax cut, but, the *Congressional Quarterly* reported, "it bore almost no resemblance to what Carter had proposed."[65] The tax cuts were, in large part, tilted toward upper income taxpayers. Carter was indignant.[66] Schultze argued that despite the disappointing result of the reform effort, a tax cut was nevertheless necessary to maintain the upper thrust of the economy.[67] He later recalled that "if Blumenthal or I, or, perhaps either one of us, had come in and said we don't need that tax cut, if you want to veto it, for other reasons, go ahead and veto it, he would have done it, I am morally certain."[68] Schultze continued in the interview, "if I had known what was coming up on oil, which had both a recessionary and an inflationary influence, I might have said from the depths of my soul, well, we are going to need some more unemployment to keep the inflation from going up so much, and maybe he shouldn't sign it."[69] Carter signed the bill in late 1978. It was a step that added stimulus to an economy already under inflationary pressure.

The year 1978 turned out to be a strong year. In the second quarter, real gross national product increased by 8.7 percent, as reported in the 1979 *Economic Report*.[70] Economic advisers became aware that the economy was expanding more rapidly than they previously thought, but their concern was focused on another issue. "The GNP is not far from the track we had been forecasting," Schultze reported to Carter, "but," he added, "unemployment has fallen by almost 1 percentage point faster than past relationships with GNP would have led us to expect."[71] The point made by Schultze requires further comment.

"Okun's Law," which relates the growth in GNP to changes in the unemployment rate, was discussed in an earlier chapter. The rule of thumb, based on historical data, suggested that a 3 percent increase in the GNP would reduce the unemployment rate by 1 percent. The sharp decline in the productivity growth rate—it actually became negative in 1979—changed Okun's ratio from 3–1 to 2–1. With lower output per worker, it now took more workers to increase GNP than was previously the case. Put in another way, an increase in national output would reduce the unemployment rate at a faster pace than previously experienced. The unemployment rate fell from 7.5 percent in the first quarter of 1977 to 6.0 percent in the second quarter of 1978. This surprising drop put the administration a year ahead of schedule in its unemployment target.

THE FALL IN PRODUCTIVITY

The productivity decline was one of the major causes of the policy mistakes made by Carter's economists. Because of the fall, the amount of output the economy was capable of producing was overestimated, along with the amount of slack, which determined how much they could push the economy before inflationary pressures would develop. There was less room for stimulus than they thought. Among the bad things that happened to the administration, Schultze has said, "one of them we didn't even recognize, the slowing growth in productivity. Well that is so subtle; even the statistics were revised on us. We didn't even know about it until it was already going on for quite a while."[72] One student of the period has said that "the measurement problems could be attributed in large part to changes in the trend growth of productivity in the economy which, though clearly seen in the data with the benefit of hindsight, was virtually impossible to ascertain in real time."[73]

The economic advisers thought of the slowdown as temporary. In a memorandum in mid-1978 to Anthony Solomon, undersecretary of the treasury, Schultze wrote that for "nonfarm private business firms, productivity rose by only 0.6 percent over the past year (2Q 1978 vs. 2Q 1977), compared to an expected rise at this stage of the cycle of perhaps 1.8 percent. This loss of productivity growth raised costs, and undoubtedly is affecting prices. The causes of the sudden loss (most of which occurred in the first six months of this year) are obscure. We have not been able to explain it, but see no reason to assume that this very bad experience will persist."[74] The anti-inflation program announced in October 1978, the program that introduced the wage and price guidelines, assumed that productivity would increase by 1.75 percent. "This assumption," Eizenstat wrote the president, "is basic to the bottom-line objective of a 6½ percent underlying rate of inflation. Any shortfall from this figure must be added to the underlying rate.... You may ask Charlie [Schultze] and Barry [Bosworth] how confident they are about this productivity assumption."[75]

Lyle Gramley recalled in an interview that "we were simply not willing to acknowledge that productivity growth had slowed as much as it had. We kept thinking, it couldn't possibly be this bad. Maybe there were measurement problems, or something of this sort."[76] Economic advisers less ambitious in terms of what could be done by way of fine tuning would have also had to deal with the drop in productivity, but would have left themselves less vulnerable to the unexpected development.

MOVEMENT TOWARD RESTRAINT

With the economy in danger of exceeding potential output, Carter's advisers began to rethink their policy strategy. In a May 1978 memorandum to the president, entitled "some disturbing thoughts about the economic outlook," Charles Schultze wrote that "we are considering strategies to reduce the Fiscal Year 1979 and Fiscal Year 1980 budget deficits, and we will probably be seeking an appointment with you this week to discuss the matter."[77]

Carter was also disturbed. More fiscally conservative from the beginning than his advisers, he underlined the sentence about reducing the deficits and wrote in the margin, "a new convert?"

There were two budgets involved. The first, the 1979 Fiscal Year budget, had already been submitted in January 1978; it would begin in October 1978 and end in September 1979. This was the budget that contained the proposal for a $25 billion tax cut to stimulate the economy. It was still under consideration by Congress. In a modification of his previous position, in which he argued vigorously for the cut, Schultze suggested that the cut needed to be reduced in size. How they would handle what would look like an abrupt turnaround was discussed in the memorandum. The administration had already been branded as inconsistent in its withdrawal of the tax rebate in the previous year. Congress was required by its own rules to complete action on a first concurrent budget resolution for the 1979 Fiscal Year budget by May 15, 1978. The House resolution, already agreed upon, provided for a $20 billion tax cut effective October 1, 1978. The Senate resolution called for a $25 billion tax cut effective January 1, 1979. Schultze suggested working with these differences as a way of avoiding the charge of inconsistency and at the same time getting a reduction in the tax cut. "If the Senate accepted the lower House amount for the size of the cut," Schultze wrote to the president, "and the House accepted the Senate's later enactment date, the FY 1979 budget deficit could be lowered by $9 billion."[78]

There is another important shift in Schultze's thinking revealed in this memorandum. Schultze now talked in terms of a higher full employment-unemployment target than the 4.9 percent accepted at the beginning of the administration. "The recent upcreep in the rate of wage advance suggests that we would take risks with inflation if we pushed the rate of unemployment below about 5¾ percent. This is not a hard and fast boundary, and we cannot be sure of the consequences of going beyond it. But we now have to err on the side of caution. . . . That is the price of having reduced the unemployment rate to 6 percent without having gotten inflation moving down. We have little room for error."[79] The level of potential GNP was also lowered; but not enough. Administration economists forecast a productivity growth of 1.5 percent annually over the next five years. The 1979 productivity growth rate was a minus 2 percent.

The second budget to be dealt with was the 1980 Fiscal Year budget, which would be presented to Congress in January 1979, begin October 1, 1979, and end in September 1980. Carter discussed this budget at a May 25,

1978, cabinet meeting. According to one account, "he spoke for about 10 to 15 minutes—quietly, as always, with more emotion than was normal, and very much to the point. The economic situation worried him deeply, he said, and he was concerned that inflation not get out of control. His economic advisers would provide the specifics, but he wanted the cabinet to hear from him, at the earliest possible moment, that he had decided to propose an extremely austere 1980 budget."[80] Cutting a federal budget is a difficult undertaking. Once the "entitlement" programs, like Social Security and Medicare, are accounted for, along with defense spending, the discretionary programs that can be cut without a change in law by Congress make up only a relatively small part of the budget.[81] The problem was complicated by the fact that inflation caused indexed entitlements to increase. Higher interest rates, also due to inflation, were an additional claim squeezing the amount of discretionary choices still further.

Cabinet officers take the heat when cuts are made in programs involving their constituencies. "And—which made it harder," one insider commented, "this was a Democratic president asking a Democratic cabinet to support budget restraint. The request ran against the grain of almost 50 years of accepted party practice, tried and true rhetoric, and hardened ideology. Jimmy Carter had the enormous misfortune to be a Democratic president who was required to acknowledge the existence of budgetary limits and to try to alter strong-running budgetary currents."[82] Unfortunately, the midterm Democratic convention met in Memphis in December 1978. The plan to hold down the 1980 budget to be presented to Congress in January 1979 had already been leaked to the press. Senator Kennedy, the leader of the liberal wing of the party, used the occasion to attack Carter's budget decision. "I support the fight against inflation," he said in his speech to the convention. "But no such fight can be effective or successful unless the fight is fair. The party that tore itself apart over Vietnam in the 1960s cannot afford to tear itself apart over budget cuts in basic social programs."[83]

THE 1981 FISCAL YEAR BUDGET

The discussion within the administration in preparation of Carter's final budget was strongly influenced by the upcoming 1980 election. The Republican opposition in Congress was pushing hard for the Kemp-Roth bill, which called for a 10 percent cut in taxes for three straight years. Ronald Reagan, who was running for the Republican nomination, endorsed the bill. After the election he submitted to Congress a slightly modified version. In

1980 the idea of tax relief had a strong appeal to voters whose rate of taxation was rising due to inflation. There was a growing awareness within the administration of the political effects of "bracket creep."

Carter's advisers strongly recommended that he include in the 1981 Fiscal Year budget, to be presented to Congress in January 1980, a provision for a tax cut. In a memorandum to the president in mid-1979 asking for Carter's directions for consultations with Congress, the Economic Policy Group wrote that "at the Spring Budget Review, you directed OMB to hold current FY 1981 outlay plans to a level allowing budget balance, absent a recession. The oil price increase may well push us into a recession that would make a balanced budget impractical or perverse on economic grounds."[84] Carter was firm. He refused to include a tax cut in the new budget even after repeated requests. Inflation had become his concern with top priority.

Events were soon to make the issue moot. Just before the 1981 budget was announced in January 1980, the Office of Management and Budget, which monitors revenue receipts and outlays during the budget year, updated its forecast for the size of the deficit for the 1980 budget then in progress and ending in September 1980. The administration, at some political cost, had designed the budget submitted in January 1979, as I have already explained, to keep the deficit below $30 billion. The OMB estimated, in its revision, that the deficit would be 50 percent larger. Most of the increase was due to automatic adjustments in program levels due to an inflation rate higher than projected and to higher interest rates. Financial markets reacted strongly. If the administration missed by such a large margin on the 1980 budget, Wall Street concluded, it could do so on the new budget proposed in January 1980. The bond market, as explained in the opening chapter in this book, became chaotic. The prime rate went to 21 percent. Carter announced in February a reopening of the 1981 Fiscal Year budget just submitted to Congress. In an unusual episode—reminiscent of parliamentary government in Europe—the administration and the leadership of Congress worked in meetings for seven straight days to make cuts in the budget. Paul Volcker, who, as we will see later, had been recently appointed to head up the Federal Reserve, sat in on meetings with Carter's economic advisers. A new budget designed to produce balance for the 1981 Fiscal Year was announced by the president in a speech in March.

Finalizing a budget is a continuous process, lasting from the time the president submits it in January to the final passage by Congress in time for the new budget year to begin on October 1. The matter of a tax cut continued to be discussed by the president's advisers at the periodic budget

Meeting on budget revision, early 1980. Sitting opposite Carter, *left to right*, are Charles Schultze, Alfred Kahn, William Miller, and Paul Volcker, chairman of the Federal Reserve. Courtesy of the Jimmy Carter Library.

reviews over the course of 1980. Even though a revised budget had just been submitted, some type of tax cut gesture in the election year seemed necessary.

Schultze later gave an interesting account of Carter's position. An interviewer asked Schultze "how much did the political question of the elections dominate thinking at this time?" Schultze responded that

> Carter was very good. I no longer remember the specifics, but about August of 1980 we all wanted an economic program for the second term that would be something for Carter to run on. Also in the mid-year projection of the budget, we wanted him to put in a contingency line on a business tax cut. . . . He said no, no tax cuts, no fiscal action whatsoever. . . . He wasn't going to do anything. This was August. I remember going down to Sea Island [Georgia], the hottest day I ever spent in my life. And my memory is now vague, but he overruled all of his economic advisers in terms of having a contingency tax cut. He had sent to the congress a mid-year budget estimate; that's what gave him this occasion.

I remember pleading up to the very last minute for him to put a small business tax cut in the economic program finally announced in September, something to be an answer to Reagan's supply-side economics. But he wouldn't do it. And he became very adamant that we were not going to do anything that gives the budget a stimulus.[85]

In his "economic renewal speech" delivered at the end of August, Carter said that "now, in the heat of an election year, is not the time to seek votes with ill-considered tax cuts that would simply steal back in inflation in the future the few dollars that the average American tax payer might get. . . . I will not accept a pre-election bill to cut taxes."[86] He did make a small concession, recommending additional weeks of unemployment insurance. An increase in depreciation allowances and an investment tax credit, he said, would be considered in the coming year.

A FINAL NOTE

It is a difficult task to assess the degree to which Carter and his advisers contributed to the inflation of the late 1970s and the degree to which they were the victims of unusual events. "In the 1970s, particularly that period at the end of the seventies," Alice Rivlin, director of the Congressional Budget Office, said in an interview, "it was just almost impossible to say what good economic policy would have been. Nobody had thought through what you do when we have stagflation. Through most of that period we had relatively high unemployment and inflation. It was easy to criticize what they were doing, but it wasn't clear, even in hindsight, what should have been done."[87]

Advisers who participated in the formation of Carter's policies have reflected on their decisions. "A President will only make two or three seminal economic decisions and they had better be the right ones," Eizenstat has said. "Our biggest mistake on economic policy was . . . misjudging the strength of inflationary forces in early 1977 and having an economic policy which over-stimulated the economy."[88]

Charles Schultze recognizes, in looking back, that they were too aggressive, but doesn't view their fiscal policy as the main cause of the inflationary problem. "My own view," he has said, "is that in 1978 we probably added, by excessive demand stimulus, perhaps one-half percent, perhaps a bit more, and one percent to the rate of inflation. [A total of 1.5 percent.] And that was a mistake. But in the context of going from what I considered to be core 6 percent to core 10 percent, that stimulus was a relatively modest part of it."[89]

Lyle Gramley has, in retrospect, taken a different view. "If there was any very large mistake that we made in terms of belief in accepted wisdom and what it implied about the way things were going, it was that one could measure the full employment-unemployment rate with sufficient precision so that one could feel fairly sure that, if the unemployment rate were at 5½ percent or above, the inflation surely ought to unwind. If there was enough slack, between actual unemployment and the full employment-unemployment rate, one could plan the course of policy with fairly aggressive objectives and fairly ambitious goals and expect the inflation rate to unwind in the process. Charlie was a lot stronger believer in that point of view than I was. As Charlie looks back on what happened during that period, he comes, to this day, to quite different conclusions than I do. I think we made some very serious mistakes. He is inclined to the view that we had some very bad luck. And those are two quite different interpretations of those four years with the Carter administration."[90]

Reading the documents in the Carter Library files, one gets the impression that Carter was more aware of the danger of inflation than were his advisers. In internal memoranda over the course of the administration, there are repeated expressions of concern. Alfred Kahn, who came into the White House as the inflation czar after mistakes had already been made in 1977–78, observed in an interview: "I believe that the President increasingly felt that if he'd listened to his own instincts rather than his economic advisers, he would have been better off. I think that's correct."[91] Stuart Eizenstat spoke along similar lines. "I think his instincts, as it turned out, were more accurate than all of ours. His instinct was to question the stimulus, to be more leery of it, to be more concerned with inflation; and I think a lot of us pushed him, a lot of his economists pushed him, in a direction with which he didn't feel fully comfortable."[92]

There is another major part of this inflation story that needs to be told; the role of the Federal Reserve and the management of monetary policy. To this I return in a later chapter.

CHAPTER 10 | **GOVERNMENT ACTIONS AND INFLATION**

At the same time that the Carter administration was attempting to implement its broad economic strategy, it also, from the very beginning, had to deal with narrower, microeconomic decisions that also influenced the inflation outcome. It is worthwhile, in this chapter, to interrupt our discussion of broad macroeconomic strategy to take a look at the more important of these micro decisions.

SOCIAL SECURITY

As is the case with every new administration, policy issues were already on the table in Congress when Carter came into office. The *Wall Street Journal* reported in December 1976, that "transition planners for Carter search for early 'time bomb' problems."[1] Among agenda items listed by the *Journal* were a Social Security tax increase and an increase in the minimum wage.

The Social Security program has gone through repeated amendments since the first monthly Social Security check was paid to Ida Mae Fuller of Brattleboro, Vermont, in 1940.[2] Coverage has been expanded beyond the provisions of the original legislation. Only 60 percent of the labor force was covered until 1950. In that year Congress made eligibility almost universal. It also authorized generous increases in benefits. Social Security has been the most successful of our social legislation programs. It has drastically reduced the poverty rate among the nation's elderly. But keeping the program financially viable—given changes in the age composition of the population, the expansion of benefits, and the method of financing—is a problem with which each president has had to deal. In 1977 it was Jimmy Carter's turn.

Congress originally thought of Social Security as self-financing, based on a large reserve built up through accumulated payroll taxes. This approach was abandoned in 1939 and in its place a pay-as-you-go arrangement was introduced, financing benefits out of current payroll taxes. Part of the reason for abandoning the original intent was the fear that if public retirement insurance were fully funded, the buildup of reserves would be so large that it would impose a drag on the economy. In 1939 the economy still had not fully recovered from the Great Depression. In the early days of Social Security this pay-as-you-go arrangement was not a problem because the number of eligible retirees was small compared to the number of workers paying Social Security taxes, and reserves accumulated. As the number of retirees has increased and as the number of active workers relative to eligible recipients is dropping, there has been a continuing concern about the financial soundness of the program.

A forecast of the financial condition of Social Security for several decades ahead is less a forecast and more like an informed guess. Estimating revenues from Social Security payroll taxes—revenues that depend on such things as employment levels and the employment mix—is a tenuous business. Predicting benefit outlays, with estimates depending, among other things, on the reliability of actuarial studies, is also difficult. A Social Security Advisory Council report in 1971 advised Congress that the program was over-financed and would amass enormous reserves in the early twenty-first century. Congress responded by increasing benefits by 20 percent and cutting future payroll tax rates. Benefits were also indexed, to adjust automatically for inflation. It was soon recognized that the forecast was wildly optimistic. The economy went into a recession, while inflation moved toward a double-digit range. Because of higher unemployment, payroll tax revenues did not increase as expected, and inflation caused a sharp rise in benefits.

Something even more fundamental was also at work in the 1970s. In the period after World War II, wages rose more rapidly than prices so that the real wage also went up. In the 1970s, inflation, and a decrease in the growth of output per worker, caused real wages to decline. Money wages grew more slowly than prices, with a consequent loss in worker purchasing power. The implications for Social Security were serious. As an internal memorandum summarized the problem in mid-1979, "energy price increases and poor productivity performance have lowered real wages and thus have lowered the real value of payroll taxes per covered worker. Since benefits are indexed to the Consumer Price Index, the real value of benefits payments has not declined. This development has put enormous strain on the trust funds."[3]

An adjustment in Social Security provisions was inevitable in the early part of the Carter administration. The Social Security Amendment of 1977, passed by Congress and signed by the president at the end of the year, was a substantive enactment. The bill made important revisions in the Social Security program. As one commentator has written, "these amendments are generally considered to be the most significant Social Security legislation since 1972 and possibly since 1950."[4] The legislation corrected an error in the benefit formula of the 1972 amendment, which provided new retirees with larger payments relative to previous earnings than had been intended. The 1977 act also provided for increases in Social Security payroll taxes, unprecedented in size, to be initiated in early 1978, and in 1981, 1985, and 1990.

While the legislation helped to alleviate the financial crisis in Social Security, additional steps were necessary in the early part of the Reagan administration. Carter's staff realized that a later adjustment would have to be made. "Even if the 1981 scheduled payroll tax increases go into effect," said one internal memorandum, "it now appears that the social security trust funds will not have sufficient revenue to pay benefits in the early 1980s."[5] The chairman of a commission appointed by President Reagan to study, again, the financial viability of the Social Security program was Alan Greenspan, later to become chairman of the Federal Reserve Board.[6] While the increases under Carter were necessary to resolve an approaching financial crisis, they also had an inflationary effect as increased payroll taxes raised labor costs, costs passed on by business in the form of higher prices.

MINIMUM WAGE

With a Democrat now in the White House, Democrats in Congress put their wish list on the table. Included on the list was an increase in the minimum wage, a favorite Democratic initiative. President Roosevelt signed the Fair Labor Standard Act in 1938. It provided for a minimum hourly wage of 25 cents. The wage was not indexed to adjust for inflation. As a result, its purchasing power eroded over time with increases in the general price level. Demands for an increase in the minimum came up in Congress with predictable regularity. A pattern became established: a jump in the minimum wage due to an amendment to the original act, followed by a decline in the purchasing power of this higher wage due to inflation. In due course, the erosion of the wage would lead to another legislatively approved increase. All of the presidents since Roosevelt have had to deal with this politically sensitive and recurring issue.[7]

The last increase in the minimum wage before Carter was in 1974, and, with the high rate of inflation in the three years that followed, the minimum provided for in law had gotten out of alignment with the average manufacturing wage. A bill was submitted by John Dent, congressman from Pennsylvania. The Dent proposal involved a substantial jump in the minimum wage. It provided for an increase in two stages: an immediate raise in pay 30 days after passage of the bill, and a further step-up starting January 1, 1978. The final increase would be from the existing $2.30 an hour to $3.30, a level which would bring the minimum wage up to 60 percent of average hourly earnings in manufacturing. Historically the minimum wage had varied between 42 and 56 percent of manufacturing wages, with an average ratio since 1960 of 50 percent. The AFL-CIO (American Federation of Labor and Congress of Industrial Organizations) informed the White House in mid-March that it would push for an increase close to the Dent proposal: $3.00 an hour and indexing at 60 percent of average hourly wages in manufacturing starting January 1, 1978.

Carter's economic policy advisers were divided over the size of the increase. The arguments on both sides can be traced in a series of memoranda circulated among the advisers and to the president. Secretary of Labor Ray Marshall argued vigorously for a large increase. In the tradition of labor secretaries he acted throughout the debate as the main contact with labor, "in constant negotiations with them," he said in a later interview, "about what the President was going to agree to and what we thought we could get through the congress, which was another kind of political reality."[8] The constituency of the Labor Department is labor. The constituency of the Commerce Department is business. Commerce opposed Marshall's position. Treasury, the Council of Economic Advisers, and the Office of Management and Budget were also in opposition.

The key issue debated—the same issue debated each time an increase in the minimum wage comes before Congress—was the economic effect. The Council of Economic Advisers argued, to start with, that the minimum wage was a relatively inefficient way of redistributing income to the poor, the purpose of the original legislation. There was only a loose correlation between the minimum wage and income, the Council argued. The correlation was fairly strong for adults, but only 2.5 million out of 9.5 million low-wage workers were heads of households. Many teenagers working for minimum wages were from families with above-poverty incomes. Less than 7 percent of teenage low-wage workers were in poverty line families. If income distribution were the desired goal, it would be better to attack it from another approach.[9] In the meantime, there would be two adverse consequences of going the minimum wage route. The increase would have a negative effect on employment for those in the lower wage categories, and would boost the inflation rate.[10]

Common sense, and a fundamental premise in economics, suggest that if the wage rate is raised, fewer workers are hired by businesses. This was conceded by all parties to the discussion. The matter in dispute was the size of the employment loss. To put the matter in another way, how sensitive is the demand for workers to an increase in wages?[11] This is a technical issue that was argued vigorously in the memoranda circulated within the administration; it is still argued intensely today. The Council of Economic Advisers cited the estimates of displaced workers made in a number of studies. According to these projections, between 170,000 and 340,000 workers, mainly teenagers, would become unemployed if the minimum wage were set at $2.94 and indexed at 60 percent of the average hourly wage in manufacturing. This combination of wage and index arrangements was close to the numbers pushed by the AFL-CIO. Labor Secretary Marshall took an opposite view of the disemployment effect. He cited studies done by the Department of Labor staff showing no significant job loss.[12]

The impact of the pay raise on the inflation rate—fast becoming the critical policy issue occupying the attention of the administration—was analyzed as coming in three stages. There was, first of all, the direct effect on prices of the increase in pay of low-wage workers. The increased cost would presumably be passed on to consumers in the form of higher prices. The second-stage impact depended on the "emulation effect," the extent to which the increase in minimum wage had a ripple effect on the earnings of above-minimum-wage workers pushing to maintain the pay differential. The third effect depended on the extent to which initial price increases, due to a rise in wages, triggered another round of wage boosts.[13] The Council of Economic Advisers recognized that the total inflation impact of the increase in the minimum was a matter of controversy. Using conservative estimates, the council argued that the full effect of an increase close to the AFL-CIO demands would raise the inflation rate by 1.8 percentage points.[14] The Labor Department disagreed with the estimates. The inflationary impact of the direct effect on prices of the increase in the minimum wage, they argued, depends on the extent to which employers increase productivity or reduce profits. Such actions would moderate the inflationary impact. The second- and third-round effects would increase the inflation rate. The final result depends on the size of these positive and negative effects. The analysis presented by the Council of Economic Advisers, Marshall argued in a memorandum to the president, ignored the offsetting outcomes of increases in productivity and reduced profit margins. The Department of Labor's analysis concluded that the total effect on inflation would be only 0.25 percent.[15]

Conflicting memoranda containing the details of these statistical analyses were sent to the president. The minimum wage debate is one of the best examples of the situations in which Carter was faced with technical, minute details. This was not the first time that he had heard arguments about the economic effects of minimum wage increases. While governor, Carter received a memorandum from staff on the economic impact of a minimum wage bill passed by Congress in 1973 and awaiting Nixon's signature. As in the Carter administration, Nixon's economists argued that the effect of the increase would be inflationary, while the Labor Department "documented the fact that when the minimum is raised, the wage spread is narrowed and there is no general upward movement of total prices and wages."[16] Carter presumably had an interest in the issue, while governor, and requested the information. That a president, however, would be left to choose between the conflicting results of the statistical analyses of his experts seems inappropriate. A report of the president's reorganization project issued in mid-1977, and referred to earlier, used the case of the minimum wage as an example to support its conclusion that "the Economic Policy Group is not effective as currently operating. As a result, the President does not always receive a full and systematic staffing of economic issues."[17] A number of observers have noted that the disarray was due partly to Carter. Lyle Gramley recalls that too much paperwork went to the president on the issue of minimum wages. "But, again," he said, "the way the Carter administration had set itself up to run as a cabinet government, the objectives it had set out in the campaign, the kind of people that he had assembled to work for his administration, made it very, very difficult to end up with anything else except a lot of conflict. Ray Marshall was at one extreme, Charlie was at another, in terms of their thinking on this particular issue."[18]

A number of specific proposals for the size of the wage increase were presented in the exchange of memoranda. Blumenthal reported to the president that discussion had reduced the disagreement to two options.[19] Option one was sponsored by the Department of Labor and supported by the Department of Housing and Urban Development. It called for an immediate increase to $2.70, 53 percent of the average manufacturing wage, with a second-stage increase to $3.10, 57 percent of the manufacturing wage average. The Treasury, the Council of Economic Advisers, the Office of Management and Budget, and the Department of Commerce backed a second option calling for a raise from the current minimum, $2.30, to $2.40, 47 percent of manufacturing earnings, and indexed thereafter "with an estimated increase to $2.57 per hour on July 1, 1978."[20]

Given the lack of a presidential assistant authorized to force compromise, Carter turned to Stuart Eizenstat, as he often did, to coordinate the decision process. Eizenstat summarized for the president the final numbers proposed by the opposing advisers and suggested that he make a final decision somewhere in between. He suggested starting with an immediate increase to $2.50, 50 percent of manufacturing wages, and increasing in three stages to arrive at a 53 percent ratio.[21] The final 53 percent number had a strong political implication.

As part of his "war on poverty," President Johnson asked his staff for an estimate of the income level that would define a poverty condition. The administration popularized the figure $3,000 for a family of four as the minimum needed for a satisfactory standard of living.[22] Adjusted periodically for inflation, the poverty level income became a litmus test of economic welfare. Liberal critics of the president were demanding that the minimum wage be above the poverty level income. Eizenstat pointed out in his memorandum to Carter that "since the 53 percent index would raise a four person family out of poverty by 1981, you could take credit for having responded to criticisms of the poverty group." In a statement reflecting the running tension between Carter and the liberal wing of the party, Eizenstat added that "the votes on this issue will unite the administration and the Republicans against the more liberal Democrats. This will force very difficult choices on the moderate Democrats who will hold the decisive vote."[23]

In the legislation passed by Congress, the result leaned toward Carter's final recommendation. In the end, the proponents of a large increase in the minimum wage didn't have the votes. Tip O'Neill, the House majority leader, had been quoted as predicting that "Congress would come down halfway between Carter and Kirkland [secretary-treasurer of the AFL-CIO]." They came down closer to Carter. In a final memorandum, Eizenstat summarized the bill passed by Congress and recommended that he sign it. All of the advisers joined ranks and also recommended signing. The bill called for a four-step increase beginning with $2.65 starting in January 1978 and ending with $3.35 in January 1981. The minimum wage was not indexed in the congressional version as it was in Carter's. The House voted decisively against indexing. When this difference is taken into consideration, the president's numbers and those of the final legislation were quite close. "The bill represents a compromise," wrote Eizenstat, "which, while not identical to our position, is generally quite consistent with it."[24]

The president signed the bill in early November. An increase in the minimum wage was inevitable given the sharp deterioration of its purchasing power due to inflation. Carter did succeed in holding it down from the minimum wage level first proposed by Congressman Dent and the AFL-CIO. The lower minimum finally arrived at moderated the adverse economic outcome on the unemployment and inflation rates, but the effects, combined with the impact of the increase in Social Security contributions, were still substantial. The Council on Wage and Price Stability reported, in its review of the first quarter of 1978, that "hourly compensation, a comprehensive measure of labor costs which includes supplements, rose at a record annual rate of 13.2 percent. . . . The first quarter acceleration of wage and compensation gains can be explained, for the most part, by increases in the Social Security tax and the minimum wage."[25]

The minimum wage story did not end there. As inflation worsened in 1978, it remained a matter of discussion. Attached to an agenda announcement for a meeting of the steering committee of the Economic Policy Group in September 1978, is a discussion paper on the minimum wage. "Without further policy action the ongoing pattern of repetitive price and wage increases in the range of 6–7 percent annually will continue into the foreseeable future. This pattern is periodically fed by one-time inflationary impulses associated with government-mandated cost increases."[26] The paper presented two options for action. The first suggested postponement of scheduled increases for all workers. A second option suggested the possibility of postponing the increase for teenagers. In November 1978, the same type of argument for considering postponement of the increase was made again, though recognizing that the 1977 amendment would be hard to reverse because it was the result of careful negotiations. Whether the president became involved in this second round of discussion, and how seriously the options were considered, are not clear. In any event, a proposal to Congress to delay the minimum wage increases already scheduled was not made.

In addition to the problem of the effect on prices of the increase in the Social Security payroll tax and the minimum wage, the administration faced other microeconomic policy decisions with inflationary implications. In a memorandum shortly after the inauguration, Schultze briefed the president on "government actions affecting prices."[27] Attached is a long list of pending federal actions that would have an inflationary effect, ranging from regulation of air emission standards for heavy-duty engines imposed by the Environmental Protection Agency to a mandatory airbag standard imposed by the Department of Transportation. Schultze forwarded another memorandum, entitled "inflation scorecard" in the latter part of the year. "The scorecard presents an estimate of the effect on the price level and the rate of inflation of government actions taken or proposed this year."[28] It contains a long list and concludes that, counting the direct and indirect effects, "for the period 1977–1981, the actions will, on average, add between 0.6 and 0.8 percent to the annual inflation rate. The energy program is about one-third of the total, and higher prices there are unavoidable. But these are the effects of less than one year of the administration's life. If we ignore energy, regard Social Security as nonrecurring, but continue at the same pace of the rest, we will have added almost 1 percent to the average rate of inflation between now and 1981." One positive step toward easing the pressure on prices was deregulation.

ECONOMIC DEREGULATION

For most of our nation's history, government regulation of business was directed at economic activity—the pricing of services and the entry and exit of firms into and out of an industry. Social regulation, regulatory enactment to protect the health and safety of workplaces and products and the quality of the environment, did not appear on the scene until the 1960s.

The first substantive economic regulation of a major industry came in 1887, with the creation of the Interstate Commerce Commission for the regulation of railroads. Trucks became available in numbers to haul freight by the 1920s and 1930s. Competing freely against the railroads, unregulated trucking began to provide serious competition for rail transport. By 1925 three-fourths of the states had passed some type of trucking regulation. Political pressure exerted by the rail industry, experiencing poor times during the Great Depression, led to passage at the federal level of the Motor Carrier Act of 1935. The act provided for minimum rates charged for shipments and for control of entry by common carrier trucks. Regulation of the airlines began in 1938.

The traditional argument advanced in favor of regulation was the need for protection of the public interest in cases of market failure. Natural monopolies like public utilities provided the classic case of firms not subject to the discipline of market competition. Government control was thought to be necessary to prevent exploitation by these monopolies. This argument for regulation was generally accepted by economists.

A major shift in professional opinion took place in the 1960s and 1970s. The view emerged that regulation does not serve the economic welfare of the public, as it was intended to do, but the entrenched interests of producers and organized workers in an industry. This narrowly defined group, it was argued, exercises political influence to turn government regulation to its own advantage, against the interest of the broader class of uninformed consumers. It was also argued that regulation distorts prices and resource allocation, and inhibits innovation. Researchers associated with the University of Chicago made a major contribution, with a series of theoretical papers, in convincing the majority of economists that deregulation was desirable. Analytical and empirical studies were contributed by other economists.[29] The Ford Foundation provided funds for a series of studies by scholars associated with the Brookings Institution. Twenty-two books and monographs on regulation with an applied focus and of interest to policy makers were published by Brookings over the decade prior to Carter's election.[30] Economists were an early influence in changing the mood of policy makers.

At a more practical level, experiments in California and Texas with deregulation of intrastate airlines provided convincing evidence that restoring free competition results in lower ticket prices and improved service. Flights within the state, not subject to the Civil Aeronautic Board, consistently had lower fares than flights controlled by the federal regulating agency.

Carter announced his support for reform of economic regulations on a number of occasions during his 1976 campaign. In his proposals to the platform committee of the Democratic Party just prior to the convention, Carter stated his position that "priority attention should be given to restructuring the nation's antiquated system of regulating transportation. The present patch-work scheme of rail, truck, and airline regulation at the federal level needlessly costs consumers billions of dollars every year. However valid the original purpose of promoting fledgling industry and protecting the public from the tyranny of monopoly or the chaos of predatory competition, the present system has, more often than not, tended to discourage desirable competition."[31] Included in the summary of campaign promises, prepared by Stuart Eizenstat at Carter's request, are "moving decisively to reform regulation of airline industry; granting greater freedom to airline companies to make decisions concerning fares, service levels and routes; promoting price as well as service competition."[32]

When Jimmy Carter became president, the time was ripe for major changes in regulatory practices. Not only had research provided the scholarly arguments in favor of reform; Carter also fell heir to the groundwork already laid by President Ford and Senator Ted Kennedy in the political forum. Attempts to introduce regulatory reform were, to an unusual degree, a bipartisan affair. Gerald Ford made a major effort and took the political risk of offending groups with vested interest in the existing system. He asked Congress to create a national commission on regulatory reform. When Congress failed to act, he set up within the administration a task force that met weekly to work on the deregulation problem. He submitted bills for reform of airline and trucking regulation to Congress in 1975.[33]

Senator Ted Kennedy, in his capacity as chairman of the Subcommittee on Administrative Practice and Procedure of the Senate Judiciary Committee, held widely reported hearings on the Civil Aeronautics Board in 1975. Economists and advocates of consumer groups, like Ralph Nader, testified before the committee. "The function of the hearing," one account reports, "was to provide vivid, concrete confirmation of the academic and populist critiques of economic regulation in a form readily accessible to the national press."[34] A full day was devoted to the deregulation experience of California and Texas. By the time Carter came into office, the issue of deregulation was on the public agenda. "We fell heir," Charles Schultze was to say later, "to some very good work that had been done by the Kennedy subcommittee. It was the distinct strategic, philosophical view of Carter to move in the direction of deregulation."[35]

The first target was the airlines. Early in his administration Carter appointed Alfred Kahn to the post of chairman of the Civil Aeronautics Board. Kahn had developed an expertise on regulation while on the faculty at Cornell University. He published a major two-volume work, which, "measured by its impact on practitioners—both business executives and commissioners—remains," according to one student of the period, "the most influential work written on the subject."[36] In 1974 Kahn was appointed chairman of the New York Public Service Commission, the most important state regulatory post in the country. It regulated, at the time, forty industries, from electric utilities to docks and wharves, and employed 650 people. He successfully introduced analytical economics into the pricing of utility services. He modified rate structure to reflect true cost. He introduced differential pricing in the use of electricity to replace the flat rate then charged for service regardless of whether consumed at off-peak or peak hours. He gained national recognition for his innovations in New York, which were imitated in other states and became the basis later for federal legislation. He was widely respected for his expertise when Carter brought him to Washington.[37] Because of his wry sense of humor he was a favorite of the media. At a press conference called to announce a proposal to eliminate regulation of interstate trucking, Kahn said "the bill was being put forward in the name of anti-inflation efforts, energy conservation, competition, regulatory reform, and free enterprise. 'Motherhood and apple pie' are being taken care of in other legislation."[38]

When Carter appointed Kahn to be chairman of the Civil Aeronautics Board (CAB), its practices were in serious need of reform. "The overall effect of Board policies," according to one student of the agency, "tended to freeze the industry more or less in the configuration of 1938. . . . Over the entire history of the CAB, no new trunkline carrier had been permitted to join the sixteen that existed in 1938."[39] By the mid-1970s, the airlines were in trouble. Since price competition was restricted by the regulatory body, rivalry took the form of in-flight frills and a large number of flights, with frequent departures at prime hours. The number of passengers per trip was down. Rising fuel costs and declining revenues due to the reduced load factor and the recession of 1974–75 had cut into profits. Since regulation prevented free competition, the industry had trouble adjusting.

The gathering momentum in Congress and the media in favor of reform encouraged the chairmen of the CAB to explore the limits of interpretation of its rather broad powers. A series of court rulings that questioned anticompetitive decisions of both the CAB and the ICC [Interstate Commerce Commission] also added to a more permissive environment for initiating reforms by administrative action. Kahn's predecessor, John Robson, appointed as chairman of the CAB by Gerald Ford, had used the rather broad powers of the Civil Aeronautics Board for a more liberal interpretation of regulatory law. When Kahn assumed the chairmanship, he moved aggressively to give airlines more freedom to lower fares and to permit easier entry. Carriers began to experiment with marketing strategies such as discount fares. Concern was expressed by some members of Congress that regulators were preempting congressional action.[40]

In early 1978 Nebraska senator Howard Cannon and Senator Ted Kennedy jointly sponsored a bill to deregulate the airlines. Cannon, chairman of the Senate Commerce Committee, which had jurisdiction in the matter, was initially skeptical of deregulation but became, in time, a strong supporter. The majority of airlines and the unions opposed deregulation strenuously but could not block legislative action. Support for the idea of freeing up the airlines had become overwhelming. In October 1978, Congress passed the Airline Deregulation Act. It allowed carriers to set fares competitively, gave them authority to choose routes, and opened up the industry by allowing free entry. It provided for a complete phasing out of the Civil Aeronautics Board over a seven-year period.

Carter originally wanted to act on both airline and trucking deregulation in the early part of his term. "The President was committed to trucking deregulation," one administration staff member has commented. "There was just something in him that liked it. Partly, I think, from his experience as governor of Georgia; the truckers and others always asked for protection."[41] White House aides persuaded him to hold up on trucking until airline deregulation was completed. The trucking industry was a more difficult political challenge than airlines. Unlike the case of the airlines, owners and workers were spread geographically across the country, with representation in almost every congressional district. After the airline bill was signed, the administration delayed again on trucking, deciding that railroad deregulation should come next. There was a second reason for holding up on trucking. The Teamsters Union contract was to expire at the end of March 1979. The Teamsters had demanded a wage increase in excess of the wage-price guidelines announced by the administration in the previous October, and the new contract would be a test for the success of the program. It was a delicate time to push trucking deregulation, which the union strongly opposed.[42] Senator Kennedy upset the administration's time schedule by introducing a bill to deregulate trucking. The administration acted to keep from losing the initiative to Kennedy, who was beginning to look like a potential challenger for the 1980 nomination. In early June 1979, Carter accepted Kennedy's invitation to join forces.[43] Fred Kahn, who by now had moved to the White House to assume the role of chief inflation fighter, played an active role in the trucking debate. Trucking legislation passed in July 1980. The provisions were not as sweeping as in the case of airlines. The jurisdiction of the Interstate Commerce Commission remained, but the bill contained significant changes in regulatory provisions governing the industry. Market entry was liberalized and more flexibility was introduced into rate setting.

Trucking was followed by two other major deregulation decisions: the railroads and financial institutions. The Staggers Rail Act, which liberalized railroad freight rate setting, passed in 1980. The Depository Institutions Deregulation and Monetary Control Act, also passed in 1980, gave savings and loan associations and mutual savings banks broader authority in lending, and provided for elimination of interest rate ceilings for both banks and thrift institutions. The deregulation of airlines, trucks, rails, and financial institutions, when added to decontrol of oil, was a major achievement, perhaps Carter's biggest economic success. By the end of his administration, the de jure economic deregulation of industry was close to complete.

One student of the deregulation movement called the economic deregulation of American industry "one of the most important experiments in economic policy in our time. In 1977, 17 percent of U.S. Gross National Product [GNP] was produced by fully regulated industries. By 1988, following ten years of partial and complete economic deregulation of large parts of the transportation, communications, energy, and financial industries that total had been cut significantly—to 6.6 percent of GNP."[44] The British ambassador to Washington in the late 1970s, Peter Jay, has been quoted as saying that "in retrospect, the years 1977–1980 will be notable in United States domestic affairs for the bringing of a profound and quiet revolution: the deregulation of huge tracts of American industry and commerce. Although the cooperation of Congress and the drive of Edward Kennedy played an essential part in this, it was a Carter administration policy that carried through against special interests."[45] The pace of the movement through the deregulation enactments was surprisingly rapid. A student of the period says that "not one economist in a hundred practicing in the early 1970s predicted the sweeping changes that were soon to happen."[46]

SOCIAL DEREGULATION

If the move to reform economic regulation was a success, attempts to recast social regulation were less satisfying. The nation became more aware, by the early 1960s, of the potential damage to the environment and public health coming from the widespread use of chemicals in agriculture, and from industrial processes and auto emissions. Rachel Carson's *Silent Spring*, an impassioned indictment of the pesticide industry, published in 1962, and on the *New York Times* best-seller list for thirty-one weeks, contributed to a rising consciousness of environmental concerns. The American historian Stephen Fox called it "the *Uncle Tom's Cabin* of modern environmentalism."[47] The first Earth Day was celebrated in 1970. A consensus had developed in the country that government protection of the environment and public health was necessary.

In the 1960s and the 1970s a regulatory explosion took place when a large number of agencies were created by Congress to protect the environment, and promote health and safety in industry. One study reported that "prior to 1964, only one regulatory agency, the FDA [Food and Drug Administration], had been established with the primary goal of protecting the well-being—as opposed to the economic interests—of consumers, workers, or the public. Between 1964 and 1977, eleven regulatory agencies were created to meet these goals."[48] In 1962 the Federal Food and Drug Administration, created by law in 1931, was given more power with the establishment of a pre-market certification process. The National Highway Safety Traffic Administration was created in 1966 to promote motor vehicle safety. In the early 1970s, during the administration of Richard Nixon, three key regulatory agencies were established: the Environmental Protection Agency (EPA), charged to set standards for toxic waste and for air and water pollution control; the Occupational Safety and Health Administration (OSHA), charged with setting safety and health standards in the workplace; and the Consumer Product Safety Commission (CPSC), created to protect consumers from hazardous products. These regulatory bodies were authorized with strong bipartisan support. The legislation committed the nation to an ambitious set of goals. The next several years involved experimentation with these new powers and the attempt to discover how to implement the law.

Few questioned the need for health and environmental concern. The Soviet Union provided a tragic example of the environmental destruction and the shortening of life expectancy that results when the damage of industrial pollution is ignored by policy makers. But implementation of a program to protect health, safety, and the environment requires a difficult balancing act. The challenge is to achieve the intended purpose of legislative enactments without imposing unreasonable standards and avoidable cost on the nation's productive capacity. Stories of arbitrary and unreasonable rulings by regulatory bureaucracies often appeared in press reports in the 1960s and 1970s. Attempts to introduce a sense of moderation were made by both the Nixon and the Ford administrations by setting up a regulatory review process to make explicit the cost and inflationary impact of environmental and safety standards.

Carter had deep personal convictions about protecting the environment and had acted in line with these convictions while governor of Georgia. During the 1976 campaign, he had committed himself to environmental protection, and was supported by environmental groups. He also committed himself to imposing discipline on regulatory agencies. The competing claims of social protection and the need to give recognition to cost limits caused tensions within the Carter administration, as they had during the Nixon and Ford presidencies.

One economist pointed out in the late 1970s that economic regulation tends to develop its own constraints in that market forces and public opinion limit the costs that rate setters can impose on the rest of society.... These corrective forces do not exist in most areas of social regulation.... The cost of health, safety, and environmental standards is not directly observable; there, the public cannot separate the mandatory costs [of regulation] from other costs of producing a pound of aluminum, a ton of paper, or a kilowatt-hour of electricity. And social regulation typically involves some aspect of human health or safety that a regulator can invoke to arouse strong emotional support for his actions, no matter how extreme or costly they may be.[49]

Murray Weidenbaum, chairman of Reagan's first Council of Economic Advisers, conducted widely reported research in the 1970s attempting to determine the cost of regulation. He estimated that the administrative and compliance costs in 1979 might top $100 billion, in 1976 dollars, the bulk of it related to social regulation.[50]

Carter's economists were interested in the cost of regulatory decisions, not only because of the direct burden imposed on business, consumers, and taxpayers, but also because of the effect on investment spending, which is critical for healthy gains in worker productivity and economic growth. The 1978 *Economic Report of the President* expresses this concern:

> Between 1965 and 1973 the net real stock of fixed business capital excluding pollution abatement equipment grew at 4.4 percent per year. During the same period, the labor force grew at a 1.9 percent rate per year.... By contrast, in the 1973–1976 period the annual growth rate of fixed capital stock, excluding that part devoted to pollution abatement, decreased substantially to 1.9 percent, while the private labor supply grew at 2.3 percent annually. This comparison of growth rates of labor and capital and the observed capacity shortages in 1973 are in themselves enough to arouse concern about capacity constraints in 1981 or even sooner.[51]

In this climate of sluggish investment, funds diverted to pollution control were a matter of concern. A paper prepared by staff for James McIntyre, director of the Office of Management and Budget, estimated that "approximately 18 percent of capital investment in the steel industry in 1979 was spent for pollution control equipment."[52]

Carter appointed to economic regulating agencies commissioners sympathetic to regulatory restraint; Alfred Kahn is an example. He appointed to the social regulatory units individuals whose past activities had been heavily involved with environmental and safety concerns. Prior to her appointment as head of OSHA by Carter, Eula Bingham, a respected toxicologist, had headed an OSHA committee that set controversial coke-oven emission standards. She was also proposed for the position as head of OSHA by the AFL-CIO, a nomination that raised concerns with business leaders.[53] Douglas Costle, appointed head of the EPA, had strong environmental connections. There is a natural tension between regulators and economic advisers. Social regulators have a narrow focus. They are charged to carry out specific actions. A president's economic advisers, just as the president himself, have broader concerns, not only for the danger of environmental damage but also for the impact of regulatory actions on the total economy.

Modifying regulations with inflationary impact became a matter of priority with Charles Schultze, who was struggling with ways to moderate the rise in prices. Schultze proposed a plan to improve on the program initiated by President Ford requiring agencies to publish inflation impact statements when new regulations were proposed. As described in a memorandum to the president, an economic analysis broader than that required by Ford would be asked of each agency, including an examination of possible alternatives.[54] If two options were equally effective, the lower cost standard should be used. A review group would be created, to examine a small number of proposed regulations each year "to give close administration scrutiny to those regulations with the greatest potential economic effects." Among the problems in regulatory reform that would have to be dealt with was a partly unanswered question about the president's power to intervene with agencies in their execution of statutory responsibilities, and the requirement that the process be public. The peer review group, Schultze wrote, was initially meant to operate informally, "but the legal procedures surrounding the rule-making process in regulatory matters make it impossible to discuss proposed regulations in an informal fashion, as we do budget requests of proposed new legislation. The results of the review will be placed in the record of public comments on the regulation at various stages in the review process."[55]

Regulatory agencies opposed the idea of a review group, but Carter accepted the Schultze plan.[56] The Regulatory Analysis Review Group (RARG) was established by Carter in March 1978. It was officially headed by Schultze, as chairman of the Council of Economic Advisers (CEA), though he delegated responsibility to other members of the CEA. The Office of Management and Budget was assigned responsibility of ensuring submission of proper regulatory analysis. In a memorandum to James McIntyre, the OMB director, Carter wrote in handwriting in the margin, "Jim, devote top effort to enforcement. I will help you personally."[57] The *National Journal* quoted William Nordhaus, the member of the council who had responsibility for the operation, as saying that in the first year, RARG "intervened in 14 proposed regulations whose potential cost to the economy was estimated at $50 billion."[58] Carter supplemented RARG with a Regulatory Council consisting of representatives of the regulatory agencies.[59] The council was charged with preventing redundancy by coordinating agencies' policies involving similar problems or related to the same industry. Also required was a unified regulatory calendar stating, according to Carter's memorandum, "the goals and benefits, legal requirements, and expected timetables of the regulations, along with available estimates of economic impacts."[60] Critics argued that the Regulatory Council, chaired by Douglas Costle, would provide a forum for agencies to coordinate resistance to outside control. In fact, the relationship between RARG and the council was reasonably productive. The council encouraged coordination and its calendar was useful to the Office of Management and Budget in its work of enforcing the regulatory process.

There was a serious gap in the review arrangement. There was no provision for resolving an impasse, in cases where an agency and the review group could not reach a compromise, except to go to the president for a decision. This omission was a problem in other administrations. Placing a president in the center of controversial environmental and health disputes is a less than satisfactory administrative and political solution. The need for Carter's intervention came early in the process. In the December before Carter took office, OSHA announced a cotton dust standard designed to protect textile workers. Long-term exposure to cotton dust is a cause of byssinosis, an irreversible medical condition commonly known as brown lung disease. The standard required the installation of expensive air-cleaning equipment and specified the maximum dust allowed per cubic meter of air. The Council of Economic Advisers and the Council on Wage and Price Stability objected to the standard. They wanted an alternative to air-cleaning equipment allowed, such as the use of respirators, and less stringent levels of exposure than permitted by the OSHA standard. Compromise could not be reached and the matter was taken to Carter for resolution.

The intensity of feelings about worker health issues is reflected in a letter to the president from a small group of members of Congress expressing concern that the OSHA decision was being reconsidered. The letter read: "482,000 employees presently work under conditions of exposure to excessive levels of cotton dust. We all have the highest regard for your determination to vigorously fight inflation. However, the sacrifice of workers' lungs and lives is neither an effective nor a just means of combating inflation."[61] George Meany joined the protest in support of OSHA. The debate within the administration was intense. Carter decided in favor of the agency, though there was a compromise in the exposure levels permitted and a delay in the time set for compliance to give industry time to adjust. Stuart Eizenstat replied to the letter from the members of Congress after the revised standard was announced. "The administration's objective was never to reduce costs by weakening the standard of protection," he wrote, "but rather to assure that the standard was imposed in a manner which minimized disruption and uncertainty within the textile industry, and which encouraged firms to continue to seek the most economical means to comply."[62] Revisions in the standard were estimated to reduce compliance cost from $700 to $500 million.[63]

Carter was caught in a no-win situation. He recalled the episode after he left the presidency. "In the private office, not in the Oval Office, but in the private office I had in back, I spent hours with that particular decision. That's one of the things I didn't want to be involved in, but it was so significant to many people that I finally let Stu Eizenstat and Charles Shultze come in and give me a briefing."[64] The competing claims of the opposing constituencies made the decision difficult, along with the basic merits of the case. Textile mills were numerous in the South and Carter was not unfamiliar with the industry's problems and had sympathy for the workers.

No one was satisfied with the decision. Both labor and business sued over the matter. The compromise was eventually upheld by the Supreme Court. Advisers were disappointed by Carter's decision. In a memorandum to the president, Schultze wrote, in a surprisingly direct way, that "the cotton dust episode was seen as a 'defeat' for the [review] program and its advocates. As reported by the press, the outcome confused participants about the degree of Presidential support."[65] William Nordhaus later recalled that the "President's economic advisers, and through them RARG, grew hesitant in the wake of the cotton dust episode about bringing controversial regulatory issues directly to the President's desk."[66] It was Carter's only intervention in a major regulatory dispute.

While economic deregulation was a major administration success, social regulatory reform was less so. Economic deregulation was a matter of direct legislative action at a time when a consensus for reform existed, whereas social regulatory reform required continuing administrative battles. The president's freedom to act was limited by statutory requirements enacted by Congress, by the intense feelings of the various constituencies, and by sharp differences within the administration. Both Ford and Carter have been criticized for the effectiveness of their review programs.[67] But I find another interpretation advanced by two students of the period to be convincing. Their opinion is that the president has "extremely limited abilities to control such a complex process as social regulation. It [their opinion] views the White House and executive office primarily as institutions that can set the tone for an administration's regulatory efforts, help raise issues that otherwise might go unexplored, and encourage policy experimentation that individual agencies, given their natural constituencies, would find difficult to initiate on their own."[68] In this interpretation, the Carter efforts, within reasonable bounds, were productive.

Reform of regulatory behavior, both economic and social, was intended, in addition to the effort to achieve market efficiency, as an anti-inflationary action. In a lengthy memorandum to the president in early 1978 outlining the steps "aimed at getting a gradual reduction in the rate of inflation over the next two years," there is included, among government contributions, "substantially improved review, control and simplification of the government regulatory process."[69] Regulatory reforms made an important contribution to improving market efficiency, to a more efficient allocation of resources, and to price moderation over the longer run. Unfortunately, the effect in containing inflation over the short term of Carter's presidency was probably marginal.

TRADE RESTRICTION ISSUES

Jimmy Carter was in favor of free trade, as presidents since Roosevelt generally have been. He was also aware of the impact of trade restrictions on the inflation problem with which he was having to deal. Like all presidents he was pressured with demands for trade protection; and also like other presidents, he accepted some measures of relief for troubled industries. The first major test case came in the early months of the administration and involved shoes.

A memorandum addressed to the Economic Policy Group summarized the condition of the shoe industry. "Since 1968 there has been a steady and significant decline in U.S. production of shoes from 643 million to 444 million pairs annually. In the same period, imports have risen from 182 million to 370 million. The number of U.S. shoe manufacturers has fallen from 600 to 378, and employment has dropped by 70,000 persons from 233,000 to 163,000."[70] Shoe manufacturing is labor intensive, and "many plants," the report went on to say, "represent the exclusive or principal source of employment in a particular community." Workers in the industry were spread over 36 states. Estimates stated that 170 of the 380 firms in the industry were in serious trouble: "Some of the 170 troubled companies may be in such serious straits that they cannot be saved." The competition came from low-wage countries producing inexpensive nonrubber footwear.

The International Trade Commission, in response to a petition from shoe producers, found in favor of the industry, recommending that a tariff of 40 percent be imposed on most nonrubber footwear imports above the 1974 level. The International Trade Commission (ITC) was created by Congress as a source of appeal when an industry felt it was subject to unfair trade. The president could, by law, reject the commission's recommendation, but the ruling put the president in a difficult position. If he did not uphold the commission, he was left alone to take the political heat. Aides advised Carter that it would be useful for him to attend a meeting of the Economic Policy Group scheduled to discuss the shoe problem. It was, he was told, the largest escape clause case in history, involving $1.4 billion of imports. In addition, "as the first major trade decision, it will be a signal to other industries contemplating protectionist appeal."[71] The case also had international implications. A decision to uphold the commission's recommendation would "hurt the political atmosphere for the Economic Summit" coming up shortly in London.

While the Economic Policy Group opposed the Trade Commission recommendation, some advisers believed that it was necessary to grant some type of relief for the industry. Eizenstat argued in a memorandum to the president that "the ITC has twice found, and congress and the public would generally agree, that the domestic shoe industry has been injured by imports. Refusal to grant any import relief may result in an override or, at the least, a major battle with congress. . . . We do not think that shoes are the proper item to kick off our anti-inflation program."[72]

Robert Strauss, the special trade representative, suggested an alternative to denying any import relief and to adopting tariff rate quotas. He recommended the negotiation of "orderly marketing agreements" under which these foreign suppliers would "voluntarily" agree to limit their exports to the United States. Such an approach had been used by Presidents Johnson and Nixon. Even though an OMA (orderly marketing agreement) is equivalent in its effect to a tariff or quota, it has the appearance of being less confrontational. The president would have ninety days to negotiate the agreements. It would be possible, then, to delay a final decision until after the London summit, at which Carter would be pushing forward plans for the multinational trade negotiations to be completed later in Tokyo. Charlie Schultze opposed the orderly marketing agreements, and stated, according to Eisenstat's notes, "that if it was just this one decision, it would not have such an important impact on consumers, but there was a problem of symbolism. He stated even with relief, the shoe industry would be in the same situation in five years."[73]

Carter decided to go along with an OMA, but "that we should emphasize the extraordinary nature of the shoe problem. He stated that his natural reluctance to impose import constraints was outweighed here by the extreme problem with employment in the industry."[74] He also asked his agency heads to cooperate in helping the domestic nonrubber footwear industry with whatever resources were available for trade adjustment assistance programs.

The direct inflationary effect of a protectionist decision in the case of shoes was estimated to be quite small. Shoe prices made up only 1.4 percent of the consumer price index according to administration estimates.[75] Steel, however, was another matter. Because steel was used as an input by a large number of industries, the administration was particularly conscious of the behavior of steel prices and the effect of increases on the pricing actions of steel users. Robert Strauss reported to the president in July 1977, that United States Steel had announced increases in certain steel prices to be effective in September.[76] Republic Steel, the second largest in the industry, and two smaller steel firms followed United States Steel's action with price increases. Charles Schultze pointed out to the president a few days later that the prices for finished steel, counting the newly announced increases, rose by 12.4 percent over the previous year in contrast to the 7.2 percent rate of increase in industrial prices generally.[77] Strauss listed basic types of government actions that could be used to pressure the steel industry. They included lowering existing tariffs and quotas applied to steel imports and modifying the "buy American" advantage given to United States steel producers. Under the "buy American" policy, domestic firms enjoyed a 6 percent price preference over foreign suppliers in government procurements. In the case of Department of Defense purchases, the preference was 50 percent. The practical effect of these steps, however, Strauss informed the president, would be small. Tariffs were already low and not an important barrier to foreign steel, and government purchases of steel mill products were a small percent of the United States steel market. Policy options available to pressure domestic producers to hold the price line were complicated by the fact that steel was approaching the condition of a "sick" industry. An ironic part of Strauss's memorandum informing the president of the coming steel price increase is the report that the industry was preparing to go to Congress to obtain quantitative restrictions on foreign steel imports.

American industry dominated the world steel market in the period following World War II. Production facilities in Europe and Japan were badly damaged during the conflict. In the after-war period domestic producers enjoyed a seller's market. As part of the postwar recovery, firms in other industrialized nations made major investments to bring steel capacity back on line. Much of the new production facilities abroad were at the cutting edge of technology. Some domestic facilities were obsolete—the Youngstown plant, closed in 1977, was 70 years old—and management was slow to introduce new technologies already in use by foreign competitors. By the time Carter came into office, the domestic steel industry was experiencing intense foreign competition.

Not only was American industry hurting because of increased capacity abroad; certain advantages the industry had always enjoyed were disappearing. Charles Schultze reported to Carter, in a summary of a Council on Wage and Price Stability report, that "most of the earlier U.S. competitive advantage in raw material costs has been lost; sharp improvements in shipping costs have reduced the disadvantage to the Japanese of buying U.S. coal." Further, Schultze reported to Carter, while new American facilities were not inferior to new facilities abroad, sharply higher construction costs had increased the cost of steel modernization. Operating costs had also risen. "Between 1967 and 1977 average wages in the U.S. economy rose 97 percent—steel workers' wages rose 142 percent, and coal wages (coking coal is an important cost) rose 124 percent."[78] Japanese production costs were 15 to 20 percent below those in the United States. Lower costs in Japan enabled Japanese producers to underprice American steel products within large parts of the American market without selling below cost, the traditional test for a case of "dumping." Environmental, health, and safety regulations were not a part of the competitive problem; while they raised American production costs, other countries were doing as much or more.[79]

The long-term problems of the industry were aggravated by cyclical events. A worldwide boom in steel in 1973 and the first half of 1974 led to further increases in capacity. The harsh recession that hit the industrialized countries in 1974 and 1975 meant sharply reduced operating rates. The sluggish recovery from the recession left world markets with weak demand and excess capacity. A background paper prepared for the Economic Policy Group in mid-1977 estimated that "world steel making capacity will exceed demand through 1980 and most probably through 1985. The United States is the only major steel market that allows for relatively free trade in steel, and therefore the excess supply pressure may seek an outlet through increased exports to the U.S."[80] The large integrated American firms, like most oligopolistic producers, did not respond to weakening demand by dropping price. "In contrast," the background paper continued, "foreign producers exhibit considerable export price flexibility in response to fluctuating demand." Price flexibility on the part of foreign suppliers was necessary to maintain markets, since mass layoffs were unacceptable and producers were faced with high fixed capital charges. Furthermore, domestic prices in these countries could be insulated from falling export prices.

United States employment in steel rose in the economic expansion of the early 1970s from 427,000 in January 1972 to a peak of 495,000 in the summer of 1974. By the spring of 1975 almost 100,000 steel workers had lost their jobs due to the recession. Some recovery took place in 1976. Domestic industry was operating at 85 percent by mid-1977, but conditions remained critical. Foreign suppliers were making heavy inroads into American markets. In October Secretary Blumenthal reported to Carter, in preparation for a White House conference on steel, that about 18,000 workers had been laid off since July. During the first 8 months of 1977, imports were 30 percent above 1976, with Japan accounting for 46 percent and the European Community for another 31 percent.[81]

The administration came under heavy pressure to propose relief. Steel caucuses had been formed in the Senate and House with members from the states and districts most severely affected. Unemployment was concentrated in a few regions: 55 percent of unemployed workers were in Ohio, Pennsylvania, and New York. Carter met with the members of the steel caucuses. It was a rough meeting. Marty Russo, congressman from Illinois, apologized in a letter to Carter for "the manner in which you were treated by my Democratic colleagues."[82] It seemed necessary to propose some form of relief before Congress reacted with strong protectionist legislation. Voluntary restraint agreements had been negotiated with Japan and the European Economic Community in the late 1960s. They expired in 1974 and were not renewed.[83] Treasury Secretary Blumenthal informed the president that "Under Secretary, Anthony Solomon, will lead a small and select task force, drawn from several agencies, to develop comprehensive policy alternatives for both domestic and international aspects of the problem." The report would be due by late November. Blumenthal also informed the president that Secretary Marshall, Secretary Kreps, and Jack Watson, the cabinet secretary, would make personal visits to the communities hard hit by layoffs. "All of us involved will meet with the 'steel caucus' members to assure the congress of our concern and our commitment to take reasonable action quickly. We must work hard to avoid protectionist legislation prior to the congressional adjournment."[84]

The summary of the report that emerged contained a number of recommendations, including proposals to assist the industry in modernization of facilities, to reexamine regulatory processes of EPA to ensure regulations do not present unnecessary barriers to upgrading, and to provide trade adjustment assistance for impacted workers.[85] The central part of the recommendations was the proposal for a "trigger price mechanism," meant as an alternative to disruptive cuts in imports that would result from a large number of antidumping cases submitted in administrative and judicial actions. A trigger price would be set by the Treasury based on the full cost of production, including transportation, of the most efficient producers—who, at the time, were the Japanese. Imports below Japanese costs would "trigger" fast-track remedial procedures—such as expediting Treasury investigation and application of appropriate remedies, "including possible retroactive application of antidumping duties."[86] The plan should substantially eliminate injury, the report continued, but not eliminate all possibility of price competition, "an element missing in solutions featuring quantitative restraint. . . . We have concluded that if unfair competition, as defined by the law, is effectively deterred through the 'fast track-trigger price system,' that industry can recapture a substantial share of the market. . . . Absent price increases significantly out-of-line with cost increases, there should be a decline from the current 20 percent level of total consumption accounted for by imports to a level of 14 percent (which is closer to the historical average of the last decade.)"[87]

The trigger price mechanism gave the industry temporary relief. According to a Congressional Budget Office report, import prices were only 2 percent below the price of domestic steel in 1979 compared to 14 percent below in 1977.[88] One study found that the trigger price mechanism accounted for 25 percent of the increase in the price of imports. A large part of the increase was explained by the fall in the value of the dollar—an event that would have occurred regardless of the administration's actions in the steel case—a decrease that made foreign goods more expensive. Secretary Miller reported to the president that the industry, which had suffered profit losses in 1977, made a profit of $1.3 billion in 1978. While this was an improvement, it was still, as a percent of capital, about half that of all manufacturing industries. Profit improvement continued in the first three quarters of 1979, but in the fourth quarter, United States Steel suffered record losses. Since Japanese costs provided the standard for the trigger mechanism, Japanese producers could price below American firms without setting off the trigger, provided they did not sell below their own costs. A problem of the arrangement for domestic producers was that European suppliers, whose costs were above those of the Japanese, could sell in the United States at a price below their own costs, provided they did not go below the costs of producers in Japan. In the first quarter of 1980, United States Steel filed new anti-dumping suits against European companies.

The trigger price arrangement was originally negotiated with the industry with the understanding that steel firms would refrain from submitting formal petitions for relief. The whole point of the mechanism was to avoid anti-dumping complaints. When United States Steel filed petitions the administration, after much internal discussion, suspended the trigger price mechanism. Carter made the announcement just before the Democratic primary in Pennsylvania, where he was being challenged for the nomination by Senator Ted Kennedy. Pennsylvania was one of the states seriously impacted by foreign competition. A revised version of the price mechanism was reintroduced in late 1980. Alfred Kahn recalled in a later interview that "we were absolutely convinced that the Department of Commerce decision on dumping was going to come out and it was going to be worse and so we had no choice."[89]

One study estimated that the trigger price mechanism caused roughly a 1 percent increase in the price of domestic steel.[90]

OVERALL EFFECT OF MICROECONOMIC DECISIONS

Some of the shocks adding to the inflationary pressure during the Carter years—food price shocks, increases in energy costs, the decline in the productivity growth rate—were outside the control of the administration. Other shocks were within the discretion of the administration: the increases in the minimum wage and the Social Security payroll tax, regulatory decisions, and actions involving protection for domestic industries from international competition. They have been described as "self-inflicted wounds."[91] It is difficult to estimate the precise effect on inflation of the microeconomic decisions of the Carter administration, but it is clear that the impact was not unimportant. Barry Bosworth has reported that the minimum wage increase and the Social Security tax increase, along with an increase in the unemployment insurance tax, contributed three-fourths of a percentage point to the inflation rate in 1978. Decisions by EPA and OSHA contributed another three-fourths of a percentage point.[92]

The members of the Council of Economic Advisers were the most concerned about the effect of microeconomic decisions. "The Carter administration shot itself in the foot repeatedly on the micro side," Lyle Gramley said in a later interview, "and we in the CEA were far more conscious of this than anybody else. We used to write memos to the President, we used to fight like tigers at inter-agency meetings to ward off some of these programs that were going to add to the inflation on the micro side, but we were by-and-large unsuccessful."[93] Charles Schultze, also reflecting on these episodes later, bemoaned what he viewed as micro mistakes, but thought that the effect was not a major one. "There were a lot of things coming on, such as, regulatory policy and minimum wages. But my recollection of the numbers was that in no one year was it important. But it contributed."[94]

In judging the effect of the microeconomic decisions, it is clear that some of the them could not have been avoided. Maintaining the solvency of the Social Security system gave the administration little choice in raising the payroll tax. Pressures on administrations to raise periodically the minimum wage in response to inflation is a routine happening. Some type of relief for the steel industry seems inevitable. Had the administration not acted, Congress would have, and perhaps in a more stringent way. A reasonable conclusion seems to be that the effect of the microeconomic decisions that were within the power of the administration to avoid was modest in explaining an inflation rate that finally moved into the double-digit range.

CHAPTER 11 | **ENTER PAUL VOLCKER**

In July 1979, President Carter retreated to Camp David for ten days to consult with a large number of invited experts and to reflect on the status of his administration. As a result of his retreat at Camp David he decided to shake up his cabinet. One of the resignations that followed was that of Secretary of the Treasury Michael Blumenthal. A number of prominent potential candidates declined to be considered for his vacated position. Because of instability in foreign exchange markets and in the domestic financial system, it was important that the post be filled as soon as possible. The president decided to ask William Miller to move to the Treasury. "That leaves a hole at the Fed," Stuart Eizenstat said as he recalled events. "During this whole time, financial markets are very nervous, for obvious reasons. Then, having first created a hole we couldn't fill quickly at Treasury, we now have a hole created at the Fed. Whom do you now appoint at the Fed? Better go with somebody who will calm financial markets. That's how Volcker came up; people had no earthly idea of where Volcker really stood."[1] Paul Volcker, who would have major impact on American monetary policy and break the momentum of inflation, came on stage as the result of chance circumstances.

He had an unusually strong background for the job. Following graduate studies in economics at Princeton, he worked in private banking. Among other assignments he was director of planning at the Chase Manhattan Bank. He served at the Treasury as undersecretary for monetary affairs, a position in which he gained extensive experience interacting with foreign finance ministers and central bank officials. At the time of Miller's departure

William Miller and Carter. At the time this photograph was taken, Miller was secretary of the treasury. He had previously been chairman of the Federal Reserve. He is the only person to have served in both positions. Courtesy of the Jimmy Carter Library.

from the Federal Reserve, Volcker was president of the New York Federal Reserve bank, which is responsible for carrying out the directions of the Open Market Committee and is also the Federal Reserve System's main link with international financial markets. The search for the new chairman was handled out of Vice President Mondale's office. Volcker's name was brought up for consideration by Anthony Solomon, the undersecretary of the treasury.[2]

Carter did not know Volcker personally, but from advisers' comments the New York Fed president sounded to him like the type of person he needed. Lyle Gramley has described his impression of Carter's thinking. "He was beginning to see," Gramley said in a post-presidency interview,

> in a way that others in the administration were seeing, that what he had done, up to this point, was simply not dealing effectively with the inflation problem. He was searching for guidance as to what might be done. When Volcker came over there to see Carter, he said to Carter in effect, "now look, I'll tell you, in no uncertain terms, that I'm going to be independent. If you don't like that, then I am not your man." In many

respects, his willingness to accept Paul Volcker as Federal Reserve chairman, which he did despite reservations expressed by the Council of Economic Advisers through Charlie, was, I think, because in part he felt that he just had to do something; that Volcker did have a reputation of being very tough on inflation, and he might be successful in dealing with the problem. I don't think he had any conception what this would mean, in terms of the course Volcker would take. Neither did anybody else, as far as that goes.[3]

Volcker's account verifies Gramley's impressions. When he was asked to come to see Carter, he later recalled, he "went to Washington without any particular expectation, mainly concerned that the president not be under any misunderstanding of my own concern about the importance of an independent central bank and the need for tighter money—tighter than Bill Miller had wanted."[4] Carter's recollection of the meeting is consistent with Volker's. I mentioned to the president in an interview that he never said anything in his memoir *Keeping Faith* about the appointment of Paul Volcker, perhaps his most important appointment. "I probably should have said something about him," the president replied. "That was a very important decision for me to make. It was in a time of economic concern for me. I didn't really know whether Paul Volcker was a Democrat or Republican. I didn't care. He came in my office with his six-and-a-half foot frame and sprawled on a couch, and I think he was smoking a cigar, and he made it plain, and it was mutual, that if he took the job he would want to do it in accordance with my previously expressed policy, that I wouldn't try to put pressure on him or interfere in his best judgment in that important role."[5]

In his first appearance before Congress in late summer, 1979, Volcker made clear the priority of price stability in his thinking. "The traditional response throughout the postwar period to any prospect of declining production and rising unemployment has been a sharp shift in monetary and fiscal policy toward expansion and the enhancement of aggregate demand—even at the risk of adding to inflation. A decade or two ago, with prices historically fairly stable, that risk was discounted. But now we have to face squarely the adverse consequences of premature or unduly large moves to stimulate the economy. . . . Ultimately the perceived 'trade-off' between unemployment and inflation would only be worsened. That is the lesson of the 1970s, not just in the United States but elsewhere."[6] It is interesting that Paul Volcker was appointed only about two months before the second-year standards of the wage-price control program were announced. Whether it was recognized at the time or not, the administration's efforts to control inflation through incomes policy had become secondary in the anti-inflation game. The ball was now in the hands of Paul Volcker.

The new chairman attended a meeting of the International Monetary Fund (IMF) in Belgrade in early October. On the flight to Europe he filled in William Miller, the new secretary of the treasury, and Charles Schultze on some of his thinking. "They were not enthused," Volcker has written, "but I got some psychological reinforcement when we stopped off at Hamburg, hometown of Helmut Schmidt, who had become chancellor of the West German Republic. We spent part of the day with him and with Otmar Emminger, who had become president of the Bundesbank. Schmidt was at his irascible worst—or best, depending upon one's point of view. He dominated the conversation and left no doubt that his patience with what he saw as American neglect and irresolution about the dollar had run out."[7] Volcker received similar complaints from other European representatives.

Much was made in the media of his departure from the IMF meeting a day early to return to the United States. His leaving was taken as a symbol of his sense of urgency. This interpretation has been downgraded by Volcker.[8] He did, however, call a secret Saturday meeting of the Federal Reserve Board on October 6, 1979, now an important date in Federal Reserve history. The Board decided on several actions. The discount rate, for example, was raised by a full percentage point, an unusually large increase. But the key part of the announcement was a change in the procedure that the Fed used to conduct monetary policy. To understand what happened requires a brief aside.[9]

As discussed earlier, the Federal Reserve could target either interest rates or the quantity of money—in the lingo of the trade, the federal funds rate or the "monetary aggregates."[10] The Fed can slow down the creation of new money, which is generated through bank loans to the public, by raising interest rates. Or it can more directly limit loans and new money creation by controlling bank reserves. The Fed has traditionally preferred to target interest rates, and for a specific reason. If the Fed uses interest rates as the policy variable, they tend to be more stable. Erratic behavior of rates can be a critical problem for banks and other financial institutions, a problem that the Fed would like to minimize. Banks live in a world of interest rates; they lend money at one rate and attract funds into deposits at another. Fluctuating rates make it more difficult to maintain a profitable spread between the two. By exercising control through interest rates, the Fed can dampen instability in financial markets. There is a downside to this approach. "With the best staff in the world," Volcker has written, "and all the computing power we could give them, there could never be any certainty about just the right level of the federal funds rate to keep the money supply on the right path and to regulate economic activity."[11]

When Volcker convinced the Federal Reserve Board to use "monetary aggregates," the quantity of reserves and money, as the target, he had several purposes in mind. First of all he wanted to gain tighter control over the money supply. A second purpose was to dramatize his commitment to an anti-inflationary policy. Money control is a simpler type of control and sends a clearer signal to the public. "More focus on the money supply also would be a way of telling the public that we meant business," Volcker has written. "People don't need an advanced course in economics to understand that inflation has something to do with too much money; if we could get out the message that when we say we're going to control money, we mean we're going to deal with inflation, then we would have a chance of affecting ordinary people's behavior."[12]

There was a third, more subtle advantage to adopting the money target, an advantage which requires a word of explanation. Jimmy Carter had run for office on a platform of lowering the unemployment rate, but he recognized early that inflation was also a potential problem. His concern over inflation is the reason he canceled the temporary tax rebate that was part of his original stimulus package. Even if he had fully understood the danger of inflation as it eventually unfolded, he—or a Republican president for that matter—could not have introduced the draconian measures necessary to stop it in its tracks. The country had just gone through the worst recession since the Great Depression. Voters would not have accepted a policy severe enough to stop the rise in prices at the cost of another recession. Carter did not have the mandate. Herbert Stein, economic adviser to Nixon, has said that we do not know that President Ford, if he had been reelected in 1976, would have followed a course of moderation sufficient to keep inflation in check. "But we do know that the basis for the persistence of such a course had not been laid. . . . In February 1978, Arthur Burns was replaced by Carter's own man, G. William Miller, as chairman of the Fed. The performance of the Fed was not, however, chiefly a reflection of the personalities involved. It was a response to a prevailing attitude in the country about the goals of economic policy."[13]

By the time Volcker came into the chairmanship of the Fed, the mandate was there. Having had a taste of double-digit inflation, the country was now ready for a strong anti-inflation initiative.[14] It would be helpful, though, once the tight money and painfully high interest rates began to bite, to deflect the political backlash. Reducing the Fed's exposure was a side benefit of the move to money targets. Schultze has explained.

> Either consciously or unconsciously, Volcker was absolutely dead right on the politics of it. In order to do what had to be done to stop and reverse inflation, the Fed had to jack interest rates up to unprecedented heights. Now if the Fed had gone about doing it the way it used to do things, every month picking the federal funds target, then, in the eyes of the public, the Fed would have been driving those rates up. And the genius of what Volcker did, during the period when you had to get the public used to this, was to adopt a system which came to the same thing, but in which he said we are not raising interest rates, we are just setting a non-inflationary path for the money supply, and the markets are raising the interest rates. It enabled the Fed to do politically, during that transition period, what it couldn't have done in a more direct way.[15]

Volcker's adoption of money targets fit in with previously expressed congressional directives. Concurrent Resolution 133, passed in 1975, required the Federal Reserve to report to Congress its objectives for annual growth of the money supply. This directive was formalized in the Humphrey-Hawkins Act, passed in October 1978. The effect of these congressional actions, however, was relatively limited. While the chairman of the Federal Reserve Board announced the Fed's money target in his periodic testimony before Congress, it was stated in the form of a range rather than a specific number, giving the Fed some latitude in its actual decisions. There are also several definitions of money, which do not always move by the same amount or even in the same direction This variety of targets makes the behavior of money somewhat difficult to interpret. The Fed was able to miss the target with relative impunity. Meanwhile variation in the federal funds rate was kept within a narrow boundary. In effect the Fed continued to target interest rates with only a modest nod in the direction of the aggregates. Volcker moved the Fed to serious money targeting.[16]

Schultze was opposed to the Fed's approach; not necessarily to the tightening of credit, but to the method of carrying it out. Once you adopt money targets, he felt, you get trapped in them. "If you convince the world that virtue consists in sticking with those money targets," he has said, "even when they don't make sense, then you have a hard time getting out of it."[17] He also thought the new procedure risky in terms of the effect that volatile interest rates—likely to follow under money supply targeting—would have

Paul Volcker in conversation with William Miller and Alfred Kahn. The person on the left is Alonzo McDonald, assistant to the president. Courtesy of the Jimmy Carter Library.

on financial markets. The Fed was moving into unexplored territory. Interest rates did, in fact, rise to unexpected heights once the policy was implemented. Gramley later said in an interview, "we were taking some enormous chances. Because we really didn't know how the economy, how the response of money stock and interest rates in the economy were going to work in this new regime. And I began to worry quite seriously, in the spring of 1980, that we might be on a course of action that was cyclically very destabilizing. And there might be explosive oscillations setting in, in term of movements of interest rates and money GNP [gross national product]. It didn't turn out that way."[18] Volcker, himself, was concerned about the effects of the new policy on financial markets and the economy in general. Building contractors, who work in an interest-sensitive and particularly vulnerable industry, were particularly hard hit. They mailed foot-long pieces of "two-by-fours" to the Federal Reserve with letters that said they didn't need them anymore.

Despite his misgivings Schultze defended the Fed to outside critics. Congressman Jim Wright wrote Carter expressing his concern about the Fed's move. Schultze replied on behalf of the president. "The Federal Reserve's actions on October 6 were designed to deal with painfully difficult circumstances in our economy and in financial markets. Inflation has shown no sign of abatement. Supplies of money and credit were growing at much too rapid a pace.... Most outside economists, of varying political persuasion, have agreed that the Federal Reserve had no choice but to act vigorously."[19] A decade later Schultze, with the advantage of hindsight, would reflect on the role of the Fed following the October 6 decision. "For Carter to stop the inflation," he said at a conference on the Carter administration held in the late 1980s, "unemployment would have had to go from 6 percent to 10 percent. No democratically elected president can or would do it (neither Carter or Reagan). You have to have an independent central bank. If I had said this 30 years ago, I would have thrown rocks at myself."[20]

Within the administration Carter's advisers had passed on to him their concerns that the new policy might have unpredictable results. "But it was significant to me," Volcker has said, "that while the president would strongly prefer that we not move in the way we proposed, with all its uncertainties, he was not going to insist on that judgment in an unfamiliar field over the opinion of his newly appointed Federal Reserve chairman."[21] Carter refrained from criticizing the Fed's actions. Interest rates went through the ceiling in the first part of 1980, fell in the middle of the year, and rose again during the latter part while the election campaign was heating up. Carter's support for the Fed must have been, at times, painful. His instincts on monetary policy were those of a small businessman. He had dealt with bankers while running his peanut-processing business, and had faced high interest charges. He shared the convictions of Harry Truman, whose haberdashery failed in a money crunch in the 1920s. A poignant moment in Truman's presidency occurred when the president interviewed William McChesney Martin in the oval office, before appointing him to head the Federal Reserve, and sought some type of assurance that Martin would not raise interest rates.

Despite Carter's outward support of Volcker, he had his moments of frustration. I reminded the president in a later interview of a handwritten memorandum addressed to Secretary of the Treasury William Miller, sent when interest rates had reached historic levels. The memorandum read: "I think the bankers are cheating the public by keeping the prime rate too high. Advise me immediately what I or we can do." The president commented on the memorandum in the interview a decade later, "well that's an arbitrary decision for bankers to make. If you talked with Bert Lance you know that I had an early incompatibility with most bankers."[22] Bankers, of course, were simply reacting to Federal Reserve pressure. But in this case the president was sympathetic to businessmen who had to face the end results of a money crunch. Both Presidents Truman and Carter had populist views of the banking industry.

In public appearances he supported the Volcker strategy. In a question-and-answer session with editors and broadcasters from Minnesota in late October 1979, a reporter told Carter that the president of the AFL-CIO (American Federation of Labor and Congress of Industrial Organizations) in Minnesota "suggests you find a way of getting rid of Mr. Volcker. Do you have a comment on that?" Carter replied: "Well, first of all, it's not possible to get rid of Mr. Volcker under the American law. And, secondly, the Federal Reserve has very wisely been isolated from political influence exerted by the White House or the congress. It's an independent agency, and I think it ought to be independent. Interest rates are almost directly related to the rate of inflation, and I think it would be expecting too much for the interest rate charges to be lower than the rate of inflation. The best way to get interest rates down is to lower inflation."[23]

"Jimmy Carter would never have let us attack the Fed strongly in the last days of the campaign," Schultze has said.[24] But the president lapsed on one occasion, a month before the 1980 election. As discussed earlier in the introductory chapter, the state of the economy in that campaign was seriously damaging for an incumbent seeking reelection. Inflation was in the double-digit range, interest rates were at historic highs with the three-month Treasury bill rate over 15 percent in late 1980, the bond market was shaky, and the unemployment rate had returned to the level it was when Carter took office. At an appearance in Pennsylvania, an economics major in the audience asked Carter a technical question: "About a year ago the Fed changed its way of dealing with monetary policy. Since that time do you think that the experience has been that this new method has shown us that the monetary supply can be, in fact, controlled by the Government, that it is a better way to deal with the problems of inflation? And finally, how would you evaluate Mr. Volcker's performance in dealing with the new policy?" Carter replied:

> The Fed is independent of the president. It's just like the judicial system. I don't have any influence on it, but that doesn't mean I have to sit mute. My own judgment is that the strictly monetary approach to the Fed's decision on the discount rate and other banking policies is ill-advised. I think the Federal Reserve Bank Board ought to look at other factors and balance them along with the supply of money. . . . I think that the Fed

ought to look at the adverse consequences of increased interest rates on the general economy as a major factor in making their own judgments.... I think Paul Volcker is an outstanding Chairman ... but I think they put too much of their eggs in the money supply basket.[25]

The Council of Economic Advisers prepared a clarification statement following Carter's Pennsylvania appearance. "Under the new system," the statement read,

> the Federal Reserve now concentrates its attention heavily on one objective, controlling the growth of the money supply within predetermined targets, letting interest rates go where they will (within a very broad range). In answering the question, the President stated that in his view controlling the growth of money was a very important factor that should be taken into account.... Obviously all of us have to be concerned about fighting inflation and about controlling the money supply, and also about the effects of rising interest rates in slowing the current economic recovery especially in housing and autos. What is obviously at stake here is the proper balance among these important objectives and this is precisely what the President had in mind.[26]

CONSUMER CREDIT CONTROLS

The recession, which had been expected by both administration and private forecasters for a year and a half, finally came in the second quarter of 1980. It was deep—one of the sharpest drops on record—but it was short, lasting for only a quarter. It happened for a number of reasons. The decline in consumer purchasing power due to the inflation was part of it. The tight money policy was another. Still another was the imposition of consumer credit controls in early 1980.

The Federal Reserve has, in its history, implemented its policies by imposing a general type of control. In a period of inflation it simply reduces the total amount of credit and money available. The market is left to decide freely how the available credit is to be allocated. Quantitative restrictions aimed at specific borrowers or industries are seldom used and require specific authorization by Congress. Consumer credit controls were imposed during World War II and again during the Korean War.[27] Under Carter the use of credit controls had an appeal to some groups like labor unions. Selective controls make it possible, the argument goes, to avoid a harsh shutdown on overall credit and the recession that would follow. George Meany approached Carter about the use of credit controls as early as mid-1978, when the inflation rate began to accelerate. Meany was anticipating that the Federal Reserve might soon begin to tighten. Carter agreed that "we should avoid excessive reliance on monetary restraint to fight inflation. I do not agree, however, that the time has come to resort to selective credit controls."[28]

The use of consumer credit controls in 1980 is a program without a parent. One gets the impression from interviews that most of the advisers were opposed or regretted that it was initiated. Charles Schultze, for example, in a post-presidency interview, recalled that "the whole thing was literally a comedy of errors. To start with, the argument for doing it was weird. It was an argument from the White House political people that if we were going to do all these 'anti-liberal' things, like raise the discount rate, cut social programs and all that, we've got to do something the 'liberals' want. . . . So let's have credit controls."[29] Alfred Kahn is one of the few advisers that can be identified as in favor of controls. "Direct credit restraints?" he responded in an interview. "Yes. I think I was the only one among the economic advisers—no, there was Stu Eizenstat as well—who was attracted by the notion that capital markets did not work perfectly, and I do not find it offensive, though it may be difficult, to direct credit."[30]

Misgivings about controls may have been expressed verbally by advisers, but formal memoranda circulated within the administration recommended their implementation. As early as mid-March 1979, a year before credit controls were imposed, Schultze suggested in a memorandum to Carter the possibility of introducing selective controls; "it might be a plausible strategy."[31] Two weeks later Secretary Blumenthal wrote to the president that "it is the unanimous opinion of your advisers that our anti-inflation program needs the strengthening of a somewhat more restrictive monetary policy." The memorandum goes on to say that "your advisers also agree unanimously that action should be taken to limit the most liberal terms on consumer credit. Such action would require you to invoke the Credit Control Act of 1969 and to request that the Federal Reserve Board take steps to put consumer credit controls into effect."[32] The controls were not introduced in 1979. They were included in a new anti-inflation initiative announced in mid-March 1980.

In an interview conducted after Carter left office, Lyle Gramley said that

> the credit control program that was put together by the Carter administration, with the assistance of the Federal Reserve, was a reaction to the uncertainty generated by dramatic changes in interest rates and the fear

that those interest rates could tear the economy apart. That maybe we could slow down the credit expansion machinery a bit by dumping some sand in it through credit controls. That's the genesis of that program. At this point, I can't remember where we started out. Once it got under way, we tried to shape it in ways that would make it effective. But, I just can't recall at this point, whether we were initially opposed to the idea.[33]

While the 1969 act empowered the president to authorize the Fed to impose selective controls, it did not require the Fed to implement them. Volcker was reluctant to impose consumer credit controls, as was the Fed in general. He didn't want to deal with the morass of administering detailed controls. The idea for controls was finally accepted by the Fed with the condition that they would be mild.

Consumer credit controls imposed in the post–World War II era had provisions that limited the number of months over which a loan could be financed. The result was to increase the size of monthly payments and so discourage credit use. The controls implemented in March 1980 had no such provisions. They called for a "voluntary" limitation on total loan expansion by banks. The Fed established a special deposit requirement of 15 percent for increases in the types of credit covered. Basically the controls were bank administered. Loans for the purchase of automobiles, furniture and appliances, and for home improvement expenditures and mortgages were excluded from the controls. The restraint was directed primarily at revolving credit in the use of credit cards. Credit cards had only recently become a part of the American experience and were used by many consumers mainly for their convenience. Outstanding loans were paid off at the end of the month. "I recall," Lyle Gramley said in a later interview, "that the monetary economist that worked for me came in, after we saw the final program that the Fed had put together with consultations from representatives of the administration, and she was screaming that those people don't understand how markets work at all; this program will be totally ineffective." She was right in her skepticism, but, as Gramley said, "of course it hit like a ton of bricks. We had no idea that was going to happen."[34]

The controls were mild but the effect was dramatic. Manufacturers and retailers bombarded the White House with the complaints that consumer spending, particularly for big ticket items, was falling through the floor. "Nobody contemplated that the response would be so enormous," Kahn later observed. "It was clearly associated with the reaction. Some people sent me credit cards, wrote irate letters to the effect that Sears Roebuck was still soliciting credit card accounts. They said that's unpatriotic."[35] Apparently the "voluntary" limitation on total loan expansion had an effect. Schultze reported to the president that "there is anecdotal evidence that banks are responding to the limitation by rejecting very large numbers of auto loans, so they can reserve their limited loan extensions for business customers."[36] The unexpected experience with credit controls, along with a large drop in interest rates in mid-1980, which made the argument for direct controls less relevant, led to their removal in July. They may have contributed to blurring the effects of the Volcker monetary policy and prolonging the transition to a noninflationary environment.

AFTERMATH

Volcker continued his restrictive monetary policy into the Reagan administration in order to break the inflation. Carter's advisers were right that stopping an inflation with fiscal and monetary policies imposes a high cost. The recession of 1981–82, the second stage that followed the one-quarter drop in production in 1980, was as severe as the recession of 1974–75 during the Ford years. Unemployment rose in the early 1980s to a record level. But the payoff was impressive. Stabilizing the price level paved the way for the rather remarkable stretch of low unemployment and low inflation that characterized the latter part of the 1980s and the 1990s, and which continued into the early twenty-first century.[37]

The experience of the Great Inflation has left a permanent mark on the consciousness of the major industrial states. Price stability is now a worldwide priority of central banks. The historic rise in prices also enhanced the banks' independence, an independence that gives them the freedom to concentrate their attention on the goal of price stability. One of the first steps of Prime Minister Tony Blair when he assumed office in Britain in 1997 was to grant authority to the Bank of England to set the bank rate, a prerogative it did not previously have. The fact that the change was made by the head of the liberal Labour Party dramatizes how pervasive the change in priorities is.[38]

In an earlier chapter I examined the extent to which the administration abetted the inflation of the later 1970s by pursuing a stimulative fiscal policy in the early Carter years. There would probably be a consensus among economists that monetary policy contributed more than fiscal decisions to the rise in the price level. To judge the contribution of money to the Great Inflation, one has to consider the entire decade, not just the Carter years. As a result of the breakdown of the Bretton Woods arrangement in the early

1970s, world liquidity increased dramatically. Over the period 1970–72 the nominal money supply rose at an annual rate of over 13 percent in Germany and a little over 27 percent in Japan, as both nations intervened in support of the dollar. Nominal balances increased by almost 8 percent in the United States, just under double the average annual growth over the course of the 1960s. These large increases in the money supply in the early 1970s were a major cause of the inflation of the decade. The rapid expansion of money preceded the rise in oil prices in 1973 and 1974. The prices of nonfarm commodities, other than oil, increased before the Organization of Petroleum Exporting Countries shock, suggesting that the expansion of money was already exerting pressure on the market for industrial materials.[39] One economist, in citing the loss of international discipline on the creation of money that followed the fall of the Bretton Woods system, has written: "with the double whammy of the loss of an external constraint, and an inadequately responsive monetary rule in place, the inevitable result was the Great Inflation."[40]

Monetary policy was overly expansionary in the early 1970s under the chairmanship of Arthur Burns. Burns was an authority on business cycles. How did he allow money to get out of control? The mishap is partly explained by his view of how the economy works. "Burns did not consider money to be a major independent influence on economic activity or inflation," one student of the period has written. "For Burns, the fundamental determinant of economic activity was the confidence of businessmen. As a result, Burns emphasized not the rate of growth of money but its short-run velocity, which he believed reflected that confidence."[41] The annual rate of increase in money was 5.9 percent for M-1 and 9.0 percent for M-2 for Burns's eight years as chairman of the Federal Reserve Board of Governors. For the previous eight years, it was 4.6 percent for M-1 and 7.2 percent for M-2. Not only did money increase more rapidly, it was, according to another Burns scholar, procyclical in its behavior, increasing at a faster rate in economic expansions than it did in contractions. "It is hard to avoid the conclusion that monetary policy contributed to the many woes of the 1970–1978 period."[42]

Those who point to monetary policy as a major cause of the price increases of the 1970s cite the renewal of monetary expansion in the years following the recession of 1974–75. Policy was stimulative in Germany and Japan in 1978, as well as in the United States, and added to the effect of the expansionary fiscal policies following the meeting of the Group of Seven at

Bonn.[43] Both oil price shocks of the 1970s were preceded by expansionary monetary policies.

External shocks, such as food and energy, are temporary in their effects; they work themselves out, economists would say, over the longer period. But presidents don't live in the long run. The problems of a four-year span create their reality. The effects of the food and energy shocks were a dominant influence on inflation in the Carter years, more so than they are today. The oil price increase of the 1970s had not only the direct effect of raising the cost of energy and petrochemicals to industry and consumers. It had the secondary effect of feeding into wage increases and making the shock effect more permanent by becoming embodied in the underlying rate. It is this second-stage effect that the incomes policy of the Carter administration was meant to prevent. A recent study suggests that the impact on wages of an oil price increase would be less in today's economy than it was during Carter's term. "Since around 1980," the study concludes, "oil price changes seem to affect inflation mostly through their direct share in a price index, with little or no pass-through into core measures. By contrast, before 1980 oil shocks contributed substantially to core inflation."[44] Jimmy Carter had the misfortune that the shocks hit heavily during his term in office.

A balanced analysis of the Great Inflation would seem to be that the shocks had a major effect; but the expansionary monetary policy that preceded them made the economy more vulnerable to these outside inflationary pressures. Most of the monetary damage was done before Carter came into office. Arthur Burns controlled Federal Reserve decisions from 1970 to the early part of 1978. Policy during the Miller years in office can be classified as loose, when a tighter regime would have been appropriate. It is to Carter's credit that he appointed Paul Volcker, who broke the back of the Great Inflation, to the chairmanship of the Federal Reserve.

CHAPTER 12 | **JIMMY CARTER AND THE AGE OF LIMITS**

"Jimmy Carter was the first Democratic president since Roosevelt to be faced with limits," Charles Schultze commented in an interview after the administration left office.[1] These economic limits set the boundaries of Carter's policy options and moved him in a more conservative direction. The limits, in turn, were due to events over which he had little control. "In no other area of domestic affairs," Stuart Eizenstat has said, "is a president so much at the mercy of external forces as in the critical area of economic policy."[2] In this final chapter we look carefully at these limits that helped to define the presidency of Jimmy Carter.

The Great Inflation dominated Carter's years in office. The pressure he exerted on unions to moderate wage demands put him in conflict with the Democratic Party's historic constituency. The inflation forced him into a restrictive fiscal mode in the last two years of his administration, a policy that stood in contrast to the policies of his Democratic predecessors. His budget decisions were strongly opposed by the more liberal elements of the party.

As discussed in detail earlier, much of the room in the budget that made possible the New Frontier and the Great Society had been exhausted when Carter came into office in 1977. The cost of entitlements created by the social initiatives grew with the increase in population, surpassing the cost of the original programs. The steady increase in the number of citizens eligible for the social entitlements created by legislation enacted during the Roosevelt administration on through the Johnson one—and the indexing of benefits to adjust for inflation—left little room for expansion of existing programs or creation of new ones. In addition, these programs were originally financed, in large part, by a "fiscal dividend," the increased federal revenues generated by the healthy economic growth rates of the 1950s and 1960s. When the growth rate slowed under Carter, he no longer had the option of paying for them with revenues from a growing economic pie.

Jimmy Carter came into office as a fiscal conservative. He was attuned to public concern about the string of budget deficits accumulated in the decades before him, and he promised in the 1976 campaign to balance the budget by 1980. He also knew that the public had growing doubts about the effectiveness of some social programs.[3] Yet he was also liberal on social issues. "He felt deeply about problems of poverty," Eizenstat has said. "He'd come from the rural south. He knew what poverty was all about."[4] There was continuing tension between his liberal instincts and his sense of fiscal prudence. But in the end, his natural inclination toward fiscal discipline and his liberal instincts were both, in part, irrelevant. The inflation, which had reached frightening proportions in the latter part of his administration, left him little choice but to move toward fiscal restraint.[5]

Of all the shocks that hit the administration and defined the limits of Carter's presidency, the most important was the slowdown in the rate of growth of productivity. If one had only one piece of data to use to monitor the health of an economy, the productivity growth rate would be the best indicator. Slower productivity growth meant, first of all, that increases in worker efficiency were not sufficient to compensate for wage increases and to prevent labor costs from rising. Higher labor costs were passed on by employers to consumers in the form of higher prices. The inflationary effects of higher food and energy cost eventually dissipate; but this combination of high money wages and low productivity gains became embedded in the core inflation rate. There is an even more important long-run consideration. Increases in output per worker are the main source of advances in the standard of living that Americans have routinely come to expect. The rising prosperity from generation to generation throughout our history is rooted in increases in the efficiency of workers and management. When real wages failed to increase during Carter's term as they had in the past, frustration among voters, most of whom were not aware of why this was happening, gradually began to set in.

PRODUCTIVITY AND ECONOMIC GROWTH

The earliest economists were not primarily concerned with recessions or with short-term "crises" that occurred periodically. They concentrated on what causes an economy to grow over time. They focused on the long-term gains in our potential to produce, rather than the short-term ups and downs, which they thought to be self-correcting. Adam Smith, who wrote the first significant book on economics in 1776, entitled his treatise *The Wealth of Nations*. He attempted to explain what causes the wealth of nations to grow from generation to generation. This preoccupation with long-run growth dominated professional economic thought over the next century and a half.[6]

It was a subject of pressing importance. The industrial revolution of the eighteenth century led to an historic breakthrough in our ability to provide the necessities and luxuries of life. Economic growth helps everyone. As John Kennedy once said, "a rising tide lifts all boats." Yet the poor benefit most from economic growth. The rich in every age live well, but economic growth lifts the poor from famine and destitute hunger to a share in the increasing abundance of an expanding economy.

The Great Depression in the 1930s shifted economists' attention to the short-run problem of the failure of an economy to fully use its factories and productive facilities accumulated over time. Massive unemployment forced them to deal with the paradox of productive capacity sitting idle while workers were without jobs. The economist who made this problem the focal point of his intellectual energies was John Maynard Keynes. Economists of the next three decades followed him in concentrating their attention on the causes and cures of economic slowdowns. Paul Romer, a modern economic growth theorist, has commented on this shift in time perspective: "Remember that we experienced major macroeconomic calamities in the inter-war period. These depressions were sufficient to wipe out 30 to 40 years' worth of growth. Economists who grew up during this era certainly didn't have any trouble thinking about something else besides long-run growth. They naturally focused on avoiding these calamities."[7]

Keynes, himself, wrote little about economic growth. What may be his only statement on the subject is an essay entitled, "Economic Possibilities for Our Grandchildren."[8] His outlook for the long term, as reflected in this essay, was optimistic. Depressions eventually pass and, beyond that, the problem of providing for the material needs of mankind would be solved in a hundred years through economic growth. The real challenge then would be what to do with the increased leisure.

An interesting connection to Keynes's essay is found in the Carter administration story. In July of 1979 Carter retired to Camp David for ten days of discussions with invited scholars and prominent leaders and for quiet reflection. Returning to Washington he delivered what has come to be called the "malaise" speech in which he talked of a "crisis of confidence" affecting the national will.[9] The nationally televised speech was well received by the public, but the president stepped on his headlines by shaking up his cabinet a few days later.[10] It was in this shake-up that Blumenthal resigned as secretary of the treasury. The Camp David retreat, the speech, and the cabinet shake-up are a well-known episode of the Carter years. The president was influenced in his decision to go to Camp David by a lengthy memorandum prepared by an aide, Patrick Caddell, who had long had a working relationship with Carter. In the memorandum there is a lengthy quotation from Keynes's little-known essay.[11]

While Keynesian economists took a mostly short-term focus, they did not ignore the growth problem. At the urging of his advisers, President Kennedy proposed a tax cut specifically targeted to encourage investment in capital goods, the first policy experiment of this type in the postwar period. On the academic level, a classic research piece on the theory of economic growth was written by Robert Solow, of the Massachusetts Institute of Technology, who was a member of the staff of the Council of Economic Advisers under Kennedy. Solow won the Nobel prize in economics for his work in growth theory, and his 1956 article is still the starting point for research on the subject.[12] Solow's work fostered an interest in "growth accounting," an attempt to quantify precisely the contribution to growth of the variables included in his model—factors like capital investment and improvements in education. A fascinating, and surprising, result of this research was the finding that approximately 40 percent of the historic growth of the American economy could not be explained, a result which one economist working in the area, Moses Abramovitz, called "the measure of our ignorance."[13]

Someone has said—perhaps it was Winston Churchill—that there is nothing that so focuses your attention like being shot at. The attention of economists was again sharply focused on the growth problem when productivity increases, previously taken for granted, abruptly slowed in the late 1960s and early 1970s. William Nordhaus, who was a member of the Council of Economic Advisers under Carter, has written that "if we ignore the wiggles, there was more or less a constant rate of productivity growth from World War I to the middle 1960s. Starting about 1966, however, there has been a slow but steady downward creep from an average of 2 to 2.5 percent annually to a level of slightly under one percent in 1979. Moreover, the smoothed rate of productivity growth in 1979 was lower than any year since 1933, and one would have to go back before 1920 to find a markedly worse year."[14] This drop in productivity, along with the energy crisis, was experienced by the typical voter as a fall in income. *Business Week* reported that between 1967 and 1973, real disposable income per person increased by 17.5 percent; over the next six years the gain fell to a meager 5.5 percent. And beginning in 1979 the numbers actually turned negative."[15] This slowdown in productivity gains and income was also experienced by other industrialized nations.

It took a while for observers monitoring the economy using real time data to recognize what was happening. When it became clear that a drop in productivity gains and a slowing of the pace of economic growth was taking place, growth accountants attempted to explain the reason. The results were inconclusive.[16] Just as we have a problem in accounting for all the factors that have contributed to growth, we are also not sure what caused the slowdown. The slowdown that occurred from the late 1960s and early 1970s to at least the middle of the 1990s—healthier growth seems to have reappeared in President Clinton's second term in office—made economic growth one of the most emphasized topics in recent research in macroeconomics.[17]

Jimmy Carter was not familiar with this professional literature on economic growth, but he had long been interested in the productive potential of the world's economies. His interest was stimulated by a strand of futuristic literature popular in the early 1970s. While governor he came into contact with a representative piece, the Club of Rome's *The Limits to Growth*.[18] The Club of Rome, a loose association of scientists, technocrats, and politicians, emerged from a meeting held in Rome in 1968.[19] Within a few years it had seventy-five members from twenty-five countries. The club members were concerned about the side effects of economic growth in a world of finite resources. They were interested in such problems as the environmental damage done by industrialization, excessive population growth, and the deterioration of urban centers.

The club became aware of work done by Jay Forrester, a professor of engineering and management at the Massachusetts Institute of Technology (MIT). At a rather young age Forrester was director of MIT's Digital Computer Lab. He developed a computer simulation model designed to track the interconnectedness of factors contributing to future world problems. Forrester agreed to form a team to do a study using his computer model for the Club of Rome. The result was *The Limits to Growth*.[20] While such things as the potential damage to the environment arising from economic growth, and the limitation of fossil fuels, were widely recognized, the conclusions of *The Limits to Growth* were considered unnecessarily alarmist.

If current trends in population, pollution, industrialization, and resource usage continued, the report argued, limits to exponential growth would be reached within a century. "The authors recommended, among other things, a 40 percent reduction in industrial investment, a 20 percent reduction in agricultural investment, a 40 percent reduction in the birth rate, and a massive transfer of wealth from rich to poor countries."[21] The implications for humanity of the study's conclusions echoed the dire prediction of Robert Malthus, in his eighteenth-century *Essay on Population*, that population would grow more rapidly than the food supply. *The Limits to Growth* had a big impact. By the end of the 1970s it had sold four million copies in thirty languages. The study was sharply criticized by economists for failure to recognize the potential of technology for pollution abatement to counter the negative impact of industrialization, and for omitting the power of the market pricing mechanism to induce the substitution of available alternatives for scarce resources.[22]

President Carter read the Club of Rome report while governor. He cited it in a speech to the American Society for Information Science in 1974. "The Club of Rome reports meld together," he said, "the accumulation of scientific data extracted from computers and extrapolate trends toward the future to show a dismal prospect, even for the survival of mankind, if we fail to change some of those trends quickly."[23] I referred to his speech and *The Limits to Growth* in a post-presidency interview. "I remember vividly," he said, "and the follow-up was our Global 2000 report on which we worked for three years, the last three years I was in office. The Club of Rome report was filled with errors and mistakes and improper assumptions. But it was a first effort to analyze what's going to happen fifteen or twenty years in the future if we don't correct the problems of population explosion and the decimation of the forests, and so forth. I was impressed by it."[24] The Global 2000 report, to which the president referred, was completed in July of his last year in office. The study involved the efforts of thirteen federal agencies that were deemed to have an impact on shaping the long-term future of our country. They were directed, President Carter said in his interview, "to take a look at the year 2000, and say where will we be in that year, what will be the source of raw materials, what will be the level of our work force, what we anticipate in all the different phases. And that was a major commitment of mine that was derived from our early reading of the Club of Rome report, and then my subsequent realization of the fallacies and mistakes that were made in their first attempt."[25]

The Global 2000 report is more cautious than *The Limits to Growth*. The projections of the study, it says, "do not predict what will occur. Rather, they depict conditions that are likely to develop if there are no changes in public policies, institutions or rates of technological advance.... A keener awareness of the nature of the current trends may induce changes that will alter these trends and the projected outcome."[26] Madeleine Albright, then on the staff of the National Security Council, provided an evaluation of the report in an internal memorandum. "The Report is credible. The criticism of pessimistic bias leveled against *Limits to Growth* does not apply to the Global 2000 projections, which include assumptions of rapid technological advance and the effects of price rises in restraining demand for resources."[27] By the time the report was finished, Carter was in the middle of an Iranian crisis, a tough presidential campaign, and out-of-control inflation. The report is a footnote in history, but it provides insight into Carter's view of the nation's challenges.

Carter brought to the Oval Office a strong sense of limits. In his inaugural speech he sounded the theme. "We have learned that more is not necessarily better, that even our great Nation has it recognized limits, and that we can neither answer all questions nor solve all problems. We cannot afford to do everything, nor can we afford to lack boldness as we meet the future. So, together, in a spirit of individual sacrifice for the common good, we must simply do our best."[28]

CARTER AND THE DEMOCRATIC PARTY

Carter attempted during his term in office to move the Democratic Party toward the political center to adapt to the changing conditions of the 1970s. "Looking back," James McIntyre later said, "I see that the Carter years were a transitional period during which the optimism of the 1960s was confronted, and we began to realize that we couldn't have it all. In the 1960s, there was rapid economic growth, increased productivity, and rapid expansion of government programs. And there was a general feeling that we could do everything. This continued into the 1970s. People thought that the growth and expansion would continue indefinitely, and that the oil shocks of the 1970s were only temporary aberrations. The Carter administration recognized—and was the first to deal with—the concept of limited resources."[29]

Eizenstat has described Carter as a neoliberal. "He was fiscally moderate and socially liberal; and that was a new sort of liberal. He didn't fit neatly in the existing wings of the party. He was neither a typical southern conservative nor a Kennedy liberal."[30] The liberal wing of the party led by Senator Ted Kennedy never accepted the idea of a need for retrenchment. "It wouldn't be altogether fair," said a scholar interviewing Schultze after the administration left office, "to say that Carter lacked political skill. He had no coalition that wanted to go where he wanted to go." "Exactly," said Schultze. "What he was doing was managing. He was trying to manage in a direction which, while not a hundred and eighty degrees, was to some degree in a different direction than his team of horses wanted to go."[31] The attempt to find a compromise between his own sense of a need for restraint, and the demands of some members of the party for a continuation of the spirit of the 1960s, gave the appearance of indecisiveness. "He was continually torn," Schultze said, "between his own basically correct, substantive instincts and the need to satisfy the coalition that elected him. And so what happened was, one day he would satisfy his basic instincts and listen to one group of advisers, essentially on the somewhat more conservative side, and the next day he would do something to please labor or the liberals. He went back and forth and gave the appearance of not knowing where he was going, and that isn't quite so much true as, like I say, Democrats ever since have never quite figured out how to square that circle."[32]

At the Democratic midterm convention held in Memphis in late 1978, the mood of the convention approached hostility. Senator Kennedy was openly critical of the administration and was giving serious consideration to opposing the president in the Democratic primary in 1980. One Carter scholar has described the scene at the convention. "On Dember 8, the President was received politely when he outlined administration accomplishments and warned that uncontrolled inflation would threaten 'compassionate and progressive government.'" But the soul of the party was with Ted Kennedy. "The next day, speaking at a forum on national health insurance," the account continues, "Kennedy wowed the delegation with the plea to sail against the 'rising wind of conservatism.'"[33]

The antagonism of the liberal wing became sharper as the president's term approached its end. The historian Arthur Schlesinger Jr., author of the best known biography of President John Kennedy and long a leading intellectual in the liberal wing of the party, wrote in an article published while the 1980 campaign was under way: "The reason for Carter's horrible failure in economic policy is plain enough. On such matters he is not a Democrat—at least in anything more recent than the Grover Cleveland sense of the word."[34]

The speech that best describes Carter's underlying theme for economic policy—and one of the best speeches of his presidency—is the one he delivered at the dedication of the John Kennedy Library in 1979. He devoted more time than usual to this piece, working closely with his chief speech writer, Rick Hertzberg.[35] In it he embellishes on the theme of limits and the implications for the party. I asked Schultze if he was involved in this speech. As he recalled, he was not, at least not to a significant extent. "My guess is it sounds like something Stu Eizenstat would write. Stu was, correctly, pushing that line. But recognizing the line intellectually, which I do, and knowing what to do about it, are two different matters."[36] Eizenstat had, indeed, himself delivered a speech on the "New Realities" to the Women's National Democratic Club in January of 1979. It was delivered, in Eizenstat words, "when we were going to come up with our next budget which was going to have some cuts really for the first time." It came some months before Carter spoke at the Kennedy Library. "You ought to read it," he told me in an interview. "It gets into this question of limits. You see what happened, the liberal wing saw this [new administration] as a resurrection of the Great Society. They thought they could resurrect the 1960s and they couldn't. We were in a transition era. Inflation was higher, deficits were more of a problem, and the country was much more conservative."[37] "Our Party and the President who carries the Party's banner," Eizenstat said in his speech, "face a new era—an era in which we will continue to build on the traditional beliefs and commitments of our Party and continue to extend hope to those in need—but in which we must adjust to new realities. Every president must face the reality he inherits; he must govern based on facts and situations handed to him. He cannot recreate the 1960s when he must govern with the far different problems of the 1970s."[38]

The Kennedy Library speech was delivered in October 1979, before seven thousand people, seated, as the scene was described by one reporter, "on folding chairs in front of the nine-story white concrete and glass library designed by I. M. Pei."[39] The audience consisted mostly of Kennedy partisans. By this time everyone knew that Ted Kennedy would probably challenge Carter for the party nomination. The president was preceded at the podium by Joseph Kennedy, son of Robert Kennedy, whose personal papers are also stored in the Kennedy Library. "The sharpest political language came not from the two probable rivals for the Democratic Presidential nomination but from Joseph P. Kennedy, 2nd., the 27-year old son of the late Robert F. Kennedy," the news story reported. He regretted the lack of zeal of the current administration in attacking the problems of the poor and the weak. "'Now we are told by the Chairman of the Federal Reserve that we have to reduce our standard of living,' he continued. 'But what about the standard of living of the people on the boards of the oil companies? Who's stopping them?' "[40] He turned and looked directly at the president who was seated on the podium behind him.[41]

When he arose to speak Carter continued the theme set out by Eizenstat. Carter's words recall an often cited speech that President Kennedy delivered at Yale University in June 1962. In his talk Kennedy presented a defense of his innovative tax cut proposals designed to alleviate the problem of the early 1960s, to "get the country moving again," to stimulate the economy operating at less than full employment. Defending his Keynesian remedy, a cut in income taxes that would move the budget toward deficit, he decried the myth that the budget must always be balanced.[42] The initiative he discussed in his speech was basically a policy to deal with the short-run problem of a sluggish economy. In contrast, in another age, Carter turned his attention to the long-run problem of the economy.

> I believe that America is now ready to meet the challenges of the 1980s with renewed confidence and with renewed spirit. These challenges are not the same ones that confronted us a generation ago. . . . President Kennedy was right: Change is the law of life. The world of 1980 is as different from what it was in 1960 as the world of 1960 was from that of 1940. Our means of improving the world must also be different. After a decade of high inflation and growing oil imports, our economic cup no longer overflows. Because of inflation, fiscal restraint has become a matter of simple public duty. We can no longer rely on a rising economic tide to lift the boats of the poorest in our society.[43]

President Carter did not succeed in pulling the party to the center during his term in office. The time was not yet right. But he was more prescient than other Democratic leaders of his time in his diagnosis of the fundamental economic problem that had to be faced. It has been said that Carter was a precursor to President Clinton. If this statement is understood to mean that Clinton is the Democratic leader who finally had to recognize the reality of an economy of limits, as did Carter two decades before him, there is truth in the saying. After three defeats in presidential elections, the party returned to the voters in 1992 with a modified political position. Clinton's declaration as president in a State of the Union Message that the "era of big government is over," his move toward a balanced budget policy, his attempt to reduce the federal debt, and his consent to reform of the welfare program, all represent adjustment to a new type of economy.

It is sometimes said that Carter's was a failed presidency. One historian has, perhaps, given a more realistic interpretation of the Carter years. "Carter was a Democratic president trying to govern at a time when the bases for Democratic governance had effectively decomposed. It is from this basic perspective that any judgments of the Carter administration's success or failure must be made."[44]

NOTES

Abbreviations

JCL   Jimmy Carter Library, Atlanta, Georgia (The Eizenstat Papers, not yet open to the public, were consulted as well.)

Miller Center   Interviews, Project on the Carter Presidency, White Burkett Miller Center of Public Affairs, University of Virginia, Charlottesville, Virginia

Schultze Papers   Charles L. Schultze Papers, Brookings Institution Library, Washington, D.C.

UCL   Special Collections, University of California Library, Davis, California

Preface

1. Maier, *The Politics of Inflation*, 4.
2. The phrase is used in Levy, *Dollars and Dreams*, 4.
3. Williamson, "Keynes and the International Economic Order," 87.
4. See, for example, Stein, *Presidential Economics*, 23, 219–21; Hargrove and Morley, *The President and the Council of Economic Advisers*, 459–501; Hargrove, *Jimmy Carter as President*, 69–109; and Ribuffo, "Jimmy Carter and the Ironies of American Liberalism." See also an interpretive piece by a member of the administration: Kahn, "America's Democrats: Can Liberalism Survive Inflation?"

Chapter One

1. Carter interview, Miller Center, 61–62.
2. Sick, *October Surprise*, 15.
3. Stuart Eizenstat, "The Presidency in Trouble," 93–94.
4. Carter interview, Miller Center, 61–62.
5. Eizenstat, Address, University of Chicago Law School, 15.
6. Jordan, *Crisis*, 307.
7. The Conference Board of New York publishes a "Help Wanted Index" based on the amount of help wanted advertising placed monthly by employers in a sample of newspapers. It is a rough measure of the national supply of jobs. Since 1951 incumbents have been reelected when job availability, as measured by the Help Wanted Index, was high and have lost when job availability was low. Medoff, "Job Growth." For a detailed analysis of the relationship between presidential elections and the economy, see Fair, "Econometrics and Presidential Elections." See also studies cited therein.
8. *The Gallup Opinion Index*, no. 181 (September 1980):25. Anderson was chosen as best qualified by 11 percent. The remaining respondents selected "don't know."

9 Ibid., 15.
10 White's observation on the similarity of the Iranian problem and the inflation is taken from Kahn interview, Miller Center, 124.
11 Stein, *Presidential Economics*, 220.
12 Memorandum, Charles Schultze to the President, April 1, 1980, Schultze Papers.
13 *Economic Report of the President, 1978*, 41.
14 Minarik, *The Size Distribution of Income During Inflation*. Research since the Manarik paper has generally found that inflation does not have a major adverse effect on the income of the poor. For a short survey of the literature, see Powers, "Inflation, Unemployment, and Poverty Revisited." Using a measurement approach different from previous research, Powers finds, however, that inflation may harm the poor more than thought. Inflation can cause unemployment, and the effect of unemployment on the poor is, as one would expect, significant. See also Shiller, "Why Do People Dislike Inflation?" Shiller reports on a survey of popular attitudes toward inflation. In his summary of the results of the survey, Shiller writes that "the concerns people mention first regarding inflation are that it hurts their standard of living, and a popular model they have that makes such an effect plausible apparently has some badly behaving or greedy people causing prices to increase, increases that are not met with wage increases." Ibid., 57.
15 House Committee on the Budget, *Hearings on the Economic Outlook at Mid-Summer*, 292.
16 Ibid.
17 "Yields on Long-Term Obligations of U.S. Rise Decidedly Above 11% for First Time," *Wall Street Journal*, January 30, 1980, 35.
18 Memorandum, Charles Schultze to the President, April 1, 1980, Schultze Papers.
19 Hertzberg, "Troubled Haven," 1.
20 Memorandum, Al McDonald to the President, February 2, 1980, Presidential Handwriting File, Box 169, JCL
21 Hertzberg, "Troubled Haven," 1.
22 *Economist*, February 23, 1980, 89.
23 *Wall Street Journal*, February 2, 1980, 6.
24 Schultze interview with the author.
25 Eizenstat, "The Presidency in Trouble," 74.
26 Ibid., 71.
27 Cutter, "The Presidency and Economic Policy," 483.
28 A classic history of interest rates is Homer and Sylla, *A History of Interest Rates*.
29 Eizenstat, "The Presidency in Trouble," 65.
30 "As Bush Ratings Sink Some Sense Parallels With Carter in 1980," *Wall Street Journal*, March 5, 1992.
31 "Bond Prices End Slightly Lower After More Signs of Economic Strength Initially Spur a Sell-Off," *Wall Street Journal*, March 4, 1992.
32 Woodward, *The Agenda*, 84.
33 Ibid., 145.
34 *Public Papers of the Presidents of the United States: Jimmy Carter, 1980–1981*, 3:2129–30.

35 Carter interview with the author.
36 Eizenstat interview, Miller Center, 105.
37 See Hargrove, *Jimmy Carter as President* and Jones, *The Trusteeship Presidency*.
38 For a comparison of Hoover and Carter, see Lee, "The Politics of Less."
39 *The Gallup Opinion Index*, no. 183 (December 1980):2.
40 Jordan's comment is found in Rosenbaum and Ugrinsky, *The Presidency and Domestic Policies of Jimmy Carter*, 165.
41 Cutler interview, Miller Center, 14.

Chapter Two
1 *The Gallup Opinion Index*, no. 106 (April 1974).
2 Ranney, "The Carter Administration," 4.
3 There is a large literature on the Democratic electoral reforms of 1968 and 1972. See, for example, Polsby, *Consequences of Party Reform*.
4 Ibid., 11.
5 Carter interview, Miller Center, 2.
6 For a discussion of the memo, see Witcover, *Marathon*, 110–13. The original memo, over fifty pages in length, is not yet available to researchers in the Carter Library. A portion of it is reproduced in Schram, *Running for President, 1976*, 55–61.
7 Jordan's 1974 memo is available at the Jimmy Carter Library. See the Peter Bourne File, Campaign 1974 Source Book DNC, August 8, 1974, Box 1, JCL. See the discussion of this memo in Witcover, *Marathon*, 134–38.
8 *Time*, June 6, 1977, 20.
9 Eizenstat interview, Miller Center, 3. Eizenstat also discussed the preparation of these issue papers in his exit interview, January 10, 1981, JCL. Presumably some of them involved economic topics. I have been unable to locate any of the papers.
10 For a discussion of the work of the Trilateral Commission, see Gill, *American Hegemony*.
11 Brzezinski interview, Miller Center, 58.
12 Jordan, *Crisis*, 45. The Trilateral papers were substantive background pieces prepared by specialists on the topics discussed. Two examples of the papers that Carter read are Campbell et al., "Trilateral Task Force on the Political and International Implications of the Energy Crisis" and Gardner et al., "Trilateral Task Force on Relations with Developing Countries." These pieces can be found in the Eizenstat Papers, box titled "Early Seventies." (I have had access to Eizenstat files that are in the Jimmy Carter Library but not open to the public. I have labeled these, as in this note, the "Eizenstat Papers." They should not be confused with the files labeled, "Domestic Policy Staff—Eizenstat," which are available to the public.)
13 Eizenstat, "The Presidency in Trouble," 15.
14 Ibid. Eizenstat discussed these conversations with Carter in his Miller Center interview, 3. He discussed them further in an interview with the author. Precisely what was said in these sessions between Carter and Eizenstat would be interesting to know. Unfortunately the tapes, transcripts, and notes of the meetings have not been located.
15 Witcover, *Marathon*, 128.

16 The Strauss prediction is reported in Moore and Fraser, *Campaign for President*, 2.
17 Carter interview, Miller Center, 44.
18 Jones, *The Trusteeship Presidency*, xx.
19 Polsby, *Consequences of Party Reform*, 75–76.
20 Reeves, *Convention*, 3.
21 Eizenstat interview, Miller Center, 4.
22 *Washington Post*, October 17, 1976, C1 and C2.
23 Carter interview, Miller Center, 3–4.
24 Eizenstat, "The Presidency in Trouble," 10–11.
25 Ibid., 12.
26 Anderson, *Revolution*, 162.
27 Committee on House Administration, *The Presidential Campaign, 1976, Jimmy Carter*, vol. 1, pt. 1:153.
28 Eizenstat interview, Miller Center, 7–8. Eizenstat also discussed the forming of the policy group in his White House exit interview, available in JCL, 6–7.
29 Carp and Rubenstein interview, Miller Center, 2.
30 See Corrigan and Havemann, "The Issues Teams."
31 Ibid., 1167.
32 The organization of the task forces is discussed in Eizenstat interview, Miller Center, 20. See also Corrigan and Havemann, "The Issues Teams," 1169.
33 For a sketch of the professional career of Lawrence Klein, see his autobiographical chapter in Breit and Spence, *Lives of the Laureates*, 21–41. See also Klein, "My Professional Life Philosophy," 180–89.
34 Information on how Klein came into contact with Carter was obtained from a Klein interview with the author.
35 Ibid.
36 Ibid.
37 Paul A. Samuelson, "Carter's Economists," 59.
38 Klein interview with the author.
39 The position paper is reproduced in Committee on House Administration, *The Presidential Campaign, 1976, Jimmy Carter*, vol. 1, pt. 1:141–48.
40 Klein interview with the author.
41 Eizenstat interview, Miller Center, 17.
42 Charles Schultze, who actually received the appointment as chairman of the council, is of the opinion that Klein would have been selected had he wished to serve. "I am morally certain that if Klein had wanted to be CEA chairman he could have been. I don't know this for a fact, but I'm morally certain and I think he turned it down." Schultze interview with the author. Klein himself has written: "In 1976 I served as Jimmy Carter's coordinator of his economics task force. During his administration I tried to be helpful in various White House economic matters. . . . That was very interesting . . . but I feel more comfortable in academia." Breit and Spence, *Lives of the Laureates*, 39.
43 Milton Friedman, who served as adviser to Goldwater, describes himself as a "liberal" but uses the term in the nineteenth-century sense of the word, which is more consistent with the word "conservative" as it is used today.

44 Stein, *Presidential Economics*, 3d ed., 95. The economic advisers that Kennedy assembled were an unusually bright group. The leader was Walter Heller, professor at the University of Minnesota, one of the more articulate economists to work in Washington. Others, who were either members of the Council of Economic Advisers or served on its staff, included James Tobin of Yale, Kenneth Arrow, then of Harvard and later of Stanford, and Robert Solow of the Massachusetts Institute of Technology. These last three were all later to win Nobel prizes in economics.

45 The Dutch economist, Jan Tinbergen, produced the first macroeconometric models in the late 1930s. He published a model of the Dutch economy in 1936. Tinbergen was awarded the first Nobel prize in economics, which was initiated in 1969. His pioneering efforts were extended to the next level of technical sophistication by scholars at the Cowles Foundation, which was set up in the United States in 1932 to do econometric research with the financial support of Alfred Cowles. Lawrence Klein was hired by the Cowles Foundation to develop a new model for the United States, a model which was the first of the postwar generation of macroeconometric models. Klein's *Economic Fluctuations in the United States, 1921–1941* was published in 1950 as Cowles Commission Monograph 11. Klein went on to develop the famous Wharton model at the University of Pennsylvania. See Morgan, *The History of Econometric Ideas*, 101–30 and 251–58.

46 See chapter 2, "Econometrics, Politics, and Public Policy," in Roberts, *The Supply-Side Revolution*, 34–68. For a discussion of the use of the large-scale econometric models by the Congressional Budget Office, see Reischauer, "Getting, Using, and Misusing Economic Information," 38–66. For an example of a critical review of the Congressional Budget Office's use of demand-oriented models, see Meiselman and Roberts, "The Political Economy of the Congressional Budget Office," 283–333. For a reply to these critics, see Rivlin, "A Comment on the Meiselman and Roberts Paper," 355–62. Rivlin was the first director of the Congressional Budget Office. It is interesting to note that Keynes was not himself enthusiastic about econometric models even though the large macromodels are usually thought of as Keynesian. For a comment on the use of large-scale econometric models in Great Britain, see Britton, *Macroeconomic Policy in Britain, 1974–1987*, 87–90.

47 Schlesinger, *The Coming of the New Deal*, 406.

48 Smith, *Morality, Reason and Power*, 242.

49 For a comparison of the postwar recessions, see table 1 in McNees, "The 1990–91 Recession in Historical Perspective," 4–5.

50 The relation between growth in the economy and the unemployment rate is governed by what is known as "Okun's Law," named after the late Arthur Okun, chairman of the Council of Economic Advisers under Lyndon Johnson and, later, a fellow at the Washington think tank, the Brookings Institution. While at Brookings, Okun was an outside adviser to President Jimmy Carter. The word "law" is a somewhat strong term for what should be thought of more accurately as an empirical regularity. By comparing historical changes in national output and changes in unemployment, Okun was able to provide a rule of thumb for connecting the two. Okun's Law was originally stated in Arthur M. Okun, "Potential GNP: Its Measurement and Significance," in Proceedings of the Business and Economics Statis-

tics Section, American Statistical Association, 1962, 98–103. Reprinted in Okun, *Economics for Policy Making*, 145–58.
51 Eizenstat, "The Presidency in Trouble," 69.
52 Committee on House Administration, *The Presidential Campaign, 1976, Jimmy Carter*, vol. 1, pt. 1:509.
53 Committee on House Administration, *The Presidential Campaign, 1976, Jimmy Carter*, vol. 1, pt. 2:703.
54 Committee on House Administration, *The Presidential Campaign, 1976*, vol. 3, pt. 1:147.
55 Committee on House Administration, *The Presidential Campaign, 1976*.
56 Carter, *Campaign Promises, 1976*. A copy is available at JCL. Carter's intention in requesting the list was to remind himself of the commitments he had made to the voters. The press soon became aware of the project, which had, of course, the potential for political embarrassment when decisions made during the presidency did not conform to campaign promises.
57 *Time*, June 28, 1976, 54.
58 Committee on House Administration, *The Presidential Campaign, 1976, Jimmy Carter*, vol. 1, pt. 2:225.
59 Ibid., 199.
60 *Economic Report of the President, 1962*, 44.
61 The full title of the bill is "The Full Employment and Balanced Growth Act of 1976," HR 50, S50.
62 The measure of value of the nation's annual output was termed the "gross national product" in the 1970s. It is now called the "gross domestic product." I have followed the 1970s usage throughout the book.
63 Samuelson, "My Life Philosophy," 238.
64 *Time*, June 28, 1976, 54. For a summary report on the Humphrey-Hawkins bill, see Singer, "The Humphrey-Hawkins Bill—Boondoggle or Economic Blessing?"
65 Committee on House Administration, *The Presidential Campaign, 1976, Jimmy Carter*, vol. 1, pt. 1:156.
66 Committee on House Administration, *The Presidential Campaign, 1976, Jimmy Carter*, vol. 1, pt. 1:369.
67 Ibid, 228.
68 Ibid., 200.
69 Ibid., 143.
70 Ibid., 146.
71 See Stein, *The Fiscal Revolution in America*, 220–32; and Matusow, *Nixon's Economy*, 76–78, 91–93.
72 Klein interview with the author.
73 Klein interview with the author.
74 Witcover, *Marathon*, 235.
75 Committee on House Administration, *The Presidential Campaign, 1976, Jimmy Carter*, vol. 1, pt. 2:771.
76 Ibid., 143.
77 Ibid., 787.

78 Committee on House Administration, *The Presidential Campaign, 1976, Jimmy Carter*, vol. 1, pt. 1:144. These proposals were also included in Carter's proposals to the Democratic Party platform committee.
79 Ibid., 143.
80 Ibid., 148.
81 Ibid., 144.
82 Ibid., 535.
83 Ibid., 144.
84 Ibid., 145.
85 See Stein, *On the Other Hand*, 65.
86 For an insider's account of the introduction of controls under Nixon, see Stein, *Presidential Economics*, 3d ed., 161–87. See also Hockoff, *Drastic Measures*, 200–233.
87 Committee on House Administration, *The Presidential Campaign, 1976, Jimmy Carter*, vol. 1, pt. 1:145.
88 Committee on House Administration, *The Presidential Campaign, 1976, Jimmy Carter*, vol. 1, pt. 2:789.
89 *Wall Street Journal*, December 3, 1976, 1.
90 *Newsweek*, December 13, 1976, 77.
91 *Wall Street Journal*, December 3, 1976, 1.
92 Stuart Eizenstat made a record of what occurred at the meeting. The quotation is from notes prepared by Eizenstat for a lecture given at the Kennedy School of Government at Harvard. These lecture notes are entitled "Economy." Mr. Eizenstat has given me access to these notes.

Chapter Three

1 Schultze interview, Miller Center, 26. Bert Lance has added to the Schultze account in his memoir. "One of those meetings at our house was a classic example of how decisions of great importance are often made in the plainest of surroundings, without any crystal chandeliers, high ceilings, and mahogany conference tables that are the standard trappings for affairs of state. Charles Schultze, who became Carter's White House economist, came to the house with Mike Blumenthal one evening so we could put together the economic program for the new administration. None of us could type, so we sat there in the shank of the night writing everything out in longhand on legal pads. . . . But the three of us couldn't very well submit our economic recommendation for the future of the nation to the president-elect in longhand. So I recruited our son, David, a college student at the time, who not only knew how to type, but was the only one in the house with a typewriter. As the rest of us slept, David set up office in the bathroom so as not to keep us awake and finished his contribution to the future of the country at 6:30 in the morning." Lance, *The Truth of the Matter*, 87.
2 For a discussion of the Troika, see Okun, "The Formulation of National Economic Policy."
3 Blumenthal has written a history of German-Jewish relations: Blumenthal, *The Invisible Wall*.
4 Carter interview, Miller Center, 13.

5 Carter has commented in an interview: "Mike [Blumenthal] always saw himself as the leader of the entire economic advisory group. Bert, however, who didn't understand perhaps as well as Mike the theory of economics, was much closer to me and I think it was obvious to everyone that if they wanted to get to me with an economic message that Bert was the avenue to follow." Carter interview, Miller Center, 12.
6 Lance was cleared of federal charges of banking irregularities in 1980. He has given his account of his relationship with Carter and his own legal difficulties in Lance, *The Truth of the Matter*.
7 "I spent every single day with him for about a year," McIntyre recalls, "going over strategy, drafting the legislation for how we would deal with various proposals so that they would be constitutional; how we could draft them so that they would be more palatable to the legislature. And we spent about a year together, including weekends, literally, working on that reorganization for the legislature." McIntyre interview with the author.
8 Schultze interview with the author.
9 Eizenstat interview with the author.
10 Hargrove and Morley, *The President and the Council Of Economic Advisers*, 479.
11 The operation of the Ford group is described by Roger Porter in *Presidential Decision Making*.
12 Quoted by Porter, Ibid., 3.
13 Memorandum, Blumenthal and Schultze to the President-Elect, January 6, 1977, White House Central File, FG 6-3, Box FG-76, JCL.
14 Memorandum, Blumenthal and Schultze to President Carter, February 12, 1977, EPG Folders, Eizenstat Papers, JCL.
15 Ibid.
16 The functions of this small staff are spelled out in Memorandum, Ernest H. Preeg to Michael Blumenthal and Jack Watson, April 4, 1977, EPG Folders, Eizenstat Papers, JCL.
17 Memorandum, Blumenthal and Schultze to President Carter, February 12, 1977, EPG Folders, Eizenstat Papers, JCL.
18 Eizenstat interview, Miller Center, 21.
19 Fallows, "The Passionless Presidency," 39.
20 Carter was influenced in his views on cabinet government by Stephen Hess, a scholar at the Brookings Institution. See Hess, *Organizing the Presidency*.
21 One of Carter's early projects was a study of the Executive Branch for purposes of reorganization. The Economic Policy Group was one of the case studies submitted. The report stated: "The Economic Policy Group is not effective as currently operating. As a result, the President does not always receive a full and systematic staffing of economic issues." President's Reorganization Project—Decision Analysis Report, June 28, 1977, Hamilton Jordan File, Box 36, JCL.
22 My source on this point is a short unpublished paper prepared by Stuart Eizenstat entitled "The Brief History of the Economic Policy Group of the Carter Administration." Mr. Eizenstat provided me with a copy. Four members of Carter's cabinet, in addition to Charles Schultze, have Ph.D.s in economics, probably a record.

James Schlesinger, secretary of energy, has a Ph.D., as do Blumenthal, Kreps, and Marshall.

23 Hamilton Jordan wrote to the president: "We will get continual criticism for not having a black person who participates directly in the formulation of economic policy." Memorandum, Hamilton Jordan to President Carter, no date, FG 6-18, Box 95, Folder 1/20/77–1/20/81, JCL. Stuart Eizenstat concurred: "I agree with Hamilton that we will be plagued with a continuous political problem if the economic policy of the administration is made by eight whites." Memorandum, Stuart Eizenstat to Rick Hutcheson, February 3, 1977, same location as the Jordan memo.

24 For example, thirty-two people, principals and staff, attended a meeting in April 1977. Minutes of the Executive Committee, 1977, EPG Folders, Eizenstat Papers, JCL.

25 Hargrove and Morley, *The President and the Council of Economic Advisers*, 468.

26 Memorandum, Schultze to the President, March 7, 1977, Staff Secretary File, Box 11, Folder 3/9/77, JCL. In his response to Schultze's memorandum, Carter wrote to the policy group: "After an initial six weeks of experience as co-Chairman of the Economic Policy Group, Chairman Schultze believes that such a position may be incompatible with his role as personal economic adviser to the President. I concur in that judgment." Memorandum, President to Members of the Economic Policy Group, March 5, 1977, White House Central File, FG 6-3, Box FG-76, JCL.

27 The staff was headed by Curtis Hessler for over two years. He had been preceded for the early months of the administration by Ernest Preeg. Randy Kau replaced Hessler upon his departure and served for a little over a year. Before coming into the administration, Hessler had worked under Jack Watson on the Carter transition staff with responsibility for matters related to the Treasury. He is the coauthor, along with Ben W. Heineman Jr., of a book critical of Carter's ability to set priorities and build support for programs: *Memorandum for the President*. Heineman served during the Carter administration first as executive assistant to Health Education and Welfare Secretary Joseph Califano and later as assistant secretary.

28 Eizenstat, "The Brief History of the Economic Policy Group," 4.

29 "In light of your most recent comments . . . we have met with Stu Eizenstat to discuss proposals for restructuring the EPG to meet your concerns. . . . Neither the EPG nor the steering committee would attempt to coordinate or 'broker' the detailed decisions involved in developing specific legislation or policy proposals. That coordination function would rest with Stu Eizenstat's Domestic Policy staff." Memorandum, Blumenthal, Lance and Schultze to the President, July 13, 1977, EPG Folders, Eizenstat Papers, JCL.

30 In a somewhat sharply worded handwritten memorandum to the members of the steering committee on May 15, 1979, Carter wrote: "I want the EPG more closely to coordinate economic policy advice coming to me in the future, and to provide better policy implementation after I have made a decision. . . . Submit to me expeditiously an outline of how to implement this change. Use existing staff levels. If you all cannot reach consensus, I will quickly resolve any differences." Memorandum, President to Mike, Charlie, Jim Mc, Fred, Stu, May 15, 1979, EPG Folders, Eizenstat

Papers, JCL. This memorandum is followed by another to heads of executive departments and agencies reaffirming that the EPG is the "exclusive vehicle for coordinating the formulation, execution, and presentation of the administration's domestic and international economic policies." Memorandum, the President to Heads of Executive Departments and Agencies, the White House Staff, May 30, 1979, EPG Folders, Eizenstat Papers, JCL. The steering committee, which had met in Blumenthal's office in the Treasury Department, would now meet in the White House. What specific incidents provoked these communications is not clear, but it is evident that the process of economic advice had continuing problems well into the administration.

31 Memorandum, Blumenthal to EPG Members, May 11, 1977, EPG Folders, Eizenstat Papers, JCL.

32 Eizenstat, "Economists and White House Decisions," 69. Van Ooms, whom McIntyre recruited from the Senate Budget Committee to be his chief economic adviser, recalled in an interview: "The President, believe it or not, had to resolve disputes over how interest rates should be handled in the budget projections. That was a debate that could not be resolved in the economic policy group." McIntyre, Hubert Harris, Van Ooms interview, Miller Center, 29. He added details on the interest rate matter in an interview with the author: "There were too many things which went to the president that shouldn't have gone to the president. I remember one issue which went to the president. It was a technical question as to how we would handle interest rate projections in the budget. Treasury and the Office of Management and Budget had traditionally straightlined the interest rates. They didn't want to do an interest rate forecast; they argued that would be telling the markets. Under the Ford administration, to the extent they published economic assumptions, they just published a flat interest rate from using the market rate before they went to press or something like that. [During the Carter years] interest rates became, of course, terribly sensitive, as a budgetary matter, because suddenly the debt was a lot larger and interest rates were going all over the place, and it seemed kind of silly to use an interest rate that nobody believed in to drive a large part of the budget estimate. So there was some discussion as to what kind of interest rates should be used. This ultimately went to the president, because the Council and OMB, as I remember, felt fairly strongly that we should use a different system that gave us a better projection of where we thought interest cost would be. As I remember, Blumenthal hung tough on this to the very end and finally had to go to the president to resolve the issue and that's not the sort of issue that you ought to have to go to the president with. It was crazy. There were some other ones like that from time to time." Van Ooms interview with the author.

33 Schultze interview with the author.

34 Eizenstat interview, Miller Center, 76. Eizenstat later commented that an economic policy coordinator was needed in the Carter White House: "The Ford administration had developed an appropriate model, which we should have employed." Eizenstat, "Economists and White House Decisions," 69.

35 Ibid. Eizenstat had, with actual White House experience, changed his earlier views on the need for a strong coordinator. In a memorandum prepared during the transi-

tion period following Carter's election, he had written: "I agree that the present White House structure, in which the chief domestic adviser is also chairman of the Domestic Council and the National Security Adviser is also chairman of the National Security Council, should be continued. And I agree that this pattern should be complemented by having the chief economic adviser be chairman of the CEA. (At present the chief economic adviser on the White House staff is not Alan Greenspan, the CEA chairman, but rather William Seidman. This type of division should be eliminated.)" Memorandum, Stuart Eizenstat to Greg Schneider, December 12, 1976, Transition Memorandum, Eizenstat Papers, JCL.

36 Okun interview, Lyndon Baines Johnson Library. Okun was not a member of the Kennedy Council of Economic Advisers, but he served under Johnson and was close to Kennedy's advisers.

37 Schultze interview with the author. Kennedy appointed to the Council of Economic Advisers economists with a strong Keynesian orientation. Dillon, a Republican, came to government from the world of finance. He often disagreed with the economists of the council. While the two sides were able to resolve many of their difficulties, unresolved issues were often taken to the president. See Seymour E. Harris, *Economics of the Kennedy Years*, particularly chap. 3.

38 Schultze, *The Public Use of Private Interests*.

39 Schultze interview, Miller Center, 10.

40 Schultze's interest level in an interview with me was noticeably elevated as he related anecdotes from the Johnson White House. "You liked Johnson, didn't you?" I asked. "About ten different verbs," he said. "Liked, feared, occasionally hated, respected, stood in awe of." For Schultze's role in the Johnson administration, see the Schultze interviews done for the Lyndon Baines Johnson Library, March 28, 1969, and April 10, 1969.

41 McIntyre interview with the author.

42 *Economist*, December 21, 1991–January 3, 1992, 52. For a sketch of Brookings Institution history, see Smith, *The Idea Brokers*, 130–34.

43 For Nourse's account of his service under Truman, see Nourse, *Economics in the Public Service*.

44 Memorandum, Henry Owen to President Carter, October 9, 1979, White House Central File, Subject File, BE, Box BE-1, JCL.

45 Schultze interview, Miller Center, 23.

46 The Schultze contacts, privately and in groups, are recorded in the Presidential Diary File, JCL.

47 Hargrove and Morley, T*he President and the Council of Economic Advisers*, 500.

48 Carter interview with the author.

49 Marshall is the only one of Carter's economic advisers, other than the Georgia contingent, who knew the president when he was governor, though Marshall has said it "was not a very lengthy or important involvement. He was there when I was director of the task force on southern rural development. He also served on that task force. He would read things that we'd write and respond and seemed to take a strong interest in rural development." Thompson, *The Carter Presidency*, 46. For Marshall's role in the Carter administration, see Fink, "F. Ray Marshall."

50 Gary Fink reports in his article on Marshall that before accepting the nomination for secretary of labor, Marshall "secured assurances that he would have a voice in economic policy development and that he would be free to speak out when he disagreed with administration policies." Fink, "F. Ray Marshall," 466.
51 Thompson, *The Carter Presidency*, 51.
52 Carter said in an interview that he wanted people around him who had been loyal to him in the campaign and in whom he had trust. Then he added: "But I wasn't trying to have my whole dependence upon a group of Georgians like me who didn't understand Washington. I thought that Mondale and the breadth of the cabinet was an adequate compensation for it." Carter interview, Miller Center, 9. Mondale's comment on his relationship with Carter: "My relations with the President have been widely reported. I think it was the most successful presidential-vice presidential relationship maybe in the history of my beleaguered office." Thompson, *The Carter Presidency*, 241.
53 Eizenstat interview, Miller Center, 56.
54 The young staffer was John Farmer. Schultze interview with the author.
55 Eizenstat interview with the author. See also Gillon, *The Democrats' Dilemma*, 202.
56 Hargrove, *Jimmy Carter as President*, 40.
57 "There was a sense [at the Camp David meeting] that there was not enough cohesion; that agencies were going out on their own. . . . And at least one of the decisions made was that there should be a stronger coordinative role for our staff. I frankly think that by that time it was really more a ratification of what was already happening . . . but at least it did put a clear Presidential imprint on what was evolving or what had already evolved by that time." Eizenstat interview, Miller Center, 32–43.
58 Carter interview, Miller Center, 18–19.
59 The files of the Council of Economic Advisers at the Carter Library have not yet been opened to the public. They are quite large in size and probably consist, primarily, of technical papers prepared for the members of the council by staff. The memoranda of the CEA and the EPG sent to the president and circulated within the administration, which are open to the public, utilized the input of the staff's analytical work.
60 Lyle Gramley was appointed to the Board of Governors of the Federal Reserve System in 1979.
61 Gramley interview with the author.
62 Ibid. The interaction between model and forecaster, as described by Gramley, was common practice in the 1970s as it is today. See McNees, "The Forecasting Record for the 1970s," 33–53. For Charles Schultze's description of the forecasting process, with details consistent with Gramley's account, see Hargrove and Morley, *The President and the Council of Economic Advisers*, 495–96. Schultze makes the point that in forecasting, "you simply cannot afford to get very far outside the consensus projection. . . . You lose your credibility. Now you can edge one way or the other. So that's my first proposition: if Data Resources, Wharton and all the other blue chip forecasters are fairly close together (and they very often are), you pretty much have to be within their forecast range." Ibid.

63 Rivlin interview with the author.
64 Eizenstat, "The Presidency in Trouble," 34–135. Rivlin has said that "there were frequent instances where there were different estimates. One that I remembered being acrimonious—it was acrimonious within the Hill—had to do with the energy program. That was very early in the Carter administration. Carter characterized his energy program as the moral equivalent of war. We did an analysis for the Congress of what the Carter energy program would actually do and we had some differences. They were not actually major differences. But we were skeptical about some of the estimates. We thought that the coal conversion program, as I remember it, would not produce as much oil saving as the administration was claiming. And so we released a report saying that to the Congressional committee. And I did an interview, perhaps with the *Washington Post*, and I think in answer to the question, is this the moral equivalent of war, I said no, it doesn't seem like a very big problem to me, or something like that, and that got quoted. And this bears on the question of Carter's friends. It was the speaker, it was Tip O'Neill, who was very angry for what seemed to him to be criticism of the president. And O'Neill was there trying to get the president's program through the Congress, and I worked for the Congress and why was I criticizing, as he interpreted it, the president's program. In fact, we weren't criticizing it, it wasn't our role to do that. It was our role to analyze whether the program would, in fact, produce as much savings as the administration was claiming. And we mostly thought it would. Our differences were really quite small. O'Neill was pretty mad." Rivlin interview with the author.
65 At the Naval Academy, Carter had a one-hour course entitled "Leadership and Personal Finance," which included, it would seem from the catalogue description, personal finance topics like insurance and at best a smattering of elementary economics. The course was clearly not the equivalent of a basic introductory course in the subject. Letter to the author from the deputy for operations, U.S. Naval Academy, April 25, 1990.
66 Thomassen had worked as a consultant to the revenue department prior to his appointment as economic adviser to the governor.
67 Thomassen interview with the author.
68 Memorandum, Henry Thomassen to Governor Carter, March 26, 1974, Record Group 1–15, Accession Number 75-32A, Box 64, Location Number 4265-19, Georgia State Archives.
69 Memorandum, Henry Thomassen to Governor Carter, August 15, 1973, Record Group 1–15, Accession Number 75-32A, Box 64, Location Number 4265-19, Georgia State Archives.
70 See White House Central File, June 22, 1978, BE 4-2, Box BE-16, JCL.
71 White House Central File, April 12, 1978, BE 4-2, Box BE-16, JCL.
72 In interviews I did with members of Carter's administration and in interviews done at the Miller Center, Carter is described as unusually bright. In Eizenstat's opinion, "he's one of the brightest political officials with whom I have dealt and indeed one of the brightest men." Eizenstat interview, Miller Center, 21. Lyle Gramley has described him as "so knowledgeable and so bright." Gramley interview with the author.

73 Memorandum, President Carter to Eizenstat, May 2, 1977, White House Central File, Subject Files, CM9, Box CM-6, JCL. Carter became aware of econometric models while governor. His economic adviser, Henry Thomassen, reported to him in early 1974 that economists at the University of Georgia had developed a Georgia econometric forecasting model, a "satellite" "of the well-known and well-tested national model devised and run by Wharton Econometric Forecasting Associates of Philadelphia." The Wharton model is the one developed by Lawrence Klein. Thomassen suggested to the governor that the Georgia model might be adapted for state use. Carter wrote in the margin: "Sounds like a good investment. Probe possibilities. Give me sample questions we may ask [of the model] in 1974." Memorandum, Henry Thomassen to Governor Carter, January 17, 1974, Record Group 1–15, Accession Number 75-32A, Box 64, Location Number 4265-19, Georgia State Archives. The background in economics of the various presidents is of some interest. Herbert Stein, economic adviser to Nixon, tells this story: "I once asked Richard Nixon whether he had studied economics in college. He told me that he had had a course at Whittier College, taught by the college preacher. According to Nixon, the preacher, 'didn't know his — from first base about economics,' and Nixon finished the course not knowing any more than that." Stein, *On the Other Hand*. 86. Nixon learned a lot of economics later, particularly from the tutelage of his adviser, Arthur Burns. The first President Bush, among modern presidents, had the most formal training in economics. He majored in the subject at Yale.

74 Schultze interview, Miller Center, 79.

75 Hargrove and Morley, *The President and the Council of Economic Advisers*, 464.

76 "I was trained by Rickover," Carter has said. [Admiral Rickover, father of the nuclear submarine service.] "I'm an engineer at heart, and I like to understand details of things that are directly my responsibility." Carter interview, Miller Center, 7.

77 Gramley interview with the author.

78 Hargrove and Morley, *The President and the Council of Economic Advisers*, 465.

79 Eizenstat interview with the author.

80 Memorandum, Schultze to the President, December 14, 1979, Eizenstat Papers, JCL.

81 McNees, "The Forecasting Record for the 1970s," 51.

82 Carter interview, Miller Center, 67.

83 Quoted in Flash, *Economic Advice and Presidential Leadership*, 25.

84 Jimmy Carter, *Why Not the Best*, 15. Carter has also told the story of his childhood in *An Hour Before Daylight*.

85 Agee and Evans, *Let Us Now Praise Famous Men*, xiii.

86 Spears, *Agee*. For a discussion of the documentary, see Coles, "Camera on James Agee."

87 *Public Papers of the Presidents of the United States: Jimmy Carter, 1979*, 2:1979–83.

88 Jimmy Carter has written a poem on Ms. Lillian's experience with leprosy in India: "Ms. Lillian Sees Leprosy for the First Time," in Jimmy Carter, *Always a Reckoning*, 21. The letters she wrote home from India have been published. Carter and Spann, *Away From Home*. She returned to Plains in weakened health. The children built her a house next to a small pond outside of town. It was in the Pond

House where transition teams met to work out the details of the new administration's programs.

89 Carter, *Addresses of Jimmy Carter*, 191.

90 One of the best sources for insight into Carter's reading and thinking prior to his entry into national politics is the Law Day speech he gave at the University of Georgia in 1974. The main speaker that day was Senator Ted Kennedy. After Carter heard Kennedy's speech he tore up his own and spoke from notes which he quickly jotted down. The speech reads like a stream of consciousness as he spills out his feelings on social justice and on those thinkers who have influenced him the most in the formation of his own sense of social values. One of those cited is Reinhold Niebuhr. Niebuhr, who taught at Union Theological Seminary, had a strong influence in the 1940s and 1950s on progressive politicians like Hubert Humphrey, George McGovern, and Adlai Stevenson. Carter became aware of Niebuhr's writings in the early 1960s when a friend gave him a copy of a compilation of the theologian's writings. See David and Good, *Reinhold Niebuhr on Politics*. The book had a major effect on Carter and became for him, in the words of his friend, "a political Bible." Niebuhr is the source of one of Carter's often repeated quotations: "The sad duty of politics is to establish justice in a sinful world." Carter has been influenced by a surprisingly varied range of writers and thinkers in the course of his intellectual development. His favorite poet is Dylan Thomas. When visiting Westminster Abbey while president, he was disappointed to find no plaque commemorating the work of the Welsh poet. He was told that the poet's moral behavior was below the standard necessary for inclusion. He mounted a low-keyed and successful campaign to have the poet honored there with an epitaph on stone. Carter has told the story of the Thomas epitaph in "A President Expresses Concern on a Visit to Westminster Abbey," in Carter, *Always a Reckoning*, 71. An American performer, who also affected Carter's thinking and is cited in his Law Day speech, is the singer Bob Dylan whose songs, a combination of folk music and blues, came out of the tradition of protest music in the genre of the work of Woody Guthrie and Pete Seeger. The appeal of his songs with their strong social message—"the times they are a'changin"—was to postwar baby boomers, a young generation sensitized by the movement for racial equality and the war in Vietnam to the problem of social injustice. Carter had met the writer-singer when his son Chip, a Dylan fan, invited him to the governor's mansion one night after a concert in Atlanta. Carter and Dylan talked to the early morning hours. One of Dylan's songs led Carter to reflect on those who worked on his father's farm. "I grew up a landowner's son," he said in his Law Day speech. "But I don't think I ever realized the proper interrelationship between the landowner and those who worked on a farm until I heard Dylan's record, 'I Ain't Gonna Work on Maggie's Farm No More.'" Law Day Speech, May 4, 1974, *Addresses of Jimmy Carter*, 257. Carter later quoted Dylan in his Democratic convention acceptance speech. For an insight into the personality of Jimmy Carter, see Miller, *Yankee from Georgia*.

91 Rubenstein and Carp interview, Miller Center. Carter was not entirely self-taught in Spanish. He had selected it as an elective at the Naval Academy. He listened to records to develop conversational proficiency.

92 Eizenstat interview with the author.
93 Committee on House Administration, *The Presidential Campaign, 1976, Jimmy Carter*, vol. 2, pt. 1:162
94 Hargrove and Morley, *The President and the Council of Economic Advisers*, 463.

Chapter Four

1 See House Committee on the Budget, *Hearings on the Economy and Economic Stimulus Proposals*.
2 Hargrove and Morley, *The President and the Council of Economic Advisers*, 477.
3 Briefing Paper, "1976 Campaign or Transition," December 20, 1976, Eizenstat Papers, JCL. The Eizenstat "1976 Campaign or Transition" material consists of three boxes of documents. The overall content of the early draft of the stimulus package is also given in Memorandum, Schultze to Economic Policy Group, January 22, 1977, Domestic Policy Staff—Eizenstat, [O/A 6338] [6], Box 144, JCL; and, Memorandum, Economic Policy Group to the President, January 22, 1977, Domestic Policy Staff—Eizenstat, [O/A 27] [2], Box 192, JCL.
4 Briefing Paper, "1976 Campaign or Transition," Eizenstat Papers, JCL.
5 Memorandum, Schultze to Economic Policy Group, January 22, 1977, Domestic Policy Staff—Eizenstat, [O/A 6338] [6], Box 144, JCL.
6 Hargrove and Morley, *The President and the Council of Economic Advisers*, 477. Schultze's statement was made about seven years after the design of the stimulus package. In his recollection of events, he probably meant to say that an investment tax credit rather than a depreciation allowance was one of the two choices.
7 Eizenstat, "Economy." This paper, prepared for use in lectures delivered at the Kennedy School, Harvard University, is based on notes Eizenstat made at the meetings of the advisory group.
8 Memorandum, Economic Policy Group to the President, January 22, 1977, Domestic Policy Staff—Eizenstat, Economic Stimulus Package—General, [CF, O/A 27] [2], Box 192, JCL.
9 Friedman, *A Theory of the Consumption Function*. Another piece of research that is a part of the literature on this subject is Ando and Modigliani, "The Life-Cycle Hypothesis of Saving."
10 Relevant articles on the debate over the 1968 surcharge include Okun, "The Personal Tax Surcharge and Consumer Demand, 1968–1970"; Springer, "Did the 1968 Surcharge Really Work?"; Okun, "Did the 1968 Surcharge Really Work? A Comment;" and Springer, "Did the 1968 Surcharge Really Work? A Reply." For a brief discussion of the technical difficulties in resolving the issue of the effectiveness of a temporary change in taxes in constraining or stimulating the economy, see Summers, "The Scientific Illusion in Empirical Macroeconomics," 136–37, 140–41. For research suggesting that the variation in consumption in reaction to changes in current income is greater than the permanent income hypothesis would suggest, see Carroll, "The Buffer-Stock Theory of Saving"; and Hall, "Macro Theory and the Recession of 1990–1991."
11 For a discussion of Ford's program see chapter 6 in Stein, *Presidential Economics*, 3d

ed. See also Balz and Havemann, "State of the Union"; and Romer and Romer, "What Ends Recessions?" 34–35.
12 Balz and Havemann, "State of the Union," 118.
13 See Congressional Quarterly, "Congress Votes Largest Tax Cut in History."
14 House Committee on the Budget, *Hearings on the Economy and Economic Stimulus Proposals*, 209.
15 Memorandum, Schultze to the President, March 7, 1977, Domestic Policy Staff—Eizenstat, Economic Stimulus Package—Program Taxes [CF, O/A 27] [2], Box 193, JCL.
16 *Public Papers of the Presidents of the United States: Jimmy Carter, 1977*, 1:50.
17 Charles Schultze interview in Hargrove and Morley, *The President and the Council of Economic Advisers*, 478.
18 Saunders and Klau, *The Role of the Public Sector*, table 1, 29.
19 Schultze, "Is There a Bias Toward Excess in U.S. Government Budgets or Deficits?" 38.
20 Schultze, "Federal Spending, Past, Present, and Future," 329. The numbers used here to represent federal spending as a proportion of GNP (gross national product) are from the same source. Over the course of economic expansions and contractions, GNP fluctuates in the short run. Government recession-related outlays also vary with the business cycle. In order to remove the distortions in the spending/GNP ratio caused by the recession-induced variations in the numerator and denominator, all spending comparisons are made relative to the full employment GNP. See ibid., 327–28.
21 Saunders and Klau, *The Role of the Public Sector*, 91. For a survey of the extensive literature on the reasons advanced for the growth of government worldwide, see ibid., 91–95. See also Aronson and Ott, "The Growth of the Public Sector."
22 Schultze, "Federal Spending, Past, Present, and Future," 324.
23 Schultze et al., *Setting National Priorities*, 398. For Schultze's views, a decade after the administration left office, on the historic growth of the federal budget, see Schultze, "Is There a Bias Toward Excess in U.S. Government Budgets or Deficits?"
24 Carter, *Keeping Faith*, 76.
25 Committee on House Administration, *The Presidential Campaign, 1976, Jimmy Carter*, vol. 1, pt. 1:152.
26 Carlson, "Federal Budget Trends and the 1981 Reagan Economic Plan," 21.
27 Schultze, *The Politics and Economics of Public Spending*.
28 McIntyre interview with the author. In comments made at a conference on the Carter administration held at Hofstra University, McIntyre added the Defense Department as doing well with zero-based budgeting, and said "the Environmental Protection Agency (EPA) did extremely well." Rosenbaum and Ugrinsky, *The Presidency and Domestic Policies of Jimmy Carter*, 418.
29 Rivlin interview with the author.
30 Briefing Paper, "1976 Campaign or Transition," December 20, 1976, Eizenstat Papers, JCL.

31 See House Committee on the Budget, *Hearings on the Economy and Economic Stimulus Proposals*, table 1, 211.
32 Ibid., 211.
33 Ibid., 210.
34 Ibid.
35 Ibid., 211.
36 Congressional Budget Office, *The Disappointing Recovery*, 20.
37 Ibid., 26–36.
38 Senate Committee on the Budget, *Hearings on the Economy and Budgetary Policy for Fiscal Year 1978*, 8.
39 House Committee on the Budget, *Hearings on the Economy and Economic Stimulus Proposals*, 78.
40 Ibid., 81.
41 House Committee on Ways and Means, *Hearings on the Tax Aspects of President Carter's Economic Stimulus Program*, 210.
42 Ibid.
43 Eizenstat, "The Presidency in Trouble," 235.
44 Eizenstat, "Economy."
45 House Committee on Ways and Means, *Hearings on the Tax Aspects of President Carter's Economic Stimulus Program*, 199. The book from which Heller took the expression is Schumacher, *Small Is Beautiful*.
46 For background on public employment programs and the role of CETA, see Baumer and Van Horn, *The Politics of Unemployment*; and Franklin and Ripley, *CETA: Politics and Policy, 1973–1982*.
47 Eizenstat, "Economy."
48 Ibid.
49 Ibid.
50 Gramlich, "Stimulating the Macro Economy through State and Local Government," 180.
51 Research in 1974 and 1975 that suggested a high rate of substitution included Fechter, *Public Employment Programs*; and National Planning Association, *An Evaluation of the Economic Impact Project*.
52 Memorandum, James McIntyre to Steering Group, November 15, 1977, "OMB Paper on Public Service Employment," Eizenstat Papers, JCL.
53 Nathan et al., *Monitoring the Public Service Employment Program*. The study was done by Nathan and colleagues at the Brookings Institution. See a short summary of the results of the study in Baumer and Van Horn, *The Politics of Unemployment*, 111–13. Many critics of the public employment program were not convinced by the Brookings study.
54 Quoted in the *Congressional Quarterly Almanac* (1976):365.
55 Eizenstat, "Economy."
56 Hargrove and Morley, *The President and the Council of Economic Advisers*, 478.
57 Schultze interview with the author. President Carter continued to think positively about the jobs program as he looked back later on his period in office. See Carter, *Keeping Faith*, 74–75.

58 Sunley, "A Tax Preference Is Born," 394.
59 Memorandum, Charles Schultze to the President, March 7, 1977, Domestic Policy Staff—Eizenstat, Economic Stimulus Package—Program Taxes [CF, O/A27] [2], Box 193, JCL.
60 See the discussion in Sunley, "A Tax Preference Is Born," 398–402.
61 Memorandum, Michael Blumenthal to President Carter, January 28, 1977, Domestic Policy Staff—Eizenstat, Economic Stimulus Package—Program, Taxes [CF, O/A 27] [2], Box 193, JCL. For Schultze's analysis of the Ullman proposal, see Memorandum, Charles Schultze to President Carter, January 28, 1977, Domestic Policy Staff—Eizenstat, Economic Stimulus Package—Program Taxes [CF,O/A 27] [1], Box 193, JCL. The Ways and Means Committee could also make the argument that the choice given businesses by the administration would create a distortion in input choices. It would arbitrarily encourage capital-intensive firms to become more capital intensive and labor-intensive firms to be more labor intensive.
62 Memorandum, President Carter to Congressman Ullman, February 9, 1977, Domestic Policy Staff—Eizenstat, Economic Stimulus Package—Program Taxes [CF, O/A 27] [1], Box 193, JCL.
63 Eizenstat, "Economy."
64 Memorandum, Michael Blumenthal to the President, February 3, 1977, White House Central File, Subject File, BE4, Box BE-13, JCL.
65 Eizenstat, "Economy."
66 Perloff and Wachter, "The New Jobs Tax Credit." For a more favorable assessment of the impact of the tax credit, see Bishop and Haveman, "Selective Employment Subsidies."
67 Eizenstat, "Economy."
68 Hargrove and Morley, *The President and the Council of Economic Advisers*, 480.
69 Ibid., 478.
70 Eizenstat, "Economy."
71 Shogan, *Promises to Keep*, 229.
72 Eizenstat, "Economy."
73 Ibid.
74 Carter interview, Miller Center, 12.
75 Klein interview with the author.
76 Eizenstat interview, Miller Center, 68.
77 Lance interview, Miller Center, 34.
78 For a detailed list of the projects, see Jones, *The Trusteeship Presidency*, 145–47.
79 Letter, President to Congress, March 16, 1977, White House Central File, FG 33, 1/20/77–1/20/81, Box FG-150, JCL.
80 Johnson, *In the Absence of Power*, 158. See an account and analysis of the water projects incident in Jones, "Keeping Faith and Losing Congress," 437–38.
81 *Keeping Faith*, 78.
82 Ibid.
83 Ibid.
84 Shogan, *Promises to Keep*, 227.
85 Eizenstat, "Economy."

86 Eizenstat, Address, University of Chicago Law School.
87 *Keeping Faith*, 79.
88 Carter interview, Miller Center, 55.
89 *Congressional Quarterly Almanac* (1977):96.
90 Jones, *The Trusteeship Presidency*, 153.
91 Memorandum, W. Bowman Cutler to the President, May 20, 1977, Domestic Policy Staff—Eizenstat, Economic Stimulus Package—Program Taxes [CF, O/A 27] [1], Box 193, JCL.
92 Romer and Romer, "What Ends Recessions," 35.
93 Minutes of the Executive Committee, April 18, 1977, Eizenstat Papers, JCL.
94 For information on what happened in the development of the economic package, during the transition and in the first few months of the administration, I have had access to detailed notes taken by Stuart Eizenstat who attended all the meetings. These notes are in the Carter library though not yet available to the general public.
95 The quotation from *Time* is from the December 31, 1965, issue, 640–67B.
96 Memorandum, Charles Schultze to the President, "Background on Inflation," March 14, 1977, Schultze Papers.
97 De Long, "America's Peacetime Inflation," 247.
98 Charles Schultze to the President, "Background on Inflation," March 14, 1977, Schultze Papers.
99 For a discussion of worldwide food shortages beginning in early 1973, see Matusow, *Nixon's Economy*, 220–29.
100 Volcker and Gyohten, *Changing Fortunes*, 114.
101 Eizenstat, "Economy," 2.
102 Carter interview, Miller Center, 68.
103 Senate Committee on the Budget, *Hearings on the Economy and Budgetary Policy for Fiscal Year 1978*, 12.
104 Ibid., 21–22.
105 Ibid., 38.
106 Ibid., 57, 59.
107 House Committee on Ways and Means, *Hearings on the Tax Aspects of President Carter's Economic Stimulus Program*, 210.
108 Matusow, *Nixon's Economy*, 220.
109 Eizenstat, "Economy," 9.
110 Pierce, "The Political Economy of Arthur Burns," 85.
111 Hargrove and Morley, *The President and the Council of Economic Advisers*, 431–32.
112 Alan Greenspan is under the impression that Burns met frequently with Carter. "He saw Carter quite often, one-on-one," Greenspan recalled in the same interview in which he described Burns's role in the Ford administration (Ibid., 432). The record of Carter's daily schedule shows that Greenspan is under an incorrect impression. Burns met with Carter, one-on-one, only two times in thirteen months. He met two additional times with Carter when Vice President Mondale and Hamilton Jordan were present (Presidential Diary, JCL, various entries). One Fed historian has said that Carter and Burns got off to a bad start. Burns was of-

113 fended by some Carter statements during the campaign. Kettl, *Leadership at the Fed*, 167. Kettl's report is based on an interview with Burns.
113 Hargrove and Morley, *The President and the Council of Economic Advisers*, 482.
114 Memorandum, Charles L. Schultze to the President, March 7, 1977, Presidential Handwriting File, Box 11, JCL.
115 Schultze interview, Miller Center, 21. Schultze goes on to add: "The real usefulness came when you'd sit down one-on-one with the secretary of the treasury, and the chairman of the Fed, or I'd sit down. Every once in a while the President would call or talk to the Fed chairman personally and he'd do something with that." Carter talked to Burns by phone nine times over the thirteen months of Burns's service as chair. The average duration for the calls was three minutes (Presidential Diary, various entries, JCL). In August 1977, Stuart Eizenstat wrote to the president urging him to make a call to the Federal Reserve chairman "concerning the possibility that Federal Reserve actions may raise interest rates." Memorandum, Stuart Eizenstat and Robert Ginsberg to the President, August 12, 1977, Domestic Policy Staff—Eizenstat, Box 207, JCL. Carter made the call.
116 Memorandum, Charles Schultze to President Carter, April 26, 1977, White House Central File, FI, Box FI-1, JCL.
117 Memorandum, Charles Schultze to President Carter, July 25, 1977, Schultze Papers.
118 Memorandum, Charles Schultze to President Carter, September 28, 1977, Schultze Papers.
119 Ibid.
120 For a summary of the Fed's intentions and the actual results of its actions over the course of the Carter administration, see the various *Annual Reports* of the Board of Governors of the Federal Reserve System, and the annual reviews of the operations of the Federal Open Market Committee prepared by the Federal Reserve Bank of New York. The transcripts of the meetings of the Federal Open Market Committee are not available for the Carter years. For a survey of Burns's views on the proper conduct of monetary policy and a critique of his record over his term in office (February 1970 to December 1977), see Hetzel, "Arthur Burns and Inflation." For two highly critical reviews of Burns's record, see Poole, "Burnsian Monetary Policy"; and Pierce, "The Political Economy of Arthur Burns."
121 Board of Governors, Federal Reserve System, *Sixty-forth Annual Report*, 1977, 45.
122 Memorandum, Michael Blumenthal and Charles Schultze to the President, December 10, 1977, Lipschutz File, Federal Reserve Board, Box 10, JCL.
123 President Carter interview with the author.

Chapter Five

1 Bergsten, *The International Economic Policy of the United States*, 6.
2 House Committee on Banking, Finance, and Urban Affairs, *Hearings on Conduct of Monetary Policy*, 9.
3 Cooper, *The Economics of Interdependence*.
4 Keohane, "U.S. Foreign Economic Policy Toward Other Advanced Capitalist States," 94.

5 Ibid.
6 Office of Economic Cooperation and Development, *Economic Outlook*, 12. At the 1976 ministerial meeting, the OECD members agreed that an average growth rate of 5 percent for the OECD area as a whole for the 1976–80 period would be consistent with a gradual reduction of inflation and sustained expansion. The administration was a little more conservative. In a briefing paper for Secretaries Blumenthal and Vance, who were to attend the ministerial meeting of the OECD in June 1977, it was suggested that: "The individual targets to which countries may be prepared to commit themselves, given the need for continued differentiation of policy among the countries and the need to avoid a resurgence of inflation, seems likely to result in a figure less than 5 percent for the OECD as a whole. Ministers could, however, state a conclusion that some increase in the rate of growth for the area as a whole in 1978 over that now in prospect for 1977, such as to bring about a significant reduction in unemployment, appears both desirable and consistent with continued reduction in the rate of inflation." "Informational Briefing of OECD, Paris, June 23–24," June 17, 1977, White House Central File, [O/A, 3150] [8 of 8], JCL.
7 Office of Economic Cooperation and Development, *Economic Outlook*, 81 and 86.
8 See the discussion in Putnam and Bayne, *Hanging Together*, 85.
9 Brookings Institution, *Tripartite Report by Sixteen Economists*, 10–11.
10 Cooper, "Global Economic Policy in a World of Energy Shortage," 84.
11 *Economic Report of the President, 1977*, 124.
12 Memorandum, Charles Schultze to the EPG Executive Committee, February 25, 1977, Domestic Policy Staff—Eizenstat, Economics, 1977 [CF, O/A 21] [2], Box 194, JCL.
13 The memorandum also pointed out that the CEA estimated that total American imports in 1977 would be $2 billion larger than they would have been if the stimulus package were not introduced.
14 See Solomon, *The International Monetary System, 1945–1981*, 307–11.
15 Craig R. Whitney, "A Refreshed and Newly Confident Schmidt Resumes Active Role," *New York Times*, January 24, 1977, quoted in Putnam and Henning, "The Bonn Summit of 1978," 130. The Putnam-Henning article is a particularly useful source for events related to Carter's international policy. The authors interviewed a number of administration officials involved in the international area. Interviews are particularly important in the coverage of international issues during the Carter years because the number of documents on this subject open to researchers in the Carter Library is limited due to the sensitivity of matters contained in internal memoranda and in communications with the various countries.
16 *Washington Post*, May 26, 1977, quoted in Putnam and Henning, "The Bonn Summit of 1978," 131 n. 53.
17 Putnam and Henning, "The Bonn Summit of 1978," 36.
18 Schmidt, *Men and Power*, 187.
19 For a discussion of the German inflation episode, see Dornbusch, "Lessons from the German Inflation Experience of the 1920s," 337–66.
20 Galbraith, *A Journey Through Economic Time*, 37.
21 Nölling, *Monetary Policy in Europe After Maastricht*, 4.

22 Stein, *The Fiscal Revolution in America*, 340.
23 Marsh, *The Most Powerful Bank*, 12.
24 Sommariva and Tullio, *German Macroeconomic History, 1880–1979*, 8. The text of the letter is reproduced in appendix 3.
25 For a recent study of how central banks have assumed more independence from political influence, see Eijffinger and Schaling, "Central Bank Independence." For a review of how the Bundesbank operated, see Clarida and Gertler, "How the Bundesbank Conducts Monetary Policy," 363–412.
26 For a survey of postwar German performance, see chapter 1 in Giersch et al., *The Fading German Miracle*.
27 See ibid., 4 table 1.
28 Ibid.
29 Destler and Mitsuyu, "Locomotives on Different Tracks," 248.
30 Hadley, "The Diffusion of Keynesian Ideas in Japan," 291. The brief survey of Japanese experience with deficit financing which follows draws on the Hadley article.
31 Takafusa Hakamura in Dore and Sinha, *Japan and World Depression*, 64. Quoted in Hadley, "The Diffusion of Keynesian Ideas in Japan," 295.
32 "As late as the early 1960s, the economics faculty of Tokyo University, Japan's most prestigious, was overwhelmingly Marxist." Hadley, "The Diffusion of Keynesian Ideas in Japan," 292.
33 Ibid., 292.
34 In cases where the attrition was severe and continuous—a "fundamental disequilibrium" in the words of the treaty—and an internally imposed solution was unrealistic, nations were allowed to devalue with the permission of the International Monetary Fund. In devaluing, a nation would decrease its currency's value relative to other currencies. The cheaper currency would make its exports more appealing to others. The phrase "fundamental disequilibrium" was not precisely defined and later became a source of some confusion.
35 McKinnon, *The Rules of the Game*, 2.
36 See Cooper, "The Gold Standard," 21.
37 The contradictions of the Bretton Woods arrangement were first pointed out by the Yale economist, Robert Triffin, in a book that gained widespread attention, *Gold and the Dollar Crisis*.
38 For a summary of events in the Eisenhower period, see Wallich, "Government Action," 97–113. Henry C. Wallich was a member of Eisenhower's Council of Economic Advisers.
39 Schlesinger, *A Thousand Days*, 654.
40 Arthur Burns felt out Europeans about an official change in the price of gold at Nixon's behest on a trip to Europe just before Nixon's inauguration. See Wells, *Economist in an Uncertain World*, 38. C. Fred Bergsten, who served in the Nixon administration, has written that at the start of Nixon's term the United States "did make some modest efforts to begin negotiating an adjustment mechanism in the direction of greater exchange rate flexibility. I was at the National Security Council at the time and recall that the Europeans stonewalled and reacted in a totally negative way to any such approach." Bergsten, "Discussion," 45.

41 See Solomon, *The International Monetary System, 1945–1981*, particularly chapters 11 and 12. Solomon was head of the Federal Reserve's international division at the time of the closing of the gold window. See also Gowa, *Closing the Gold Window*.

42 For a brief summary of the changes embodied in the amendment of Article IV, see Solomon, *The International Monetary System, 1945–1981*, 272–74. While the amendment formalized the floating exchange rate system, it also provided for cooperative arrangements whereby nations, at their own discretion, might link their currencies to one another, introducing, in effect, a regional Bretton Woods system. The European Monetary System is the major example.

43 Friedman's position on flexible exchange rates was presented in "The Case for Flexible Exchange Rates." Other important contributions in favor of flexible rates include Meade, "The Case for Variable Exchange Rates"; and Johnson, "The Case for Flexible Exchange Rates, 1969."

44 Volcker and Gyohten, *Changing Fortunes*, 101.

45 Henning, *Currencies and Politics in the United States, Germany, and Japan*, 126. Bergsten's testimony was before the House Banking Committee, June 3, 1976. It is reprinted in Bergsten, *Managing International Economic Interdependence*.

46 Committee on House Administration, *The Presidential Campaign, 1976, Jimmy Carter*, vol. 1, pt. 1:397. Carter, in response to a question from a reporter at a press conference at the end of the day's session, said that "the Japanese have already become aware of the concern about the inclination to buy dollars, to sell yen, to lower the price of the yen, and this trend has already been somewhat reversed because of action by the Japanese government." Ibid.

47 Bergsten interview with the author.

48 See Putnam and Henning, "The Bonn Summit of 1978," 36–37.

49 De Menil, "From Rambouillet to Versailles," 16.

50 See the survey of events in ibid., 17–18. Other sources on the summits that are particularly useful are Putnam and Bayne, *Hanging Together*; Putnam and Henning, "The Bonn Summit of 1978"; and Gerald Holtham, "German Macroeconomic Policy and the 1978 Bonn Summit."

51 The briefing paper prepared for Gerald Ford prior to the Rambouillet summit can be found in "International Economic Summit, Paris, France, November 15–17, 1975," Presidential Handwriting File, Trips Foreign—Economic Summit—1975 (1), Box 49, Ford Library. For a summary of the main points of the summit communiqués during the Carter years, from London in 1977 through Venice in 1980, see De Menil and Solomon, *Economic Summitry*, 75–78.

52 De Menil, "From Rambouillet to Versailles," 18.

53 Memorandum, Anthony M. Solomon to Michael Blumenthal, July 21, 1978, Solomon Chronological File, Folder 7/78, Box 4, JCL.

54 Putnam and Bayne, *Hanging Together*, 44.

55 Eizenstat interview, Miller Center, 74. In a memorandum during the transition period, Eizenstat wrote: "Although international economic policy has become one of the major areas of political concern in recent years, this Council has done very little to focus and coordinate that concern. Even those in the present administration widely admit that." Memorandum, Eizenstat to Greg Schneiders, December 12,

1976, 1976 Campaign or Transition, Eizenstat Papers, JCL. There is a lengthy paper in the Carter Library on the CIEP prepared by the outgoing administration as an aid to the new administration. See "Summary of Developing International Economic Issues," January 10, 1977, Domestic Policy Staff—Eizenstat, Economics (General) [O/A 6236] [2], Box 194, JCL.

56 Memorandum, Curtis Hessler to EPG Steering Committee, January 27, 1978, White House Central File, O/A 665, February 9, 1978, Box 189, JCL

57 Bergsten interview with the author.

58 Brzezinski interview, Miller Center, 45.

59 *Public Papers of the Presidents of the United States: Jimmy Carter, 1979*, 1:758.

60 See "The Summit Becomes an Institution," in Putnam and Bayne, *Hanging Together*, 44–58. According to Robert Beckel, who served in the State Department, Owen "had an enormous amount of influence with Carter on matters of international economics." Beckel interview, Miller Center, 41.

61 The statement said: "Inflation does not reduce unemployment. On the contrary, it is one of its major causes." See the discussion in Putnam and Henning, "The Bonn Summit of 1978," 42. For Henry Owen's assessment of the London summit, see "The London Summit Revisited."

62 Memorandum, Richard N. Cooper to Steering Group of the Economic Policy Group, September 28, 1977, Eizenstat Papers, Folder "EPG Meetings, September 1977," JCL.

63 Subcommittee on Trade of the House Committee on Ways and Means, *U.S. Department of Treasury News* B-532 (November 3, 1977):1. The Congressional Budget Office agreed with Bergsten on the causes of the deficit. See *The U.S. Balance of International Payments and the U.S. Economy*. For more detail on the trade deficit, see the discussion in Lawrence, "An Analysis of the 1977 U.S. Trade Deficit."

64 Lawrence, "An Analysis of the 1977 U.S. Trade Deficit," 63. The decline in domestic oil production was reversed in the latter part of 1977 with the opening of the Alaskan pipeline.

65 Ibid. Carter was aware, while he was governor, of increasing American oil imports. The issue came up in a discussion about whether deep-water ports should be built off the coast of Georgia for handling large crude carriers. There would be a need for such super-ports, one aide explained, in the future. "In the absence of any major reduction in demand or increases in domestic petroleum discoveries, the contribution of imports [to national needs] is expected to increase to 43% by 1975 and possibly to 57% by 1985." Memorandum, Jack Burris to Governor Carter, July 24, 1973, Record Group 1-15, Accession Number 75-32A, Box 64, Location Number 4265-19, Georgia State Archives.

66 Memorandum, Anthony M. Solomon to Secretary Blumenthal, July 15, 1977, Solomon File, Chronological File, Folder 7/1/77–7/15/77, Box 1, JCL.

67 For a description of the dollar's behavior in 1977 and 1978, see Solomon, *The International Monetary System, 1945–1981*, 344–50.

68 Ibid., 345.

69 Putnam and Bayne, *Hanging Together*, 70–71. For further information on events surrounding the dollar's behavior, see Cohen and Meltzer, *United States Inter-*

national Economic Policy in Action, 15–64. The authors interviewed participants in policy decisions, but on a non-attributing basis.
70 See the discussion in Whitman, "Global Monetarism," 522–26 and the sources cited there. See also Hennings, "West Germany," 488–90.
71 See Golub, *The Current-Account Balance and the Dollar*, table 1, 2.
72 Emminger, *The D-Mark*, 1.
73 McCracken et al., *Toward Full Employment and Price Stability*, 56. This report is commonly referred to as the McCracken Report.
74 Goodman, *Monetary Sovereignty*, 63.
75 Ibid.
76 Schmidt, *Men and Power*, 265.
77 Blumenthal has insisted that his remarks were misunderstood. In an interview with a *Fortune* editor in 1979, he discussed the problem for a businessman in adjusting to Washington life. Blumenthal had been president of Bendix Corporation before joining the Carter administration. Earlier in his career he had worked in Washington under Kennedy and Johnson, with responsibilities in trade negotiations but without the heightened exposure that is part of the life of a secretary of the treasury. One lesson of a Washington experience, he said, is the danger of being misinterpreted. "What you have to learn is that you have to express yourself very carefully, and that you have to build defenses against being misquoted and being misunderstood. Take the example of the dollar. I never said that I wanted the dollar to decline, yet I was quoted as saying that. What I said was that we favored flexible exchange rates agreed to in the IMF, and that this means there will be ups and downs, that we weren't pegging the rate." Blumenthal, "Candid Reflections," 37. Blumenthal made similar comments to the author in an interview two decades later.
78 See the interpretation of Blumenthal's intent—an interpretation consistent with the one given here—in Putnam and Henning, "The Bonn Summit of 1978," 49–50.
79 *Economic Report of the President, 1978*, 124–25.
80 "Remarks by the Honorable Michael Blumenthal Secretary of the Treasury of the United States at the Ministerial Meeting of OECD, Paris, France," U.S. Department of the Treasury news release, June 24, 1977, 2.
81 Solomon, *The International Monetary System, 1945–1981*, 346. The Burns statement, quoted in Solomon, appears in a reprint of the speech Burns gave at Columbia University in *The Federal Reserve Bulletin* 63, no. 5 (May 1977):456–62.
82 Memorandum, Anthony M. Solomon to Secretary Blumenthal, July 15, 1977, Solomon File, Chronological File, Folder 7/1/77–7/15/77, Box 1, JCL.
83 Memorandum, Anthony Solomon to Michael Blumenthal, July 27, 1977, Solomon File, Chronological File, Folder 7/15/77–7/31/77, Box 2, JCL. A briefing paper attached to the Solomon memorandum was prepared by Frederich L. Springborn, Office of Foreign Exchange Operations.
84 Memorandum, Michael Blumenthal to President, August 9, 1977, Solomon File, Chronological File, Box 2, JCL.
85 Cabinet Minutes, July 25, 1977, 5, JCL.
86 Cabinet Minutes, November 7, 1977, 3, JCL.

87 Memorandum, President Carter to the Secretary of the Treasury and the Chairman of the Council of Economic Advisers, January 13, 1978, Solomon File, Chronological File, Box 3, JCL.
88 Memorandum, Michael Blumenthal and Charles Schultze to President Carter, January 19, 1978, Domestic Policy Staff—Eizenstat, Economic and Budgetary Outlook, 1979–81, [CF, O/A 727] [1], Box 191, JCL.
89 Ibid.
90 *Public Papers of the Presidents of the United States: Jimmy Carter, 1977*, 2:2159–60.
91 Memorandum, Charles Schultze to President Carter, February 21, 1978, Schultze Papers.
92 Putnam and Henning, "The Bonn Summit of 1978," 52.

Chapter Six

1 Phillips's famous article is titled "The Relation Between Unemployment and the Rate of Change of Money Wage Rates in the United Kingdom, 1861–1957."
2 Biven, *Who Killed John Maynard Keynes?* 44. Phillips's paper was anticipated by Irving Fisher, the Yale economist, in 1926. See Fisher, "A Statistical Relation Between Unemployment and Price Changes." Lawrence Klein, Carter's first nationally known economic adviser, published a paper less than a year after Phillips's study attempting to explain the behavior of prices and wages. Klein found that "excess demand for labour as represented by a moving average of unemployment has been an important factor over the sample period," but he also examined the impact on wages and prices of a number of other variables. He referred, in passing, to "a recent paper by A. W. Phillips." Klein and Ball, "Some Econometrics of the Determination of Absolute Prices and Wages," 475 n. 1.
3 See chapter 21 in Keynes's *The General Theory of Employment*.
4 The Samuelson and Solow paper is "Analytical Aspects of Anti-inflation Policy."
5 Eizenstat Papers, JCL. There are five transition papers in the package containing the document quoted. This paper is not dated, but a companion paper is dated December 20, 1976.
6 The inflation rate as measured by the consumer price index was 3 percent in 1957. It declined to 2 percent in 1958, following more restrictive monetary and fiscal policy, and reached 1 percent in 1961 and 1962. See the discussion in Kahn and Weiner, "Has the Cost of Disinflation Declined?" 6–7.
7 Friedman challenged the Phillips curve idea of a stable trade-off between inflation and unemployment in his 1967 presidential address to the American Economic Association: "The Role of Monetary Policy." An argument along the lines of Friedman's was independently made by Edmund Phelps of Columbia University. See Phelps, "Money Wage Dynamics," 687–711. Friedman's lecture delivered on the occasion of his receiving the Nobel prize in 1976, again dealt with his theory of the relation between unemployment and inflation. See Friedman, "Nobel Lecture." Friedman's views on the Phillips curve eventually prevailed. Most economists now believe that a Phillips curve trade-off may be possible in the short-run in response to stimulative policy, but does not exist in the long run.
8 See Sargent and Wallace, "Rational Expectations"; and Lucas and Sargent, "After

Keynesian Economics." For a description of Lucas's contribution to economics, see Chari, "Nobel Laureate Robert E. Lucas, Jr.," 2–12.
9 Morris, "Opening Remarks."
10 Memorandum, Charles Schultze to the President, "Background on Inflation," March 14, 1977, Schutlze Papers.
11 Ibid.
12 The complete document and the shorter summary can be found in Domestic Policy Staff—Eizenstat, [O/A 6338] [7], Box 144, JCL. The report was available on March 24. The summary—"Elements of a Comprehensive Anti-Inflation Strategy, Summary"—was forwarded to the president on March 29, 1977.
13 Ibid.
14 Okun's speech, "The Formulation of National Economic Policy," is reprinted in Pechman, *Economics for Policy Making*. Okun also estimated the sacrifice in terms of unemployment. (See, Okun, "Efficient Disinflationary Policies.") He concluded that it would take three point-years of unemployment to reduce the inflation rate by one percentage point, a "point year" being a 1 percent rate of unemployment above the full-employment rate. Three point years in 1977 would cost almost three million workers their jobs. Other researchers later placed the unemployment rate cost of disinflation at two point-years. A decade after Carter left office, one study of the cost of cutting the inflation rate through the restrictive monetary policies initiated in the late 1970s and continued into the early 1980s, estimated that an eight percentage point cut in inflation cost eighteen point years of unemployment. (Kahn and Weiner, "Has the Cost of Disinflation Declined?") For cost estimates done in papers from the early 1990s, see the discussion and references in Bryant, "Comment"; and Gordon, "The Phillips Curve Now and Then." Okun's conclusions were criticized by researchers from the rational expectations school of thought. The debate over the cost of disinflation was an extension of the debate over the properties of the Phillips curve. According to the rational expectations school, if the Federal Reserve announces its intention to lower inflation by a tighter policy, and if the bank has credibility, workers and businesses would expect the inflation rate to decrease. Accordingly, they would see themselves as being in a less inflationary environment and would revise their pricing and wage decisions, lowering the price markups and moderating wage demands. Inflationary pressure would weaken and real output and employment remain unaffected. See, for example Lucas, "Expectations and the Neutrality of Money"; and Sargent and Wallace, "Rational Expectations." Unfortunately, business and unions are uncertain about the commitment of the central bank to a disinflationary policy. There is also rigidity in prices and wages, which, for a variety of reasons, adjust sluggishly. As a result, disinflation is not without cost. One should not interpret these comments as suggesting that the contribution of the rational expectations school are unimportant. Expectations were clearly an important element in the inflation of the 1970s. Many, if not most, economists would probably agree with the judgment of William Poole: "An important development—if not *the* important intellectual development throughout the past 25 years in our understanding of how the macroeconomy works—is the recognition that expectations play a central role in affecting economic behavior" (Poole, "Monetary Policy Rules?" 7).

The Federal Reserve has, over the last decade, increased its credibility by exhibiting a consistent commitment to price stability. Businesses and unions also exhibit more flexibility in wages and prices because of increased foreign competition and a decline in union power. It is not possible, in this book, to explore this matter in detail. For a survey of the state of controversy in macroeconomics during the time of the Carter administration, see Santemero and Seater, "The Inflation-Unemployment Trade-off."

15 Domestic Policy Staff—Eizenstat, Economics, General, 1977, White House Central File, [O/A 21] [1], Box 194, JCL.
16 Domestic Policy Staff—Eizenstat, [O/A 6338] [7], Box 144, JCL.
17 Carter, while governor, had been briefed on the dilemma of choosing between price stability and full employment. In 1973, Henry Thomassen, Governor Carter's economic adviser, sent a memorandum to the governor in which he discussed phase four of the Nixon administration's wage and price control program. One issue that came up in the memorandum was the possible use of a tax surcharge to slow demand. "Were the surcharge sufficiently large," Thomassen wrote, "it could be trusted to slow or reverse the growth in output. Yet, only if resulting recessionary conditions were severe and long-lasting, would the expectation of inflation be apt to disappear. Within the United States, as other advanced countries, however, substantial and prolonged unemployment is politically unacceptable, and to control inflation flowing from expectations new tools must be devised." Memorandum, Henry Thomassen to Governor Carter, "Impatience and Imprudence in Fighting Inflation," September 18, 1973, Record Group 1–15, Accession Number 75-32A, Box 64, Location Number 4265-19, Georgia State Archives.
18 Eizenstat, "Economy," 3.
19 "Elements of a Comprehensive Anti-Inflation Strategy, Summary," March 25, 1977, Domestic Policy Staff—Eizenstat, [O/A 6338] [7], Box 144, JCL.
20 *Economic Report of the President, 1962*, 185.
21 In the Kennedy guidelines, wage increases in specific industries would be guided by the average increase in productivity in the overall economy. If an industry's rate of productivity increase exceeded the overall rate, then unit labor costs would decline and the industry should lower price. If an industry had a rate of productivity increase below the average of the overall economy, then the guidelines called "for an appropriate increase in price." Ibid., 189.
22 The presidential press conference can be found in *Public Papers of the Presidents of the United States: John F. Kennedy, 1962*, 1:315–18. Carter was reminded of the Kennedy-Steel case by an aide in 1980. A copy of the press conference was attached to the memorandum. In 1980, the Carter administration was struggling with wage-price guidelines and a problem of Mobil Oil compliance arose. "Although the Mobil case is not the same as U.S. Steel, the principle is similar," the aide wrote. "Additional peer pressure and negotiations might get them to get back into compliance." Memorandum, Anne Wexler to the President, April 4, 1980, Eizenstat Papers, JCL.
23 "Elements of a Comprehensive Anti-Inflation Strategy, Summary," March 25, 1977, Domestic Policy Staff—Eizenstat, [O/A 6338] [7], Box 144, JCL.

24 Memorandum, President Carter to Charles Schultze, March 31, 1977, Presidential Handwriting File, Box 17, JCL.
25 Memorandum, Ray Marshall to the Economic Policy Group, April 8, 1977, White House Central File, BE4-2, Box BE-16, JCL.
26 Memorandum, Arthur F. Burns to the President, March 31, 1977, Domestic Policy Staff—Eizenstat, [O/A 6338] [7], Box 144, JCL.
27 Schultze interview, Miller Center, 31–32.
28 Dark, "Organized Labor and the Carter Administration," 761.
29 Quoted in ibid., 775.
30 See the discussion in Dark, "Organized Labor and the Carter Administration." See also the comments of Harold Coxson, who was the chief labor lawyer for the U.S. Chamber of Commerce at the time and who participated in the legislative struggles over the labor legislation. Coxson, "Discussion."
31 At the meeting, Meany, according to Eizenstat's notes, "took a very strong position in opposition to prenotification of union demands as an interference with the right of collective bargaining. He said that he could not favor such a program 'even if Billy Carter wants it.'" Eizenstat, "Economy," 17–18. The president's brother, Billy Carter, made for good copy and had become a regular feature in press reports from Plains because of his colorful personality. Meany's reference to Carter's brother must have been personally offensive to the president. Attached to a letter from the president to George Meany, January 16, 1978, is a handwritten note from Carter to his secretary, Susan Clough. The note reads: "Susan—Issue clear instructions. Should be to: President George Meany. I don't call him George." January 16, 1978, White House Central File, BE 4-2, Box BE-16, JCL. For Meany's account of his experience with Carter, see Robinson, *George Meany and His Times*, chap. 18. This biography uses as its main source extensive interviews with Meany, which are quoted at length. Despite the strained feelings between Carter and Meany, the administration worked closely with labor on various issues. William Cable, who served under Frank Moore, the head of the Congressional Liaison Office, and had responsibility for the House, has provided insight into the degree of cooperation between the administration and labor at the working level in Congress. "Frank would host a get-together every Friday afternoon . . . and Ken Young who was the head of the legislative operation for the AFL-CIO, and usually two or three of the other major unions' Hill people, lobbyists—I know that that's a nasty word—would come over, and we'd talk about the next day's business, the next week's business, the next month's business, and where we were going together and what we could do. And that wasn't a meeting that was ever written down as a negotiation between George Meany and the President, but it sure did make up a day-to-day, every working day, cooperative understanding that happened within that White House and the labor movement." Cable, "Discussion," 806.
32 *Public Papers of the Presidents of the United States: Jimmy Carter, 1977*, 1:622–37.
33 Memorandum, Charles Schultze to the President, April 12, 1977, Presidential Handwriting File, Box 17, JCL.
34 Stuart Eizenstat, "Economy," 28.
35 *Public Papers of the Presidents of the United States: Jimmy Carter, 1977*, 1:629.

36 Stuart Eizenstat, "Economy," 17.
37 Quoted in Robert Shogan, *Promises to Keep*, 231.
38 Schultze interview, Miller Center, 32.
39 Memorandum, Blumenthal to EPG Members, June 17, 1977, Domestic Policy Staff—Eizenstat, [O/A 6338] [5], Box 144, JCL.
40 News release, Council on Wage and Price Stability, White House Central File, BE 4, O/A 8600, Box BE-16, JCL.
41 Memorandum, Alfred Kahn and Robert Bergland to the President, March 27, 1979, Domestic Policy Staff—Eizenstat, [O/A 538], Box 146, JCL.
42 See the discussion in Glassman and Sege, "The Recent Inflation Experience."
43 *Time*, March 5, 1979, 48.
44 Ibid.
45 Memorandum, Charles Schultze to President Carter, May 11, 1977, Domestic Policy Staff—Eizenstat, [CF, O/A 21] [2], Box 194, JCL.
46 Ibid.
47 Memorandum, Charles Schultze to Stuart Eizenstat, "President's Wednesday Lunch with 'Campaign' Economists," August 23, 1977, Schultze Papers.
48 Memorandum, W. Michael Blumenthal and Charles Schultze to the President, March 15, 1978, Domestic Policy Staff—Eizenstat, [O/A 7422], Box 144, JCL.
49 Memorandum, Richard Moe to the Vice President, Jordan, Powell, Landon Butler, April 3, 1978, Domestic Policy Staff—Eizenstat, [O/A 7432] [2], Box 145, JCL.
50 Hargrove and Morley, *The President and the Council of Economic Advisers*, 488.
51 Memorandum, Charles Schultze to the President, January 1, 1978, White House Central File, BE 4-2, Box BE-16, JCL.
52 *Public Papers of the Presidents of the United States: Jimmy Carter, 1978*, 1:723–25.
53 Ibid., 724.
54 Memorandum, Robert S. Strauss to the President, May 5, 1978, Presidential Handwriting File, Box 84, JCL.
55 News release, "What the Government Has Done," White House Central File, BE4, [O/A 8600], Box BE-16, JCL.
56 Memorandum, Ray Marshall and Robert S. Strauss to the President, May 8, 1978, Presidential Handwriting File, May 8, 1978, Box 85, JCL.
57 Presidential Diary Office, Diary File, Backup Material, January 13, 1978, Box PD-23, JCL.
58 Eizenstat Diary, May 10, 1978, Pad 33A, 1978, JCL. Stuart Eizenstat kept notes of the meetings he attended. He has granted me access to these notes.
59 Ibid.
60 Memorandum, Charles Schultze and Barry Bosworth to the President, July 19, 1978, Domestic Policy Staff—Eizenstat, [O/A 6338] [4], Box 143, JCL. The data suggest that there was a shift of income from profits to labor in the 1970s in most of the industrialized economies. See Bruno and Sacks, *Economics of Worldwide Inflation*, 162–64; and Glassman and Sege, "The Recent Inflation Experience." There was a bulge in profits in the last quarter of 1978 that caused George Meany to challenge the fairness of the application of the guidelines. Over the longer term, profits had been in a declining trend since the early 1950s. There was a dip in corporate

profit's share of GNP under Carter, after removal of the effects of the business cycle. See Holloway and Wakefield, "Sources of Change in the Federal Government Deficit, 1970–1986," 31. Alan Greenspan, who was heading his own consulting firm in New York at the time, commented: "By any long-term standard, profits are still inadequate to create the type of capital investment that this country needs." "Storm Over Surging Profits," *Time*, April 2, 1979, 60. The nations of the OECD were concerned throughout the 1970s about the declining profit share of national income. (See Llewellyn, "Resource Prices and Macroeconomic Policies.")

61 Hargrove and Morley, *The President and the Council of Economic Advisers*, 488.
62 Memorandum, Robert Strauss to the President, July 21, 1978, Domestic Policy Staff—Eizenstat, [O/A 6338] [4], Box 143, JCL.
63 Memorandum, Vice President Mondale, Michael Blumenthal, Stuart Eizenstat, and Charles Schultze to the President, December 23, 1977, Lipshutz File, Federal Reserve Board, Box 10, JCL.
64 Memorandum, Charles Schultze to the President, April 4, 1978, Schultze Papers.
65 Memorandum, Charles Schultze to the President, May 6, 1978, Presidential Handwriting File, Box 84, JCL.
66 Memorandum, Charles Schultze to the President, June 27, 1978, Presidential Handwriting File, Box 93, JCL.
67 Ibid.
68 Lyle Gramley interview with the author.
69 William Miller interview with the author.
70 Ehrbar, "Bill Miller Is a Fainthearted Inflation Fighter."
71 William Miller interview with the author.
72 Ehrbar, "Bill Miller Is a Fainthearted Inflation Fighter," 42.
73 Schultze interview with the author.
74 Memorandum, Charles Schultze to the President, April 11, 1979, Domestic Policy Staff—Eizenstat, Monetary Policy [CF, O/A 538], Box 238, JCL.
75 President Carter interview with the author.
76 Silk, *Economics in the Real World*, 155.

Chapter Seven

1 Anthony Solomon to Michael Blumenthal, September 8, 1977, Solomon Files, Chronological File, Box 2, JCL.
2 For a description of the visit by subcabinet officials, and events that followed, see Destler and Mitsuyu, "Locomotives on Different Tracks," 249-56.
3 Ibid.
4 Letter, President Carter to Helmut Schmidt, January 31, 1978, NSA, Brzezinski File, Box 6, JCL. There was continuing tension between the president and Chancellor Schmidt over the course of Carter's administration. An initial irritant was a *Newsweek* interview shortly before the election in which Schmidt indicated a preference for Ford. Schmidt apologized for the indiscretion. A memorandum to Governor Carter from a staff member in late October 1976 reported that "West German Chancellor Schmidt asked his close associate and assistant, Klaus Bolling, to call Cyrus Vance last week and convey to Vance the Chancellor's concern over the inter-

view in *Newsweek* in which Schmidt expressed an apparent preference for Ford over Carter. Bolling said that Schmidt was 'embarrassed and upset' at his slip of the tongue. He has a 'high regard' for Carter from what he has heard about him and looks forward to meeting him after the election." Memorandum, Dick Holbrooke to the Governor, October 26, 1976, "1976 Campaign or Transition," Eizenstat Papers, JCL. Schmidt was to say later that he had worked closely with Ford and Carter was an unknown quantity. Schmidt, *Men and Power*, 178. A number of disputes between the two involved such things as the production of neutron weapons and their deployment in Europe. See Carter, *Keeping Faith*, 225–29. At some meetings the discussion became quite heated. See Carter's account of a luncheon session at the Tokyo summit in 1979: Ibid., 112–13. In a meeting at the Venice summit in 1980, Carter reports in his memoir, the discussion between him and Schmidt "was the most unpleasant personal exchange I ever had with a foreign leader." Ibid., 538. Schmidt's account of the same meeting is given in Schmidt, *Men and Power*, 210–19. In his evaluation of Carter, Schmidt wrote in his memoir: "I thought I completely understood Carter's psychological makeup—he was, in fact, a man who never stopped searching his soul and tended repeatedly to change his mind—and it seemed necessary to be firm with him." Ibid., 79. Carter's evaluation of Schmidt is recorded in his diary: "Helmut is strong, somewhat unstable. Postures, and drones on, giving economic lessons when others are well aware of what he is saying." Carter, *Keeping Faith*, 113. One would suppose that the strained relationship was partly caused by the fact that they came from two totally different backgrounds. Schmidt had formal training in economics. He had developed his political skills and risen to power in a competitive parliamentary system. He had headed up important ministries on his way to the top. He viewed Carter as a governor of a minor province and without national political experience. A part of the reason for the strained relationship lies also in strong differences in personality. Schmidt had a personality at times abrasive. He irritated not only American presidents, but also cabinet colleagues, by his inability at times to curb his tongue. See Carr, *Helmut Schmidt*, 62–63. On the other hand, Carter is, as Michael Blumenthal has described him in commenting on the Carter/Schmidt relationship, "a Southern gentleman." Blumenthal interview with the author. Carter and Schmidt had one thing in common—a passion for detail.

5 Memorandum, Henry Owen to the Vice President, February 2, 1978, White House Central File, CO 54-2, Box CO-26, JCL.
6 Quoted in Putnam and Bayne, *Hanging Together*, 82. The original source of the quote is the *Daily Telegraph*, February 14, 1978.
7 Memorandum, Henry Owen to the President, February 18, 1978, White House Central File, CO 54-2, Box CO-26, JCL.
8 The letters have not yet received security clearance in the Carter Library. They are referred to by Owen in a covering memorandum to Carter. Memorandum, Henry Owen to President Carter, March 24, 1978, NSA, Brzezinski, Box 6, JCL.
9 Memorandum, Henry Owen to President Carter, "Chancellor Schmidt's Messages to You About the Summit," April 8, 1978, NSA, Brzezinski, Box 6, JCL.
10 Ibid.

11 The document is entitled "Macroeconomic Assessment, May 21, 1978." It can be found in the Schultze Papers.
12 Henry Owen, Notes on International Economic Preparatory Group Meeting, May 27 and 28, Domestic Policy Staff—Eizenstat, [CF, O/A 665], Box 190, JCL.
13 Ibid.
14 Putnam and Henning, "The Bonn Summit of 1978," 71.
15 Helmstader, "The Irrelevance of Keynes to German Economic Policy," 418.
16 Putnam and Henning, "The Bonn Summit of 1978," 23.
17 "Helmut Schmidt's Prescription, the World Economy at Stake," *Economist*, February 26, 1983, 21.
18 See the discussion in Hennings, "West Germany."
19 Putnam and Henning, "The Bonn Summit of 1978," 67. The authors report that their account of German decision making "is based primarily on extensive confidential interviews with virtually all key participants in the 1978 German decisions." Ibid., 133 n.114.
20 Michael Blumenthal interview with the author.
21 Quoted in Ludlow, *The Making of the European Monetary System*, 76.
22 Ibid., 130–31.
23 The text of the communiqué can be found in *Public Papers of the Presidents of the United States: Jimmy Carter, 1978*, 2:1310–15.
24 Ibid.
25 Putnam and Bayne, *Hanging Together*, 91.
26 See Wright, "The Origins of American Industrial Success, 1879–1940," 651–68.
27 Robert O. Keohane, "The International Politics of Inflation," 93.
28 *Washington Post*, December 26, 1977.
29 Carter, *Keeping Faith*, 103.
30 Owen, "Taking Stock of the Seven-Power Summits," 660.
31 See Johnson, "The Impact of Price Controls on the Oil Industry," 110.
32 For a discussion of the Nixon period, see Shultz and Dam, *Economic Policy Beyond the Deadlines*, 179–97. For an account of the various phases of the price controls imposed by Nixon, particularly as these relate to petroleum, see Kalt, *The Economics and Politics of Oil Price Regulation*, 9–16.
33 For a survey of the energy initiatives of the Ford administration, see De Marchi, "The Ford Administration."
34 For a short sketch of Ford's attempts at oil price decontrol, see ibid., 497–502. See also Reichley, *Conservatives in an Age of Change*, 365–73.
35 The O'Neill statement is cited in Jones, *The Trusteeship Presidency*, 135.
36 Jones and Strahan, "The Effect of Energy Politics," 164.
37 Carter interview, Miller Center, 23.
38 Carter had an early interest in energy problems. He served for a year as chairman of the national Governors' Conference on Natural Resources. He also saw directly the effects of the energy shortage in the early 1970s on Georgia industries. "I think that this energy problem," he said in remarks at an energy conference held at the Georgia Institute of Technology in 1973, "is perhaps the most serious responsibility

I have on my own shoulders as the elected leader of almost five million Georgians." *Addresses of Jimmy Carter*, 210.

39 Eizenstat interview, Miller Center, 30. Eizenstat also stated in this interview that at two cabinet level meetings on energy problems, "nobody really strongly came out for deregulation in that room. Charlie Schultze, for example, who basically believed in the free market, in terms of energy was concerned about the inflationary implications of doing it. We were in the middle of a natural gas shortage and it might be a bad time to remind people of the fact that you were going to substantially raise price." "The President was persuaded to keep controls," Eizenstat has also commented, "but to lift the control price substantially to $1.42 per BTU. Because controls were maintained, even though at higher levels, production-oriented Democrats were disappointed and unsupportive, while consumer advocates on the left lashed at the proposal because it raised prices to consumers." Eizenstat Address, University of Chicago Law School, 58–59.

40 Eizenstat, "The Presidency in Trouble," 24.

41 For an account of the development of the energy package, see Hanson and Kaufman, "The National Energy Tax Act of 1978," 187–213. The authors interviewed about two-thirds of the members of the Schlesinger group.

42 Comments at a cabinet meeting; quoted in Shogan, *Promises to Keep*, 191.

43 Jimmy Carter, *Keeping Faith*, 91.

44 The Carter energy proposal is summarized in Cochrane, "Carter's Energy Policy," 556–77.

45 The 1975 legislation had a penalty provision for noncompliance, but the Schlesinger group thought it unlikely to be effective in achieving its objective. Hanson and Kaufman, "The National Energy Tax Act of 1978," 189–90.

46 Minutes of the Cabinet Meeting, April 25, 1977, JCL.

47 Eizenstat Meeting Notes, July 11, 1978, Pad 35, JCL

48 Eizenstat Meeting Notes, July 10, 1979, Pad 35, JCL.

49 Eizenstat Meeting Notes, June 22, 1978, Pad 35, JCL.

50 See the discussion in Putnam and Henning, "The Bonn Summit of 1978," 64–67.

51 Eizenstat to the President, November 14, 1979, White House Central File, Subject File, BE-2, Box BE-4, JCL.

52 *Public Papers of the Presidents of the United States: Jimmy Carter, 1977*, 1:631.

53 The DRI estimate is mentioned in Memorandum, Charles Schultze to the President, April 23, 1977, White House Central File, Subject File, BE-4, Box BE-13, JCL.

54 Memorandum, Michael Blumenthal and Charles Schultze to the President, March 15, 1978, White House Central File, [O/A 665], Box 190, JCL.

55 Memorandum, Schultze to the President, July 7, 1978, Schultze Papers.

56 Memorandum, Charles Schultze to the President, July 11, 1978, Domestic Policy Staff—Eizenstat, [O/A 6316] Box 286, JCL.

57 Memorandum, Charles Schultze to the President, "Economic Effects of Alternative Outcomes at the Summit," July 7, 1978, Schultze Papers.

58 Eizenstat Meeting Notes, July 19, 1978, Pad 35, JCL.

59 Quoted in Ikenberry, "Market Solutions for State Problems," 170. Ikenberry interviewed Eizenstat and several other participants in the intra-administration debate: Richard Cooper, Henry Owen, and James Schlesinger.

Chapter Eight

1 Memorandum, Anthony M. Solomon to Michael Blumenthal, July 21, 1978, Solomon Chronological File, Box 4, JCL.
2 At a press conference shortly after Bonn, Carter was asked about the possibility that he might "move administratively to impose import fees or quotas on foreign oil." Carter replied that it was an option, "in the absence of congressional action, for me to impose, through Executive order under the present law, either import quotas, limiting the amount of oil that could come in, or import fees, which would charge extra for oil coming into the Nation. And, of course, the other option, which is one that I think would be at the bottom of the list, would be to permit the oil companies to unilaterally increase the price of their oil very high and to let the consumers pay for it to the enrichment of the oil companies themselves." *Public Papers of the Presidents of the United States: Jimmy Carter, 1978*, 2:1442.
3 Memorandum, Schlesinger, Blumenthal, Cooper, Schultze, Kahn, McIntyre, Owen and Eizenstat to the President, January 3, 1979, White House Central File, CM II, Box CM-7, JCL.
4 Memorandum, Lyle Gramley to the President, March 22, 1979, Presidential Handwriting File, Box 123, Folder 3/23/79, JCL.
5 Memorandum, Charles Schultze to the President, March 16, 1979, Presidential Handwriting File, Box 123, JCL.
6 Memorandum, Landon Butler to Hamilton Jordan, March 18, 1979, Presidential Handwriting File, Box 123, JCL.
7 Memorandum, Schlesinger, Blumenthal, Cooper, Schultze, Kahn, McIntyre, Owen and Eizenstat to the President, January 3, 1979, White House Central File, CM II, Box CM-7, JCL.
8 Alfred Kahn interview, Miller Center, 110.
9 Memorandum, Cyrus Vance, Michael Blumenthal, James Schlesinger, Juanita Kreps, and Henry Owen to the President, March 23, 1979, Presidential Handwriting File, Box 123, JCL. Richard Cooper of the State Department had earlier made a case for phased decontrol in a memorandum to Stuart Eizenstat in mid-December. See Memorandum, Richard N. Cooper to Stu Eizenstat, December 15, 1978, White House Central File, TA 4-11, Box TA-26, JCL.
10 For a survey of the behavior of the dollar over the period in question, see Solomon, *The International Monetary System, 1945–1981*, 344–50.
11 In the first attempt to reconstruct the Bretton Woods arrangement, the band on either side of the official rate was 2.5 percent. In a second attempt to save the system, the 4.5 percent band was allowed.
12 Solomon, *The International Monetary System, 1945–1981*, 294. For a thorough treatment of the creation of the European Monetary System, see Ludlow, *The Making of the European Monetary System*. The EMS provided a buffer for the mark, but did not free it completely from the economic effects of dollar movements. When par-

ticipants in the market moved out of the dollar due to a lack of confidence, they did not move equally into all the European currencies. They moved selectively, particularly into the mark. This selective movement widened the difference between the mark and the other currencies of the EMS, leading to greater fluctuations in European currencies than would otherwise have occurred. See the discussion in Strange, "Europe and the United States."

13 For a brief survey of the European Monetary System over the period 1979 to 1992, see Neely, "Realignments of Target Zones Exchange Rate Systems," 23–34.
14 Quoted in Ludlow, *The Making of the European Monetary System*, 121.
15 Quoted in ibid., 120.
16 Ibid., 122. I have not had access to the so-called "Bergsten list." Charles Schultze prepared an "Assessment of Proposals for a New European Monetary System" for the president a few days prior to Bonn. Schultze advised Carter that "although there are some political disadvantages for the United States, we should not take a negative attitude on general principles, and indeed should support the broad objectives of European economic integration, including monetary cooperation." He did express concern over the effect on the dollar. "We must be assured unequivocally that the dollar will be free to adjust when fundamental economic conditions warrant. It must not be pegged." Memorandum, Charles Schultze to the President, July 11, 1978, Presidential Handwriting File, Box 94, JCL.
17 Presidential Handwriting File, Folder Bonn Economic Summit, 7/16/78–7/17/78–7/18/78, Box 95, JCL.
18 *Public Papers of the Presidents of the United States: Jimmy Carter, 1978*, 2:1315.
19 See Putnam and Bayne, *Hanging Together*, 94.
20 *Public Papers of the Presidents of the United States: Jimmy Carter, 1978*, 2:1315.
21 Eizenstat Meeting Notes, August 15, 1978, Pad 38, JCL.
22 Ibid.
23 Anthony Solomon noted in a report for the White House: "Market commentators attributed this reaction to perceived weakness in the program in the monetary and fiscal areas." Anthony M. Solomon, White House Report, October 26, 1978, Solomon Chronological File, Box 5, JCL.
24 Eizenstat Meeting Notes, October 19, 1978, Pad 41, JCL.
25 For an account of this meeting, see Nickel, "The Inside Story of the Dollar Rescue," 40–44.
26 Daily Diary, October 28, 1978. The meeting was a closely held secret. James McIntyre later complained to Eizenstat that he and others had not been informed in advance about the dollar action. Eizenstat had asked Solomon to brief the vice president and Hamilton Jordan. Blumenthal reported to Eizenstat that he had asked the president about this and Carter had said no. "He feels it has to be kept close." Eizenstat Meeting Notes, November 1, 1978, Pad 41, JCL.
27 Eizenstat has given an account of that weekend. "I was on a synagogue retreat in West Virginia on a rare weekend off when Secretary of the Treasury Michael Blumenthal, in his finest hour, met with the President in the Cabinet Room on Saturday and Sunday and convinced him that international financial markets would be impressed only with dramatic action to raise interest rates to end the run on

the dollar by drawing foreign investment to the U.S. and to curb inflation by de-stimulating the economy. I was kept closely informed, in what became a makeshift office for me at the retreat, by Secretary Blumenthal, Charlie Schultze, and Vice President Mondale." Stuart Eizenstat, "The Presidency in Trouble," 70.
28 Hickel, "The Inside Story of the Dollar Rescue," 42.
29 The idea for the Carter bonds seems to have come first from Arthur Burns when he was still chairman of the Federal Reserve Board. "In his meeting with me this morning," Carter wrote to Blumenthal and Schultze in January 1978, "Chairman Burns spoke about issuing Treasury securities in foreign currencies. I would like your preliminary views on this." Memorandum, President Carter to the Secretary of the Treasury and the Chairman of the Council of Economic Advisers, January 13, 1978, Solomon Papers, Chronological File, Box 3, JCL. Blumenthal and Schultze replied a week later. "This approach could provided us with substantial intervention resources that would not have to be repaid in the short term." But there are major disadvantages. Among these disadvantages: "U.S. willingness to issue such bonds would trigger strong demands by OPEC and others for exchange rate guarantees on their large dollar holdings—OPEC has been pressing for such 'indexation' for some time." Memorandum, Michael Blumenthal and Charles Schultze to the President, January 19, 1978, Domestic Policy Staff, Economic and Budgetary Outlook, 1979–81 [CF, O/A 727] [1], Box 191, JCL.
30 Memorandum, Anthony M. Solomon to the President, December 27, 1977, Solomon Papers, Chronological File, Box 3, JCL.
31 Eizenstat, "The Presidency in Trouble," 70.
32 Memorandum, Schlesinger et al. to the President, January 3, 1979, White House Central File, CM 11, Box CM-7, JCL.
33 Ibid.
34 These inflation effects represent increases over and above the consumer price increases expected if there were no change in current policy (the "base case"). The base case increases in the CPI were estimated to be four-tenths of one percent in 1979, two-tenths in 1980, and one-tenth in 1981.
35 Memorandum, Schlesinger et al. to the President, January 3, 1979, White House Central File, CM 11, Box CM-7, JCL.
36 Memorandum, Stuart Eizenstat and Kitty Schirmer to the President, March 16, 1979, Presidential Handwriting File, Box 123, JCL.
37 Memorandum, Michael Blumenthal to the President, March 16, 1979, Presidential Handwriting File, Box 123, JCL.
38 Blumenthal's comments, as well as those of other participants in the meeting, are recorded in the Eizenstat Meeting Notes, March 19, 1979, Pad 50, JCL.
39 Memorandum, Eizenstat and Schirmer to the President, March 16, 1979, Presidential Handwriting File, Box 123, JCL.
40 Eizenstat Meeting Notes, March 19, 1979, Pad 50, JCL.
41 The attendees at Camp David included, in addition to the president, vice president, and Fed chairman: Brock Adams, Michael Blumenthal, Stuart Eizenstat, Fred Kahn, Juanita Kreps, Ray Marshall, James McIntyre, James Schlesinger, Charles Schultze, and Robert Strauss. Eizenstat comments in his meeting notes on the large

number of attendees. "Mike and Charlie complain on JC inviting such a large group to Camp David for the economic discussion.... This is the underlying problem with economic policy—too many people." Eizenstat Meeting Notes, March 19, 1979, Pad 50, JCL.

42 Memorandum, Charles Schultze to the President, March 16, 1979, Presidential Handwriting File, Box 123, JCL.

43 Eizenstat Meeting Notes, March 19, 1979, Pad 50, JCL.

44 The same argument was used by opponents of decontrol in the Nixon administration. George Shultz, who served in the Nixon government and later under President Reagan, and Kenneth Dam have given an account of the dispute: "Advocates of rationing and controls further maintained that consumption of oil products, unlike other goods, would not be responsive to higher prices because the demand for oil products is more or less fixed. Price, it was said, is not a factor in deciding how much gasoline is used. People have to drive to work, whatever the price of gas. This position which may be termed 'elasticity pessimism,' assumed that the responsiveness (elasticity) of demand for oil products to price was very low." Schultz and Dam, *Economic Policy Beyond the Headlines*, 186. Schultz and Dam go on to point out that consumers become more sensitive to price changes over the longer run and that, even in the short run, people do adjust by forming car pools and buying smaller cars.

45 Producers would oppose the tax for obvious reasons. Congressional liberals, whom the authors of the memorandum had in mind, would withhold support for a tax in order to prevent decontrol.

46 Memorandum, Cyrus Vance, Michael Blumenthal, James Schlesinger, Juanita Kreps, and Henry Owen to the President, March 23, 1979, Presidential Handwriting File, Box 123, JCL.

47 Memorandum, Stuart Eizenstat and Kitty Schirmer to the President, March 16, 1979, Presidential Handwriting File, Box 123, JCL.

48 Martin Tolchin, "Carter to End Price Control on U.S. Oil and Urge Congress to Tax Any 'Windfall Profits,'" *New York Times*, April 6, 1979.

49 Eizenstat, "The Presidency in Trouble," 93.

50 Memorandum, Stuart Eizenstat and Frank Moore to the President, March 23, 1979, Presidential Handwriting File, Box 123, JCL.

51 Memorandum, Frank Moore to the President, March 23, 1979, Presidential Handwriting File, Box 123, JCL.

52 Eizenstat Meeting Notes, January 3, 1979, Pad 45, JCL. Similar sentiments were repeated at a meeting on March 19. Eizenstat Meeting Notes, March 19, 1979, Pad 50, JCL.

53 Eizenstat Meeting Notes, March 27, 1979, Pad 51, JCL.

54 Eizenstat Meeting Notes, March 23, 1979, Pad 51, JCL. There was an occasional case of inconsistency in his position. At a press conference held while he was on a visit to Iowa in early May, a month after he had already announced decontrol, a reporter asked Carter how he would react if Congress voted to extend price controls on oil beyond the 1981 date on which they were scheduled to end. Carter replied that "if the House and Senate pass this legislation [to extend price controls] and

send it to me, I will certainly not veto it. We will live with it." *Public Papers of the Presidents of the United States: Jimmy Carter, 1979*, 3:801. In reaction to Carter's statement, Eizenstat sent a strongly worded memorandum to the president. "I am extremely concerned about the statement you made in Iowa, indicating you would not veto a bill extending controls.... This gives the impression of an absence of leadership—that you really do not care one way or another whether controls are extended or not." White House Central File, BE-2, Subject File, Box BE-3, JCL.

55 Memorandum, Richard N. Cooper to Stuart Eizenstat, December 15, 1978, White House Central File, TA 4-11, Box TA-26, JCL.
56 Memorandum, Cyrus Vance, Michael Blumenthal, James Schlesinger, Juanita Kreps, Henry Owen to the President, March 23, 1979, Presidential Handwriting File, Box 123, JCL.
57 For the decontrol speech, see *Public Papers of the Presidents of the United States: Jimmy Carter, 1979*, 1:609–14. One of the first acts of Ronald Reagan as president was to end oil price controls ahead of schedule.
58 For Carter's remarks on the occasion of the signing of the bill, see *Public Papers of the Presidents of the United States: Jimmy Carter, 1980*, 1:584–90.
59 Eizenstat, "The Presidency in Trouble," 26.
60 Eizenstat Meeting Notes, March 22, 1979, Pad 51, JCL.
61 Stuart Eizenstat to President Carter, June 28, 1979, Presidential Handwriting File, Box 137, JCL.
62 For a survey of tensions that developed between the United States and Japan after the Bonn summit over the issue of whether or not the Japanese were weakening in their commitments, see Destler and Mitsuyu, "Locomotives on Different Tracks," 256–62. The tensions were amicably resolved before the Tokyo summit, which met in 1979.
63 De Menil, "From Rambouillet to Versailles," 26.
64 For a detailed discussion of this issue, see Holtham, "German Macroeconomic Policy."
65 Ibid., 147.
66 Solomon, "A Personal Evaluation," 48.
67 See Holtham, "German Macroeconomic Policy," 150–53.
68 The actions of the Bundesbank caused tensions to develop between the bank and the Schmidt government. See the discussion in Goodman, *Monetary Sovereignty*.
69 Cooper, "Global Economic Policy in a World of Energy Shortage," 102.
70 De Menil, "From Rambouillet to Versailles," 27.
71 *Monthly Report*, January 1983. Quoted in Hollerman, *Japan, Disincorporated*, 158.
72 For a summary of the literature on the subject, see Bryant, *International Coordination*, 6–34 and 74–87. See also Frankel, *Obstacles to International Macroeconomic Policy Coordination*. For another treatment of uncertainty applied to international cooperation, see Ghosh and Masson, *Economic Cooperation in an Uncertain World*.
73 Bryant, *International Coordination*, 77–78.
74 Frankel, *Obstacles to International Macroeconomic Policy Coordination*, 18.
75 See Bryant et al., *Empirical Macroeconomics*. The twelve models included, among others, a Federal Reserve model, a Japanese model, an OECD model, and two

United States models frequently used for forecasting—the Wharton and Data Resources models. The simulations were for the United States and the rest of the OECD countries taken collectively.
76 Frankel and Rockett, "International Macroeconomic Policy Coordination."
77 See, for example, Bryant, *International Coordination*, 83–86.
78 Ibid., 44.
79 "Comments," by Paul R. Masson, ibid., 136.
80 See the account in Funabashi, *Managing the Dollar*.
81 Solomon, "A Personal Evaluation," 48.

Chapter Nine

1 Schultze interview with the author.
2 Memorandum, Stuart Eizenstat to the President, July 22, 1978, Domestic Policy Staff—Eizenstat, [O/A 6338] [4], Box 143, JCL. I have not been able to locate the original Marshall memorandum. Marshall refers to it in a memorandum to the President, September 18, 1978, Domestic Policy Staff—Eizenstat, [O/A 7432] [1], Box 145, JCL. "I support the basic anti-inflation program recommended to you by the EPG. Fundamentally, the program is based on principles I recommended to you in the concept paper dated July 15."
3 Memorandum, Michael Blumenthal to the President, September 13, 1978, Domestic Policy Staff—Eizenstat, [O/A 7432] [1], Box 145, JCL.
4 The formula used to obtain the 5.75 percent price rule added increases in employment taxes, 0.5 percent, to the 7 percent wage increase and subtracted from this sum a projected 1.75 percent increase in productivity. (7% + 0.5% − 1.75% = 5.75%). Ibid.
5 Memorandum, Michael Blumenthal to the President, September 13, 1978, Domestic Policy Staff—Eizenstat, [O/A 7432] [1], Box 145, JCL.
6 Memorandum, Charles Schultze to the President, September 26, 1978, Domestic Policy Staff—Eizenstat, [O/A 7432] [2], Box 145, JCL.
7 The address to the nation is found in *Public Papers of the Presidents of the United States: Jimmy Carter, 1978*, 2:1839–45.
8 Schultze interview, Miller Center, 33
9 "Address to the Nation," *Public Papers of the Presidents of the United States: Jimmy Carter, 1978*, 2:1841.
10 Memorandum, Stuart Eizenstat and Robert Ginsburg to the President, September 18, 1978, Domestic Policy Staff—Eizenstat, [O/A 7432] [1], Box 145, JCL.
11 Memorandum, Charles Schultze to the President, September 26, 1978, Domestic Policy Staff—Eizenstat, O/A 7432, Box 145, JCL. Blumenthal gave his views to the President in Memorandum, Michael Blumenthal to the President, September 27, 1978, Domestic Policy Staff—Eizenstat, [O/A 7432] [2], Box 145, JCL.
12 Memorandum, Vice-President to the President, September 25, 1978, Domestic Policy Staff—Eizenstat, [O/A 7432] [2], Box 145, JCL.
13 Schultze interview, Miller Center, 34. The budget submitted to Congress in January 1979 did project a $30 billion deficit.
14 Memorandum, Secretary Marshall to the President, February 7, 1979, Domestic Policy Staff—Eizenstat, [O/A 726] [1], Box 143, JCL.

15 Hargrove and Morley, *The President and the Council of Economic Advisers*, 490.
16 Memorandum, Charles Schultze to the President, October 5, 1978, Domestic Policy Staff—Eizenstat, [O/A 7432] [2], Box 145, JCL.
17 Hargrove and Morley, *The President and the Council of Economic Advisers*, 496–97.
18 *Public Papers of the Presidents of the United States: Jimmy Carter, 1978*, 2:1843.
19 In the memorandum to the President, Schultze did not mention a large oil price increase as one of the negative things that could happen. He did list others. "For example, if we experience only a ¾ percent rise in productivity [the productivity growth rate turned out to be negative]; a further 7 percent depreciation of the dollar [the actual depreciation was less than 7 percent, though still substantial at over 4 percent]; a 10 percent rise in food prices [food prices actually rose by almost 11 percent]." Memorandum, Charles Schultze to the President, October 5, 1978, Domestic Policy Staff—Eizenstat, [O/A 7432] [2], Box 145, JCL.
20 Hargrove and Morley, *The President and the Council of Economic Advisers*, 497–98.
21 Memorandum, Stuart Eizenstat and Alfred Kahn to the President, June 2, 1979, Eizenstat Papers, JCL.
22 General Accounting Office, *The Voluntary Pay and Price Standards*, 8.
23 Memorandum, Charles Schultze to the Economic Policy Group, March 13, 1979, Eizenstat Papers, JCL.
24 Lyle Gramley and Daniel Brill, Draft of "Talking Points for Consultations with Labor, Business, and Congress," June 11, 1979, Eizenstat Papers, JCL.
25 Minutes of the EPG Steering Committee, June 25, 1979, Eizenstat Papers, JCL. Part of the inflation in agricultural prices was due to feedback from the nonagriculture part of the economy. The increased cost to farmers of inputs used in the production process was passed on in higher prices for farm output. Oil-based inputs like fuel and fertilizer rose rapidly as a result of the oil shock in 1979.
26 See Bullard, "Historical CPI Inflation."
27 See Gordon, "Measuring the Aggregate Price Level," 260–61.
28 In 1999, only 20 percent of union contracts had a provision for cost-of-living adjustments.
29 *Economic Report of the President*, 1980, 35.
30 Lyle Gramley and Daniel Brill, Draft of "Talking Points for Consultations with Labor, Business, and Congress," June 11, 1979, Eizenstat Papers, JCL.
31 Eizenstat, "The Presidency in Trouble," 83.
32 Memorandum, Lyle Gramley and Daniel Brill to the Economic Policy Group's Steering Committee, May 16, 1979, Eizenstat Papers, JCL.
33 House Committee on Ways and Means, *Hearings on the Advisability of a Tax Reduction in 1980 Effective for 1981*.
34 Memorandum, EPG Steering Committee to the President, June 20, 1979, Eizenstat Papers, Economic Policy Group, 1979, JCL.
35 Poole, "Comments," 85.
36 For the announcement of the National Accord, see *Public Papers of the Presidents of the United States, 1979, Jimmy Carter* 2:1777–78.
37 Schultze recalled in a post-presidency interview: "In fact we turned it (determining the pay standard) over to this committee. Now we didn't actually turn it over be-

cause there was then a continuing struggle. I had a continuing nasty messy year with that committee. . . . And they [labor] were always threatening to walk out." Schultze interview, Miller Center, 43. For Alfred Kahn's description of the origin of the Pay Advisory Committee, see Alfred Kahn interview, Miller Center, 51–53.

38 The inflation speech can be found in *Public Papers of the Presidents of the United States: Jimmy Carter, 1980–1981*, 1:476–82.
39 Alfred Kahn interview, Miller Center, 46.
40 Memorandum, Alfred Kahn to the Steering Committee of the Economic Policy Group, June 11, 1980, Eizenstat Papers, JCL.
41 Memorandum, Council on Wage and Price Stability to the Economic Policy Group, June 12, 1980, Eizenstat, EPG 1980, Eizenstat Papers, JCL.
42 Memorandum, Secretary Miller to the President, July 30, 1980, Eizenstat, EPG 1980, Eizenstat Papers, JCL.
43 "Recommendations of the Pay Advisory Committee with Respect to the Wage Guidelines Program and Regulation," Washington, November 17, 1980. The statement is quoted in Vicusi, "The Political Economy of Wage and Price Regulation," 160.
44 General Accounting Office, *The Voluntary Pay and Price Standards*. The report was undertaken at the initiative of the General Accounting Office and at the request of the Subcommittee on Commerce, Consumer, and Monetary Affairs of the House Committee on Government Operations. Senator Ted Kennedy, on behalf of the Energy Subcommittee of the Joint Economic Committee, also asked the General Accounting Office "to look at certain activities of the Council, particularly the area of regulatory review and the Council's allocation of its internal resources." Ibid., 1.
45 Ibid., 1–2.
46 *Economic Report of the President, 1981*, 59. The GAO report had a monetarist tone underlying the discussion. The differences between the GAO and the administration were not just about facts, but also about the basic model to be used for interpreting how the economy works. The discussion in the report and in the administration economists' replies represent a good example of the controversy within the profession during the Carter administration. In his comments on the report, published in an appendix, Alfred Kahn wrote: "I regret to say that the draft GAO report is, essentially, an ideological polemic against all incomes policies, on principle, rather than an objective analysis of the effectiveness of the President's present standards . . . in terms of what they were designed to accomplish. What is disturbing is that the GAO report represents so clearly and essentially the adoption of a particular set of preconceptions representing the position of one segment of the economics profession, and that the predisposition has precluded a fair characterization of what the standards might reasonably have been expected to accomplish." Ibid., 171.
47 Schultze interview with the author.
48 Gramley interview with the author.
49 Blinder, "The Anatomy of Double-Digit Inflation." This article is a more detailed treatment of the analysis found in Blinder, *Economic Policy and the Great Stagflation*. During an interview, Charles Schultze cited the Blinder article as an interpretation

with which he agreed. For another piece not unsympathetic to the "external shock" view, see Bruno and Sacks, *Economics of Worldwide Inflation.*

50 Blinder, "The Anatomy of Double-Digit Inflation," 264.
51 See, for example Taylor, "How Should Monetary Policy Respond?" and DeLong, "America's Peacetime Inflation." See also Taylor's comments on DeLong's article, same volume, 276–80.
52 See DeLong, "America's Peacetime Inflation," 268–70.
53 See the summary in Carlson, "Federal Fiscal Policy," 28.
54 See Herbert Stein, *Presidential Economics,* 214.
55 Pechman, *Setting National Priorities,* 3.
56 Hargrove and Morley, *The President and the Council of Economic Advisers,* 453.
57 Memorandum, Charles Schultze to Michael Blumenthal, June 27, 1977, Schultze Papers.
58 Memorandum, T-2 Forecasting Group to Michael Blumenthal, Juanita Kreps, James McIntyre, Ray Marshall, and Charles Schultze, October 5, 1977, Domestic Policy Staff—Eizenstat, [O/A 6236] [1], Box 194, JCL.
59 Memorandum, Lyle Gramley to the Steering Committee, October 19, 1977, Eizenstat Papers, JCL.
60 The general problem of errors in policy making due to misperceptions of the economy's performance is discussed in Orphanides, "The Quest for Prosperity Without Inflation."
61 The Long/Ullman resistance is reported in Hargrove, *Jimmy Carter as President,* 99.
62 For a summary of the content of the reform bill, see *Economic Report of the President, 1978,* 74–75.
63 Memorandum, Charles Schultze to the President, December 18, 1977, Schultze Papers.
64 Memorandum, Stuart Eizenstat and Charles Schultze to President Carter, January 16, 1978, Domestic Policy Staff—Eizenstat, [O/A 6343] [8], Box 290, JCL. After the statement that inflation was not heating up, Eizenstat and Schultze added: "But neither is there much hope that it will decline from the current 6 to 6½ percent. . . . Your decision on this year's budget and tax reduction will not overcommit us in the future."
65 *Congressional Quarterly Almanac* (1978):218
66 For an account of the fate of the reform bill, see Birnbaum and Murray, *Showdown at Gucci Gultch.*
67 Memorandum, Charles Schultze to the President, September 27, 1978, Domestic Policy Staff—Eizenstat, [O/A 6343] [6], Box 289, JCL.
68 Schultze interview with the author.
69 Ibid.
70 The 1980 *Economic Report* reduced this number to 8.3 percent.
71 Memorandum, Charles Schultze to the President, May 6, 1978, Presidential Handwriting File, Box 84, JCL.
72 Schultze interview with the author.
73 Orphanides, "The Quest for Prosperity Without Inflation," 4.

74 Memorandum, Charles L. Schultze to Anthony Solomon, July 31, 1978, Schultze Papers.
75 Memorandum, Stuart Eizenstat and Robert Ginsburg to the President, September 18, 1978, Domestic Policy Staff—Eizenstat, [O/A 7432] [1], Box 145, JCL.
76 Gramley interview with the author.
77 Memorandum, Charles Schultze to the President, May 6, 1978, Presidential Handwriting File, Box 84, JCL.
78 Memorandum, Charles Schultze to the President, May 9, 1978, Presidential Handwriting File, May 10, 1978, Box 85, JCL.
79 Ibid.
80 Cutter, "The Presidency and Economic Policy," 477–78.
81 The administration had announced in June 1977 a decision to increase the defense budget by 3 percent in real terms. The decision was made, in part, in order to convince other NATO members to raise their quotas. Since the commitment was made in real terms, the amount devoted to defense in nominal dollars went up automatically with inflation.
82 Cutter, "The Presidency and Economic Policy," 479.
83 The quotation originally appeared in the *New York Times*. It is quoted in ibid., 481.
84 Memorandum, Economic Policy Group Steering Group to the President, June 20, 1979, Eizenstat Papers, JCL.
85 Hargrove and Morley, *The President and the Council of Economic Advisers*, 494–95.
86 *Public Papers of the Presidents of the United States: Jimmy Carter, 1980–1981*, 2:1586.
87 Rivlin interview with the author.
88 Eizenstat, Address, University of Chicago Law School, 49.
89 Hargrove and Morley, *The President and the Council of Economic Advisers*, 483. Schultze's interpretation of the inflationary process is developed in articles completed after leaving the administration. See Schultze, "Some Macro Foundations for Micro Theory"; Schultze, "Microeconomic Efficiency and Nominal Wage Stickiness" (his presidential address to the American Economic Association); and Schultze, *Other Times, Other Places*. See also Barry Bosworth's interpretation, which closely parallels Schultze's, in Bosworth, "Nonmonetary Aspects of Inflation."
90 Gramley interview with the author.
91 Kahn interview, Miller Center, 119.
92 Eizenstat interview with the author. Eizenstat's notes taken at a staff meeting on March 28, 1977, report the same assessment as his post-administration interview. "J. C. very concerned about inflation—bad news recently." In a marginal note in the same entry, probably added later after the Carter Presidency was over, Eizenstat comments: "He had an earlier sense of it than others." Eizenstat Meeting Notes, March 28, 1977, Pad 12, JCL.

Chapter Ten

1 *Wall Street Journal*, December 3, 1976, 1.
2 For a detailed survey of the Social Security program, see Berstein and Berstein, *Social Security*. For a survey of the Social Security problem at the time Carter entered office, see Munnell, *The Future of Social Security*, particularly, 93–111. See also

Boskin, *The Future of Social Security*, and Capra et al., "Social Security: An Analysis." For a recent discussion of Social Security problems, see Triest, "Social Security Reform." The Triest article summarizes the papers presented at a conference sponsored by the Boston Federal Reserve and held in June 1996.

3. Memorandum, Kau to Economic Policy Group Steering Committee, July 29, 1979, Eizenstat Papers, JCL.
4. Robertson, "The Outlook for Social Security," 272.
5. Memorandum, Kau to Steering Committee, July 29, 1979, Eizenstat Papers, JCL.
6. See "How to Save Social Security," *Business Week*, November 29, 1982, 78–85.
7. For a brief survey of the debate during President Clinton's term in office over the Fair Minimum Wage Act of 1999, see Neumark et al., "Will Increasing the Minimum Wage Help the Poor?"
8. Ray Marshall interview, Miller Center, 37.
9. See Memorandum, Council of Economic Advisers to the Economic Policy Group, March 17, 1977, White House Central File, LA 6, Box LA-10, JCL.
10. Ibid.
11. In terms used by economists, the estimate of the number of workers affected by an increase in the minimum wage depends on the wage elasticity of the demand for such workers. A large number of studies had been done by 1977 estimating the elasticity. The analytical work on which the Council of Economic Advisers depended for their conclusions was done by Barry Bosworth of the Council on Wage and Price Stability. A paper, "Background Material," March 17, 1977, is attached to a memorandum from Stuart Eizenstat and Bill Johnson to the President (March 22, 1977, White House Central File, LA 6, Box LA-10, JCL.) The author of this paper is not identified but clearly was Barry Bosworth. Lyle Gramley recalled in an interview: "I remember that it was Barry Bosworth that did the analytic leg work for the CEA on the minimum wage thing. It forms the basis for Charlie's position." The Bosworth analysis relied heavily on research done by Edward Gramlich of the University of Michigan. See Gramlich, "Impact of Minimum Wages."
12. Memorandum, Secretary Marshall to the President, March 22, 1977, White House Central File, LA-6, Box LA-10, JCL.
13. "Background Material," March 17, 1977, attached to Memorandum, Stuart Eizenstat and Bill Johnson to the President, March 22, 1977, White House Central File, LA 6, Box LA-10, JCL.
14. Ibid.
15. Memorandum, Ray Marshall to the President, March 22, 1977, White House Central File, LA 6, Box LA-10, JCL.
16. Memorandum, David Scott to Governor Carter, August 7, 1973, Record Group 1–15, Accession Number 75-32A, Box Number 64, Location Number 4265-19, Georgia State Archives.
17. President's Reorganization Project—Decision Analysis Report, June 28, 1977, Hamilton Jordan File, Box 36, JCL.
18. Lyle Gramley interview with the author.
19. Memorandum, Michael Blumenthal to the President, March 21, 1977, White House Central File, LA 6, Box LA-10, JCL.

20 Ibid.
21 Memorandum, Stuart Eizenstat to the President, June 6, 1977, White House Central File, LA-6, Subject-Executive, Box LA-10, JCL.
22 See the *Economic Report of the President, 1964*, 57–58. A leading scholar attempting to define in dollar terms a minimum income was Robert Lampman. See his analysis of the definition and breadth of poverty prepared for the Joint Economic Committee: Lampman, *The Low Income Population*.
23 Memorandum, Stuart Eizenstat to the President, June 6, 1977, White House Central File, LA-6, Subject-Executive, Box LA-10, JCL.
24 Memorandum, Stuart Eizenstat to the President, June 6, 1977, White House Central File, LA-6, Subject-Executive, Box LA-10, JCL.
25 Council on Wage and Price Stability, "Inflation Update," May 22, 1978, White House Central File, BE 4 [O/A 8600], Box BE-16, JCL.
26 Memorandum, Curt Hessler to the EPG Steering Committee, September 28, 1978, Domestic Policy Staff—Eizenstat, [O/A 7432] [1], Box 145, JCL.
27 Memorandum, Charles Schultze to the President, February 10, 1977, White House Central File, BE 4-1, Box BE-15, JCL.
28 The Schultze scorecard memorandum is attached to a memorandum by Rick Hutcheson to the Vice President, November 17, 1977, White House Central File, BE 4-2, Box BE-16, JCL.
29 The most frequently cited paper produced by the Chicago school is Stigler, "The Theory of Economic Regulation." For a discussion of deregulation literature at the time of the Carter administration, see Levine, "Revisionism Revised?"
30 See Derthick and Quirk, *The Politics of Deregulation*.
31 U.S. Committee on House Administration, *The Presidential Campaign, 1976, Jimmy Carter*, vol. 1, pt. 1:235–36.
32 Carter, *Campaign Promises, 1976*, 97, JCL.
33 For a summary of Ford's efforts, see Derthick and Quirk, *The Politics of Deregulation*, 45–50.
34 Ibid., 44. Stephen Breyer, later to be appointed to the Supreme Court by President Clinton, served as special council to the subcommittee. Breyer came to the subcommittee from Harvard where he had specialized in economic regulation. He was the coauthor of a Brookings monograph: Breyer and MacAvoy, *Energy Regulation by the Federal Power Commission*.
35 Schultze interview, Miller Center, 48–49.
36 Kahn's two-volume work is *The Economics of Regulation: Principles and Institutions*. The quotation is from McGraw, *Prophets of Regulation*, 236. Kahn served as Dean of the College of Arts and Sciences at Cornell from 1969 to 1974. For a profile, see Sobel, *The Worldly Economists*, 233–44.
37 For an account of Kahn's activities at the New York Commission, see Anderson, *Regulatory Politics and Electric Utilities*. Kahn, himself, recommended this source. Alfred Kahn interview, Miller Center, 147.
38 Robyn, *Braking the Special Interests*, 38.
39 McGraw, *Prophets of Regulation*, 263. The Civil Aeronautics Board had, over its history, admitted to the industry a large number of airlines, but only to provide spe-

cialized or geographically limited services. See Kahn, "Applications of Economics to an Imperfect World," 7 n. 5.

40 For a detailed account of the Board's movement away from its historic positions, see Derthick and Quirk, *The Politics of Deregulation*.

41 Ronald Lewis, Alfred Kahn interview, Miller Center, 82. Lewis served under Kahn during the Carter administration as deputy adviser for regulatory affairs, Council on Wage and Price Stability.

42 The Teamsters endorsed Ronald Reagan in the 1980 election in retaliation for Carter's support of trucking deregulation.

43 For a detailed account of the events surrounding the trucking deregulation initiatives, see Robyn, *Braking the Special Interests*. Robyn interviewed participants in the deregulation effort from both the White House and Congress. She also interviewed trucking executives and union leaders.

44 Winston, "Economic Deregulation," 1263.

45 The quotation appears in Dumbrell, *The Carter Presidency*, 14.

46 Sam Peltzman, "The Economic Theory of Regulation after a Decade of Deregulation," 3.

47 The Fox statement is quoted in Sale, *The Green Revolution*, 4.

48 Gerston et al., *The Deregulated Society*, 28. This citation is a good source for a short survey of the creation of the new regulatory agencies.

49 Crandall, "Curbing the Costs of Social Regulation," 1–2.

50 Weidenbaum, "On Estimating Regulatory Costs," 14.

51 *Economic Report of the President, 1978*, 157.

52 A copy of the paper is attached to a memorandum, Josh Gotbaum to Stuart Eizenstat, June 2, 1980, Domestic Policy Staff–Eizenstat, Industrial Policy, [CF, O/A 728], Box 224, JCL.

53 OSHA, in the organizational arrangement, was in the Labor Department. According to one historian's profile of Labor Secretary Ray Marshall, he was given full authority to make appointments and he chose Bingham as head of OSHA. Bingham was aware of OSHA's negative image in the business community and with many members of Congress. "With Marshall's encouragement and support, Bingham reorganized OSHA, streamlined its rules and procedures." Fink, "F. Ray Marshall" 477.

54 Memorandum, Charles Schultze to the President, October 7, 1977, Domestic Policy Staff–Eizenstat, Economics (General), [CF, O/A 21] [1], Box 194, JCL.

55 The power of the president to intervene in regulatory decisions was challenged in court.

56 The plan was actually developed by a task force set up to study the problem of monitoring regulatory decisions, but Schultze played a major role.

57 Memorandum, President to James McIntyre, March 18, 1978, White House Central File, FG, Box FG-2, JCL.

58 *National Journal*, October 13, 1979.

59 Memorandum,: President to Heads of Executive Departments and Agencies, October, 31, 1978, White House Central File, FG, Box FG-2, JCL.

60 Ibid.

61 Domestic Policy Staff—Eizenstat, June 29, 1978, Cotton Dust Standards, Box 106, JCL.
62 Ibid.
63 Gerston et al., *The Deregulated Society*, 182.
64 Comments made in a seminar with Georgia Tech students. Copy in possession of the author.
65 Memorandum, Charles Schultze to the President, September 29, 1978, White House Central File, FG, Box FG-2, JCL. In the seminar with Georgia Tech students referred to in the previous note, Carter said: "Schultze was one of those economic advisers who had a very balanced attitude. He was genuinely concerned about workers' health. He wasn't just a hard nosed economist who didn't care about textile workers. He really did care. I don't know if I took the wind out of his sails [an expression a student in the seminar used in a question to Carter]. That's a much more drastic statement than I would have thought would be warranted on that decision."
66 Litan and Nordhaus, *Reforming Federal Regulation*, 76.
67 See the discussion in Eads and Fix, *Relief or Reform?*
68 Ibid., 67. George Eads was on the Council of Economic Advisers in the latter part of the Carter administration.
69 Memorandum, Charles Schultze to the President, January 7, 1978, White House Central File, BE 4-2, Box BE-16, JCL.
70 Memorandum, Sidney Harman to the Economic Policy Group, June 19, 1977, White House Central File, [O/A 3150] [7 of 8], JCL.
71 Memorandum, Ernest H. Preeg to Jack Watson, March 24, 1977, White House Central File, [O/A 3150] [3 of 8], JCL.
72 Memorandum, Stuart Eizenstat and Bob Ginsburg to the President, March 29, 1977, White House Central File, [O/A 3150] [3 of 8], JCL.
73 Eizenstat, "Economy," 22.
74 Ibid., 23.
75 Memorandum, Ernest H. Preeg to Jack Watson, March 24, 1977, White House Central File, [O/A 3150] [3 of 8], JCL. For a detailed account of the shoe agreements and the effect on American producers, see Congressional Budget Office, *Has Trade Protection Revitalized Domestic Industries?* The voluntary quotas ended in 1981, though the industry was left more protected by tariffs than the average for all manufacturing. For the fate of the industry over the next decade, see Congressional Budget Office, *Trade Restraints*.
76 Memorandum, Robert S. Strauss to the President, July 25, 1977, White House Central File, CM 8, Executive, Box CM-7, JCL.
77 Memorandum, Charles Schultze to the President, July 27, 1977, White House Central File, CM 8, Executive, Box CM-7, JCL.
78 Memorandum, Charles Schultze to the President, September 27, 1977, White House Central File, CM 8, Executive, Box CM-7, JCL.
79 Ibid.
80 "World Steel Situation," paper prepared for the July 18, 1977, meeting of the Economic Policy Group, Eizenstat Papers, JCL.

81 Memorandum, Michael Blumenthal to the President, October 12, 1977, White House Central File, CM 8, Executive, Box CM-7, JCL.
82 Letter to the President, October 31, 1977, White House Central File, CM 8, Executive, Box CM-7, JCL.
83 Voluntary restraint agreements were reintroduced in 1984 under President Reagan when the International Trade Commission ruled that the industry was hurt by import competition.
84 Memorandum, Michael Blumenthal to the President, September 27, 1977, White House Central File, CM 8, Executive, Box CM-7, JCL.
85 A summary of the report is attached to a memorandum for the president from Michael Blumenthal. See Memorandum, Michael Blumenthal to the President, November 23, 1977, White House Central File, CM 8, Executive, Box CM-7, JCL.
86 Ibid.
87 Ibid.
88 Congressional Budget Office, *Has Trade Protection Revitalized Domestic Industries?* 53.
89 Alfred Kahn interview, Miller Center, 38. For a case study of the trigger price mechanism, see Hufbauer et al., *Trade Protection in the United States*, 107–12.
90 Crandall, *The U.S. Steel Industry*, 107–12.
91 See Jon Frye and Robert J. Gordon, "Government Intervention in the Inflation Process."
92 Barry Bosworth, "Anti-Inflationary Policies," 120.
93 Lyle Gramley interview with the author.
94 Hargrove and Morley, *The President and the Council of Economic Advisers*, 487.

Chapter Eleven
1 Eizenstat interview with the author.
2 Eizenstat, Address, University of Chicago Law School; and Lyle Gramley interview with the author.
3 Gramley interview with the author.
4 Volcker and Gyohten, *Changing Fortunes*, 164.
5 President Carter interview with the author.
6 House Committee on the Budget, *Hearings on the Economic Outlook at Mid-Summer*, 293–94.
7 Volcker and Gyohten, *Changing Fortunes*, 168.
8 Ibid.
9 As background for understanding Volcker's initiative, see Meulendyke, "A Review of Federal Reserve Policy Targets."
10 During the Carter years there was a problem of finding an appropriate definition of money to use for operational purposes. The measure traditionally followed by the Fed included cash and checking accounts (M-1). Savings and loan associations and mutual savings banks were allowed to offer checkable deposits in the latter part of the 1970s. These had to be added to M-1. Other liquid assets also had to be considered as possessing "moneyness." Examples include traditional savings accounts, short-term certificates of deposits, overnight repurchase agreements, and overnight

Eurodollar liabilities. In February 1980, there was a redefinition of monetary aggregates (M-1, M-2, and M-3) that is basically accepted today.
11 Volcker and Gyohten, *Changing Fortunes*, 166.
12 Ibid., 167.
13 Stein, *Presidential Economics*, 215, 218.
14 For a similar comment, see DeLong, "America's Peacetime Inflation."
15 Schultze interview with the author.
16 The idea of using money as the Federal Reserve's target was a main theme of the school of monetarism led by Milton Friedman. Friedman would have liked to see the Fed set a money target and follow it without change regardless of cyclical movements in the economy. One of his arguments for this policy is that there are long and variable lags before the effect of monetary policy is transmitted to the economy. Since it is not possible to forecast the timing of the effect, fine tuning of the monetary target does more harm than good. While Volcker found some features of monetarism useful, he did not subscribe completely to the theory. He expressed his views in detail shortly before becoming chairman of the Federal Reserve Board. See Volcker, "The Contributions and Limitations of 'Monetary Analysis'"; and Volcker, "The Role of Monetary Targets in an Age of Inflation." Friedman criticized Volcker's policy because of the wide range of the annual targets and a lack of commitment to the target on a month-by-month and year-by-year basis.
17 Hargrove and Morley, *The President and the Council of Economic Advisers*, 486.
18 Lyle Gramley interview with the author. Gramley also commented that "ostensibly the purpose of changing the method of implementation of monetary policy was to obtain more precise control of the growth of the money stock. Now there is just absolutely no analytic substantive basis for believing that that ever could have worked. There had been very substantial analytic work done at the Federal Reserve during the time I was there as a staff member, and it was reiterated during the period prior to the change in policy, indicating that you could control the growth of money stock quite as precisely by setting the federal funds rate, as by using non-borrowed reserves as the operating instrument variable of monetary policy. Paul was well aware of this and ninety-eight percent of the reason for going in this direction was a cover. He felt, and perhaps quite justifiably, that the central bank could not take responsibility for setting interest rates, when interest rates might have to go as high as they did, in order to stop inflation."
19 Letter, Charles Schultze to Jim Wright, November 28, 1979, White House Central File, FG 143, Box FG-188, JCL.
20 The papers delivered at this conference on Carter are reprinted in Rosenbaum and Ugrinsky, *The Presidency and Domestic Policies of Jimmy Carter*. Schultze's remarks were made in a commentary on one of the papers. They are not included in the conference volume. They are available on tape.
21 Volcker and Gyohten, *Changing Fortunes*, 169.
22 President Carter interview with the author.
23 *Public Papers of the Presidents of the United States: Jimmy Carter, 1979*, 2:2051.
24 Hargrove and Morley, *The President and the Council of Economic Advisers*, 499.
25 *Public Papers of the Presidents of the United States: Jimmy Carter, 1980–1981*, 3:2040–

41. Schultze identified the questioner as a Ph.D. student. Schultze interview, Miller Center, 107.
26. The statement is dated October 7, 1980, and is included in a packet sent by Anne Wexler and Al McDonald to the Cabinet, October 10, 1980, White House Central File, BE4, Box BE-14, JCL.
27. For a short historical survey of the use of selective credit controls and their implementation under Carter, see Schreft, "Credit Controls: 1980." The control of margin credit for use in financing stock purchases, which has long been a part of the Federal Reserve arsenal, represents the exception to the Fed's avoidance of selective controls.
28. Letter, President Carter to George Meany, June 5, 1978, Domestic Policy Staff—Eizenstat, [OA 6338] [2], Box 143, JCL.
29. Schultze interview with the author.
30. Alfred Kahn interview, Miller Center, 97.
31. Memorandum, Charles Schultze to the President, March 16, 1979, Lipschutz File, Federal Reserve Board, Box 21, JCL.
32. Memorandum, Michael Blumenthal to the President, March 30, 1979, Domestic Policy Staff—Eizenstat, Monetary Policy, [CF, O/A 538], Box 238, JCL.
33. Lyle Gramley interview with the author.
34. Ibid.
35. Fred Kahn interview, Miller Center, 98.
36. Memorandum, Charles Schultze to the President, May 5, 1980, Charles Schultze Papers, Brookings Institution Library.
37. The Federal Reserve decided to ease up on its monetary policy in late summer 1982. The Fed acted because an international crisis was developing. The United States was still suffering from the 1981–82 recession, the other industrial economies were struggling, and the developing countries were in serious trouble. The Mexican debt crisis was threatening the stability of other Latin American countries and endangering the United States banks that were holding sizable amounts of Mexican obligations. The minutes of the meeting in August 1982, when the Fed made the decision to ease, are not yet available to the public. Lyle Gramley, who attended the meeting as a member of the Board of Governors, gave me a brief account in an interview. It was customary for Volcker to be the last person to speak. At this meeting, he departed from his usual approach. He announced that he would like to make some preliminary remarks. He did a survey of conditions in the United States, Europe and Japan, and the developing countries. We have to act, he said. The whole world is counting on us. The economy needed a massive monetary stimulus, a stimulus that would have been difficult to execute if the Fed continued to target M-1. The method of operating, in place since October 1979, was abandoned. The Fed returned to setting the funds rate, a practice it continues today. The Federal Reserve is still required by law to report its money targets to Congress, but the announcement is more a ritual act than a realistic report on Federal Reserve strategy. Economists have cited a technical problem in the Fed's use of monetary aggregates. Success in using money targets requires a predictable velocity. If the turnover rate of money cannot be forecast, the quantity of money necessary to achieve a desired level of to-

tal spending is uncertain. Over the postwar decades preceding the Carter years, the velocity was relatively stable, increasing at a constant rate with, at most, small deviations from trend. In the early 1980s the turnover rate became difficult to predict, for a variety of reasons, making the use of a money target less workable. The instability of velocity is thought of by economists as the instability of the money demand function. The literature on this subject is massive. For a survey of research done at the time of the decision of the Fed to go back to interest rate targets, see Judd and Scadding, "The Search for a Stable Money Demand Function."

38 For a survey of the move toward more independence for central banks, see Chang, "Policy Credibility and the Design of Central Banks."
39 See the discussion in Barsky and Kilian, "Money, Stagflation, and Oil Prices."
40 Taylor, "An Historical Analysis of Monetary Policy Rules," 27. See also McKinnon, "Currency Substitution and Instability in the World Dollar Standard."
41 Hetzel, "Arthur Burns and Inflation," 34.
42 Poole, "Burnsian Monetary Policy," 475.
43 See the survey of the various nations' actions and their handling of the oil shock in Hutchison, *Aggregate Demand, Uncertainty and Oil Prices*.
44 Hooker, "Are Oil Shocks Inflationary?" 1.

Chapter Twelve

1 Schultze interview with the author.
2 Eizenstat, "The Presidency in Trouble," 62.
3 Issues other than the economy were moving the country toward a more conservative mood: racial tensions, Vietnam, and changes in lifestyle. This shift has been examined at length by social and political commentators. See, for example, Edsall and Edsall, *Chain Reaction*.
4 Eizenstat interview, Miller Center, 102.
5 How much budget deficits actually contribute to inflation is open to debate. But the view that deficits contribute to inflation was widely held when Carter was president, certainly by the financial community, which came under enormous stress in the late 1970s because of the surge in prices.
6 The economic growth of the last two centuries is an impressive story. For a popular account, see Rosenberg and Birdzell, *How the West Grew Rich*.
7 Snowdon and Vane, *Conversations with Leading Eonomists*, 296.
8 The essay is included in his collection: Keynes, *Essays in Persuasion*.
9 Carter, "Energy and National Goals." Carter did not actually use the word "malaise" in the speech. The label "malaise speech" was coined by commentators and critics. For an account of events surrounding the Camp David retreat and the speech, see Holland, "The Great Gamble."
10 Rick Hertzberg, Carter's speech writer, has said, "that speech elicited the greatest volume of favorable mail of any presidential speech in history." Hertzberg interview, Miller Center, 66.
11 I was curious as to how this rather obscure piece got included in Carter's reading material. I asked Caddell, in a passing conversation, about the origin of the Keynes quotation. He said the essay was recommended by a *Washington Post* reporter. Cad-

dell's memorandum to Carter, "Of Crisis and Opportunity," April 23, 1979, can be found in Press-Powell, [CF, O/A 519], Box 40, JCL.
12. Solow, "A Contribution to the Theory of Economic Growth."
13. The expression is found in Abramovitz, "Resources and Output Trends."
14. Nordhaus, "Economic Policy," 134.
15. *Business Week*, January 28, 1980, 73.
16. The literature on this problem is large. For a few examples, see Denison, *Accounting for Slower Growth*; Munnell, "Why Has Productivity Growth Declined?"; and Baumol et al., *Productivity and American Leadership*.
17. William Baumol has argued that the lower growth of the late 1960s and the 1970s is a relative thing. The "golden age of growth" of the 1950s and 1960s was itself an aberration. Slower growth, he has written, is more consistent with the historic trend. (Baumol, "Productivity Growth, Convergence and Welfare.") Recent work by other economists, the "new growth theory," has concentrated on eliminating the "residual" of unexplained growth common to earlier studies. The leaders of the "new growth theory" are Paul M. Romer and Robert E. Lucas.
18. Meadows et al., *The Limits to Growth*.
19. For a brief description of the Club of Rome and the origins of the report it sponsored, see McCormick, *Reclaiming Paradise*, 74–77.
20. The team that produced the report was made up of relatively young people. The director of the study, Dennis Meadows, was twenty-eight years old. His wife, Donella, a researcher in nutrition and food at MIT, was part of the team.
21. See McCormick, *Reclaiming Paradise*, 77.
22. William Nordhaus, among others, wrote a detailed criticism of *Limits to Growth* prior to joining the administration. Nordhaus, "World Dynamics." A later piece done by Nordhaus is "Lethal Model 2." His criticisms were those emphasized by most economists.
23. Carter, "Address to the American Society for Information Science."
24. Carter interview with the author.
25. Ibid. The published version of the 2000 report is Council on Environmental Quality and the Department of State, The *Global 2000 Report to the President*.
26. *Global 2000 Report*, 1:1.
27. Memorandum, Madeleine Albright to Jerry Oplinger, June 6, 1980, National Security Affairs, Staff Material, Press and Congressional Relations, Box 5, JCL.
28. Jimmy Carter, "Inaugural Speech," 2.
29. McIntyre interview, Miller Center, 417.
30. Eizenstat interview with the author. Eizenstat has given, in a number of places, a partial list of Carter's liberal feelings and actions: "Environmental protection: He was the first governor to block a corps of engineers dam and was the most consistently proenvironmental president since Theodore Roosevelt. . . . A suspicion of big institutions: the medical and legal professions, whom he felt cared less about those they served than their own self-aggrandizement; big oil, big business, big labor, all of whom he saw as self—interested advocates. . . . Civil rights for minorities and social justice for the disadvantaged. Indeed, I believe that his greatest and least appreciated domestic accomplishment was to bring the South back into the political

mainstream of the Union, on terms of racial harmony and tolerance the South and the nation could accept with dignity." (Eizenstat, "The Carter Presidency," 5.) "We appointed more blacks to the judiciary than every President of the United States up to that point combined, as well as more women." Eizenstat interview, Miller Center, 127–28. Eizenstat has also cited Carter's human rights theme in international policy.
31 Schultze interview, Miller Center, 47.
32 Schultze interview with the author.
33 Ribuffo, "'I'll Whip His Ass,'" 11.
34 Schlesinger, "The Great Carter Mystery," 21.
35 Hertzberg interview, Miller Center, 10.
36 Schultze interview with the author.
37 Eizenstat interview with the author.
38 Eizenstat, "Remarks, Women's National Democratic Club," January 4, 1979. Copy in author's possession.
39 *New York Times*, October 21, 1979, 1.
40 Ibid.
41 Joseph Kennedy's remarks are preserved in a video available in the Carter library.
42 Kennedy, "Commencement Speech at Yale University."
43 Carter, "Remarks at Dedication Ceremonies for the John F. Kennedy Library," 1981.
44 Dark, "Organized Labor and the Carter Administration," 780.

BIBLIOGRAPHY

Manuscript Collections
Atlanta, Georgia
  Jimmy Carter Library
    Stuart Eizenstat manuscripts in possession of the author: "The Brief History of the Economic Policy Group of the Carter Administration," "The Economy," "The Presidency in Trouble"
  Georgia State Archives
Charlottesville, Virginia
  Interviews, Project on the Carter Presidency, White Burkett Miller Center of Public Affairs, University of Virginia. Also available at the Jimmy Carter Library.
Davis, California
  Special Collections, University of California Library at Davis. Interviews with Lyle Gramley, January 10, 1995, and Charles Schultze, November 11, 1995, Washington, D.C.
Washington, D.C.
  Charles L. Schultze Papers, Brookings Institution Library

Interviews Conducted by Author
C. Fred Bergsten, assistant secretary of the treasury, Carter administration, March 26, 1996, Washington, D.C.
Michael Blumenthal, secretary of the treasury, Carter administration, April 23, 1996, New York, N.Y.
President Jimmy Carter, October 7, 1993, Atlanta, Ga.
Stuart Eizenstat, assistant to the president for domestic policy, Carter administration, November 5, 1990, Washington, D.C.
Lyle Gramley, member, Council of Economic Advisers, Carter administration, November 4, 1990, Washington, D.C.
Alfred Kahn, inflation adviser to the president, Carter administration, November 16, 1990, Carter Conference, Hofstra University.
Lawrence Klein, chair, Economic Task Force, Carter campaign, 1976, June 26, 1991, Washington, D.C.
Bert Lance, director, Office of Management and Budget, Carter administration, October 30, 1990, Calhoun, Ga.
James McIntyre, director, Office of Management and Budget, Carter administration, November 6, 1990, Washington, D.C.
William Miller, secretary of the treasury, Carter administration, May 23, 1991, Washington, D.C.

Van Doorn Ooms, economic adviser, Office of Management and Budget, Carter administration, May 23, 1991, Washington, D.C.
Alice Rivlin, director, Congressional Budget Office, June 24, 1991, Washington, D.C.
Charles Schultze, chair, Council of Economic Advisers, Carter administration, May 23, 1991, Washington, D.C.
Thomas Stelson, undersecretary of energy, Carter administration, June 8, 1990, Atlanta, Ga.
Henry Thomassen, economic adviser to the Georgia governor, May 23, 1989, Atlanta, Ga.

Public Documents

Board of Governors, Federal Reserve System. *Annual Report*. Washington, D.C., various years.
Economic Report of the President. Washington, D.C.: Government Printing Office, various years.
Public Papers of the Presidents of the United States. Washington, D.C.: Federal Register Division, National Archives and Records Service, various years.
U.S. House Committee on Banking, Finance and Urban Affairs. *Hearings on Conduct of Monetary Policy*. 95th Cong., 1st sess., 1977.
U.S. House Committee on House Administration. *The Presidential Campaign, 1976*. 3 vols. Washington, D.C.: Government Printing Office, 1978.
U.S. House Committee on the Budget. *Hearing on the Economy and Economic Stimulus Proposals*. 95th Cong., 1st sess., 1977.
——. *Hearings on the Economic Outlook at Mid-Summer*. 96th Cong., 1st sess., 1979.
U.S. House Committee on Ways and Means. *Hearings on Tax Aspects of President Carter's Economic Stimulus Program*. 95th Cong., 1st sess., 1977.
——. *Hearings on the Advisability of a Tax Reduction in 1980 Effective for 1981*. 96th Cong., 2nd sess., 1980.
U.S. Senate Committee on the Budget. *Hearings on the Economy and Budgetary Policy for Fiscal Year 1978*. 95th Cong., 1st sess., v. 4, 1977.

Newspapers and Periodicals
Business Week
Congressional Quarterly Almanac
Economist
Fortune
National Journal
Newsweek
New York Times
Time
Wall Street Journal
Washington Post

Books and Reports
Agee, James, and Walker Evans. *Let Us Now Praise Famous Men*. Boston: Houghton Mifflin, 1960.

Anderson, Douglas D. *Regulatory Politics and Electric Utilities: A Case Study in Political Economy*. Boston, Mass.: Auburn House, 1981.
Anderson, Martin. *Revolution*. San Diego, Calif.: Harcourt Brace Jovanovitch, 1988.
Barsky, Robert B., and Lutz Kilian. "Money, Stagflation, and Oil Prices: A Reinterpretation." Manuscript (1999), Federal Reserve Bank of Philadelphia.
Baumer, Donald C., and Carl E. Van Horn. *The Politics of Unemployment*. Washington, D.C.: Congressional Quarterly Press, 1985.
Baumol, William J., et al. *Productivity and American Leadership: The Long View*. Cambridge, Mass.: MIT Press, 1989.
Bergsten, C. Fred. *The International Economic Policy of the United States: Selected Papers of C. Fred Bergsten, 1977–1979*. Lexington, Mass: Lexington Books, 1980.
———. *Managing International Economic Interdependence: Selected Papers of C. Fred Bergsten, 1975–1976*. Lexington, Mass.: D. C. Heath, 1977.
Berstein, Merton C., and Joan Bradshaug Berstein. *Social Security: The System That Works*. New York: Basic Books, 1988.
Birnbaum, Jeffrey H., and Alan S. Murray. *Showdown at Gucci Gultch: Lawmakers, Lobbyists and the Unlikely Triumph of Tax Reform*. New York: Random House, 1987.
Biven, W. Carl. *Who Killed John Maynard Keynes?* Homewood, Ill.: Richard D. Irwin, 1989.
Blinder, Alan S. *Economic Policy and the Great Stagflation*. New York: Academic Press, 1981.
Blumenthal, W. Michael. *The Invisible Wall: Germans and Jews, a Personal Exploration*. New York: Counterpoint, 1998.
Boskin, Michael J., ed. *The Future of Social Security*. San Francisco: Institute for Contemporary Studies, 1977.
Breit, William, and Roger W. Spence, eds. *Lives of the Laureates: Ten Nobel Economists*. Cambridge, Mass.: MIT Press, 1990.
Breyer, Stephen G., and Paul W. MacAvoy. *Energy Regulation by the Federal Power Commission*. Washington, D.C.: Brookings Institution, 1974.
Britton, Andrew. *Macroeconomic Policy in Britain, 1974–1987*. New York: Cambridge University Press, 1991.
Brookings Institution. *Tripartite Report by Sixteen Economists: Economic Prospects and Politics in the Industrial Countries*. Washington, D.C.: Brookings Institution, 1977.
Bruno, Michael, and Jeffrey D. Sacks. *Economics of Worldwide Inflation*. Cambridge, Mass.: Harvard University Press, 1985.
Bryant, Ralph. *International Coordination of National Stabilization Policies*. Washington, D.C.: Brookings Institution, 1995.
Bryant, Ralph, et al., eds. *Empirical Macroeconomics for Interdependent Economies*. Washington, D.C.: Brookings Institution, 1988.
Campbell, John C., et al. "Trilateral Task Force on the Political and International Implications of the Energy Crisis; Energy: The Imperative for a Trilateral Approach." Trilateral Commission, June 1974.
Carr, Jonathan. *Helmut Schmidt: Helmsman of Germany*. New York: St. Martin's, 1985.
Carter, Jimmy. *Always a Reckoning and Other Poems*. New York: Times Books, 1994.
———. *Campaign Promises, 1976*. Transition Planning Group, 1976.

———. *An Hour Before Daylight: Memories of My Rural Boyhood*. New York: Simon and Schuster, 2001.
———. *Keeping Faith: Memoirs of a President*. New York: Bantam Books, 1982.
———. *Why Not the Best?* Nashville: Broadman, 1977.
Carter, Lillian, and Gloria Carter Spann. *Away From Home*. New York: Simon and Schuster, 1977.
Cohen, Stephen D., and Ronald I. Meltzer. *United States International Economic Policy in Action*. New York: Praeger, 1982.
Congressional Budget Office. *The Disappointing Recovery*. Washington, D.C.: Government Printing Office, 1977.
———. *Has Trade Protection Revitalized Domestic Industries?* Washington, D.C.: Government Printing Office, 1986.
———. *Trade Restraints and the Competitive Status of the Textile, Apparel, and Nonrubber-Footwear Industries*. Washington, D.C.: Government Printing Office, 1991.
———. *The U.S. Balance of International Payments and the U.S. Economy*. Washington, D.C.: Government Printing Office, 1978.
Cooper, Richard N. *The Economics of Interdependence*. New York: McGraw Hill, 1968.
Cooper, Richard N., et al. *Can Nations Agree? Issues in International Economic Cooperation*. Washington, D.C.: Brookings Institution, 1989.
Council on Environmental Quality and U.S. Department of State. *The Global 2000 Report to the President*. New York: Penguin Books, 1982.
Crandall, Robert. *The U.S. Steel Industry in Recurrent Crisis*. Washington: D.C.: Brookings Institution, 1981.
David, Harry R., and Robert C. Good, eds. *Reinhold Niebuhr on Politics: His Political Philosophy and Its Application to Our Age as Expressed in His Writings*. New York: Charles Scribners' Sons, 1960.
De Menil, George, and Anthony M. Solomon, eds. *Economic Summitry*. New York: Council on Foreign Relations, 1983.
Denison, Edward F. *Accounting for Slower Economic Growth: The United States in the 1970s*. Washington, D.C.: Brookings Institution, 1979.
Derthick, Martha, and Paul J. Quirk. *The Politics of Deregulation*. Washington, D.C.: Brookings Institution, 1985.
Dore, Ronald, and Radha Sinha, eds. *Japan and World Depression*. New York: St. Martin's, 1987.
Dumbrell, John. *The Carter Presidency: A Re-evaluation*. Manchester, England: Manchester University Press, 1993.
Eads, George C., and Michael Fix. *Relief or Reform?* Washington, D.C.: Urban Institute Press, 1984.
Edsall, Thomas B., and Mary D. Edsall. *Chain Reaction: the Impact of Race, Rights, and Taxes in American Politics*. New York: W. W. Norton, 1991.
Eizenstat, Stuart. "The Brief History of the Economic Policy Group of the Carter Administration." Manuscript.
———. "Economy." Manuscript.
———. "The Presidency in Trouble." Manuscript.

Emminger, Otmar. *The D-Mark in the Conflict Between Internal and External Equilibrium, 1948–1975.* Princeton Studies in International Finance, no. 122. Princeton, N.J.: Princeton University Press, 1977.

Fechter, Alan. *Public Employment Programs.* Washington, D.C.: American Enterprise Institute, 1975.

Flash, Edward S., Jr. *Economic Advice and Presidential Leadership.* New York: Columbia University Press, 1965.

Frankel, Jeffrey A. *Obstacles to International Macroeconomic Policy Coordination.* Princeton Studies in International Finance, no. 64. Princeton, N.J.: Princeton University Press, 1988.

Franklin, Grace A., and Randall B. Ripley. *CETA: Politics and Policy, 1973–1982.* Knoxville, Tenn.: University of Tennessee Press, 1984.

Friedman, Milton. *A Theory of the Consumption Function.* Princeton, N.J.: Princeton University Press, 1957.

Funabashi, Yoichi. *Managing the Dollar: From the Plaza to the Louvre.* Washington, D.C.: Institute for International Economics, 1989.

Galbraith, John Kenneth. *A Journey Through Economic Time: A Firsthand View.* New York: Houghton Mifflin, 1994.

Gallup, George. *The Gallup Opinion Index.* Various issues.

Gardner, Richard N., et al. "Trilateral Task Force on Relations with Developing Countries; OPEC, the Trilateral World, and the Developing Countries: New Arrangements for Cooperation, 1976–1980." Trilateral Commission, December 1974.

General Accounting Office. *The Voluntary Pay and Price Standards Have Had No Discernible Effect on Inflation.* Washington, D.C.: Government Printing Office, 1980.

Gerston, Larry N., et al. *The Deregulated Society.* Pacific Grove, Calif.: Brooks/Cole, 1988.

Ghosh, Atish R., and Paul R. Masson. *Economic Cooperation in an Uncertain World.* Oxford: Basil Blackwell, 1994.

Giersch, Herbert, et al. *The Fading German Miracle: Four Decades of Market Economy in Germany.* New York: Cambridge University Press, 1992.

Gill, Stephen. *American Hegemony and the Trilateral Commission.* New York: Cambridge University Press, 1990.

Gillon, Steven M. *The Democrats' Dilemma: Walter F. Mondale and the Liberal Legacy.* New York: Columbia University Press, 1992.

Golub, Stephen S. *The Current Account Balance and the Dollar: 1977–1978 and 1983–1984.* Princeton Studies in International Finance, no. 57. Princeton, N.J.: Princeton University Press, 1986.

Goodman, John B. *Monetary Sovereignty: The Politics of Central Banking in Western Europe.* Ithaca, N.Y.: Cornell University Press, 1992.

Gordon, Robert J. "The Phillips Curve Now and Then." Working Paper 3393, National Bureau of Economic Research, June 1990.

Gowa, Joanne. *Closing the Gold Window: Domestic Politics and the End of Bretton Woods.* Ithaca, N.Y.: Cornell University Press, 1983.

Hargrove, Edwin C. *Jimmy Carter as President: Leadership and the Politics of the Public Good.* Baton Rouge: Louisiana State University, 1988.

Hargrove, Edwin C., and Samuel A. Morley, eds. *The President and the Council of Economic Advisers.* Boulder, Colo.: Westview Press, 1984.

Harris, Seymour E. *Economics of the Kennedy Years.* New York: Harper and Row, 1964.

Heineman, Ben W., Jr., and Curtis A. Hessler. *Memorandum for the President: A Strategic Approach to Domestic Affairs in the 1980s.* New York: Random House, 1980.

Henning, C. Randall. *Currencies and Politics in the United States, Germany, and Japan.* Washington, D.C: Institute for International Economics, 1994.

Hess, Stephen. *Organizing the Presidency.* Washington, D.C.: Brookings Institution, 1976.

Hockoff, Hugh. *Drastic Measures: A History of Wage and Price Controls in the United States.* New York: Cambridge University Press, 1984.

Hollerman, Leon. *Japan, Disincorporated: The Economic Liberalization Process.* Stanford, Calif.: Hoover Institution Press, 1988.

Homer, Sidney, and Richard Sylla. *A History of Interest Rates.* New Brunswick, N.J.: Rutgers University Press, 1991.

Hooker, Mark A. "Are Oil Shocks Inflationary?" Working Paper, Federal Reserve Board, December 1991.

Hufbaurer, Gary Clyde, et al. *Trade Protection in the United States: 31 Case Studies.* Washington, D.C.: Institute for International Economics, 1986.

Hutchison, Michael M. *Aggregate Demand, Uncertainty and Oil Prices: The 1990 Oil Shock in Comparative Perspective.* Basel, Switzerland: Bank for International Settlements, 1991.

Johnson, Haynes. *In the Absence of Power.* New York: Viking, 1980.

Jones, Charles O. *The Trusteeship Presidency: Jimmy Carter and the United States Congress.* Baton Rouge: Louisiana State University Press, 1988.

Jordan, Hamilton. *Crisis: The Last Year of the Carter Presidency.* New York: Putnam, 1982.

Kahn, Alfred E. *The Economics of Regulation: Principles and Institutions.* New York: John Wiley, 1970–71.

Kalt, Joseph P. *The Economics and Politics of Oil Price Regulation: Federal Policy in the Post-Embargo Era.* Cambridge, Mass.: MIT Press, 1981.

Kettl, Donald L. *Leadership at the Fed.* New Haven: Yale University Press, 1986.

Keynes, John Maynard. *Essays in Persuasion.* New York: Harcourt, Brace and Co., 1932.

——. *The General Theory of Employment, Interest, and Money.* New York: Harcourt, Brace and Co., 1936.

Klein, Lawrence R. *Economic Fluctuations in the United States, 1921–1941.* New: York: John Wiley, 1950.

Kraus, Sidney, ed. *The Great Debates, Carter vs. Ford, 1976.* Bloomington: Indiana University Press, 1979.

Lampman, Robert J. *The Low Income Population and Economic Growth.* Joint Economic Committee, Study Paper no. 12. Washington, D.C.: Government Printing Office, 1959.

Lance, Bert. *The Truth of the Matter: My Life In and Out of Politics*. New York: Summit Books, Simon and Schuster, 1991.

Levy, Frank. *Dollars and Dreams*. New York: Russell Sage Foundation, 1987.

Litan, Robert E., and William D. Nordhaus. *Reforming Federal Regulation*. New Haven: Yale University Press, 1983.

Ludlow, Peter. *The Making of the European Monetary System*. Boston, Mass.: Butterworth Scientific, 1982.

Maier, Charles S., ed. *The Politics of Inflation and Economic Stagflation*. Washington, D.C.: Brookings Institution, 1985.

Marsh, David. *The Most Powerful Bank: Inside German's Bundesbank*. New York: Times Books, 1992.

Matusow, Allen. *Nixon's Economy: Booms, Busts, Dollars, and Votes*. Lawrence: University Press of Kansas, 1998.

McCormick, John. *Reclaiming Paradise*. Bloomington: Indiana University Press, 1989.

McCracken, Paul, et al. *Toward Full Employment and Price Stability: A Report to the OECD by a Group of Independent Experts*. Paris: Organization for Economic Cooperation and Development, 1977.

McGraw, Thomas K. *Prophets of Regulation: Charles Francis Adams, Louis D. Brandeis, James M. Landis, and Alfred E. Kahn*. Cambridge, Mass.: Harvard University Press, 1984.

McKinnon, Ronald I. *The Rules of the Game: International Money and Exchange Rates*. Cambridge, Mass.: MIT Press, 1996.

Meadows, Donella H., et al. *The Limits to Growth*. 3 vols. New York: New American Library, 1972.

Miller, William Lee. *Yankee from Georgia: The Emergence of Jimmy Carter*. New York: Times Books, 1978.

Minarik, Joseph J. *The Size Distribution of Income During Inflation*. Washington, D.C.: Brookings Institution, 1980.

Moore, Jonathan, and Janet Fraser. *Campaign for President: The Managers Look at 76*. Cambridge, Mass.: Ballinger Publishing, 1977.

Morgan, Mary S. *The History of Econometric Ideas*. New York: Cambridge University Press, 1990.

Munnell, Alicia H. *The Future of Social Security*. Washington: Brookings Institution, 1977.

Nathan, Richard, et al. *Monitoring the Public Service Employment Program*. Washington, D.C.: National Commission for Manpower Policy, 1978.

National Planning Association. *An Evaluation of the Economic Impact Project of the Public Employment Program*. Washington, D.C.: National Planning Association, 1974.

Nölling, Wilhelm. *Monetary Policy in Europe After Maastricht*. New York: St. Martin's, 1993.

Nourse, Edwin. *Economics in the Public Service*. New York: Harcourt, Brace and Co., 1953.

Okun, Arthur. *Economics in Policy Making*. Cambridge, Mass.: MIT Press, 1983.

Organization for Economic Cooperation and Development. *Economic Outlook.* December 1976.
Orphanides, Athanasios. "The Quest for Prosperity Without Inflation." Manuscript, May 1999. Washington, D.C.: Board of Governors of the Federal Reserve System.
Pechman, Joseph A., ed. *Setting National Priorities: the 1978 Budget.* Washington, D.C.: Brookings Institution, 1977.
Polsby, Nelson W. *Consequences of Party Reform.* New York: Oxford University Press, 1983.
Porter, Roger. *Presidential Decision Making: The Economic Policy Board.* New York: Cambridge University Press, 1980.
Putnam, Robert D., and Nicholas Bayne. *Hanging Together: The Seven Power Summits.* Cambridge, Mass.: Harvard University Press, 1984.
Reeves, Richard. *Convention.* New York: Harcourt, Brace, Jovanovich, 1977.
Reichley, A. James. *Conservatives in an Age of Change: The Nixon and Ford Administrations.* Washington, D.C.: Brookings Institution, 1981.
Roberts, Paul Craig. *The Supply-Side Revolution.* Cambridge, Mass.: Harvard University Press, 1984.
Robinson, Archie. *George Meany and His Times.* New York: Simon and Schuster, 1981.
Robyn, Dorothy. *Braking the Special Interests: Trucking Deregulation and the Politics of Policy Reform.* Chicago: University of Chicago Press, 1987.
Rosenbaum, Herbert D., and Alexej Ugrinsky, eds. *The Presidency and Domestic Policies of Jimmy Carter.* Westport, Conn.: Greenwood Press, 1994.
Rosenberg, Nathan, and L. E. Birdzell Jr. *How the West Grew Rich: The Economic Transformation of the Industrial World.* New York: Basic Books, 1986.
Sale, Kirkpatrick. *The Green Revolution.* New York: Hill and Wang, 1993.
Saunders, Peter, and Friedrich Klau. *The Role of the Public Sector: Causes and Consequences of the Growth of Government.* Paris: Organization for Economic Cooperation and Development, 1985.
Schlesinger, Arthur, Jr. *The Coming of the New Deal.* Boston: Houghton Mifflin, 1960.
——. *A Thousand Days: John F. Kennedy in the White House.* Boston: Houghton Mifflin, 1965.
Schmidt, Helmut. *Men and Power: A Political Perspective.* New York: Random House, 1989.
Schram, Martin. *Running for President, 1976.* New York: Stein and Day, 1977.
Schultze, Charles L. *Other Times, Other Places.* Washington, D.C.: Brookings Institution, 1986.
——. *The Politics and Economics of Public Spending.* Washington, D.C.: Brookings Institution, 1968.
——. *The Public Use of Private Interests.* Washington, D.C.: Brookings Institution, 1977.
Schultze, Charles L., et al. *Setting National Priorities: The 1972 Budget.* Washington, D.C.: Brookings Institution, 1972.
Schumaker, Ernest F. *Small Is Beautiful: A Study of Economics As If People Mattered.* London: Bland and Briggs, 1973.
Shogan, Robert. *Promises to Keep: Carter's First Hundred Days.* New York: Thomas Y. Crowell, 1977.

Shultz, George P., and Kenneth W. Dam. *Economic Policy Beyond the Headlines*. New York: Norton, 1978.
Sick, Gary. *October Surprise*. New York: Times Books, 1991.
Silk, Leonard. *Economics in the Real World*. New York: Simon and Schuster, 1984.
Smith, Gaddis. *Morality, Reason and Power*. New York: Hill and Wang, 1986.
Smith, James Allen. *The Idea Brokers, Think Tanks and the Rise of the Policy Elite*. New York: Free Press, 1991.
Snowdon, Brian, and Howard R. Vane. *Conversations with Leading Economists*. Northhampton, Mass.: Edward Elger, 1999.
Sobel, Robert. *The Worldly Economists*. New York: Free Press, 1980.
Solomon, Robert. *The International Monetary System, 1945–1981*. New York: Harper and Row, 1982.
Sommariva, Andrea, and Giuseppe Tullio. *German Macroeconomic History, 1880–1979*. New York: St. Martin's, 1987.
Stein, Herbert. *The Fiscal Revolution in America*. Washington, D.C.: American Enterprise Press, 1990.
———. *On the Other Hand: Essays on Economics, Economists, and Politics*. Washington, D.C.: American Enterprise Institute Press, 1995.
———. *Presidential Economics: The Making of Economic Policy From Roosevelt to Reagan and Beyond*. 3rd ed. New York: Simon and Schuster, 1994.
Thompson, Kenneth W., ed. *The Carter Presidency: Fourteen Intimate Perspectives of Jimmy Carter*. New York: University Press in America, 1990.
Triffin, Robert. *Gold and the Dollar Crisis*. New Haven: Yale University Press, 1960.
Volcker, Paul A., and Toyoa Gyohten. *Changing Fortunes: The World's Money and the Threat to American Leadership*. New York: Times Books, 1992.
Wells, Wyatt C. *Economist in an Uncertain World: Arthur Burns and the Federal Reserve, 1970–1978*. New York: Columbia University Press, 1994.
Witcover, Jules. *Marathon: The Pursuit of the Presidency, 1972–1976*. New York: Viking Press, 1977.
Woodward, Bob. *The Agenda: Inside the Clinton White House*. New York: Simon and Schuster, 1994.
Wooten, James. *Dasher: The Roots and the Rising of Jimmy Carter*. New York: Summit Books, 1978.

Articles

Abramovitz, Moses. "Resources and Output Trends in the United States Since 1870." *American Economic Review* 46, no. 2 (May 1956): 5–23.
Ando, Albert, and Franco Modigliani. "The Life-Cycle Hypothesis of Saving: Aggregate Implications and Tests." *American Economic Review* 54, no. 1 (March 1963): 53–84.
Aronson, J. Richard, and Attiat F. Ott. "The Growth of the Public Sector." In *Companion to Contemporary Economic Thought*, edited by David Greenway et al., 523–46. New York: Routledge, 1991.
Ball, Lawrence. "What Determines the Sacrifice Ratio?" In *Monetary Policy*, edited by N. Gregory Mankiw, 155–88. Chicago: University of Chicago Press, 1994.

Balz, Daniel J., and Joel Havemann. "State of the Union, Ford Pushes Program in Face of Strong Criticism." *National Journal Reports* (January 25, 1975): 115–222.

Baumol, William J. "Productivity Growth, Convergence, and Welfare: What the Long-Run Data Show." *American Economic Review* 76, no. 5 (December 1986): 1072–85.

Bergsten, C. Fred. "Discussion." In *The International Monetary System*, edited by Peter B. Kenen et al., 43–50. New York: Cambridge University Press, 1994.

Bishop, John, and Robert Haveman. "Selective Employment Subsidies: Can Okun's Law be Repealed?" *American Economic Review* 69, no. 2 (May 1979): 124–30.

Blinder, Alan S. "The Anatomy of Double-Digit Inflation in the 1970s." In *Inflation: Causes and Effects*, edited by Robert E. Hall, 261–82. Chicago: University of Chicago Press, 1982.

Blumenthal, W. Michael. "Candid Reflections of a Businessman in Washington." *Fortune* (January 29, 1979): 36–49.

Bosworth, Barry P. "Anti-Inflationary Policies in a Democratic Free Market Society." In *After the Phillips Curve: Persistence of High Inflation and High Unemployment*, 117–23. Conference Series 19, Federal Reserve Bank of Boston, June 1978.

———. "Nonmonetary Aspects of Inflation." *Journal of Money, Credit, and Banking* 12, no. 3 (August 1980): 527–39.

Bryant, Ralph C. "Comment." In *Price Stabilization in the 1990s*, edited by Kumihara Shigehara, 84–89. London: MacMillan, 1993.

Bullard, James. "Historical CPI Inflation Under Current Calculations Methods." *National Economic Trends* (August 1999). Federal Reserve Bank of St. Louis.

Cable, William H. "Discussion." In *The Presidency and Domestic Policies of Jimmy Carter*, edited by Herbert D. Rosenbaum and Alexej Ugrinsky, 805–6. Westport, Conn.: Greenwood Press, 1994.

Capra, James R., et al. "Social Security: An Analysis of Its Problems." In *Quarterly Review* (Federal Reserve Bank of New York) 7, no. 3 (Autumn 1982): 1–17.

Carlson, Keith M., "Federal Budget Trends and the 1981 Reagan Economic Plan." In *Review* (Federal Reserve Bank of Saint Louis) 71, no. 1 (January/February 1989): 8–31.

———. "Federal Fiscal Policy Since the Employment Act of 1946." *Review* (Federal Reserve Bank of St. Louis) 69, no. 4 (December 1987): 14–29.

Carroll, Christopher D. "The Buffer-Stock Theory of Saving: Some Macroeconomic Evidence." *Brookings Papers on Economic Activity* 2 (1992): 61–135.

Carter, Jimmy. "Address to the American Society for Information Science." In *Addresses of Jimmy Carter, Governor of Georgia 1971–1975*, 34–38. Atlanta: Georgia Department of Archives and History, 1975.

———. "Energy and National Goals, Address to the Nation." In *Public Papers of the Presidents of the United States: Jimmy Carter, 1979*, vol. 2, 1235–41. Washington, D.C.: Federal Register Division, National Archives, 1979.

———. "Inaugural Speech." *Public Papers of the Presidents of the United States: Jimmy Carter, 1977*, vol. 1, 2. Washington, D.C.: Federal Register Division, National Archives, 1977.

———. "Remarks At Dedication Ceremonies for the John F. Kennedy Library." *Public*

Papers of the Presidents of the United States: Jimmy Carter, 1979, vol. 2, 1981. Washington: D.C.: Federal Register Division, National Archives, 1979.

Chang, Roberto. "Policy Credibility and the Design of Central Banks." *Economic Review* (Federal Reserve Bank of Atlanta) 83, no. 1 (first quarter 1998): 4–15.

Chari, V. V. "Nobel Laureate Robert E. Lucas, Jr.: Architect of Modern Macroeconomics." *Quarterly Review* (Federal Reserve Bank of Minneapolis) 23, no. 2 (Spring 1999): 2–12.

Clarida, Richard, and Mark Gertler. "How the Bundesbank Conducts Monetary Policy." In *Reducing Inflation: Motivation and Strategy*, edited by Christina D. Romer and David H. Romer, 363–412. Chicago: University of Chicago Press, 1997.

Cochrane, James L. "Carter's Energy Policy and the Ninety-fifth Congress." In *Energy Policy in Perspective: Today's Problems, Yesterday's Solutions*, edited by Craufurd D. Goodwin, 556–77. Washington, D.C.: Brookings Institution, 1981.

Coles, Robert. "Camera on James Agee." *New Republic* (November 3, 1979): 23–28.

Congressional Quarterly. "Congress Votes Largest Tax Cut in History." *Congressional Quarterly Almanac* (1975): 95–111.

Cooper, Richard N. "Global Economic Policy in a World of Energy Shortage." In *Economics in the Public Service: Papers in Honor of Walter W. Heller*, edited by Joseph A. Pechman and N. J. Simler, 85–107. New York: W. W. Norton, 1982.

———. "The Gold Standard: Historical Facts and Future Prospects." *Brookings Papers on Economic Activity* 1 (1982): 1–45.

Corrigan, Richard, and Joel Havemann. "The Issues Team: The People Who Prepare Jimmy Carter for the Presidency." *National Journal* (August 21, 1976): 1166–72.

Coxson, Harold P. "Discussion." In *The Presidency and Domestic Policies of Jimmy Carter*, edited by Herbert D. Rosenbaum and Alexej Ugrinsky, 807–11. Westport, Conn.: Greenwood Press, 1994.

Crandall, Robert W. "Curbing the Costs of Social Regulation." *Brookings Bulletin* (Winter 1979).

Cutter, W. Bowman. "The Presidency and Economic Policy: A Tale of Two Budgets." In *The Presidency and the Political System*, edited by Michael Nelson, 471–93. Washington, D.C.: Congressional Quarterly, 1984.

Dark, Taylor. "Organized Labor and the Carter Administration: The Origins of Conflict." In *The Presidency and Domestic Policies of Jimmy Carter*, edited by Herbert D. Rosenbaum and Alexej Ugrinsky, 761–82. Westport, Conn.: Greenwood Press, 1994.

De Long, Bradford. "America's Peacetime Inflation: The 1970s." *In Reducing Inflation: Motivation and Strategy*, edited by Christina D. Romer and David H. Romer, 247–76. Chicago: University of Chicago Press, 1997.

De Marchi, Neil. "The Ford Administration: Energy as a Political Good." In *Energy Policy in Perspective: Today's Problems, Yesterday's Solutions*, edited by Craufurd D. Goodwin, 475–546. Washington: D.C.: Brookings Institution, 1981.

De Menil, George. "From Rambouillet to Versailles." In *Economic Summitry*, edited by George De Menil and Anthony M. Solomon, 9–41. New York: Council on Foreign Relations, 1983.

Destler, I. M., and Hisao Mitsuyu. "Locomotives on Different Tracks: Macroeconomic

Diplomacy, 1977–1979." In *Coping with U.S.-Japanese Economic Conflicts*, edited by I. M. Destler and Hideo Sato, 249–56. Lexington, Mass.: D. C. Heath, 1982.

Dornbusch, Rudiger. "Lessons from the German Inflation Experience of the 1920s." In *Macroeconomics and Finance: Essays in Honor of Franco Modigliani*, edited by Rudiger Dornbusch and J. Bossons, 337–66. Cambridge, Mass.: MIT Press, 1987.

Ehrbar, A. F. "Bill Miller Is a Fainthearted Inflation Fighter." *Fortune* (December 31, 1978): 40–43.

Eijffinger, Sylvester, and Erich Schaling. "Central Bank Independence: Searching for the Philosopher's Stone." In *The New Europe: Evolving Economic and Financial Systems in East and West*, edited by Donald E. Fair and Robert J. Raymond, 263–79. Boston: Kluwer, 1993.

Eizenstat, Stuart. Address, University of Chicago Law School. Manuscript, April 18, 1989. Copy in possession of the author. A condensed version of the address is available: "The State of the Modern Presidency; Can It Meet Our Expectations?" Occasional Papers from the Law School, University of Chicago, no. 26.

———. "Economists and White House Decisions." *Journal of Economic Perspectives* 2, no. 3 (Summer 1992): 65–71.

———. "The Carter Presidency: Two Perspectives." In *The Presidency and Domestic Policies of Jimmy Carter*, edited by Herbert D. Rosenbaum and Alexej Ugrinsky, 1–16. Westport Conn.: Greenwood Press, 1994.

Fair, Ray. "Econometrics and Presidential Elections." *Journal of Economic Perspectives* 10, no. 3 (Summer 1996): 89–102.

Fallows, James. "The Passionless Presidency." *Atlantic Monthly* (May 1979): 39.

Fink, Gary M. "F. Ray Marshall: Secretary of Labor and Jimmy Carter's Ambassador to Organized Labor." *Labor History* 37, no. 4 (Fall 1996): 463–79.

Fisher, Irving. "A Statistical Relation Between Unemployment and Price Changes." *International Labor Review* 13, no. 6 (June 1926): 185–92.

Frankel, Jeffrey A., and Katharine E. Rockett. "International Macroeconomic Policy Coordination When Policy Makers Do Not Agree on the True Model." *American Economic Review* 78, no. 3 (June 1988): 318–40.

Friedman, Milton. "The Case for Flexible Exchange Rates." In *Essays in Positive Economics*, 157–203. Chicago: University of Chicago Press, 1953.

———. "Nobel Lecture: Inflation and Unemployment." *Journal of Political Economy* 85, no. 3 (June 1977): 82–110.

———. "The Role of Monetary Policy." *American Economic Review* 58, no. 1 (March 1968): 1–17.

Frye, Jon, and Robert J. Gordon. "Government Intervention in the Inflation Process: The Econometrics of 'Self-Inflicted Wounds.'" *American Economic Review* 71, no. 2 (May 1981): 288–94.

Glassman, James E., and Ronald A. Sege. "The Recent Inflation Experience." *Federal Reserve Bulletin* 67, no. 5 (May 1981): 389–97.

Gordon, Robert J. "Measuring the Aggregate Price Level: Implications for Economic Performance and Policy." In *Price Stabilization in the 1990s*, edited by Kumiharu Shigehara, 233–67. London: MacMillan, 1993.

Gramlich, Edward M. "Impact of Minimum Wages on Other Wages, Employment, and Family Incomes." *Brookings Papers on Economic Activity* 2 (1976): 409–51.
———. "Stimulating the Macroeconomy Through State and Local Government." *American Economic Review* 69, no. 2 (May 1979): 180–85.
Hadley, Eleanor M. "The Diffusion of Keynesian Ideas in Japan." In *The Political Power of Economic Ideas: Keynesianism Across Nations*, edited by Peter A. Hall, 291–310. Princeton: Princeton University Press, 1989.
Hall, Robert E. "Macro Theory and the Recession of 1990–1991." *American Economic Review* 83, no. 2 (May 1993): 275–79.
Hanson, Lee, and Michael S. Kaufman. "The National Energy Tax Act of 1978: Taxation Without Rationalization." *Harvard Environmental Law Review* 3 (1979): 187–213.
Helmstader, Ernst. "The Irrelevance of Keynes to German Economic Policy and to International Economic Cooperation in the 1980s." In *Keynes and Economic Policy: The Relevance of the General Theory After Fifty Years*, edited by Walter Eltis and Peter Sinclair, 411–27. Hampshire, England: MacMillan Press, 1990.
Hennings, Klaus Hinrick. "West Germany." In *The European Economy*, edited by Andrea Bolto, 472–501. New York: Oxford University Press, 1982.
Hertzberg, Daniel. "Troubled Haven: Bond Market Becomes Increasingly Volatile With Some Big Losses." *Wall Street Journal*, February 21, 1980.
Hetzel, Robert L. "Arthur Burns and Inflation." *Economic Quarterly* (Federal Reserve Bank of Richmond) 84, no. 1 (Winter 1998): 21–44.
Hickle, Herman. "The Inside Story of the Dollar Rescue." *Fortune* (December 4, 1978): 40–44.
Holland, J. William. "The Great Gamble: Jimmy Carter and the 1979 Energy Crisis." *Prologue* (Spring 1990): 63–79.
Holloway, Thomas M., and Joseph C. Wakefield. "Sources of Change in the Federal Government Deficit, 1970–1986." *Survey of Current Business* 65, no. 5 (May 1985): 25–32.
Holtham, Gerald. "German Macroeconomic Policy and the 1978 Bonn Summit." In *Can Nations Agree? Issues in International Economic Cooperation*, edited by Richard N. Cooper et al., 141–77. Washington, D.C.: Brookings Institution, 1989.
Ikenberry, G. John. "Market Solutions for State Problems: The International and Domestic Politics of American Oil Decontrol." *International Organization* 42, no. 4 (Winter 1988): 151–77.
Johnson, Harry. "The Case for Flexible Exchange Rates, 1969." In *Further Essays in Monetary Economics*, 198–228. Cambridge, Mass.: Harvard University Press, 1972.
Johnson, William A. "The Impact of Price Controls on the Oil Industry: How to Worsen an Energy Crisis." In *Energy: The Policy Issue*, edited by Gary Eppen, 99–121. Chicago: University of Chicago Press, 1975.
Jones, Charles O. "Keeping Faith and Losing Congress: The Carter Experience in Washington." *Presidential Studies Quarterly* 14, no. 3 (Summer 1984): 437–45.
Jones, Charles O., and Randall Strahan. "The Effect of Energy Politics on Congressional and Executive Organization in the 1970s." *Legislative Studies Quarterly* 10, no. 2 (May 1985): 151–79.

Judd, John P., and John L. Scadding. "The Search for a Stable Money Demand Function." *Journal of Economic Literature* 20, no. 3 (September 1982): 993–1023.

Kahn, Alfred E. "America's Democrats: Can Liberalism Survive Inflation?" *The Economist*, March 7, 1981, 21–25.

———. "Applications of Economics to an Imperfect World." *American Economic Review* 69, no. 2 (May 1979): 1–13.

Kahn, George A., and Stuart E. Weiner. "Has the Cost of Disinflation Declined?" *Economic Review* (Federal Reserve Bank of Kansas City) 75, no. 2 (May–June 1990): 5–24.

Kennedy, John F. "Commencement Speech at Yale University." In *Public Papers of the Presidents of the United States: John F. Kennedy, 1962,* 470–75. Washington, D.C.: Federal Register Division, National Archives.

Keohane, Robert O. "The International Politics of Inflation." In *The Politics of Inflation and Economic Stagnation,* edited by Leon N. Lindberg and Charles S. Maier, 458–62. Washington, D.C.: Brookings Institution, 1985.

———. "U.S. Foreign Economic Policy Toward Other Advanced Capitalist States: The Struggle to Make Others Adjust." In *The Eagle Entangled: U.S. Foreign Policy in a Complex World,* edited by Kenneth A. Oye et al., 91–122. New York: Longman, 1979.

Klein, Lawrence R. "My Professional Life Philosophy." In *Eminent Economists: Their Life Philosophies,* edited by Michael Szenberg, 180–89. New York: Cambridge University Press, 1992.

Klein, Lawrence R., and R. J. Ball. "Some Econometrics of the Determination of Absolute Prices and Wages." *Economic Journal* 69, no. 275 (September 1959): 465–82.

Lawrence, Robert Z. "An Analysis of the 1977 U.S. Trade Deficit." *Brookings Papers on Economic Activity* 1 (1978): 159–89.

Lee, David D. "The Politics of Less: The Trials of Herbert Hoover and Jimmy Carter." *Presidential Studies Quarterly* 13, no. 2 (Spring 1983): 305–12.

Levine, Michael E. "Revisionism Revised? Airline Deregulation and the Public Interest." *Law and Contemporary Problems* 44, no. 1 (Winter 1981): 179–95.

Llewellyn, John. "Resource Prices and Macroeconomic Policies: Lessons From Two Oil Shocks." *OECD Economic Studies* 1 (Autumn 1983): 197–212.

Lucas, Robert E. "Expectations and the Neutrality of Money." *Journal of Economic Theory* 4, no. 2 (April 1972): 103–24.

Lucas, Robert E., and Thomas J. Sargent. "After Keynesian Economics." In *After the Phillips Curve: Persistence of High Inflation and High Unemployment. Federal Reserve Bank of Boston, Conference Series* 19 (June 1978): 49–72.

McKinnon, Ronald I. "Currency Substitution and Instability in the World Dollar Standard." *American Economic Review* 72, no. 3 (June 1982): 320–33.

McNees, Stephen K. "The Forecasting Record for the 1970s." *New England Economic Review* (Federal Reserve Bank of Boston) (September/October 1979): 33–53.

———. "The 1990–91 Recession in Historical Perspective." *New England Economic Review* (Federal Reserve Bank of Boston) (January/February 1992): 4–22.

Meade, James E. "The Case for Variable Exchange Rates." *Three Banks Review* 27, no. 3 (September 1955): 3–27.

Medoff, James L. "Job Growth and the Reelections of Presidents." Manuscript, October 1, 1992. Harvard University.

Meiselman, David I., and Paul Craig Roberts. "The Political Economy of the Congressional Budget Office." In *Three Aspects of Policy and Policy Making*, edited by Karl Brunner and Allan H. Meltzer, 283–333. New York: North-Holland Publishing, 1979.

Meulendyke, Ann-Marie. "A Review of Federal Reserve Policy Targets and Operating Guides in Recent Decades." *Quarterly Review* (Federal Reserve Bank of New York) 13, no. 3 (Autumn 1988): 6–17.

Morris, Frank E. "Opening Remarks." In *After the Phillips Curve: Persistence of High Inflation and High Unemployment. Federal Reserve Bank of Boston, Conference Series* 19 (June 1978): 7–8.

Munnell, Alicia H. "Why Has Productivity Growth Declined? Productivity and Public Investment." *New England Economic Review* (Federal Reserve Bank of Boston) (January–February 1990): 3–22.

Neely, Christopher J. "Realignments of Target Zones Exchange Rate Systems: What Do We Know?" *Review* (Federal Reserve Bank of Saint Louis) 80, no. 5 (September/October 1994): 23–24.

Neumark, David, et al. "Will Increasing the Minimum Wage Help the Poor?" *Economic Commentary* (Federal Reserve Bank of Cleveland) (February 1999).

Nickel, Herman. "The Inside Story of the Dollar Rescue." *Fortune* (December 4, 1978): 40–44.

Nordhaus, William D. "Economic Policy in the Face of Declining Productivity Growth." *European Economic Review* 18 (1982): 131–57.

———. "Lethal Model 2: The Limits to Growth Revisited." *Brookings Papers on Economic Activity* 2 (1992): 1–45.

———. "World Dynamics: Measurement Without Data." *Economic Journal* 83, no. 4 (December 1973): 1156–83.

Okun, Arthur. "Did the 1968 Surcharge Really Work? A Comment." *American Economic Review* 67, no. 1 (March 1977): 166–69.

———. "Efficient Disinflationary Policies." *American Economic Review* 68, no. 2 (May 1978): 348–52.

———. "The Formulation of National Economic Policy." In *Economics for Policy Making: Selected Essays of Arthur M. Okun*, edited by Joseph A. Pechman, 584–91. Cambridge, Mass.: MIT Press, 1983.

———. "The Great Stagflation Swamp." In *Economics for Policy Making: Selected Essays of Arthur M. Okun*, edited by Joseph A. Pechman, 49–62. Cambridge, Mass.: MIT Press, 1983.

———. "The Personal Tax Surcharge and Consumer Demand, 1968–1970." *Brookings Papers on Economic Activity* (1971): 167–212.

———. "Potential GNP: Its Measurement and Significance." *Proceedings of the Business and Economics Statistics Section, American Statistical Association* (1962): 98–103.

Owen, Henry. "The London Summit Revisited." *Trialogue* no. 16 (Winter 1977–78): 1–2.

———. "Taking Stock of the Seven-Power Summits: Two Views." *International Affairs* 60, no. 4 (Autumn 1984): 657–51.

Peltzman, Sam. "The Economic Theory of Regulation After a Decade of Deregulation." *Brookings Papers on Economic Activities, Microeconomics* (1989): 1–41.

Perloff, Jeffrey M., and Michael L. Wachter. "The New Jobs Tax Credit: An Evaluation of the 1977–1978 Wage Subsidy Program." *American Economic Review* 69, no. 2 (May 1979): 173–79.

Phelps, Edmund S. "Money Wage Dynamics and Labor Market Equilibrium." *Journal of Political Economy* 73, no. 4 (July–August 1967): 687–711.

Phillips, A. W. "The Relation Between Unemployment and the Rate of Change of Money Wage Rates in the United Kingdom, 1861–1957." *Economica* 25, no. 100 (November 1958): 283–99.

Pierce, James L. "The Political Economy of Arthur Burns." *Journal of Finance* 34, no. 2 (May 1979): 485–96.

Poole, William. "Burnsian Monetary Policy: Eight Years of Progress?" *Journal of Finance* 34, no. 2 (May 1979): 473–96.

———. "Comments." *Brookings Papers on Economic Activity* 1 (1980): 79–85.

———. "Monetary Policy Lessons of Recent Inflation and Disinflation." *Journal of Economic Perspectives* 2, no. 3 (Summer 1988): 73–100.

———. "Monetary Policy Rules?" *Review* (Federal Reserve Bank of St. Louis) 81, no. 2 (March 1999): 3–12.

Powers, Elizabeth T. "Inflation, Unemployment, and Poverty Revisited." *Economic Review* (Federal Reserve Bank of Cleveland) 31, no. 3 (Quarter 3, 1995): 2–13.

Putnam, Robert D., and C. Randall Henning. "The Bonn Summit of 1978: A Case Study in Coordination." In *Can Nations Agree?*, edited by Richard N. Cooper et al., 12–140. Washington, D.C.: Brookings Institution, 1989.

Ranney, Austin. "The Carter Administration." In *The American Election of 1980*, edited by Austin Ranney, 1–36. Washington, D.C.: American Enterprise Institute, 1981.

Reischauer, Robert D. "Getting, Using, and Misusing Economic Information." In *Making Economy Policy in Congress*, edited by Allen Schick, 38–66. Washington, D.C.: American Enterprise Institute, 1983.

Ribuffo, Leo R. "'I'll Whip His Ass': Jimmy Carter, Edward Kennedy, and the Latest Crisis of American Liberalism." Manuscript, Speech to the Organization of American Historians, Atlanta, April 15, 1994.

———. "Jimmy Carter and the Ironies of American Liberalism." *Gettysburg Review* 1, no. 4 (Fall 1988): 738–49.

Rivlin, Alice. "A Comment on the Meiselman and Roberts Paper." In *Three Aspects of Policy Making*, edited by Karl Brunner and Allan H. Meltzer, 355–62. New York: North-Holland Publishing, 1979.

Robertson, A. Haeworth. "The Outlook for Social Security." *American Economic Review* 69, no. 2 (May 1979): 272–74.

Romer, Christina D., and David H. Romer. "What Ends Recessions?" In *NBER Macroeconomics Annual, 1994*, edited by Stanley Fischer and Julio J. Rotemberg, 113–56. Cambridge, Mass.: MIT Press, 1994.

Samuelson, Paul A. "Carter's Economists." *Newsweek* (June 28, 1976): 59.

———. "My Life Philosophy: Policy Credos and Working Ways." In *Eminent Economists: Their Life Philosophies*, edited by Michael Szenberg, 236–47. New York: Cambridge University Press, 1992.

Samuelson, Paul A., and Robert M. Solow. "Analytical Aspects of Anti-inflation Policy." *American Economic Review* 50, no. 2 (May 1960): 177–94.

Santemero, Anthony M., and John J. Seater. "The Inflation-Unemployment Trade-off: A Critique of the Literature." *Journal of Economic Literature* 16, no. 2 (June 1978): 499–544.

Sargent, Thomas J., and Neil Wallace. "Rational Expectations: The Optimal Monetary Instrument and the Optimal Money Supply Rule." *Journal of Political Economy* 83, no. 2 (April 1975): 241–54.

———. "Rational Expectations and the Theory of Economic Policy." *Journal of Monetary Economics* 12, no. 2 (April 1976): 169–84.

Schlesinger, Arthur, Jr. "The Great Carter Mystery." *New Republic* (April 12, 1980): 18–21.

Schreft, Stacey L. "Credit Controls: 1980." *Economic Review* (Federal Reserve Bank of Richmond) 76, no. 4 (November/December 1990): 25–55.

Schultze, Charles L. "Federal Spending, Past, Present, and Future." In *Setting National Priorities*, edited by Henry Owen and Charles L. Schultze, 323–69. Washington, D.C.: Brookings Institution, 1976.

———. "Is There a Bias Toward Excess in U.S. Government Budgets or Deficits?" *Journal of Economic Perspectives* 6, no. 2 (Spring 1992): 25–43.

———. "Microeconomic Efficiency and Nominal Wage Stickiness." *American Economic Review* 75, no. 1 (March 1985): 1–15.

———. "Some Macro Foundations for Micro Theory." *Brookings Papers on Economic Activity* 2 (1981): 521–92.

Shiller, Robert J. "Why Do People Dislike Inflation?" In *Reducing Inflation: Motivation and Strategy*, edited by Christina D. Romer and David H. Romer, 13–70. Chicago: University of Chicago Press, 1997.

Singer, James W. "The Humphrey Hawkins Bill—Boondoggle or Economic Blessing?" *National Journal* (June 12, 1976): 812–15.

Solomon, Anthony M. "A Personal Evaluation." In *Economic Summitry*, edited by George De Menil and Anthony M. Solomon, 42–54. New York: Council on Foreign Relations, 1983.

Solow, Robert M. "A Contribution to the Theory of Economic Growth." *Quarterly Journal of Economics* 39, no. 1 (February 1956): 65–94.

Spears, Ross. *Agee: A film*. Johnson City, Tenn.: James Agee Film Project, 1978.

Springer, William L. "Did the 1968 Surcharge Really Work?" *American Economic Review* 65, no. 4 (September 1975): 644–59.

———. "Did the 1968 Surcharge Really Work? A Reply." *American Economic Review* 67, no. 1 (March 1977): 170–72.

Stigler, George J. "The Theory of Economic Regulation." *Bell Journal of Economics and Management Science* 2, no. 1 (Winter 1971): 3–21.

Strange, Susan. "Europe and the United States: The Transatlantic Effect of Inflation: A Comparative Analysis." In *The Politics of Inflation: A Comparative Analysis*, edited by Richard Medley, 65–76. New York: Pergamon, 1982.

Summers, Lawrence. "The Scientific Illusion in Empirical Macroeconomics." *Scandinavian Journal of Economics* 93, no. 2 (1991): 129–48.

Sunley, Emil M. "A Tax Preference Is Born: A Legislative History of the New Jobs Tax Credit." In *The Economics of Taxation*, edited by Henry J. Aaron and Michael J. Boskin, 391–408. Washington, D.C.: Brookings Institution, 1980.

Taylor, John B. "An Historical Analysis of Monetary Policy Rules." National Bureau of Economic Research, Working Paper 6768, 1988.

———. "How Should Monetary Policy Respond to Shocks While Maintaining Long-Run Price Stability? Conceptual Issues." In *Achieving Price Stability, Symposium*, 181–95. Kansas City: Federal Reserve Bank of Kansas City, 1996.

Triest, Robert K. "Social Security Reform: An Overview." *New England Economic Review* (Federal Reserve Bank of Boston) (November/December 1997): 1–17.

Vicusi, W. Rip. "The Political Economy of Wage and Price Regulation: The Case of the Carter Pay-Price Standards." In *What Role for Government?*, edited by Richard J. Zeckhauser and Derek Leebaert, 159–74. Durham, N.C.: Duke University Press, 1983.

Volcker, Paul A. "The Contribution and Limitations of 'Monetary Analysis.'" *Quarterly Review* (Federal Reserve Bank of New York) (Special 75th Anniversary Issue): 35–41.

———. "The Role of Monetary Targets in an Age of Inflation." *Journal of Monetary Economics* 4, no. 4 (1978): 329–39.

Wallich, Henry C. "Government Action." In *The Dollar in Crisis*, edited by Seymour E. Harris, 97–113. New York: Harcourt, Brace and World, 1961.

Weidenbaum, Murray L. "On Estimating Regulatory Costs." *Regulation* (May–June 1978): 14–17.

Whitman, Marina v. N. "Global Monetarism and the Monetary Approach to the Balance of Payments." *Brookings Papers on Economic Activity* 3 (1975): 522–26.

Williamson, John. "Keynes and the International Economic Order." In *Keynes in the Modern World*, edited by David Worswick and James Trevithick, 87–127. London: Cambridge University Press, 1983.

Winston, Clifford. "Economic Deregulation: Days of Reckoning for Microeconomists." *Journal of Economic Literature* 31, no. 3 (September 1993): 1263–89.

Wright, Gavin. "The Origins of American Industrial Success, 1879–1940." *American Economic Review* 80, no. 4 (September 1990): 651–68.

INDEX

Abramovitz, Moses, 256
Anderson, John, 12

Bergsten, C. Fred, 95, 168
Bingham, Eula: head of Occupational Safety and Health Administration, 225
Blumenthal, Michael: secretary of treasury, 41; accused of "talking down" dollar, 117–18, 290 (n. 77); position on Bonn oil price commitment, 160; resignation, 237
Bonn summit: pre-summit pressure on Germany to stimulate economy, 146–47; U.S. urged to control inflation and energy use, 147–48, 160; pressure on Schmidt to accept stimulus, 149–51; final agreement, 151–52, 162; pre-summit congressional resistance to energy bill, 159–60; conflict among advisers over oil price commitment, 160; discussion of behavior of dollar, 168–69; evaluation of, 178–79; German appraisal of effect on Germany, 178–79; Japanese evaluation of, 179
Bretton Woods, 104–6
Brookings Institution: as source of advisers for presidents, 47–48
Budget: unexpected deficit for 1980, 8–11, 204; growth of in decades preceding Carter, 65–66; voter disaffection with government spending, 66–68; zero-based, 68–69; restraint pledged in October 1978 anti-inflation package, 186–88; movement toward restraint in 1978 and 1979 budgets, 201–3; fiscal restraint and tension within Democratic Party, 203; reworking of 1980 budget, 204; Carter refuses to ask for tax cut in 1981 budget, 204–5
Burns, Arthur: appointed to Federal Reserve by Nixon, 88; as forceful chairman, 88; interaction with Nixon administration, 88–89; Carter advisers' view of, 89–90; not reappointed by Carter, 92–93; argues for tough action by Council on Wage and Price Stability, 130–31; policy as chairman of Federal Reserve, 250; number of meetings with Carter, 284–85 (n. 112); approaches Europeans about change in price of gold, 287 (n. 40); suggests idea of Carter bonds, 302 (n. 29)

Campaign, 1976: primaries, 18–20; limited staff in early 1976, 20–23; increase in staff in late 1976, 23–24; and economics task force, 24–25; condition of economy and election results, 27–30; promises, 30, 270 (n. 56); and jobs program, 35–36; and inflation, 36–38
Carson, Rachel: *Silent Spring*, 222
Carter, Jimmy: effect of economic shocks on presidency, ix–xi; reasons for defeat in 1980, 1–5; debate with Reagan in 1980, 12; decision to run for president, 16; role in 1974 congressional campaign, 16–17; acts as chief of staff, 43; training in economics, 53–54, 277 (n. 65); ability to absorb economic advice, 54–55, 277 (n. 72); interest in economics, 55–56; confidence in economic advice, 55–56, 277 (n. 72); influence of parents during childhood, 56–59; fiscally moderate and socially liberal policy priorities, 56–60, 259; com-

petence in Spanish, 59, 279 (n. 91); conflict with liberal wing of Democratic Party, 59–60; concern for growth in government, 65–68; energy conservation plan, 156–59; fireside chat on energy, 157–58; "moral equivalent of war" statement, 158; opinion of October 1978 inflation package, 169–70; more accurate than advisers on inflation danger, 207; populist views on banking, 244; faced with economic limits, 253; deals with growth of entitlements, 253–54; tension between liberal instincts and sense of fiscal prudence, 254; constrained by slowdown in economic growth, 259; strong sense of limits, 259; attempt to pull Democratic Party to center, 259–60; lacks coalition, 259–60; speech at dedication of Kennedy Library, 260–61; as precursor to Clinton, 262; realistic interpretation of Carter years, 262–63; involvement in details, 274 (n. 32); influenced by Reinhold Niebuhr, Dylan Thomas, and Bob Dylan, 279 (n. 90); briefed on price/unemployment tradeoff while governor, 293 (n. 17); liberal programs, 318–19 (n. 30)

Carter, Lillian, 58, 278–79 (n. 88), 302 (n. 29)

Carter bonds, 170

Civil Aeronautics Board: interpretation of regulatory law under Ford, 220

Conference Board of New York, 265 (n. 7)

Congressional Budget Office: use of standard models in forecasting, 52, 269 (n. 46); differs with Carter on welfare cost estimates, 52–53; forecasts staff capability, 52–53

Consumer credit controls: appeal to labor unions, 246–47; history of, 246–47; supporters within administration, 247; advisers' views of, 247–48; dramatic effect of, 248; loose, 248; removal of, 249

Cooper, Richard, 95, 160

Costle, Douglas, 225

Cotton dust regulations, 226; Carter's final decision, 227

Council of Economic Advisers: makeup and role, 51

Council on Wage and Price Stability, 194

Crude oil equalization tax: passage resisted by Congress, 159; oil price decontrol not contingent on, 174–75; passed by Congress, 177

Depository Institutions Deregulation and Monetary Control Act, 221

Deregulation: Schultze memorandum on government actions affecting prices, 216–17; Carter's major economic success, 221–22

Deregulation, economic: traditional argument for regulation, 217; shift in economists' thinking about regulation, 218; Carter's 1976 campaign promise concerning, 218; President Ford's and Senator Ted Kennedy's attempts at reform, 219; 1978 Airline Deregulation Act, 220–21; Cannon-Kennedy bill to deregulate airlines, 220–21; Carter-Kennedy initiative to deregulate trucking, 221; 1980 Staggers Rail Act, 221

Deregulation, social, 222–28; and Rachel Carson's *Silent Spring*, 222; regulatory explosion of sixties and seventies, 222–23; Nixon's and Ford's attempts to recognize cost limits, 223; estimated costs, 224; more difficult than economic deregulation, 227–28; appraisal of Carter's program, 228; inflationary effect of, 228

D'Estaing, Giscard, 167

Eckstein, Otto, 71

Econometric models: supply-side economists criticize large-scale forecasting models, 27, 269 (n. 46); first macro-

econometric models, 269 (n. 46); Carter's familiarity with while governor, 278 (n. 73)
Economic advisers: background of Carter's, 25–27, 41–51; postelection gathering in Plains, 39–40. *See also* Economic Policy Group
Economic forecasting: by administration and Congressional Budget Office, 51–52; importance in policy decisions, 52–53; procedures under Carter, 52–53
Economic growth: effect on Carter's options, 253–54; concern of early economists, 254–55; classic solution to poverty, 255; effect of Great Depression on interest in, 255; Keynes's ideas on, 255; Keynesian economists' interest in theory of, 256; interest in current research, 256–57, 318 (n. 17)
Economic Policy Group: relation to Troika, 40–41; membership, 40–45, 273 (n. 23); compared to Ford's Economic Policy Board, 42; problems with flow of advice, 43–45
Economic stimulus package: final drafting by Blumenthal, Schultze, and Lance, 40, 211 (n. 1); content, 61–64; need for and size of, 69–72; outside opinion of, 70–72; conflict between Marshall and Schultze over jobs program, 72–75; movement through Congress, 75–79; reasons for dropping tax rebate, 77–79; final passage, 82–83; compared to Ford's, 197–98
Economic summits, 109–10
Economic task force, 1976 campaign, 24–25
Economy, 1980, 3–11
Eizenstat, Stuart: work on policy issues in 1974 congressional and 1976 presidential campaigns, 18; role in coordination of economic policy, 45–46, 50–51; opposes Bonn oil price decision, 160–61; appraisal of administration's anti-inflation policy, 206; "New Realities" speech before Women's National Democratic Club, 261
Election reforms, 1969–72, 15–16
Energy problem: fundamentals of, 155; Nixon and Ford conservation plans, 155; Carter's conservation plan, 156–58; Carter's interest in while governor, 298–99 (n. 38)
Environmental Protection Agency, 223
European monetary system, 164–68; U.S. reaction to, 167–68, 300–301 (n. 12), 301 (n. 16)

Federal Reserve: delegated by Congress to control money supply, 88; organization, 88; November 1978 actions to support dollar, 170
Financial markets: constraints on presidents, 8–11
Fiscal policy: Carter's position on in 1976 campaign, 34–35
Food and Drug Administration, 222–23
Ford, Gerald: Economic Policy Board, 42, 274–75 (n. 35); inherits stagflation, 85; energy conservation plan, 155; efforts at regulatory reform, 219
Forecasting: procedures under Carter, 52; by administration and Congressional Budget Office, 52–53; importance to policy decisions, 52–53
Forrester, Jay, 257–58
Friedman, Milton: favors flexible exchange rate system, 107, 288 (n. 43); criticizes Phillips curve reasoning, 126–27; favors use of money targets by Federal Reserve, 315 (n. 16). *See also* Phillips curve

Germany: historic fear of inflation, 99–100; anti-inflation responsibility of Bundesbank, 100–101; post–World War II economic recovery, 101; slowing growth rate in sixties and seventies, 101; effect of Bonn agreements on, 177–78
Global 2000 report, 258–59

Gramley, Lyle: leads forecasting group, 52, 276 (n. 62); thoughts on administration's biggest mistake, 206–7; thoughts on Volcker's targeting of monetary aggregates, 253

Greenspan, Alan: on Burns's attendance at meetings of Ford's Economic Policy Board, 88–89; on Burns's contacts with Carter, 284 (n. 112)

Hatch, Orrin: criticizes use of macroeconometric models, 27

Heller, Walter: economic adviser to President Kennedy, 45; criticizes size of Carter's tax cut, 72

Hessler, Curtis, 273 (n. 27)

Humphrey-Hawkins bill, 32–34

Inflation: social effects of, 4–5, 266 (n. 14); and financial markets, 5–8; as issue in 1976 campaign, 36–38; causes of under Johnson, Nixon, and Ford, 83–85; concern in early days of administration, 85–88; measurement of, 87; Carter's first anti-inflation plan, 127–30, 132–34; unemployment rejected as solution to, 128; food price shocks, 134; union rejection of unsuccessful 1978 wage-price deceleration program, 136–39; incompatibility of Bonn inflation and oil promises, 164; effect of Bonn oil price decontrol on, 164; numerical wage-price guidelines introduced in October 1978 anti-inflation speech, 185–86; debate within administration over October 1978 commitment to budget restraint, 186–88; union rejection of wage-price guidelines, 190–91; supply shocks, 191–93; in last two years of Carter administration, 191–95; excess demand as cause of, 197–200; reasons for failure of anti-inflation policy, 197–200; advisers' final evaluation of anti-inflation strategy, 206–7; effects of microeconomic decisions on, 234–35; public rejection of draconian measures to end, 241–42; monetary policy and the Great Inflation, 249–51. *See also* Supply shocks

Interest rates: behavior in 1980, 6–11

International economic cooperation: economists' skepticism about success of, 179–82

International exchange: reasons for U.S. trade deficit, 113–14; fall of dollar in 1977–78, 114; theory of exchange rate determination, 114–15; dollar depreciation a burden to Germany, 116; effect of oil price decontrol on dollar, 165–66; fall of dollar in late 1978, 169–70; defense of dollar in November 1978, 170–71

International monetary system: gold standard, 103; Bretton Woods system, 104–6; floating rate system, 106–7

International policy: responsibility of Economic Policy Group, 111; U.S. reasons for refusal to support falling dollar in early 1977, 118–19; U.S. shift to dollar support, 119–20

International Trade Commission: dealings with unfair trade issues, 229; finding in favor of shoe industry, 229

Interstate Commerce Commission: railroad and trucking regulation, 217

Iran hostage crisis, 1–2

Japan: economy after World War II, 102–3; reception of Mondale mission, 102–3; alleged "dirty float" in 1977, 107–8; assessment of Bonn outcome, 179

Jones, Reginald: congressional testimony on stimulus package, 71

Jordan, Hamilton: assessment of 1980 campaign, 13; strategy memoranda in 1976 campaign, 16; role in 1974 congressional campaign, 16–17

Kahn, Alfred, 165, 207, 219–20; inflation czar, 186; expert on economics of regulation, 219–20; sympathetic to regulatory restraint, 224; appointed to Civil Aeronautics Board, 230; supports consumer credit controls, 247

Kennedy, John: conflict with U.S. Steel, 129–30 (n. 22); Yale speech, 262; Council of Economic Advisers, 269

Kennedy, Joseph, II: comments at dedication of Kennedy Library, 261–62

Kennedy, Ted: challenges Carter in 1980 primaries, 2; and Memphis midterm convention, 203; hearings on regulatory reform, 219; view on need for government retrenchment, 259

Keynes, John Maynard: basic ideas, 26–27; meets with Franklin Roosevelt, 27; views on economic growth, 255; "Economic Possibilities for Our Grand Children," 255–56

Klein, Lawrence: head of economic task force in 1976 campaign, 24–25; early Keynesian, 26–27; declines to serve as chairman of Council of Economic Advisers, 268 (n. 42); research findings similar to Phillips curve, 291 (n. 2)

Labor: Carter's relations with, 131–32; 1977 fall in real wage increase, 135–39; opposes prenotification of union demands, 294 (n. 31)

Lance, Burt: director of Office of Management and Budget, 41; relationship to Carter, 41, 272 (n. 5); resignation, 41, 272 (n. 6)

Limits to Growth (Club of Rome report), 257–59; critique of, 258

Locomotive strategy: idea of, 95–97; other nations' pressure on Germany and Japan to adopt, 97–98; rejected by Germany, 98–101

London economic summit, 112

Long, Russell: resists passage of Carter energy program in Senate, 159

Lucas, Robert, 126; work on "new growth theory," 318 (n. 17)

"Malaise" speech, 255–56

Marshall, Ray: role in advisory process as secretary of labor, 43, 49; change in position on wage-price guidelines, 185, 305 (n. 2); argues for large increase in minimum wage, 212

Meany, George: tension with Carter, 132, 294 (n. 31); urges Carter to introduce consumer credit controls, 246–47

Midterm Democratic convention, 260

Miller, William: chairman of Federal Reserve, 140; liked by Carter advisers, 140; succeeds Blumenthal at Treasury, 237

Minimum wage: eroded by inflation, 211; debate over economic effect of increase, 212–13, 310 (n. 11); controversy in administration over size of increase, 212–14; impact on inflation rate, 213–14; and inadequate handling of policy advice, 214; Eizenstat as mediator within administration, 215; final legislation passed by Congress, 215–16; on administration agenda long after passage, 216–17

Mondale, Walter: influence on Carter's economic policy, 49–50; mission to West Germany and Japan, 95–103; German and Japanese reaction to mission, 98–103; opposes Bonn oil price commitment, 160; helps Carter in Washington, 276 (n. 52)

Monetary policy: Carter's position on in 1976 campaign, 34–35; Carter advisers' concern over 1977 Burns policy, 91–92; attempts by Carter advisers to influence Federal Reserve Board to moderate, 141–42; outside critics think 1978 policy not tight enough, 142; Carter advisers urge Federal Reserve to tighten in early 1979, 143–44; Congress directs Federal Reserve to report money supply targets, 242; Carter supports independent Federal Reserve, 245–46; problems in measuring money, 314–15 (n. 10). *See also* Burns, Arthur; Volcker, Paul

National Bureau of Economic Research: measurement of business cycles, 28
National Highway Safety Traffic Administration, 223
Natural gas deregulation, 156–57, 299 (n. 39)
Nixon, Richard: inflation under, 84–85; initiates oil price control, 154; energy conservation plan, 154–55

Occupational Safety and Health Administration, 223
Oil: foreign resentment of U.S. consumption of, 152–53; price controls under Nixon, 154; political resistance to ending price controls, 155–56, 160; effect of higher price on demand for, 174, 303 (n. 44); administration consults with Congress on price decontrol, 175–76; Carter's awareness of increasing imports of while governor, 289 (n. 65)
Oil price decontrol: Carter promise at Bonn to raise oil prices, 152, 160–62; role of price in efficient allocation of oil, 153–54; in original energy package, 158–59; Carter's options for, 164, 171–77; union resistance to, 164–65; administration's internal debate on, 173–75; Carter understands Mondale's views on, 174; administration consults with Congress on, 175–76; Carter's doubts about oil price commitment, 176–77; political fallout, 177–78
Okun's law: cost of reducing inflation by demand restraint, 128, 292 (n. 14); relationship of gross national product and unemployment, 200, 269 (n. 50)
O'Neill, Tip: clears passage of Carter energy plan in House, 159; defends Carter in Congress, 277 (n. 64)
Ooms, Van Doorn, 274 (n. 32)

Organization for Economic Cooperation and Development, 97, 286 (n. 2)
Organization of Petroleum Exporting Countries, 85
Owen, Henry: role in summit meetings, 111–12; supports Bonn oil price decision, 160

Pechman, Joseph, 198
Phillips curve: summary, 123–25; effect on administration policy, 125–27; Robert Lucas's argument against, 126; Milton Friedman's criticism of, 126–27; anticipated by Irving Fisher, 291 (n. 2); Carter briefed on price/unemployment tradeoff while governor, 293 (n. 17)
Productivity growth: decline during Carter years, x–xi, 135–56, 200–201; decline not recognized by advisers, 200–201; slowdown lowers capacity of economy, 200–201; slowdown defines limits of Carter presidency, 254; decline means fall in per capita disposable income, 257

Quadriad: first meeting with Carter, 90; role, 90

Rational expectations, 126–27, 292 (n. 14)
Recessions: dating by National Bureau of Economic Research, 28
Regulatory Analysis Review Group: proposed by Schultze to reduce regulatory costs, 225–26; role of Schultze and Office of Management and Budget, 225–26; cotton dust regulation, 226; no provision for resolving impasse, 226
Regulatory Council: responsible for regulatory calendar, 226
Rivlin, Alice: director of Congressional Budget Office during Carter term, 52; congressional testimony on stimulus package, 70–71; defends use of macroeconometric models, 269 (n. 46);

comments on Carter's "moral equivalent of war" statement, 277 (n. 64)
Robson, John, 220

Schlesinger, James, 157
Schmidt, Helmut: reaction to Mondale mission, 98–99; leads effort to establish European monetary system, 166–68; tensions with Carter, 296–97 (n. 4)
Schultze, Charles: chairman of Council of Economic Advisers, 42; Keynesian views, 46–47; experience in Washington, 46–47; personal adviser to Carter, 48–49; concerned about inflationary effects of Bonn oil price commitment, 161; briefs president on price effects of government actions, 216–17; considers modifying regulations with inflationary effects a priority, 225; reflections on Lyndon Johnson, 275 (n. 40); interpretation of inflationary process, 309 (n. 89); Carter's opinion of, 313 (n. 65)
Schumaker, Ernest, 72
Shoe industry: employment loss due to foreign trade, 228–29; trade protection issue, 228–30; Carter's decision to protect by "orderly marketing agreement," 229–30; small inflationary effect of protection of, 230
Smith, Adam, 255
Social security: history of, 209–10; continuing problem for presidents, 210–11; Carter's legislation, 211
Solomon, Anthony: supports Bonn oil price decision, 160, 163; evaluation of Bonn summit, 182–83; designs steel industry relief from foreign trade, 232–33
Solow, Robert: on Kennedy's Council of Economic Advisers, 256; wins Nobel Prize, 256
Staggers Rail Act, 221
Steel industry: decline in U.S. international competitiveness after World War II, 231–32; job losses in 1970s, 232; Carter meets with members of steel caucuses, 233; trigger price mechanism temporary relief for, 233–34
Strauss, Robert: pressures steel industry to moderate price increases, 230–31
Supply shocks: food prices, 191; housing prices, 192–93; oil prices, 193; major reason for Great Inflation, 197

Tax incentive plan: content, 188–90; rejected by Congress, 189; probable cost, 189–90
Tax rebate: part of stimulus package, 62–64; controversy over effectiveness of, 63–64, 280 (n. 10); withdrawn from congressional consideration, 77–78
Tax reform: important part of Carter's 1976 campaign, 199–200; modest reform passed by Congress, 199–200; reform bill stimulus not needed, 199–200
Thomassen, Henry: economic adviser to Carter while governor, 53–54; letters to Carter at White House, 54; briefs Carter while governor on price/unemployment tradeoff, 293 (n. 17)
Trade restriction issues, 228–34; in shoe industry, 228–30. *See also* Steel industry
Trilateral Commission: members in administration, 17; Carter's membership in, 17–18; and locomotive strategy, 96; papers read by Carter, 257 (n. 12)
Tripartite Pay Advisory Committee: created in late 1979, 194; tension with Council on Wage and Price Stability and Council of Economic Advisers, 194

Unemployment: relationship to gross national product, 28–29; top priority for Carter in 1976 campaign, 29–30; specific targets adopted in 1976 campaign, 30–34; defining full employment-unemployment rate, 31–33; sharp fall in 1977–78, 200

Volcker, Paul: education and background, 237–38; Carter's interview with, 238–39; informs Carter he will tighten monetary policy if appointed, 238–39; testifies in Congress that price stability will be first priority, 239–40; informs Schultze and Miller of monetary plan, 240; secret meeting of Federal Reserve Board in October 1979, 240; chooses monetary aggregates as target for Federal Reserve policy, 240–41; reasons for adopting money target, 241, 315 (n. 18); and country's readiness for strong monetary action, 241–42; effect of money targeting on financial markets, 242–43; Schultze opposes money target strategy of but defends Federal Reserve to outside critics, 242–43; construction industry hurt by money targeting, 243; Schultze's later views of strategy of, 244; Carter's views of policy of, 244–46; eases up on monetary policy in 1982, 316–17 (n. 37)

Wage-price controls: Carter's attitude toward standby controls in n1976 campaign, 37–38; precise numerical guidelines rejected in 1977 policy statement, 130; numerical guidelines introduced in October 1978 speech, 185–86; second-year wage-price standards and "national accord," 194; failure of, 194–95; Schultze's and Gramley's opinions on guidelines' success, 195–96; General Accounting Office's evaluation of guidelines and administration's reply, 195–96, 307 (n. 46); attempts to pressure steel industry to moderate price increases, 230–31, 293 (n. 22)

Watergate: role in 1976 campaign, 28

Water projects: conflict with Congress over deletion from first budget, 79–83

Watson, Jack: heads transition issues team, 23–24

Wiedenbaum, Murray: estimates costs of regulation, 224